The authors

Alan Murdie LLB barrister has updated the *Council Tax Handbook* since 1998. He has a long-standing interest in local taxation and has been involved in many test cases. He is chair of Council Tax Legal Services and Nucleus Legal Advice in London.

Paul Moorhouse has worked as a housing, debt and benefits adviser since 1990. He currently works part-time for Dalkeith and District CAB and is a freelance writer on welfare benefits.

Acknowledgements

A huge debt is owed to David Paterson, Paul Moorhouse and Susan Mitchell for checking the text of this edition, and to Martin Ward who wrote the first two editions, upon which this new edition is broadly based.

Many thanks to Nicola Johnston for editing and managing the production of the book, Anne Ketley for compiling the index, and Kathleen Armstrong and Pauline Phillips for proofreading the text.

Grateful thanks to the many people who have provided valuable information, comments and suggestions since the last edition. Thanks are due to staff and volunteers at Nucleus Legal Advice in Earl's Court and Ealing Advice; staff and volunteers from Council Tax Legal Services; Lyn Ryan of Manchester Citizens Advice; Alistair Chisholm of the Institute of Money Advisers and Ben Grower, former member and chairman with the Valuation Tribunal for England between 1998 and 2018. Thanks also go to the Institute of Ratings Revenue and Valuation, and the library staff of the Honourable Society of Lincoln's Inn who once again gave invaluable help with identifying and obtaining key references.

The law described in this book was correct at 1 October 2018.

Contents

Abbreviations   viii

Chapter 1   Overview
1. Introduction   1
2. Administration   2
3. Legal background and references   3

Chapter 2   Chargeable dwellings
1. Chargeable dwellings   9
2. Dwellings in England and Wales   10
3. Dwellings in Scotland   17
4. New and altered properties   19

Chapter 3   Valuation
1. Who is responsible for valuations   23
2. The listing officer's and assessor's powers   25
3. How dwellings are valued   26
4. Compiling and maintaining valuation lists   30
5. Inspecting the valuation list   30
6. Altering a valuation list   32
7. The valuation bands   42

Chapter 4   Exempt dwellings
1. Exempt dwellings in England and Wales   48
2. Exempt dwellings in Scotland   59
3. How exempt dwellings are identified   65
4. Notification of exemption   65
5. Penalties   66
6. Appeals   67

Chapter 5   Liability
1. Who is liable   70
2. Who is a resident   72
3. When the owner is always liable   77
4. Joint liability   82

5. Change of circumstances 85
6. Backdating liability 85
7. How the liable person is identified 86
8. Appeals 88

Chapter 6   Disability reductions 91
1. What is a disability reduction 91
2. When a disability reduction can be made 92
3. Getting a disability reduction 95
4. How the reduction is made 97
5. Change of circumstances 97
6. Appeals 98

Chapter 7   Discounts and premiums 100
1. 25 per cent discount for one resident 100
2. Who counts for discount purposes 101
3. Who is disregarded for discount purposes 101
4. Getting a discount 112
5. Unoccupied dwellings discounts 114
6. Miscellaneous discounts 116
7. Premiums on long-term empty and second homes 117
8. Appeals 120

Chapter 8   Council tax reduction schemes 124
1. What is a council tax reduction 124
2. How council tax reduction schemes work 128
3. Council tax reduction schemes for pensioners 131
4. Council tax reduction schemes in England 133
5. Council tax reduction schemes in Wales 137
6. Council tax reduction schemes in Scotland 137
7. Alternative maximum council tax reduction ('second adult rebate') 138
8. How council tax reduction entitlement is calculated 141
9. Applying for council tax reduction 161
10. If you disagree with a council tax reduction decision 165
11. Discretionary reductions 167
12. Future changes 168

Chapter 9   Bills and payments 173
1. Who must pay the bill 173
2. When bills should be issued 174
3. How the bill is calculated 176

4. How bills are served   179
5. Information the bill should contain   180
6. Payment arrangements   183
7. Penalties   189
8. Appeals against the amount of the bill   191

Chapter 10   Enforcement   194
1. Introduction   194
2. Statutory enforcement in England and Wales   195
3. Liability orders (England and Wales)   198
4. Recovery methods (England and Wales)   210
5. Statutory enforcement in Scotland   229

Chapter 11   Appeals   239
1. Valuation tribunals and valuation appeal committees   239
2. Matters that can be appealed   241
3. How to appeal   249
4. How appeals are dealt with   250
5. Appeal hearings   255
6. Reviews of tribunal and committee decisions   266

Chapter 12   Complaints about council tax administration   272
1. Complaints to the Ombudsman   272
2. Complaints to the local auditor   290
3. Action through the courts   291

Appendices
Appendix 1   Useful addresses   295
Appendix 2   Taking Control of Goods: National Standards   297
Appendix 3   Adjournment letter   299
Appendix 4   Abbreviations used in the notes   300

Index   306

Abbreviations

AA	attendance allowance	IB	incapacity benefit
CA	carer's allowance	IS	income support
CTB	council tax benefit	JSA	jobseeker's allowance
CTC	child tax credit	MHCLG	Ministry of Housing, Communities and Local Government
CTR	council tax reduction	MP	Member of Parliament
CTRRP	Council Tax Reduction Review Panel	NI	national insurance
DHP	discretionary housing payment	PC	pension credit
DLA	disability living allowance	PIP	personal independence payment
DWP	Department for Work and Pensions	SDA	severe disablement allowance
ESA	employment and support allowance	UC	universal credit
EU	European Union	VOA	Valuation Office Agency
HB	housing benefit	VTE	Valuation Tribunal for England
HMCS	HM Courts Service	VTW	Valuation Tribunal for Wales
HMRC	HM Revenue and Customs	WTC	working tax credit

Chapter 1

Overview

This chapter covers:
1. Introduction (below)
2. Administration (p2)
3. Legal background and references (p3)

1. Introduction

This *Handbook* describes council tax as it operates throughout England, Wales and Scotland. It should be of value to taxpayers, advisers and administrators.

Council tax is best understood as a cross between a land tax and a personal tax. It was originally introduced for the financial year beginning on 1 April 1993 by the Local Government Finance Act 1992,[1] and for all subsequent financial years, after the failure of the short-lived system of community charge, or 'poll tax', which operated in England and Wales between 1990 and 1993.[2] The scheme of the original 1992 Act has now been substantially altered by the Localism Act 2011 and Local Government Finance Act 2012. Council tax is levied on domestic dwellings, but the number of people and the type of people who are living in a dwelling affect the amount of tax to be paid and who should pay it. Increasingly, more emphasis is placed on the personal element of the tax than the property element. This *Handbook* provides a guide to the relevant rules.

Council tax bills are normally calculated on the assumption that two adults occupy a property. Where there is only one resident, a 25 per cent discount (known as a 'variation' in Scotland) applies. In some situations, a discount may be available where there is more than one adult resident in a property but the second or extra adults fall into a number of prescribed classes – eg, they are students or severely mentally impaired. Such individuals are classed as 'disregarded for discount'.

There are a number of differences in the way the council tax scheme operates in Scotland compared to England and Wales. In some chapters, these variations are indicated as they arise; in others, there are separate sections on the different arrangements. Following changes under the Local Government Finance Act 2012, there are many further local variations as to the support which is available for those on low incomes.

One of the fundamental principles upon which council tax was originally conceived was that the poorest in the community would be protected by council tax benefit (CTB) covering up to 100 per cent of their council tax liability. Between 1 April 1993 and 31 March 2013, central government funded a nationwide CTB system for those on welfare benefits or low incomes.

On 1 April 2013, CTB was abolished and replaced by locally determined council tax reduction schemes. Local schemes have created new administrative functions within the council tax system, with councils being given powers equivalent to those which existed under specified social security legislation relating to council tax. Local authorities have increased financial autonomy and responsibility for support for pensioners, those on low incomes and on benefits. The amount of support available in each area to a local taxpayer is decided by each individual local authority, and not on a national basis. As a result, the amount of support that a low-income taxpayer is entitled to receive can vary widely, so that the position of one low-income taxpayer in one part of England and Wales is no longer the same, or broadly equal to, that in another part of the UK. Over 300 different support schemes exist for authorities across England and 22 different schemes operate in Wales. The position is more consistent in Scotland.

Domestic rates are still payable in Northern Ireland. This *Handbook*, therefore, does not apply to Northern Ireland.

2. **Administration**

In England and Wales, district councils, metropolitan districts and London boroughs, unitary authorities, combined authorities, the Common Council of the City of London and the Council of the Isles of Scilly are responsible for setting the council tax, as well as billing and collection in their area. Each authority collects council tax on behalf of itself and other bodies (known as 'precepting authorities'). The authorities which issue the bills and collect the tax are known as '**billing authorities**'.[3]

In Scotland, billing and levying is performed by local authorities. Scottish local authorities are legally obliged to collect Scottish Water charges (for household water and waste water). These charges are included in the annual council tax bill.

Although local authorities set and levy the council tax in their area, in many areas, the day-to-day administration and collection of council tax is carried out by private companies acting on behalf of the local authority. These companies may also be responsible for administering benefits and enforcing non-payment of tax or undertaking certain types of enforcement, most commonly the use of enforcement agents to seize goods or begin insolvency proceedings. In England, they can also notify you about reductions, ascertain liability and collect penalties.[4]

3. **Legal background and references**

The legal framework for the council tax is contained in the Local Government Finance Act 1992, as amended by the Local Government Act 2003, the Localism Act 2011 and the Local Government Finance Act 2012. The Act includes sections and Schedules that apply throughout England, Wales and Scotland, as well as sections and Schedules that apply exclusively to one or other of the two jurisdictions.

The Acts enable the Secretary of State, the Welsh government or the Scottish government to formulate legislation (statutory instruments) in the form of regulations which contain and amend the details of the scheme. In practice, it is these regulations that govern the operation of the council tax. Some legislative provisions are shared in common between England, Wales and Scotland, while in other cases specific regulations have been created and put in place by the national assemblies in Wales and Scotland.

Different sets of statutory instruments apply to England and Wales and to Scotland. Additionally, certain statutory instruments only apply in England or to Wales or Scotland. Most of the regulations have been amended since they were first made and others substituted. The original text of many of these regulations is available at www.legislation.gov.uk but subsequent amendments are not always included or updated to reflect the most recent changes.

Each local authority is required to draw up a council tax reduction (CTR) scheme which applies from the start of each financial year. With the exceptions of pensioners and certain prescribed categories of support set out in regulations made by the Secretary of State, each local authority is left to devise the support scheme and level of support for its own area as it sees fit for persons of working age. Consequently, there is no national set scheme of support for persons of working age and there is widespread variation between different councils. Reference needs to be made to the appropriate local CTR scheme published by an individual authority. However, these rules have legal effect and are binding on the authority, and appeal rights to the valuation tribunals of England and Wales remain consistent and standardised throughout England and Wales, with separate provisions applying in Scotland.

Relevant caselaw is also identified in the appropriate paragraphs of this *Handbook*.

Electronic communication

Under powers derived from the Electronic Communications Act 2000, local authorities in England, Wales and Scotland may serve certain notices and information required for council tax by electronic means. These provisions require the agreement of the taxpayer and service upon an unauthorised third party would be insufficient to amount to valid service.[5] Information and notices may also be served electronically on local authorities by taxpayers, although to be effective in law the communication must be recorded on a local authority computer. Electronic communication can also be used to alter lists and for appeals.

Freedom of information

The Freedom of Information Act 2000 (and in Scotland, The Freedom of Information (Scotland) Act 2002) enables anyone to seek and obtain information held by state bodies, subject to certain exceptions. The Act may be used to discover information about aspects of the council tax, both national and local, in addition to information which is already available to the public (such as the valuation list). If a request to supply information is unreasonably refused, an appeal can be made to the Information Commissioner. Not all information is available – eg, personal records.

Personal data held on computer can also be obtained under the Data Protection Act 2018.[6] The person who is the subject of the data can obtain copies of the information by way of a subject access request.

A further right of access to information on local authority decisions can be obtained under the Openness of Local Government Bodies Regulations 2014.[7]

Tax capping and referendums

Under the Local Government Finance Act 1992, the Secretary of State could originally limit the amount of council tax set by individual local authorities (known as 'capping'). The government could use this power to instruct councils to set a lower budget if it considered their budget requirement and council tax to have exceeded what it considered a reasonable amount. When this power was exercised, the result was that lower bills might be issued to residents. The Welsh government still has the power to selectively cap council tax rises in Wales.

In England, the Localism Act 2011 removed this power and instead introduced that any local authority in England (including police and fire authorities) must call a referendum if it wants to raise its council tax above a set threshold where an increase is deemed 'excessive'.[8] What is deemed as 'excessive' is determined by a set of principles set annually by the Secretary of State.[9] Any amount which exceeds the relevant principle must be approved in a referendum of local voters.[10]

The Secretary of State's principles must include a comparison between the relevant basic amount of council tax for the year under consideration, and the preceding year. The principles must be set out in a report to be laid before the House of Commons by a set date. Where the report is not laid, or not approved by resolution of the House of Commons, no principles can take effect and no authority's relevant basic amount of council tax can be determined as excessive for the year.[11]

Local authorities, major precepting authorities, fire authorities and police and crime commissioners are required to determine whether the amount of council tax they plan to raise is excessive.[12] An authority proposing an excessive increase is also required to make substitute calculations, based on a non-excessive council tax level.[13]

In previous years in England, the amount had been set at 2 per cent. As a consequence, some councils increased the amount of council tax by 1.99 per cent so as to avoid the possibility of a referendum. For 2018/19, the excessive amount is 6 per cent or more (comprising 3 per cent for expenditure on adult social care and 3 per cent for general other expenditure) than an authority's 2017/18 amount of council tax.[14] For 2019/20, it is 5 per cent (2 per cent for social care and 3 per cent for general expenditure).[15]

Provision for a council tax referendum

If a local referendum takes place and the majority of voters veto the increase, the substitute calculations have effect for the financial year.[16]

The referendum can be held at any time of the authority's choosing subject to this being no later than a date in May or a date specified by the Secretary of State by order.[17] A local authority must publish a statement of reasons for the council tax increase at least 28 days before the date of the referendum.[18] The notice of such a referendum must be published no later than 25 days before the date of the referendum.[19] The poll is to be taken by a secret ballot. Proxy voting is permitted and assistance is allowed for disabled and illiterate voters who need help.[20]

The wording of the question for the referendum and the form of the ballot paper are prescribed by the Secretary of State in regulations and must explain the percentages and increase involved.[21]

If a local authority fails to hold a referendum on time, the substitute calculations have effect.

No referendums under these provisions were held in the first three years. The first referendum under took place on 7 May 2015. The Bedfordshire Police and Crime Commissioner proposed a 15.8 per cent increase in council tax for 2015/16: 30.5 per cent of voters supported the proposal and 69.5 per cent opposed it.[22]

A referendum may be challenged on a limited number of grounds in an election court or by way of judicial review.[23]

Practice notes and implementation letters

In addition to the legislation, the Ministry of Housing, Communities and Local Government (in England), the Welsh government and the local authority associations have together produced, and periodically revised, a series of 'practice notes'. These advise on the interpretation of the legislation and on administrative arrangements, and highlight a number of good practice points. There is no Scottish equivalent. The Ministry of Housing, Communities and Local Government also produces council tax 'implementation letters'. These advise local authorities about the latest changes in legislation or decisions of the courts. Points from the implementation letters are periodically included in revisions of the practice notes. While the legislation is binding on local authorities, neither the practice notes nor the implementation letters have the force of law and local authorities are not bound by them. Particularly useful comments from the practice notes are included in this *Handbook*. The Valuation Tribunal Service also issues a council tax guidance newsletter (*Valuation in Practice*), which may be consulted online, and a selection of guidance notes.

The president of the Valuation Tribunal for England has issued a practice statement applying to the conduct of hearings and the procedures to be adopted with appeals. Best practice guidance has also been issued by the Valuation Tribunal for Wales. See p240 for more details.

Notes in the *Handbook*

References to the law are given in notes at the end of each chapter. The notes usually begin with the letters E, W or S or a combination of these, indicating references to English, Welsh and/or Scottish law. The abbreviations used in the notes can be found in Appendix 4.

Legal and other references

Local authorities publish details of their local reduction schemes for council tax which should be available online.

Statutes and regulations governing council tax are available online but are not updated. Butterworth's loose-leaf work, *Ryde on Rating and the Council Tax*, reproduces all the relevant English and Welsh legislation and the practice notes. Large public reference libraries should have this two-volume work.

CPAG's Housing Benefit and Council Tax Reduction Legislation consolidates the legislation on CTR schemes in England, Wales and Scotland.

Shelter and the Chartered Institute of Housing produce *Help with Housing Costs, Volume 1: Guide to Universal Credit and Council Tax Rebates* (available from CPAG). *Atkin's Court Forms*, published by LexisNexis, covers forms typically used in council tax matters.

Rating and Valuation Reporter covers changes to council tax and reports decisions of the courts in valuation and local taxation matters. Other unreported decisions may be available on LexisNexis website, a database of court decisions and law reports; some judgments are also available at www.judiciary.gov.uk.

The most detailed guide to enforcement by way of imprisonment in England and Wales remains the Legal Action Group's *The Enforcement of Local Taxation: an advisors' guide to non-payment of council tax and poll tax* (2000).

Detailed information on proceedings in the civil and criminal courts, which may involve council tax matters, can be found in specialist works of law and procedure, published annually. Note that the rules of civil procedure which apply in the County Court and High Court do not have an equivalent in council tax proceedings in magistrates' courts. Details of appropriate procedures in the magistrates' court can be found in the annual *Stone's Justices' Manual*.

Policy changes and council tax research can be found on the Ministry of Housing, Communities and Local Government website.

Information on valuation matters and appeals can be found at the Valuation Office Agency website and the Valuation Tribunal Service website. The Valuation Tribunal Service website is regularly updated with summaries given in recent valuation tribunal decisions.

Individual local authority websites may also provide useful information on the payment and collection of council tax in local areas. It seems likely that the provision of information in this area will increase in the next few years, and some local authorities are developing schemes to share information with advice agencies, such as Citizens Advice, at a local level.

Reports of Ombudsman decisions are available at the Ombudsman websites for England, Wales and Scotland.

See Appendix 1 for the website addresses.

Notes

1. Introduction
 1 s1 LGFA 1992
 2 s100 LGFA 1992

2. Administration
 3 **EW** s1 LGFA 1992
 4 CTRS(DFE)(E) Regs

3. Legal background and references
 5 *UKI (Kingsway) Ltd v Westminster City Council* [2017] EWCA Civ 430
 6 ss44–45 Data Protection Act 2018
 7 The Openness of Local Government Bodies Regulations 2014 No.2095

 8 s52ZB(2) LGFA 1992; Schs 5 and 6 LA 2011
 9 s52ZC(1) LGFA 1992
 10 s4ZA LGFA 1992
 11 s52ZD LGFA 1992
 12 s52ZB LGFA 1992
 13 s52ZF LGFA 1992
 14 *Referendums Relating to Council Tax Increases (Principles) (England) Report 2018/19*, HC 792, 5 February 2018
 15 MHCLG, *Council tax levels set by local authorities England 2018-2019*, revised 9 April 2018
 16 s52ZH LGFA 1992

17 s52ZG LGFA 1992; The Local Authority
(Referendums Relating to Council Tax
Increases) (Date of Referendum)
(England) Order 2013 No.2862
18 Reg 11 LA(CR)(CTI)(E) Regs
19 Sch 3 para 3 LA(CR)(CTI)(E) Regs
20 Sch 3 para 28 LA(CR)(CTI)(E) Regs
21 Sch 1 LA(CR)(CTI)(E) Regs as amended
by the Local Authorities (Conduct of
Referendums) (Council Tax Increases)
(England) (Amendment) Regulations
2013 No.409
22 House of Commons Library, *Council tax:
local referendums, briefing paper number
05682*, 18 May 2015
23 Reg 20 LA(CR)(CTI)(E) Regs

Chapter 2

. . . .

Chargeable dwellings

This chapter covers:
1. Chargeable dwellings (below)
2. Dwellings in England and Wales (p10)
3. Dwellings in Scotland (p17)
4. New and altered properties (p19)

1. Chargeable dwellings

Council tax is payable on any dwelling which is not exempt (see Chapter 4). Properties on which the tax must be paid are referred to as 'chargeable dwellings'.[1] The definition of a 'dwelling' is therefore a fundamental one for council tax purposes.

In most cases, whether or not a property constitutes a dwelling is not in question. Houses, flats, bungalows, cottages and maisonettes used for domestic purposes all normally count as dwellings. However, sometimes it may not be clear whether or not a property constitutes a dwelling. This might occur, for example, if one property consists of a number of dwellings or if a number of properties constitute one dwelling. Whether or not a specific property constitutes a dwelling is one of the grounds for making a proposal to alter the valuation list (see Chapter 3) and could be the subject of an appeal (see Chapter 11).

The definition of a dwelling which applies in England and Wales differs from that which applies in Scotland. In the majority of cases, however, the effect is the same.

. . . .

Reducing the amount of council tax payable

The amount of council tax payable in respect of a dwelling may be reduced by:
– an alteration to the dwelling's valuation band (see Chapter 3);
– a fixed period or indefinite exemption (see Chapter 4);
– a disability reduction (see Chapter 6);
– a discount (see Chapter 7);
– council tax reduction (CTR) under the local support scheme (see Chapter 8);

– adopting certain payment arrangements, which may offer a discount (see Chapter 9);

– a discretionary reduction (see p167).

2. Dwellings in England and Wales

What counts as a dwelling

The legal definition of a dwelling for council tax purposes in England and Wales is not straightforward. The Local Government Finance Act 1992 defines a 'dwelling' as any property which:[2]

- would have been a 'hereditament' (ie, a rateable unit – see p11) for the purposes of section 115(1) of the General Rate Act 1967 if that Act had remained in force (see p11); *and*
- is not shown, or required to be shown, on a local or a central non-domestic rating list (see p15); *and*
- is not exempt from local non-domestic rating;[3] *or*
- is a 'composite hereditament' (see p16).

What is not a dwelling

The Act specifically excludes certain properties from being dwellings, unless they constitute part of a larger property which is itself a dwelling. These are:[4]

- a yard, garden, outhouse or other land or building belonging to, or enjoyed with, property used wholly for the purposes of living accommodation; *or*
- a private garage which either has a floor area of not more than 25 square metres or is used wholly or mainly to accommodate a private motor vehicle; *or*
- private storage premises used wholly or mainly to store domestic articles.

These exclusions mean, for example, that a garage used to keep a private car that is not part of a larger property does not constitute a dwelling and should not be included in the valuation of any other dwelling. A room occupied by a concierge may be included as domestic property forming part of a collection of dwellings chargeable to council tax.[5]

In England, property may be included in the definition of 'domestic property' if it is used for the microgeneration of electricity or heat by alternative energy sources (eg, biomass, biofuel, wind or water). However, it is not 'a dwelling' unless it forms part of a larger property which is itself a dwelling.[6]

Short-stay accommodation

Where a hotel or business provides accommodation for short periods to individuals whose sole or main residence is elsewhere, the part of the property which is wholly or mainly used is a non-domestic hereditament and is liable to non-domestic rates.[7] The accommodation must not be commercial self-contained, self-catering accommodation. The definition of business includes a property run by a charity.[8] However, small establishments such as guest houses are subject solely to council tax where:

- short-stay accommodation is provided for six people or less at any one time;
- the provider's sole or main residence is within the property; *and*
- the short-stay accommodation is subsidiary to the use of the property as a sole or main residence.

If you are housed in temporary bed and breakfast accommodation (eg, where you are homeless and in priority need and you and other dependent family members are being housed by the local authority[9]), you should not be liable for council tax. In such a case, the liability falls upon the owner of the dwelling (see Chapter 5).[10]

If a building or a self-contained part of a building is intended, in the coming year, to be available for letting commercially as self-catering accommodation for short periods totalling 140 days or more, it is not a domestic property and so not liable to council tax. In Wales, to escape council tax liability such a property must also have been let as self-catering accommodation for at least 70 days during the previous year and have been available for letting for at least 140 days. Where such a property is let for less than 70 days over the previous year as part of a larger business with other lets at the same location or within very close proximity, in some circumstances it may not be a domestic property chargeable to council tax.[11]

Hereditaments

The General Rate Act 1967 charged general rates on domestic and non-domestic property. Section 115(1) of that Act defined a **'hereditament'** as a 'property which is or may become liable to a rate, being a unit of such property which is, or would fall to be, shown as a separate rate item in the valuation list'. The exact identity of the hereditament has been the subject of numerous legal cases. Prior to 2015, in the leading case on the issue, Denning LJ said:[12]

> Where two or more properties are within the same curtilage or contiguous to one another, and are in the same occupation, they are as a general rule to be treated for rating purposes as if they formed part of a single hereditament. There are exceptional cases, however, where for some special reason they may be treated as two or more hereditaments. That may happen for instance, because they were valued at different times, or because they were at one time in different occupations, or because one part is used for an entirely different purpose. Where the two properties are in the same occupation but are not within the same curtilage nor contiguous to one another, each of them must as a general rule be treated as a separate hereditament for rating purposes: and this is the case even though they are used by the occupier for the purposes of his one whole business.

These principles were subject to revision in 2015 by the Supreme Court and a more fluid set of tests adopted. In *Woolway v Mazars*,[13] the Supreme Court looked at the degree of connectedness between two offices of the same business operating on different floors of a building. It ruled that adjacent spaces would normally possess the characteristic of being connected and treated as one hereditament, but unity was not simply a question of contiguity. If direct communication is possible between two occupied parts of a dwelling, by a door or a staircase, the occupier will usually be said to create a new and larger hereditament in place of the two which previously existed.

Where two spaces are geographically distinct, a functional test may still enable them to be treated as a single hereditament, but only where the use of the one section or unit is necessary to the effectual enjoyment of the other. This is normally decided by whether the two sections can be let separately.

Whether the use of one section is necessary for effective enjoyment of the other depends not upon the needs of the occupier, but on the physical character of the property and its objectively ascertainable characteristics.

Dwellings in a state of disrepair

In some cases, a property may be in such a state of disrepair that it cannot be classed as a dwelling at all. It could be so derelict that even with a reasonable amount of repairs, no one could be expected to live in it. Such a property ceases to be a hereditament and may be removed from the valuation list altogether.

When deciding whether a dwelling should be removed, a key test is whether a reasonable amount of repair work would make it habitable. If the answer is 'no', the dwelling can be taken off the list entirely. Past valuation tribunal decisions on this question show that the state of dereliction must be severe and it must be uneconomical to undertake repairs. A tribunal may establish that if it were unreasonable to undertake repairs and no reasonable owner would attempt them, the dwelling should be removed from the list.

Note: the actual intentions of the landlord or owner are not relevant. The tribunal looks at the actions of a hypothetical reasonable owner. Thus, an owner or landlord who is willing to spend more than what a reasonable person would to repair a property may still have the dwelling removed from the list for the period it is uninhabitable. For example, in one case, a valuation tribunal held that a dwelling with dangerous electrical wiring and lacking a gable wall should not appear in a valuation list while undergoing rebuilding.[14] The building was uninhabitable during rebuilding and failed to meet the definitions of a rateable hereditament. If a dwelling can be repaired, it should remain on the valuation list and may be entitled to an empty dwelling exemption for 12 months while the repairs are carried out. For more information on exemptions, see Chapter 4.

Self-contained accommodation and 'granny flats'

If a dwelling is considered to be a single dwelling under the definition of a hereditament (see p11), but consists of more than one 'self-contained unit' of living accommodation, the local authority will treat each self-contained unit of accommodation as a separate dwelling.[15]

A **'self-contained unit'** is a building, or part of a building, which has been constructed or adapted for use as separate living accommodation.[16] Local authority listing officers are advised to look for living and sleeping accommodation and at least minimal separate cooking and washing facilities before they decide that the property constitutes 'self-contained' living accommodation. For example, a property that contains more than one self-contained unit (eg, a large house that has been adapted to provide a separate 'granny' annex or provides separate staff accommodation) should be treated as two or more dwellings. The annex may then be an exempt dwelling if unoccupied (see Chapter 4). Key factors to be taken into account include whether a self-contained unit or annex has all the features necessary for independent living. The actual intentions of the parties are not decisive.[17]

If a living unit does not have independent outside access, it does not necessarily mean it is part of a single dwelling.[18]

The view of the occupier (eg, if s/he says that the accommodation is used as a games room rather than living accommodation) will not prevent a listing officer from deciding that a separate dwelling exists.

Identifying whether a dwelling constitutes a 'self-contained unit' takes part in stages. The listing officer must first determine that a hereditament exists and to what extent, and only then go on to consider whether the hereditament contains any self-contained units.[19]

Determining whether parts of a building are 'self-contained units' is an objective test of fact and degree in each case and includes the following considerations.[20]

- Is the part of the building identified reasonably suitable and fit for use as a self-contained dwelling?
- Are the physical characteristics of the dwelling, which may include services and fixtures, of reasonable suitability?
- What is the actual use of the self-contained part of the dwelling? While this may be relevant, it is not the key test and usually is not of significant weight in the assessment.
- What are the characteristics of the rest of the building and access?

The size of a dwelling is also relevant to determine whether it is suitable to be classed as self-contained accommodation, but the size of the areas in comparison to the rest of the building is not an issue.[21] Whether there is a door or a lock does not determine alone whether accommodation is self-contained or not,[22] but the existence of a door and its position may indicate that it has been constructed with a sufficient degree of privacy to be classed as self-contained.[23]

Council Tax Manual Practice Note 5 states:[24]

A self-contained unit should have facilities for living, sleeping, preparation and cooking of food and bathing facilities such as a bath or shower, wash hand basin and lavatory. However in exceptional circumstances the lack of a facility does not prevent a unit from being self-contained, for example, a unit having shared bathing facilities – *Clement (LO) v Bryant and Others* (2003 RA 133).

Thus, the absence of a fixture (eg, an oven) does not always stop a dwelling from being classed as self-contained, but is a factor to be considered.[25]

If you are an 'interested person' (see p34), you can make a proposal (see p35) to the listing officer not to show your home as a separate unit of accommodation on the valuation list. The test for the tribunal is one of fact and degree to determine whether the conditions for a self-contained dwelling are met.[26]

Buildings in multiple occupation

The listing officer has the discretion to treat a property which would otherwise be considered to be two or more separate dwellings as a single dwelling if it:[27]

- consists of a single self-contained unit, or such a unit together with or containing premises constructed or adapted for non-domestic purposes; *and*
- is occupied as more than one unit of separate living accommodation.

This could apply, for example, to a property occupied by more than one household, but where the residents share facilities such as kitchens or bathrooms – eg, a group of bedsits, a hostel, a care home or refuge. The deemed dwelling unit must be capable of being lived in separately to be classed as a self-contained unit. The listing officer must exercise her/his discretion reasonably and should take into account all the circumstances of the case, including the extent to which the parts of the property that are separately occupied have been structurally altered.

The listing officer's decision that a property is, or should be treated as, only one dwelling rather than several may have an impact not only on the single dwelling's valuation band but also on liability and entitlement to discounts (also known as 'variations' in Scotland) or benefits. In one case concerning general rates, it was held that at least four factors should be considered by a valuation officer when exercising her/his discretion.[28] These are:

- the degree to which facilities, such as kitchens and bathrooms, are shared;
- the degree of internal adaptations, such as entrance doors;
- the degree of identifiably separate parts;
- the degree of transience in the occupiers' residence.

The higher courts have confirmed that the above principles continue to apply with the test that is sometimes referred to as the 'bricks and mortar test', by looking at the reality of what has actually been constructed rather than at the intentions of the owner (see Chapter 5).[29] However, if two flats are converted to a single property, a new dwelling is created for council tax purposes.[30] The presence or absence of one characteristic is not normally determinative in itself, but an overall collection of features. It would be expected that a reasonable decision looking at all the facts would be taken.[31]

In Wales, a refuge must be treated as a single dwelling for council tax purposes, even if the dwelling consists of more than one self-contained unit. A property is classed as a refuge if it:[32]

- is operated on a not for profit basis; *and*
- is used wholly or mainly for the temporary accommodation of persons who have been subject to:
  - controlling, coercive or threatening behaviour;
  - physical violence;
  - abuse of any other description (whether physical or mental); *or*
  - threats of any such violence or abuse,

  from a partner with whom they are or were cohabiting.

Houses in multiple occupation have to be registered with the local authority (see Chapter 5) but a different definition applies regarding the number of people living in the property.

Converted sheds and garages

In areas with high rents and a shortage of accommodation, some people have transformed sheds and garages into places to stay for migrant workers. These may pose problems for local authorities in the future. Converted sheds and garages may be excluded from the category of 'dwelling' or may be part of the owner's dwelling. Even if they are treated as dwellings in their own right, in most cases it is likely that the owner will be held liable for the council tax (see Chapter 5).

Properties on the non-domestic rating list

Property is 'domestic' if it is used wholly for the purpose of living accommodation. If it is not in use, it is still considered to be domestic property if its next use will be domestic. Most non-domestic property, such as business or industrial property, is shown on either the local or central non-domestic rating list. Such properties are not dwellings for council tax purposes, but are subject to non-domestic rates.

Caravans and houseboats

A pitch for a caravan and a mooring for a houseboat are hereditaments (see p11) and are, therefore, capable of being considered dwellings for council tax purposes if they are occupied by a caravan or houseboat (including a boat which is no longer navigable[33]) which is someone's sole or main residence (see p72). If not in use, even if the pitch or mooring is empty, it is still considered a dwelling if it appears that its next use will be domestic, but it may be an exempt dwelling (see Chapter 4). Boats and caravans may themselves be classed as hereditaments and treated as domestic dwellings. For a boat or a caravan to constitute a hereditament, the key question is the degree of permanence in its position.

If a boat is moored at one spot or a caravan parked on the same pitch for a substantial period, its value may also be included in the valuation of pitch or mooring for banding purposes. Where a dwelling boat or caravan occupies a mooring or pitch for 12 months or more, the value of the boat or caravan should be included in the band value, even if it moves away for brief periods, of say, two to four weeks, provided it then returns to its original mooring or pitch.[34] The question to be asked is whether the occupation can be characterised as that of a 'settler' or 'wayfarer'. If the latter, then only the mooring or pitch should valued.[35]

Holiday caravans and other caravans used for non-domestic purposes are subject to non-domestic rates. However, if you keep a caravan at home for use on holidays, you are not liable to pay non-domestic rates or council tax on it.

Timeshare property

Timeshare accommodation does not count as domestic property and is subject to non-domestic rates.

Composite hereditaments

A property is a **'composite hereditament'** if only part of it is used solely for the purpose of living accommodation. For example, some rooms in a property may be used only for business purposes and others used only for domestic purposes. Council tax is payable on the domestic portion and non-domestic rates are payable on the business portion. It is possible to appeal against a decision that a property is a composite hereditament, or against a decision on the proportion of a property that is used for domestic or non-domestic purposes. The key question is whether the character of a dwelling house has been lost.[36] For example, a dwelling in which a room or garage is predominantly used for business purposes may be classed as a composite hereditament. However, the fact that someone works from home does not necessarily create a composite hereditament. In *Tully v Jorgensen (VO)*, the appellant worked from home because her disability meant she was unable to travel to work on a daily basis. The room she used had not been structurally adapted for business use and contained normal domestic furniture. Outside of office hours, the room reverted to normal family use. No one visited for business purposes and if meetings were required, they took place elsewhere. Consequently, the room was part of the ordinary domestic accommodation of the household.[37]

When valuing a composite property, a listing officer is expected initially to value the property as a whole, and then apportion the relevant amount between domestic and non-domestic parts.[38]

When assessing the domestic portion of a composite hereditament, the listing officer must take into account the amount of the property that could reasonably be attributed to domestic use. The Court of Appeal has ruled that, provided the listing officer does so, s/he can value the domestic portion by any method s/he chooses and it is not necessary to value the whole composite hereditament first.[39]

Dwellings in different locations

The location of a dwelling is a major determining factor in how much council tax is payable and whether it should be treated as one or more properties. Two properties which are occupied in common by the same person or body and used for one purpose, but which are geographically separated (eg, by a road or public street) or if there is not common possession of the whole area concerned, should normally be treated as two separate hereditaments.[40]

If a dwelling (including a dwelling that is part of a larger single property) falls within the area of two or more local authorities, or two or more parts of an authority's area, it should be treated as being in the area in which the greatest part of the dwelling is situated, or in terms of use, of greater domestic value is situated.[41]

Where no part of a composite hereditament can reasonably be ascertained to have a domestic use of greater value than any other part, the area within which the dwelling is treated as being situated is determined by agreement between the billing authorities. If they cannot agree, the matter is determined by drawing lots.[42]

3. Dwellings in Scotland

In Scotland, a **'dwelling'** means any lands and 'heritages' – ie, rights that exist with the land, such as farming and fishing rights:[43]

- which consist of one or more dwelling houses with any garden, yard, garage, outhouse or pertinent other area belonging to and occupied with the dwelling house(s); *and*
- which would, but for the fact that it is a dwelling, be entered separately in the valuation roll.

The valuation roll is now limited to recording the details of non-domestic and part-residential properties. Details of domestic dwellings are now contained in the valuation lists.

A Scottish dwelling includes:

- the residential part of part-residential property (see p19); *and*
- part of any premises that was apportioned on 1 April 1989 as a dwelling house.

It includes caravans, but only if they are your sole or main residence.

What counts as a dwelling

Certain types of property are explicitly included or excluded from the Scottish definition of a dwelling. The following properties are specifically included in the definition of a dwelling if, but for the fact that they were dwellings, they would be entered separately on the valuation roll:

- a garage, carport or car parking space wholly or mainly used, or last used, for private motor vehicles;[44]
- certain private storage premises used, or last used, wholly or mainly to store domestic articles (including cycles and other similar vehicles);[45]
- bed and breakfast accommodation operated on a commercial basis by a person living there for letting to not more than six people a night;
- student halls of residence which include shared facilities;
- accommodation owned by the Ministry of Defence which is, or is likely to be, the sole or main residence of at least one member of the armed forces;
- school boarding accommodation;
- any part of a communal residential establishment with shared facilities for residents, including those parts of a hostel or care home (as defined for the purpose of a discount – see p110) which are used wholly or mainly as the sole or main residence of a person employed there. **Note:** the other parts of this type of accommodation in which the residents live are not dwellings, but are subject to non-domestic rates.

Note: some of the above dwellings are exempt from council tax (see Chapter 4).[46]

In determining what is a dwelling, a court or tribunal may consider both the physical characteristics *and* the use made of the property as relevant considerations.[47]

What is not a dwelling

Certain properties are specifically excluded from the Scottish definition of a dwelling, but may be subject to non-domestic rates. These are:

- certain huts, sheds and bothies which are no one's sole or main residence;
- certain self-catering holiday accommodation which is no one's sole or main residence;
- women's refuges (except any part which is the sole or main residence of an employee of the voluntary organisation managing the refuge);[48]
- timeshare accommodation.[49]

If a dwelling is served by a combined heat and power station, the pipes, risers and other plant connected with the power station are not treated as part of the dwelling (and so are ignored for valuation purposes), except insofar as they fall within the solum (upper soil), garden, yard or garage of the dwelling.[50]

Thus, all pipes and risers for the transport of water between a power station and a block of flats (or tenement) are not treated as part of all the dwellings in the tenement, insofar as these pipes and risers are not located in or on land pertaining to the tenement. If the power station benefits only the tenement, it (and all the associated plant) counts as part of each dwelling. They are allocated equally between the dwellings they serve.

Buildings in multiple occupation

In Scotland, a house in multiple occupation includes dwellings that were not originally constructed or subsequently adapted for such use but are actually being used as a house in multiple occupation even if they are, at times, occupied by one person. These houses in multiple occupation must be formally registered with the local authority.[51]

Part-residential property

Certain properties with a mixed domestic and non-domestic use (eg, nursing homes and hospitals – see p18 and p110) are divided into their relevant parts. The non-domestic element is entered on the valuation roll and the domestic element is entered on the valuation list and is treated as a dwelling for council tax purposes.

Premises that are used for commercial or sporting purposes (known as '**part-residential subjects**') are treated differently. The property is shown on the valuation roll, but an apportionment note on the roll indicates the net annual value and the rateable value based on the residential and non-residential use of the property.[52] The residential part counts as a dwelling for council tax purposes. **Note:** those parts of a refuge, hostel or care home (see p110) used as accommodation for residents rather than employees are specifically excluded from the definition of part-residential subject.[53]

---

4. **New and altered properties**

A new dwelling may be created either by a new building or by the structural alteration of an existing property. A new dwelling is considered to come into existence for council tax purposes from the day a completion notice is served, or from the completion date contained on the notice, if later.[54] In the latter case, this is if a dwelling is not completed, but the local authority believes it is substantially completed and it can be completed within three months from the date the notice is served.

A new or altered dwelling does not require a completion notice once someone starts to live there.

If a new or altered dwelling is unoccupied, it may be exempt from council tax for a period (see Chapter 4). If a new dwelling is created by the structural alteration to a building, the former dwelling(s) is considered to have ceased to exist on the completion date.

Completion notices

The local authority (in England and Wales) or assessor (in Scotland) may serve a completion notice on the owner of a building which has been completed or which can reasonably be expected to be completed within three months.[55] This notice proposes a completion day for the building.

The proposed completion day becomes the actual completion day unless the owner appeals. Before the outcome of the appeal, the proposed completion day is treated as the actual completion day.

In deciding whether a completion notice should be issued, the question is whether the building is capable of occupation. The Lands Chamber of the Upper Tribunal has stated:[56]

The building is only a hereditament if it is ready for occupation...If the building lacks features which will have to be provided before it can be occupied for that purpose and when provided will provide part of the hereditament and form the basis of its valuation it does not constitute a hereditament and so does not fall to be shown in the Rating List. There is, in consequence, no scope for including in the List a building which is nearly, even very nearly, ready for occupation unless the completion notice procedure has been followed.

Appealing against a completion notice

Any disagreement over the date on a completion notice can be raised in the first instance with the local authority (in England and Wales) or the assessor (in Scotland).

In England and Wales, appeals should be made directly to the Valuation Tribunal for England or the Valuation Tribunal for Wales within 28 days of the notice being sent (see p239).[57] An out-of-time appeal may be allowed if you have failed to meet this time limit for reasons beyond your control.[58]

In Scotland, an appeal must be lodged with a valuation appeal committee within 21 days of receiving the completion notice.[59] Do this by writing to the assessor, stating the grounds of the appeal and enclosing a copy of the completion notice.

Notes

1. Chargeable dwellings

1 **EW** s4(1) and (2) LGFA 1992
S s72(6) LGFA 1992

2. Dwellings in England and Wales

2 s3(1) LGFA 1992
3 s66(1A) LGFA 1988
4 s3(4) LGFA 1992
5 *The Collection (Management) Ltd v Jackson* [2013] UKUT 166 (LC)
6 s3(4A) LGFA 1992 as defined in s66(1A) and s26(2) LGFA 1988 Climate Change and Sustainable Energy Act 2006
7 s66(2) LGFA 1988
8 s66(8) LGFA 1988
9 Either under the Housing Act 1996 or the Children Act 1989
10 CT(LO) Regs
11 s66(2BB)(d) LGFA 1988 s66 as substituted by the Non-Domestic Rating (Definition of Domestic Property) (Wales) Order 2016 No.31
12 *Gilbert (Valuation Officer) v Hickinbottom & Sons Ltd* [1956] 2 All ER 101 (CA)
13 *Woolway v Mazars* [2015] UKSC 53
14 *Z Munter Farms Ltd v Pettitt* [2006] RVR 332
15 CT(CD)O
16 Art 2 CT(CD)O
17 *Re a Dwelling in London N2* [2015] RVR 157
18 *Vaziri v Listing Officer* [2006] RVR 329
19 *Rawsthorne (Listing Officer) v Parr* [2009] EWHC 2002 (Admin)
20 *Corkish (LO) v Wright and Hart* [2014] RVR 233
21 *Re a Dwelling in London N2* App Ref 5090649355/084CAD VTE [2015] RVR 157 per President Professor Graham Zellick
22 *Jorgensen (LO) v Gomperts* [2006] RA 300
23 *Ramdhun v Coll (LO)* [2015] RVR 89
24 VOA, Council Tax Manual, Practice Note 5: Appendix 1: Case summaries relating to Disaggregation, para 2.5
25 *Beasley (LO) v YMCA* [2000] RA 249; *Kelderman v Valuation Office Agency* [2014] EWHC 159 (Admin)
26 *Corkish (LO) v Wright and Hart* [2014] RVR 233 per Popplewell, J
27 CT(CD)O, as amended by The Council Tax (Chargeable Dwellings, Exempt Dwellings and Discount Disregards) (Amendment) (England) Order 2003 No.3121
28 *James v Williams* [1973] RA 305
29 *R v London South Eastern Valuation Tribunal and Neale ex parte Moore* [2001] RVR 94; *Baker (LO) v Gomperts* [2006] All ER(D) 1 July; *Listing Officer v Callear* [2012] EWHC 3697
30 *R v East Sussex Valuation Tribunal ex parte Silverstone* [1996] RVR 203
31 *Associated Provincial Picture Houses v Wednesbury Corporation* [1948] 1 KB 223
32 Art 3B CT(CD)O inserted by art 3 Council Tax (Chargeable Dwellings) (Amendment) (Wales) Order 2014 No.2653
33 *Nicholls v Wimbledon Valuation Officer* [1995] RVR 171
34 VOA, Council Tax Manual, Practice Note 7 – Application to Council Tax to Caravan Pitches and Moorings, para 6.2
35 *Reeves (LO) v Northrop (LO)* [2013] EWCA 362
36 *Guthrie v Highland Region and Western Isles Assessor* [1995] RA 292
37 *Tully v Jorgensen (VO)* [2003] RA 233
38 *Listing Officer v Monmouth School* [2009] EWHC 2720 (Admin)
39 Reg 7 CT(SVD) Regs; *Atkinson and Others v Lord* [1997] RA 413
40 *Woolway v Mazars* [2015] UKSC 53
41 CT(SVD) Regs; see also VOA, Council Tax Manual, Practice Note 10
42 Reg 3 CT(SVD) Regs, as amended by CT(SVD)(A) Regs

3. Dwellings in Scotland

43 s72 LGFA 1992
44 Reg 2(2) CT(Dw)(S) Regs
45 Reg 2(3) CT(Dw)(S) Regs
46 CT(DPRS)(S) Regs
47 *The Old Course Ltd v Fife Council Assessor* [2016] CSIH 40 Lands Valuation Appeal Court, Court of Session

48 CT(D)(S) Regs
49 CT(Dw)(S) Regs
50 CT(Dw)(S) Regs 2010
51 Sch para 3 CT(LO)(S) Regs
52 s72(8) and Sch 5 LGFA 1992
53 CT(D)(S) Regs

4. New and altered properties
54 **EW** s17 LGFA 1992; Sch 4A LGFA 1988
    S s83(1) and Sch 6 LGFA 1992
55 **EW** s17 LGFA 1992; Sch 4A LGFA 1988
    S s83(1) and Sch 6 LGFA 1992
56 *Porter v Trustees of Gladman Sipps* [2011]
    UKUT 204 (LC)
57 **E** Reg 21(5) VTE(CTRA)(P) Regs
    W Reg 29(4) VTW Regs
58 **E** Reg 21(6) VTE(CTRA)(P) Regs
    W Reg 29(5) VTW Regs
59 **S** Sch 6 LGFA 1992

Chapter 3

Valuation

This chapter covers:
1. Who is responsible for valuations (below)
2. The listing officer's and assessor's powers (p25)
3. How dwellings are valued (p26)
4. Compiling and maintaining valuation lists (p30)
5. Inspecting the valuation list (p30)
6. Altering a valuation list (p32)
7. The valuation bands (p42)

1. Who is responsible for valuations

England and Wales

In England and Wales, the valuation of dwellings for council tax purposes is carried out by the Valuation Office Agency (VOA), which is part of HM Revenue and Customs (HMRC). There is a listing officer at the VOA for each local authority. The listing officer has various duties in relation to compiling and maintaining the valuation list, and is independent of the local authority.[1] The term 'listing officer' in this *Handbook* refers to any listing officer and any other officer appointed by HMRC's commissioners to carry out their functions.[2]

Details of your local Valuation Office and listing officer can be found at www.voa.gov.uk or by telephoning 0300 050 1501 (England) or 0300 050 5505 (Wales).

Scotland

In Scotland, the **assessor** and any deputy assessor for each local authority decides which valuation band applies to each dwelling in the area.[3] The assessor is a professional valuer who must comply with any directions on valuations given by HMRC commissioners.[4] The assessor is appointed and employed by the council.[5] Details of assessors can be found at www.saa.gov.uk.

Appointees

The commissioners (in England and Wales) and the assessor (in Scotland) have the power to appoint other people (eg, private surveyors) to carry out valuations.[6] The commissioners and the assessor are able to supply these appointees with relevant information obtained under their various powers – eg, any survey report obtained for rating purposes.[7] If the person assisting with the valuation discloses that information for reasons other than valuation purposes under the provisions of the Freedom of Information Act 2000, data protection purposes or in legal proceedings, s/he may be imprisoned for up to two years and/or fined.[8]

Complaints

If you are unhappy with a valuation decision, see p32 and Chapter 11.

To complain about maladministration (as opposed to the actual decision) of any local listing officer, initially contact the office concerned. Maladministration includes delays in dealing with enquiries and letters, providing inaccurate or misleading information and bad service from a member of staff. See p273 for more examples.

If the response to your complaint is unsatisfactory, you can ask for a 'tier two' review. If you are not satisfied with a tier two response you can put your case to the Adjudicator. The role of the Adjudicator is to review the handling of complaints brought against the Insolvency Service, HMRC and the VOA, and can recommend action to put matters right. The VOA will accept the Adjudicator's recommendations, unless there are exceptional circumstances. You can refer a complaint to the Adjudicator's Office in writing or by telephone (see Appendix 1). During 2017/2018, the Adjudicator received 23 complaints about the VOA.[9]

If you are unhappy with the Adjudicator's recommendations, you can complain to the Ombudsman. Since the VOA is a central government agency, the complaint is to the Parliamentary and Health Service Ombudsman, not the Local Government and Social Care Ombudsman/Public Services Ombudsman for Wales, whose role is described in Chapter 12. Contact your MP if you are pursuing a complaint with the Parliamentary and Health Service Ombudsman.

In Scotland, a complaint may be made to the Valuation Joint Board using the complaints form. If you are still dissatisfied at the end of the procedure, you can complain to the Scottish Public Services Ombudsman (SPSO).

The SPSO is the final stage for complaints about most public bodies that provide public services in Scotland. The SPSO will only consider a complaint after you have completed the assessor's complaints procedure. Complaints must be made to the SPSO within 12 months of when you became aware of the matter subject to complaint.

2. **The listing officer's and assessor's powers**

The listing officer and assessor have powers to:
- enter dwellings; *and*
- obtain information from a past or present owner, occupier, the local authority and certain other people.

Powers of entry

A listing officer and any assistant with written authorisation from the listing officer (in Scotland, the local assessor or deputy assessor) may enter, survey and value a dwelling.[10] At least three clear days' written notice must be given. In England, the power can only be exercised where the officer has first obtained approval from the First-tier Tribunal before exercising the power.[11] The three-day period excludes weekends and public holidays. Normally, the official concerned should try to arrange a suitable time for access and give you at least seven days' notice.

Listing officers carry identity cards and will ask your permission to take photographs.[12]

If you intentionally delay or obstruct the official, you may be liable, on summary conviction, to a fine not exceeding level 1 on the standard scale.[13]

The owner's and occupier's duty to provide information

The listing officer or assessor may require the present or past owner or occupier of a dwelling to supply information to assist her/him to carry out the valuation.[14] If the information is in the owner's or occupier's possession or control, it should be supplied within 21 days of a written notice being served. Failure to comply, without reasonable excuse, may result in a fine of up to level 2 on the standard scale.[15]

A current or past owner or occupier could be liable to be imprisoned for up to three months and/or for a fine up to £1,000 if s/he makes a false statement.[16]

The local authority's duty to provide information

The listing officer or assessor may require the local authority to supply information about a property to assist her/him to carry out the valuation. In addition, if any information comes to the notice of a local authority, which it considers would assist the listing officer or assessor in her/his duties, it should provide that information.[17] In practice, the local authority will identify new dwellings and refer existing ones that have been altered.

Right to use other sources of information

Certain other individuals and organisations, such as the former community charge registration officer and, in Scotland, the district council, must also supply information if the listing officer or assessor requests it.[18] A listing officer or assessor may also take into account any other information available from other sources.

3. How dwellings are valued

In **England and Scotland**, each dwelling is valued on the basis of what it might reasonably have been expected to realise on the open market, subject to certain valuation assumptions, if sold on 1 April 1991 by a willing seller.[19]

When valuing a property, the question asked is: 'What was this dwelling worth on 1 April 1991, assuming there was a buyer available and the valuation assumptions applied?' (see p27).

The use of 1 April 1991 for valuations has meant that adjustments for changes in prices over time have not had to be made. However, with changes in property prices since 1991, the construction of many new dwellings and the alteration of others, an assumed valuation date of 1 April 1991 has become harder to justify or maintain. As a result, the Local Government Act 2003 introduced a 10-year cycle of revaluations, but the process has so far only been completed for Wales (see below).

Plans for a general revaluation in England by 1 April 2007 were abandoned in March 2006 when the Council Tax (New Valuation Lists for England) Act 2006 was passed. This removed the requirement for a revaluation to be undertaken every 10 years, and future revaluation dates will be set by regulations. At present, the government has no plans to undertake a revaluation in England and council tax valuations will continue to be made based on a theoretical sale price on 1 April 1991.[20]

In **Wales**, a revaluation of dwellings was completed on 1 April 2005, using the relevant date of 1 April 2003.

Theoretical and actual value

The valuation for council tax purposes represents a *theoretical* value of what the property was worth on the relevant date (see above), not its actual value. So, a dwelling which, in reality, may have been in a bad state of repair is treated as though it had been in a reasonable state of repair, as this is one of the valuation assumptions applied to all dwellings regardless of the circumstances. Similarly, fixtures inside a dwelling are ignored – eg, it makes no difference whether there is a modern kitchen installed or no kitchen fittings at all. A council tax valuation must be made applying all the theoretical assumptions, regardless of what the actual situation was or might be today. The consequences of this are that the *actual price* that a property achieved when put on the market in 1991, or since, will not be its value for council tax purposes unless the two figures happen to coincide. An actual sale price would simply count as evidence towards what a property was worth for the purposes of a council tax banding valuation, applying the valuation assumptions.

A dwelling built since 1991 has to be valued by imagining it as if it had existed in 1991 and then applying the valuation assumptions to it to determine what it was worth. From this theoretical valuation, the dwelling is then allocated a valuation band.

Banding details of domestic properties can be found at www.voa.gov.uk.

The valuation assumptions

To make all valuations on a common basis, properties are not only assessed on the basis of their market value on 1 April 1991 in England and Scotland (1 April 2003 in Wales), but are also subject to certain valuation assumptions. The factors that affect the market value of a property include the number of rooms, its age, the construction materials used, the presence of a garden and the nature of the neighbouring environment. Many factors can affect value, and once these have been taken into consideration, the following statutory valuation assumptions are then applied.

Valuation assumptions

– The sale is with vacant possession.
– In England and Wales, a house is sold freehold and a flat (ie, part of a building divided horizontally to provide living units) is sold on a lease for 99 years at a nominal rent.
– In England and Wales, the dwelling is sold free from any rent charge (ie, rare rental payments on freehold land usually associated with covenants) or other duty or obligation.
– In Scotland, the dwelling is sold free from any 'heritable security' – ie, any mortgage is paid off.
– The size, layout and character of the dwelling, and the physical state of its locality, are the same as on the day the valuation was made.
– The dwelling is in reasonable repair.
– If there are common parts (eg, a shared hallway), these are in a reasonable state of repair considering the age and character of the dwelling and its locality, and the purchaser is liable to contribute to the cost of keeping them in such a state.
– Fixtures designed for a person with a physical disability, which increase the value of the dwelling, are ignored.
– The dwelling's use is permanently restricted to use as a private dwelling.
– The dwelling has no development value other than that attributable to any development for which no planning permission is required.

Note: the above assumptions are applied, whether or not they exist in fact.[21] The fact that a flat may be in shared ownership does not prevent it being valued as if a 99-year lease has been granted to a single owner.

While the effect of a rent charge will be disregarded, other forms of covenant which may affect a property may be considered when it is valued.[22] The effect of any shared ownership scheme which may apply to a flat is disregarded.[23]

Reasonable repair

The dwelling is presumed to be in a reasonable state of repair, regardless of whether it is or not.

However, a distinction may be drawn between a dwelling which is in need of repair and a dwelling which is in such a poor state that it should no longer be classified as a dwelling or hereditament (see p11), and should no longer be on the valuation list.

The High Court has accepted that there may come a point at which a property is so derelict as to be incapable of repair.[24] A valuer or tribunal must avoid confusing the concept of the existence, or continued existence, of a hereditament on the one hand, from the separate question of the proper valuation of a hereditament on the other. If a dwelling is in such a state of disrepair that it cannot be classed as a hereditament, it should be removed from the valuation list. Listing officers are expected to ask the question: 'Having regard to the character of the property and a reasonable amount of repair works being undertaken, could the premises be occupied as a dwelling?'[25]

If the answer is no, the dwelling should be removed from the valuation list. If it is yes, it should be valued using the assumption that it is in a reasonable state of repair.

Similarly, in Scotland the view has been taken that:[26]

when determining whether subjects are, or remain, a dwelling it is not correct to treat them as if they are in a state of reasonable repair if in fact they are not. The assumption…does not apply at that stage. Rather, regard has to be had to the subjects' actual state and existing use.

A mere incapacity to be lived in for a temporary period while repairs or other alteration works are being carried out is not necessarily enough to cause a dwelling to cease to be a dwelling.[27]

Fixtures for a person with a disability

'Fixtures' are items permanently attached to a dwelling, such as a sink, lavatory or lift. The value of fixtures should be ignored in the valuation if they:[28]

- are designed to make the dwelling suitable for use by a person with a physical disability; *and*
- add to the dwelling's value.

In other words, the dwelling is valued on the basis that those fixtures are not present. There is no requirement for someone with a disability to live in the dwelling. Such fixtures may have been taken into account during the valuation process. If this is the case, the listing officer or assessor should be advised of this possible oversight.

However, the presence of fittings and adaptations may be relevant to obtaining a reduction in valuation (see p33). There is also a separate disability reduction scheme (see Chapter 6).

Dwellings with mixed domestic and business use

In England and Wales, properties which include both a domestic and non-domestic component (known as 'composite hereditaments' – see p16) are valued on the proportion of the market value which might reasonably be attributed to the domestic use of the property. The valuation is based on the same rules and assumptions outlined above, except that the assumption that the property is permanently restricted for use as a private dwelling is ignored.

Scottish farmhouses, crofts and fish farms

In Scotland, dwellings such as farmhouses or cottages and croft houses connected with agriculture or fish farms are valued on the assumption that their availability is restricted to being used in that way. This lowers the value of the property and may lead to its being placed in a lower valuation band. When valuing a dwelling for council tax, the effect of a planning condition restricting occupation to a person mainly employed on a farm must not be ignored.[29]

Proposals and appeals on valuations

The use of valuation assumptions (see p27) means that a dwelling's valuation band may not reflect its actual sale price in 1991 (2003 in Wales). Consequently, the actual selling price of a dwelling would not necessarily be useful evidence to support a proposal to alter its value on the valuation list (see p32) or at a valuation tribunal or a valuation appeal committee hearing, unless the actual sale price happened to match the council tax valuation using the statutory valuation assumptions.

The valuation assumptions are applied whatever the condition of the dwelling (but see p30 if energy efficiency measures have been added). Thus, a valuation for council tax purposes may differ from a valuation for any other purpose. The assumptions are applied in every case regardless of the actual circumstances on the relevant day (ie, 1 April 1991 for England and Scotland, and 1 April 2003 for Wales) and used by valuation tribunals and valuation appeal committees and the High Court and Court of Session when considering appeals against banding decisions.

To be successful, a proposal to alter a dwelling's banding or an appeal must apply the assumptions described on p27.

Energy efficiency measures

The addition of energy efficiency or renewable energy measures, such as ground source heat pumps, insulation or solar panels, affect the value of a dwelling for council tax purposes. If the property is sold and the measures have increased the value of the dwelling into the next council tax band level, it is possible to change the dwelling's valuation. However, in practice, only substantial improvements would be likely to move a property up a band on its sale, and energy efficiency measures in isolation are unlikely to do so or will be disregarded.[30]

4. Compiling and maintaining valuation lists

The listing officer or assessor is responsible for compiling and maintaining each local authority's valuation list.[31]

Compiling the list

In **England and Scotland**, the valuation list in operation was compiled on 1 April 1993 and came into force on that day. In **Wales**, the current list came into force on 1 April 2005.

Any new lists must, as far as is reasonably practicable, be accurate on the date on which they are compiled, and so properties must be revalued before the publication of each list. As soon as is reasonably practicable after its compilation, a copy should be sent to the local authority. The local authority should deposit this at its principal office.[32]

Maintaining the list

The listing officer or assessor must maintain the list for as long as is necessary for the purposes of the council tax.[33] The listing officer or assessor notifies the local authority on a regular basis of any alterations to the compiled list to take account of new dwellings, demolitions, successful appeals and other changes. For the purpose of determining which valuation band (see p42) is applicable to a dwelling for any day, the state of affairs at the end of the day is assumed to have existed throughout that day.[34] This reflects the fact that council tax is a daily tax, payable for each day a dwelling falls into a particular valuation band.

5. Inspecting the valuation list

Everyone has the right to inspect the valuation list and an online version is available. Access to this information must be provided free of charge and at a reasonable time and place.[35]

You can check the council tax banding of an individual property and inspect the valuation list in England and Wales online by providing the address, postcode and billing authority area on the Valuation Office Agency website at www.voa.gov.uk. Valuation lists for Scottish local authorities are at www.saa.gov.uk.

You can make copies of the list. Alternatively, you can request that the local authority, listing officer or assessor supply a copy, but a reasonable charge may be made for this service. If you are intentionally obstructed from exercising your rights in relation to the valuation list, the person responsible for the obstruction may be liable, on summary conviction, to a fine not exceeding level 2 on the standard scale.[36]

What the valuation list shows

A valuation list must show the items identified below.[37] The list does not contain any personal information. The omission from a list of any matter which should be included does not make it invalid.[38]

The contents of a valuation list
- Each dwelling in the local authority's area.
- Each dwelling's valuation band.
- A reference number for each dwelling.
- A marker indicating properties with mixed domestic and non-domestic use (England and Wales only).
- The effective date on which there has been an alteration.
- An indicator showing that an alteration has been made following an order of a valuation tribunal or a valuation appeal committee or the High Court or Court of Session.
- Notes indicating that a dwelling is a private garage or domestic storage premises (Scotland only).

There is no statutory requirement for how the contents of the valuation list should be laid out. Listing officers and assessors typically order their lists alphabetically, by postal towns, then by streets within each town. Within each street, numbered addresses are shown first, then named-only addresses in alphabetical order. Addresses which cannot be allocated to any street are shown at the end of the list of addresses in each postal town under the heading 'within billing authority area'. Addresses that are not allocated to a postal town appear at the end of the list.[39]

6. **Altering a valuation list**

A current valuation list can be altered by the listing officer or assessor following:
- the receipt of a proposal from an interested party or the local authority; *or*
- a successful appeal to the Valuation Tribunal for England (VTE), Valuation Tribunal for Wales (VTW), valuation appeal committee in Scotland, or to the High Court or Court of Session.

A dwelling's valuation band may be altered if:[40]
- the listing officer or assessor is satisfied that the valuation band is incorrect – eg, because of a clerical error;
- the listing officer or assessor is satisfied that the dwelling would have been allocated to a different valuation band had the valuation been carried out correctly;
- there has been a 'material increase' (see below) in the value of the dwelling since it was placed on the list and all, or part, of it has been sold or let on a lease for a term of seven years or more;
- there has been a 'material reduction' (see p33) in the value of the dwelling;
- part of the property has started to be used, or is no longer used, for business purposes, or the balance between business and domestic use has changed;
- there has been a successful appeal against the valuation band shown on the list;
- the listing officer has made an earlier determination of a band but is subsequently satisfied that the banding decision was wrong, including a historical inaccuracy.[41]

The Valuation Office Agency (VOA) should usually tell you within two months if it has decided to alter the list.

A 'material increase' in the dwelling's value

A 'material increase' in the value of a dwelling means any increase which is caused (in whole or in part) by any building or other works.[42] This applies to work which either increases the size of the property or adds to its market value. However, the material increase only has an impact on the valuation once the dwelling (or any part of it) has been sold. In England and Wales, this also applies if the dwelling is let on a lease for seven years or more. In England, it does not apply to the installation of plant or equipment for the generation of electricity or the production of heat by a source of energy or a technology included in section 26(2) of the Climate Change and Sustainable Energy Act 2006 where:[43]
- the majority of the electricity or heat is generated or produced for use of persons in the dwelling; *or*

- the electricity/heat generated has a capacity not exceeding 10 kilowatts or 45 kilowatts thermal.

In England, the increase takes effect on the council tax banding from the day the alteration is entered on the list.[44] In Scotland and Wales, it takes effect from the date the sale or lease was completed.[45]

Even if a dwelling has not been sold or let on a lease of seven years or more, if a revaluation takes place in England in the future (see p26), all material increases will be taken into account in setting the banding for the dwelling concerned.

A 'material reduction' in the dwelling's value

A **'material reduction'** in the value of a dwelling should lead to an immediate revaluation. This, if sufficiently significant, also leads to an immediate rebanding of the dwelling. This only applies, however, if the material reduction is caused (in whole or in part) by:[46]

- the demolition (but not partial demolition during other building or engineering work) of any part of the dwelling; *or*
- any change in the physical state of the dwelling's locality; *or*
- any adaptation of the dwelling to make it suitable for a person with a physical disability.

Changes in the physical state of a locality give the greatest scope for proposals to change a dwelling's valuation band – ie, so-called 'blighting'. Such changes include, for example, a change in the character of the immediate environment brought about because of a road-widening scheme, the deterioration of surrounding property or a change in the use of nearby business premises.

The reduction in value should post-date the entry of the dwelling on the valuation list. In one case it was pointed out:[47]

...[in] some cases the reduction may follow very swiftly upon the change, in other cases it may not do so. It may take time after the change is known about before the impact of it is realised and it begins to affect the prices which people are prepared to pay for the affected dwellings.

In England and Wales, a reduction in value takes effect from the day on which the circumstances that caused the reduction arose. However, if that day cannot be reasonably established, the alteration takes effect from the day the proposal (see p34) was served on the listing officer or, in any other case, from the date it was entered on the list.[48]

In Scotland, a material reduction takes effect from the date the value fell sufficiently to affect the property's banding or the start of the financial year in which the proposal is made, whichever is later.[49]

How dwellings are revalued

When one of the conditions for the potential alteration of a dwelling's valuation band exists, there should be a revaluation. This should be made on the basis of the rules and assumptions on p27.

In England, this means that the dwelling's value, taking into account its current state, is still based on what it would have sold for on the open market by a willing vendor on 1 April 1991.[50] If the change in value is only small, it might not be sufficient to move a dwelling from one valuation band to another.

In Scotland and Wales, a material increase is assessed on the date the sale or transaction took place. In the case of a material increase in the value of the dwelling, the date of alteration takes effect from the date of the transaction, even if the increase is not identified for several years. The effective date of the alteration should be the day on which the first sale of the dwelling subsequent to the material increase is completed, not the date that you were informed or an assessor discovered it. If the change in value is only established some while after the first date of sale, the liable person may be faced with a backdated bill.[51]

If a dwelling ceases to be a composite hereditament, if there is a reduction in the domestic use of a dwelling or if a new dwelling comes into existence, the relevant date is the date of the alteration to the property. If a number of changes have taken place, the change in the valuation list is taken from the date of the last change.[52]

Obtaining an alteration

If a list is inaccurate, a '**proposal**' may be made to the listing officer or assessor for an alteration to the list. In many instances, there are time limits for this (see p35). Making a proposal is also the first stage in the appeal process (see Chapter 11).

Who can make a proposal

Any 'interested person' can make a proposal to alter the list. An '**interested person**' on any particular day is:[53]

- the owner of the dwelling;
- anyone who is liable (either solely or jointly) to pay the tax on the dwelling;
- in the case of an exempt dwelling (see Chapter 4) or a dwelling on which the council tax has been set at nil, the person who would otherwise be liable to pay the tax.

Local authorities in England can also make proposals to the listing officer.[54]

If you get council tax reduction (see Chapter 8), you are entitled to make a proposal to change the banding of the property.

Time limits

A proposal may be made at any time if:

- a property should be excluded from, or included on, the valuation list;[55]

- there has been a material increase (see p32) in the value of the dwelling and a relevant transaction;
- there has been a material reduction (see p33) in the value of a dwelling;
- part of a property starts to be used, or is no longer used, for business purposes, or the balance between business and domestic use has changed.[56]

In the following circumstances, however, there is a time limit in which to make a proposal.

- **Proposals concerning a valuation band on the original list.** Except in limited circumstances, the time limit to make a proposal has now expired.
- **Banding proposals made by a new resident/owner or concerning a new property.** A proposal can be made within a six-month period if:
  - someone first becomes liable for the council tax on a particular dwelling; *or*
  - the dwelling (eg, a new home) is first shown on the valuation list after 1 April 1993 (1 April 2005 in Wales).[57]

Such a proposal cannot be made, however, if:
  - it is based on the same facts that have already been considered and determined by the VTE, the VTW or valuation appeal committee in Scotland, or by the High Court or Court of Session; *or*
  - the new taxpayer is a company which is a subsidiary of the preceding taxpayer; *or*
  - the preceding taxpayer is a company which is a subsidiary of the new taxpayer; *or*
  - the change of taxpayer has occurred solely because a new partnership has been formed and one of the partners was a partner in the previous partnership.[58]

- **Appeal decisions concerning a comparable dwelling.** A proposal may be made within six months of an appeal decision on another comparable dwelling if this gives reasonable grounds for arguing that the valuation band of the dwelling in question should be changed.[59]
- **Proposals concerning an alteration to the list.** If the listing officer or assessor has altered the list in respect of a dwelling, a proposal can be made within six months from when the notice of the alteration was served.[60] The time limit may not apply where a delay by either the billing authority or the valuation office has meant a historical inaccuracy has arisen in the list.[61]

Making a proposal

You must make the proposal by writing to the listing officer at the local office of the VOA (the address should be on the council tax bill) or the local assessor.[62] Standard forms and explanatory notes are available from these offices to assist with the proposal. The completed form or, alternatively, a letter should contain all relevant information including:[63]

- your name and address;

- the capacity in which the proposal is being made – ie, whether you are the liable person or the owner of the dwelling;
- the dwelling to which it relates;
- the date;
- the way in which you propose the list should be altered;
- the reasons for believing the list to be inaccurate, the relevant facts, any evidence supporting those facts and any relevant dates, such as the date you first became the liable person or the date when a material reduction in the dwelling occurred.

Note: while you are awaiting the decision of the listing officer, you are usually expected to pay the council tax. However, if you do not think you should be paying council tax at all, as your proposal is that the dwelling should not be on the valuation list at all, but you have been billed for council tax, you should also contact the local authority and inform it that you are also challenging liability to the tax.

Example

Ted has proposed that his dwelling should not be on the valuation list at all as it is a room which actually forms part of a house of multiple occupation. Ted disputes both the bill and liability to tax under section 16 of the Local Government Finance Act 1992 as it is the owner who is liable (see Chapter 5). Ted can appeal the local authority decision to the valuation tribunal (see Chapter 11). If the local authority starts enforcing the bill because he has not paid and he is summonsed to the magistrates' court, Ted should seek an adjournment on the basis that he has begun the appeal process (see Chapter 10).

The proposal should be addressed to the listing officer or assessor for the relevant area and delivered or posted to the appropriate address. Keep a copy and obtain some proof of postage or, if delivered by hand, a receipt, or record online.

If you are acting on behalf of another council taxpayer to challenge a council tax band, the VOA expects you to:
- provide a form of authority to act on the taxpayer's behalf, which must be signed and dated by her/him not more than six months before it is supplied;
- check whether you are entitled to make a valid proposal on the proper form, either on the internet or supplied by the local valuation office;
- provide relevant evidence to raise doubt over the accuracy of the band;
- supply a completed property details questionnaire.

Evidence

A wide range of evidence can be used to establish value. You can use sales evidence for up to two years either side of 1 April 1991 for your property or similar properties in your locality. Evidence that similarly sized properties to yours are in a lower band may be used. There must be no more than a 10 per cent difference in size comparison between these properties and yours. Evidence of significantly larger properties within the locality in a lower band may also be accepted. No more than five comparable properties should be supplied – if you supply more than five comparable properties, only the first five are considered as part of the case.

Normally a proposal can only deal with one dwelling. In England, however, a proposal can be made for more than one dwelling if:[64]

- you make the proposal in the same capacity (eg, as the owner) and each of the dwellings is within the same building (or 'curtilage') as the other(s); *or*
- it arises because a property is shown as a dwelling when it should not be or should be shown as a number of dwellings.

Response of the listing office

In **England and Wales**, the listing officer should write within 28 days acknowledging receipt of the proposal, unless the proposal is considered to be invalid (see below). In **Scotland**, the assessor should write acknowledging receipt of the proposal within 14 days. The acknowledgement letter should include details of the procedures that will be followed.[65]

Joint proposals in Scotland

In Scotland, other interested people (see p34) may write to the assessor indicating that they wish to support the proposal.[66] Provided the proposal has not been withdrawn or referred to the local valuation appeal committee, the original proposal should then be treated as a joint proposal.

Invalid proposals

Different procedures apply to invalid proposals in England, Wales and Scotland. If the listing officer or assessor fails to identify an invalid proposal at this stage, the point can still be raised at an appeal hearing.[67]

England

In England, if the listing officer considers that the proposal is invalid, you are sent an 'invalidity notice'. This should be done within four weeks of her/his receiving the proposal. This notice gives:[68]

- the reasons why the proposal is considered invalid; *and*
- you a right to make a further proposal in relation to the same dwelling (see below) or to appeal against the invalidity notice to the VTE (see p39).

The listing officer may withdraw an invalidity notice at any time by informing you in writing.

Unless an invalidity notice has been withdrawn, you can:

- make a further proposal, but only once and only if the original proposal was made within the appropriate time limit. If you make a further proposal, the earlier proposal which resulted in the invalidity notice is treated as withdrawn; *or*

- appeal to the VTE. You must send the tribunal a copy of the invalidity notice, together with a written statement. This should include the address of the dwelling and the reasons why the proposal is considered invalid. Action on the original proposal is suspended until either the listing officer withdraws the invalidity notice, or the VTE or High Court reaches a decision on the validity of the proposal. If the listing officer withdraws an invalidity notice after an appeal has been started, s/he must inform the tribunal. See Chapter 11 for more details on tribunal hearings.

Scotland

In Scotland, a distinction is drawn between proposals that are considered invalid because:[69]

- you are not an appropriate person to make a proposal or because it is out of time; *and*
- you did not include the required information.

The assessor must write to you within six weeks of receiving the proposal giving reasons for the decision and describe your right to appeal to the assessor within four weeks. If no such appeal is made, the matter ends. If you did not include the required information, the letter must give reasons for the decision and should also identify the information that needs to be supplied. You may either:

- supply the information within four weeks; *or*
- appeal in writing to the assessor within four weeks.

If the information is not supplied or an appeal is not made within the four-week period, the assessor treats the proposal as invalidly made and that is the end of the matter.

If an appeal is made in either case but the assessor still considers the appeal invalid, s/he should inform the local valuation appeal committee in writing, within four weeks, that an appeal has been made. Details of the proposal and the assessor's reasons for considering the proposal invalid should also be given.[70]

Wales

In Wales, if the listing officer believes that a proposal has not been validly made, s/he may serve an invalidity notice on you. This must be done within four weeks. The notice must explain the reasons for her/his decision and that you can either make a further proposal or appeal to a valuation tribunal. If you make a fresh proposal, the original is treated as withdrawn. The fresh proposal must be made within four weeks of the invalidity notice being served.

After a valid proposal has been made: England and Wales

Within six weeks of receiving a valid proposal, the listing officer should send a copy to anyone else who appears to be liable for council tax on the dwelling. Copies should also be sent to the local authority if it has informed the listing officer in writing that it wishes to receive a copy of a class(es) of proposal, and your proposal falls within such a class. Each copy should be accompanied by a statement of the procedures to be followed.[71]

Following the receipt of a valid proposal:

- the listing officer may agree to the proposal (see below);
- all interested parties may agree to a different alteration to the list (see below);
- an appeal may be made to the VTE/VTW (see below);
- the proposal may be withdrawn (see p40).

The listing officer agrees to the proposal

If the listing officer agrees to the proposal, you and the liable person (if different) should be notified that the valuation list will be altered accordingly. The valuation list should be altered within six weeks of the date of the letter.[72]

Agreeing to a different alteration

Before an appeal, it is possible for the listing officer to agree an alteration to the list that is different from that proposed, but with which you agree. This requires the agreement of all interested parties. If such an agreement is reached, the listing officer should alter the valuation list within six weeks of the date of the agreement. The original proposal is treated as having been withdrawn.[73]

Appealing to the valuation tribunal

If the listing officer has made a decision and served a notice on the proposer, the taxpayer and any other competent person, an appeal can be made to the VTE/VTW (see p239):

An appeal must be made within three months. If an appeal has not been made within this time, the president of the tribunal can authorise the appeal if the delay has arisen because of circumstances beyond your control.

The appeal is started by serving the tribunal with a copy of the decision notice, together with the following information if this is not contained in the decision notice:

- the address of the dwelling;
- the reasons for the appeal;
- the name and address of:
  - the appellant;
  - the proposer (if different from the appellant);
  - the listing officer;
  - any other person who appears to be a taxpayer;
- any other interested person.

Where, after an appeal has been made to the VTE under regulation 13 of the Council Tax (Alteration of Lists and Appeals) Regulations (disagreement as to proposed alteration), the listing officer alters the list in accordance with the proposal to which the appeal relates, the listing officer must notify the VTE and the appeal is treated as having been withdrawn on the date on which the notice is served on the VTE.[74]

In rare situations where neither the local authority nor the valuation office will take responsibility for deciding whether a dwelling is on the list or should be taxed, or officials attached to both try to claim it is the responsibility of the other, you should challenge the decision letters of both bodies with two separate appeals both being made to the valuation tribunal.

Appeals are described in Chapter 11.

Note: you normally cannot make a second appeal on the same facts if one has already been determined against you by the valuation tribunal but an application may be made to a vice president to set aside a decision or an application may be made by way of judicial review.[75]

Withdrawing the proposal

You may withdraw the proposal at any time before an appeal by writing to the tribunal, or orally at the hearing. If a proposal is withdrawn at the hearing, it does not take effect unless the panel consents. Each party must be notified in writing of a withdrawal, and the date on which the proposal is withdrawn should be confirmed. Each party has the opportunity to begin a new appeal about the decision by serving a written notice. This must state that the new appellant wishes to proceed with an appeal and the reason for it.

In the past, it was not unknown for the valuation office or for local authority staff to attempt to encourage people to withdraw their proposals and appeals. Such 'persuasion' included claims that a tribunal had previously rejected a similar appeal, so an appellant had no prospect of success. Remember that a tribunal decision on any point is persuasive, but not binding, on subsequent tribunals (see Chapter 11). If you are subject to improper pressure over an appeal by an official either in the valuation office or from, or acting on behalf of, the local authority, you should make a formal complaint.

After a valid proposal has been made: Scotland

In Scotland, once a valid proposal has been received:
- the assessor may agree to the proposal (see below);
- an appeal may be made to a local valuation appeal committee (see p41);
- the proposal may be withdrawn (see p41).

The assessor agrees to the proposal

If the assessor thinks the proposal is well founded, you (and any joint proposer) should be advised of this in writing. The list should be altered within six weeks of the date of the letter.[76]

Appealing to a local valuation appeal committee

If the assessor thinks that the proposal is not well founded and it is not withdrawn, s/he should refer the disagreement to the local valuation appeal committee. This should be done within six months of the day the assessor received the proposal.[77]

If the assessor has previously issued an invalidity notice on the grounds that:

- you are not an appropriate person to make the proposal or because the proposal is out of time, the six-month period starts from the day the assessor withdrew the notice or you won the appeal against the notice;
- the proposal does not include the required information, the six-month period starts from the day that all the relevant information was supplied or the day you won the appeal against the notice.[78]

A proposal may be adopted by another interested person (see p34) if the original proposer seeks to withdraw it. In such cases, the six-month period starts from the date the person informed the assessor of her/his wish to adopt the proposal.[79]

The appeal is initiated by the assessor writing to the secretary of the valuation committee, advising of the appeal. The following information should be included the:[80]

- proposed alteration of the list;
- date on which the proposal was received;
- name and address of the proposer;
- grounds on which the proposal was made.

Appeals are described in Chapter 11.

Withdrawing the proposal

The proposal may be withdrawn at any time by writing to the assessor.[81] If none of the proposers are currently liable for the tax on the dwelling, the assessor must write to at least one currently liable person telling her/him about the proposed withdrawal. An interested person (see p34) has six weeks from the date of the letter to advise the assessor that s/he wishes to adopt the proposal. From that date, it is then treated as having been made by that person.

Notification of an alteration

Within six weeks of altering the list, the listing officer or assessor should write to the local authority stating the effect of the alteration. The local authority should alter its copy of the valuation list as soon as is reasonably practicable.[82]

England and Wales

In England and Wales, the listing officer should also write to the person who is currently liable for the tax on the dwelling within six weeks of altering the list, advising her/him of the effect of the alteration and the process by which a proposal and appeal may be made.[83] This obligation to notify does not, however, apply if the alteration was made solely to correct a clerical error, or to reflect:

- a decision of the listing officer that a proposal is well founded; *or*
- an agreed alternative alteration; *or*
- a change in the address of the dwelling concerned; *or*
- a change in the area of the billing authority; *or*
- the decision of the VTE/VTW or the High Court in relation to the dwelling concerned.

Scotland

In Scotland, the assessor must notify a liable person within six weeks of the alteration being made. Where the alteration involves the addition of the dwelling to the list, the owner must also be notified within six weeks of the alteration. The notification should include a statement about the process by which a proposal may be made.

Additionally, the assessor must notify a liable person within six weeks of the alteration being made if:

- an alteration has been agreed, but the proposer is not a liable person at the time of the alteration; *or*
- an appeal decision has led to the alteration of the list but none of the parties to the appeal is a liable person on the date of the alteration.[84]

7. **The valuation bands**

The set amount of council tax and Scottish Water charges for each dwelling depend on the valuation band to which it is allocated. Different valuation bands apply in England,[85] Scotland[86] and Wales.[87]

You can find out which band your property is in at www.gov.uk/council-tax-bands.

England and Scotland

The original bands from the 1993 valuation list apply in England and Scotland, although the ratio of calculation of tax has changed (see p44).

Valuation bands in England

Valuation band	Range of values
A	Up to £40,000
B	£40,001 to £52,000
C	£52,001 to £68,000
D	£68,001 to £88,000
E	£88,001 to £120,000
F	£120,001 to £160,000

G	£160,001 to £320,000
H	£320,001 and over

Valuation bands in Scotland

Valuation band	Range of values
A	Up to £27,000
B	£27,001 to £35,000
C	£35,001 to £45,000
D	£45,001 to £58,000
E	£58,001 to £80,000
F	£80,001 to £106,000
G	£106,001 to £212,000
H	£212,001 and over

Wales

From 1 April 2005, dwellings in Wales fall into one of the following bands, based on a theoretical valuation date of 1 April 2003.[88] These bands apply to all domestic dwellings from 1 April 2005.

Valuation bands in Wales from 1 April 2005

Valuation band	Range of values
A	Up to £36,000
B	£36,001 to £52,000
C	£52,001 to £73,000
D	£73,001 to £100,000
E	£100,001 to £135,000
F	£135,001 to £191,000
G	£191,001 to £286,000
H	£286,001 to £400,000
I	£400,001 and over

Before 1 April 2005, the valuation bands for Wales were as listed in the table below. These values apply to any calculation of council tax for a dwelling in Wales before 1 April 2005. This may arise if there is a question of backdating an exemption (see Chapter 4) or discount (see Chapter 7).

Valuation bands in Wales before 1 April 2005

Valuation band	Range of values
A	Up to £30,000
B	£30,001 to £39,000
C	£39,001 to £51,000
D	£51,001 to £66,000
E	£66,001 to £90,000
F	£90,001 to £120,000
G	£120,001 to £240,000
H	£240,001 and over

How the amount of tax payable varies between bands

The council tax payable in any local authority depends upon the valuation band in which the dwelling has been placed. The lower the value of the band, the lower the bill will be. The amount of tax payable on dwellings in the same area varies between valuation bands in **England** in the following proportions:[89]

6(A):7(B):8(C):9(D):11(E):13(F):15(G):18(H)

This means, for example, that the tax payable on a Band H dwelling is three times more than that payable on a Band A dwelling and double that of a Band D dwelling. The local authority has no discretion to vary bands or the relative proportion of tax paid within each band.

In **Wales** from 1 April 2005, the amount of tax payable on dwellings in the same area varies between valuation bands in the following proportions:[90]

6(A):7(B):8(C):9(D):11(E):13(F):15(G):18(H):21(I)

This means that those in the top Band I in Wales will pay three-and-a-half times more than those in the lowest Band A.

In **Scotland** from 1 April 2017, the following ratios and proportions apply:[91]

240 (A):280(B):320(C):360(D):473(E):585(F):705(G):882(H)

The new proportion increases the levels of tax payable for dwellings in the higher four bands (E to H) relative to that payable for dwellings in the lower four bands.

In England, Wales and Scotland, the calculation of tax for different valuation bands in any financial year is worked out by the formula:

$$A \times (N \div D)$$

where A is the average amount calculated (or last calculated) by the billing authority for each dwelling for that year, N is the number associated with the valuation band and D is the number associated with Band D.[92]

In 2018/19, the average council tax Band D payable:

- in England, is £1,671;[93]
- in Wales, is £1,491;[94]
- in Scotland, is £1,208.[95]

Notes

1. Who is responsible for valuations
1 **EW** s20 LGFA 1992
2 **EW** s26 LGFA 1992
3 s84(1) LGFA 1992
4 s86(5) LGFA 1992
5 s86(10) LGFA 1992
6 **EW** s21 LGFA 1992
   S s86(7) LGFA 1992
7 **EW** s21 LGFA 1992
   S s86(8) LGFA 1992
8 **EW** s21 LGFA 1992
   S s86(9) LGFA 1992
9 Adjudicator's Office, *Annual Report 2018*, at www.adjudicatorsoffice.gov.uk/pdf/Adjudicators-Annual-Report-2018.pdf

2. The listing officer's and assessor's powers
10 **E** s25A LGFA 1992
    W s26 LGFA 1992
    S s89 LGFA 1992
11 s25A LGFA 1992, as inserted by art 3 Council Tax and Non Domestic Rating (Powers of Entry: Safeguards) (England) Order 2015 No.982
12 VOA charter, 8 February 2016
13 **EW** s26 LGFA 1992
    S s89 LGFA 1992

14 **EW** s27 LGFA 1992
    S s90 LGFA 1992
15 **EW** s27 LGFA 1992
    S s90 LGFA 1992
16 **EW** s27 LGFA 1992
    S s90 LGFA 1992; The Criminal Justice Act 1991 (Commencement No.3) Order 1992 No.333
17 **EW** s27(6) LGFA 1992
    S s90 LGFA 1992
18 **EW** s27 LGFA 1992
    S s90 LGFA 1992

3. How dwellings are valued
19 **E** s21 LGFA 1992; CT(SVD) Regs
    W s21 LGFA 1992; CT(SVD) Regs, as amended by CT(SVD)(W)(A) Regs
    S s86(2) LGFA 1992 and CT(VD)(S) Regs
20 Response to Parliamentary Question by Rishi Sunak, Under-Secretary of State for Housing, Communities and Local Government, 19 March 2018
21 *R v East Sussex Valuation Tribunal ex parte Silverstone* [1996] RVR 203
22 *Coll (Listing Officer) v Walters* [2016] EWHC 831 (Admin)
23 *Call v Brannan; Call v Kozak and another* [2015] All ER (D) 44 (Apr)
24 *Wilson v Jo Coll (Listing Officer)* [2011] EWHC 2824 (Admin)

25 VOA, Council Tax Manual, Practice Note 4 – Disrepair, Building Works, Temporary Disabilities and Flooding

26 *Assessor Tayside Joint Valuation Board v a decision of the valuation appeal committee for Perth and Kinross* [2017] CSIH 64, para 25

27 *Assessor Tayside Joint Valuation Board a decision of the valuation appeal committee for Perth and Kinross* [2017] CSIH 64, para 25

28 **E** s21 LGFA 1992; CT(SVD) Regs
W s21 LGFA 1992; CT(SVD) Regs, as amended by CT(SVD)(W)(A) Regs
S s86(2) LGFA 1992; CT(VD)(S) Regs

29 **S** Reg 3 CT(VD)(S) Regs; *The Appeal of Grampian Valuation Joint Board* [2003] RA 167 Sc

30 Parliamentary Answer by John Healy, Minister for Local Government, 13 December 2007; reg 3 CT(ALA)(E) Regs, as amended by reg 2(2)(c) CT(ALA)(E)(A) Regs

4. Compiling and maintaining valuation lists

31 **EW** ss22 and 22B LGFA 1992
S s84 LGFA 1992

32 **EW** ss22 and 22B LGFA 1992
S s85 LGFA 1992

33 **EW** s22 LGFA 1992
S s84 LGFA 1992

34 **EW** s2(2)(b) LGFA 1992
S s71(2)(b) LGFA 1992

5. Inspecting the valuation list

35 **EW** s28 LGFA 1992
S s91 LGFA 1992

36 **EW** s28 LGFA 1992
S s91 LGFA 1992

37 **EW** s23 LGFA 1992 and CT(CVL) Regs
S s84 LGFA 1992 and CT(CVL) Regs

38 **EW** s23 LGFA 1992
S s84 LGFA 1992

39 Council Tax Guidance Manual 3.4.1

6. Altering a valuation list

40 **E** Reg 3 CT(ALA)(E) Regs, as amended by reg 2 CT(ALA)(E)(A) Regs; VTE(CTRA)(P) Regs
W CT(ALA) Regs
S r4(1)(b)(i) CT(ALA(S) Regs

41 *Adam v Listing Officer* [2014] EWHC 1110 (Admin)

42 **E** s24 LGFA 1992
S s87 LGFA 1992

43 Reg 3 CT(ALA)(E) Regs, as amended by reg 2(2)(c) CT(ALA)(E)(A) Regs

44 **E** Reg 9 CT(ALA)(E) Regs

45 **W** Reg 14(2) CT(ALA) Regs, as amended by CT(ALA)(A)(W) Regs
S Reg 19 CT(ALA)(S) Regs; *Lothian Valuation Joint Board v Campbell and Campbell* [2011] CSIH 47

46 **E** s24 LGFA 1992
S s87 LGFA 1992

47 *Tilly v Listing Officer for Tower Hamlets* [2001] RVR 250

48 **E** Reg 9 CT(ALA)(E) Regs
W Reg 14(5)(a) and (b) CT(ALA) Regs, as amended by CT(ALA)(A)(W) Regs

49 Reg 19 (5) CT(ALA)(S) Regs

50 **E** CT(SVD) Regs
W CT(SVD)(W)(A) Regs
S CT(VD)(S) Regs

51 *Lothian Valuation Joint Board v Campbell and Campbell* [2011] CSIH 47

52 **E** Reg 6 CT(SVD) Regs, as amended by CT(VALA)(E) Regs
S CT(VD)(S) Regs, as amended by CT(VD)(S)(A) Regs

53 **E** Reg 2 CT(ALA)(E) Regs
S Reg 3 CT(ALA)(S) Regs

54 **E** Reg 4 CT(ALA)(E) Regs

55 **E** Reg 4 CT(ALA)(E) Regs
S Reg 5 CT(ALA)(S) Regs

56 **E** Reg 4 CT(ALA)(E) Regs
S Reg 5 CT(ALA)(S) Regs

57 **E** Reg 4 CT(ALA)(E) Regs
S Reg 5 CT(ALA)(S) Regs

58 **E** Reg 4(5) CT(ALA)(E) Regs
S Reg 5 CT(ALA)(S) Regs

59 **E** Reg 4 CT(ALA)(E) Regs
S Reg 5 CT(ALA)(S) Regs

60 **E** Reg 4(2) CT(ALA)(E) Regs
S Reg 5 CT(ALA)(S) Regs

61 *Baiyelo v Corkish* [2017] Appeal No.5690727898/084CAD 22 May 2017, judgment of VTE President Mr Garland

62 **E** Reg 5 CT(ALA)(E) Regs
S Reg 6 CT(ALA)(S) Regs

63 **E** Reg 5 CT(ALA)(E) Regs
S Reg 6 CT(ALA)(S) Regs

64 Reg 5 CT(ALA)(E) Regs

65 Reg 7 CT(ALA)(S) Regs

66 Reg 12 CT(ALA)(S) Regs

67 **E** CT(ALA)(E) Regs
W CT(ALA) Regs
S CT(ALA)(S) Regs

68 Reg 7 CT(ALA)(E) Regs

69 Regs 8 and 9 CT(ALA)(S) Regs

70 Reg 10 CT(ALA)(S) Regs

71 Reg 8 CT(ALA)(E) Regs

72 Reg 9(3) CT(ALA)(E) Regs

73 Reg 9(4) CT(ALA)(E) Regs

74 Reg 19(7) VTE(CTRA)(P) Regs
75 *Hakeem v VTS and London Borough of Enfield* [2010] EWHC 152 (Admin); *Bailyelo v Corkish* [2017] Appeal No.5690727898/084CAD
76 Reg 14 CT(ALA)(S) Regs
77 Reg 15 CT(ALA)(S) Regs
78 Reg 15 CT(ALA)(S) Regs
79 Reg 15 CT(ALA)(S) Regs
80 Reg 15 CT(ALA)(S) Regs
81 Reg 11 CT(ALA)(S) Regs
82 **E** Reg 12(1) CT(ALA)(E) Regs
    S Reg 16 CT(ALA)(S) Regs
83 Reg 12 CT(ALA)(E) Regs
84 Reg 16 CT(ALA)(S) Regs

7. The valuation bands
85 **E** s5(2) LGFA 1992
86 **S** s74(2) LGFA 1992
87 **W** s5(3) LGFA 1992
88 **W** s5(3) LGFA 1992
89 s5 LGFA 1992
90 s5(1A) LGFA 1992
91 s74 LGFA 1992 as substituted by art 2(1) Council Tax (Substitution of Proportion) (Scotland) Order 2016
92 s36 LGFA 1992
93 MHCLG, *Council tax levels set by local authorities in England 2018-19 (Revised)*, Statistics Release, 9 April 2018. This figure includes an amount to fund adult social care. Without adult social care, the average Band D council tax would be £1,531.
94 Statistics for Wales, Council Tax levels in Wales: 2018-2019 Budget Requirement (BR1), March 2018
95 Scottish Government, Dataset: Band D Council Tax 1996-97 to 2018-19, April 2018

Chapter 4

Exempt dwellings

This chapter covers:
1. Exempt dwellings in England and Wales (below)
2. Exempt dwellings in Scotland (p59)
3. How exempt dwellings are identified (p65)
4. Notification of exemption (p65)
5. Penalties (p66)
6. Appeals (p67)

No council tax is payable on a dwelling on any day when it falls into an exempt category. The local authority must take steps each year to establish which dwellings in its area are exempt. When determining whether a dwelling is exempt, the state of affairs at the end of the day is assumed to have existed throughout that day.[1]

1. Exempt dwellings in England and Wales

An exempt dwelling is one that falls into one of 23 classes listed A–W by satisfying certain requirements. The classes of dwellings that are entitled to an exemption are set out in the Council Tax (Exempt Dwellings) Order 1992, as amended from 1 April 2013 by the Council Tax (Exempt Dwellings) (England) (Amendment) Order 2012.

Exemption classes B and D to W[2]

Class B	Unoccupied dwelling owned by a charity (up to six months). See p50.
Class D	Dwelling unoccupied by someone who is detained or in prison. See p51.
Class E	Unoccupied dwelling previously the sole or main residence of someone who has moved into a hospital, care home or certain hostels. See p53.
Class F	Dwelling unoccupied because someone has died. See p52.
Class G	Unoccupied dwelling in which occupation is prohibited by law. See p53.
Class H	Unoccupied dwelling held for a minister of religion. See p53.
Class I	Unoccupied dwelling previously the sole or main residence of someone who has moved to receive personal care. See p54.

Class J	An unoccupied dwelling which was previously the sole or main residence of someone who has moved elsewhere to provide personal care to another person. See p54.
Class K	An unoccupied dwelling previously the sole or main residence of a student who is resident elsewhere or a person who will become a student within six weeks of vacating the dwelling. See p54.
Class L	An unoccupied dwelling in the possession of a mortgage lender. See p55.
Class M	Student halls of residence. See p56.
Class N	A dwelling wholly occupied by students or school or college leavers. See p57.
Class O	Armed forces accommodation. See p58.
Class P	Visiting forces accommodation. See p58.
Class Q	An unoccupied dwelling where the person who would otherwise be liable is a trustee in bankruptcy. See p55.
Class R	Empty caravan pitches and houseboat moorings. See p58.
Class S	A dwelling wholly occupied by people under 18. See p58.
Class T	A dwelling which is an annexe and may not be let separately. See p55.
Class U	A dwelling occupied by people who are 'severely mentally impaired'. See p58.
Class V	A dwelling in which at least one liable person has diplomatic, Commonwealth or consular privilege or immunity. See p58.
Class W	A dwelling which is one of at least two dwellings in a single property occupied by a dependent relative of a person living in another dwelling in the property. See p58.

An exemption from council tax may be considered as a possession within the meaning of Article 1 Protocol 1 of the European Convention on Human Rights.[3]

Vacant homes

In England since 1 April 2013, two classes of dwelling which related to vacant homes – Classes A and C – are no longer classed as automatically exempt on a national basis but may be on a local basis if an individual council decides otherwise.[4] **Note:** in Wales, these categories remain as exempt dwellings.

Exemption Classes A and C

Class A	For a 12-month period, a vacant dwelling requiring or undergoing major repair work, or undergoing structural alteration, or having undergone either if less than six months had elapsed since the works were substantially completed.
Class C	A dwelling vacant for a six-month period or less – eg, following completion.

Properties in England falling into these two categories are no longer treated as receiving an automatic exemption and are liable for 100 per cent of the council tax. Any reduction on these two classes of property is awarded as a discount only if your local authority decides that a discount should be given (see p114).

Exemptions may still be claimed for previous years in some cases, and you should check whether your local authority makes provision for certain classes of dwelling.

In addition, a local authority may make a class of dwelling exempt by way of a discount that reduces the amount of council tax payable on a dwelling to zero (see Chapter 7).

The term 'exempt dwellings' applies to different types of dwelling which are vacant.

The term **'vacant'** refers to a dwelling which is both:[5]

• unoccupied; *and*
• substantially unfurnished.

This definition is no longer relevant to England, where the 'vacant dwelling' exemptions have been abolished.

The legislation contains no definition of 'substantially unfurnished'. In practice, many local authorities regard a dwelling as **'substantially unfurnished'** if there are insufficient furnishings to enable someone to live in the dwelling. However, the quantity of furniture present in the dwelling, in relation to its size, should be the determining factor, ignoring anything other than 'furniture' – ie, appliances, fitted wardrobes, TV and carpets. Thus, a studio flat with a table, two chairs, a sofa and a bed (plus a cooker, washer/drier and TV) would be substantially furnished, but the same goods would not make a four-bedroom house substantially furnished.

The legislation defines an **'unoccupied dwelling'** as one in which no one lives, and an **'occupied dwelling'** as one in which at least one person lives.[6] There is, however, a significant distinction between occupying a home and being solely or mainly resident in it (see p72). While the same person may occupy two or more dwellings at any one time, s/he can only be mainly resident in one of them. The local authority must consider each case on the particular facts.

Classes of exempt dwellings in England and Wales

Unoccupied dwelling owned by a charitable body

An unoccupied dwelling owned by a body established solely for charitable purposes is exempt for up to six months from the last day it was occupied. Almshouses and refuges are typical examples of properties that are exempt.

Four conditions must be met for the exemption to apply.[7]

• The dwelling must be owned by the body.
• The body must be established for charitable purposes only.

- The dwelling must have been unoccupied for a period of less than six months.
- The last occupation must have been in furtherance of the objects of the charity.

For this exemption to apply, the charity must be the freeholder or hold the most inferior (ie, shortest) leasehold interest for a term of six months or more. The dwelling may be furnished or unfurnished. The exemption only applies, however, if the dwelling was last occupied in connection with furthering the objectives of the charity. When deciding the day on which the dwelling was last occupied, any period of occupation of not more than six weeks is disregarded.[8]

It should normally be enough for there to be a short statement in writing as a representation from the charity which covers all four conditions directly and which states that:

- based on the material held by the charity, each of the conditions are met; *and*
- the statement was true to the belief of the person making the statement.[9]

To show that the last occupation was in furtherance of the aims of the charity, it is expected that the charity will supply information about the last occupier. This may include details of the history of any letting and some details of the last occupier – eg, why s/he was receiving help from the charity and what benefits s/he received where relevant. There should be sufficient evidence to show the aims of the charity were being fulfilled.[10]

This disregard was originally a way to avoid abuse of the exemption. Without the disregard, the owner could ensure that the building is occupied for a few days near the end of the six-month period and thus trigger the exemption again for a further six months. This exemption can be repeated each time the dwelling is unoccupied following a period of occupation of six weeks or more, provided the above conditions are met.

Vacant dwellings in Wales

A vacant dwelling (one that is unoccupied and substantially unfurnished, or an unoccupied caravan or houseboat) is exempt for up to six months.[11] This exemption applies both to new and previously occupied dwellings. Any one period of not more than six weeks during which the dwelling is occupied is disregarded when deciding if the dwelling has been vacant.

Dwelling unoccupied because the former resident is detained or in prison

An unoccupied dwelling is exempt indefinitely if the former resident is in prison or certain other forms of detention and the dwelling was previously her/his sole or main residence (see p72).[12] For the purpose of this exemption, a person is considered detained if s/he would be regarded as such for the purpose of a council tax discount (see p111).[13] The definition includes people detained under immigration or mental health powers, but not those in prison for non-payment of council tax.

This exemption includes not only former residents who were owners (ie, the freeholder or the leaseholder with the shortest lease of six months or more) but also a former tenant of the dwelling, whether or not s/he is the person who is liable to pay council tax on the property.[14]

The dwelling is also exempt if the owner or tenant was previously the sole or main resident and, since the end of her/his imprisonment, has been in a hospital, care home, hostel or other accommodation where care is provided, or if s/he has been providing personal care to someone else.

Example
On leaving prison, Geoff moves in with his elderly mother to look after her. Geoff's former home remains exempt.

Unoccupied dwelling in which someone has died

A dwelling is exempt if it has been unoccupied since the former resident's death and the only person liable for the tax on the dwelling would be the deceased's personal representative, and no grant of probate or letters of administration have been made.[15] In the case of rented accommodation, the exemption is designed to discourage landlords, who would become liable for the council tax following a tenant's death, from pressing for the property to be cleared immediately in order to benefit from the six-month exemption for vacant dwellings or, alternatively, from seeking to pass on to the deceased's relatives or estate the council tax payable on the dwelling which is now unoccupied, but not vacant.

The exemption applies for each day for which the executor or administrator is liable for rent and lasts up to six months after the grant of probate or letters of administration. Prior to obtaining probate or letters of administration, there is no minimum period for the exemption to last. Thus, a delay of eight years in applying for probate will not restrict the exemption, even if the ultimate beneficiary is likely to be the same person as the executor.[16]

Any one short occupation of less than six weeks following the death is disregarded. Thus, the exemption is not ended if, for instance, a relative stays at the dwelling briefly in order to arrange the deceased's affairs.

This exemption may not apply if the deceased left the dwelling to a beneficiary in her/his will who is a joint owner or who is already in occupation. In this case, the beneficiary becomes the taxpayer at the date of death, as s/he is deemed to become the owner for council tax purposes on that date. This situation may arise at the death of a spouse or partner who was living apart, or if a relative who was living in the dwelling succeeds to the tenancy. However, there may be an argument for an exemption if the executor is given any discretion over the dwelling that might affect whether the beneficiary can occupy it.

The Valuation Tribunal for England has upheld a decision by Epsom and Ewell Borough Council that members of a trust to whom a council taxpayer had transferred her bungalow to protect it from family business liabilities were not entitled to claim the exemption following her death. Although the bungalow was treated as part of the deceased's estate for inheritance tax purposes, it belonged to the trustees.[17]

Dwelling in which occupation is prohibited by law

In England and Wales, a dwelling is exempt indefinitely if its occupation is prohibited by law, including:

- a condition imposed by planning control under Part 3 of the Town and Country Planning Act 1990;[18]
- occupation otherwise prohibited by law;
- if it is kept unoccupied because of powers under any Act of parliament with a view to prohibiting occupation or to acquiring it.

Thus, property which is unoccupied because it is being acquired under a compulsory purchase order is exempt from council tax. However, a dwelling on which a local authority has served a repair notice does not qualify for an exemption, even if the occupant has to move out temporarily.[19] If the dwelling is actually occupied (eg, by squatters), the dwelling is not exempt from the charge. The squatters will normally be liable to pay the tax. See Chapter 5 for more information on liability.

Unoccupied dwelling held for a minister of religion

An unoccupied dwelling, such as a vicarage, is exempt indefinitely if it is held to be available for occupation by a minister of any religious denomination and from where s/he will perform the duties of her/his office.[20]

Dwelling unoccupied because the former resident is in hospital or a care home

An unoccupied dwelling is exempt indefinitely if it was previously the sole or main residence (see p72) of an owner, tenant or licensee:[21]

- who would be disregarded for the purpose of a council tax discount because s/he is a patient in hospital, or is in a care home or certain hostels; *and*
- who, since s/he last occupied the dwelling, has either been in that type of accommodation, in detention, or receiving or providing care elsewhere.[22] The care must be required for one of the reasons listed on p54.

During temporary stays in hospital, you remain liable for council tax at your normal address. However, if your main residence is a hospital, your previous home is exempt from council tax, provided it is unoccupied.[23]

Dwelling unoccupied because the former resident is receiving care elsewhere

An unoccupied dwelling is exempt indefinitely if it was the sole or main residence (see p72) of an owner, tenant or licensee who now has her/his sole or main residence elsewhere and where s/he is receiving personal care (but not a hospital, care home or certain hostels).[24] The personal care must be required because of her/his:

- old age; *or*
- disablement; *or*
- illness; *or*
- past or present alcohol or drug dependence; *or*
- past or present mental illness or disorder.

To qualify, the former resident must have been resident in such accommodation, or in prison or detention centre, or in a hospital, care home or hostel since the dwelling last ceased to be her/his residence.

This exemption applies if the former resident was an owner and, in England, if s/he was a tenant or licensee, irrespective of whether s/he was liable for council tax on the dwelling. In Wales, this exemption extends to former tenants only if the person has been absent for the whole period since the dwelling last ceased to be her/his residence.

Dwelling unoccupied because the former resident is providing care elsewhere

An unoccupied dwelling is exempt indefinitely if it was previously the sole or main residence (see p72) of an owner, tenant or licensee who is now solely or mainly resident elsewhere because s/he is providing personal care to someone.[25]

This exemption applies to former residents who were owners, as well as tenants or licensees, irrespective of whether they were liable for council tax on the dwelling.

The carer does not have to be disregarded for the purpose of a council tax discount. However, the person being cared for must require the care because of:

- old age; *or*
- disability; *or*
- illness; *or*
- past or present alcohol or drug dependence; *or*
- past or present mental illness or disorder.

The carer must have been absent from her/his own dwelling since it was last occupied because s/he has been providing such care.

Dwelling left unoccupied by a student owner

An unoccupied dwelling is exempt indefinitely if it was last occupied as the sole or main residence (see p72) of its owner who is now a student and s/he:[26]

- has been a student since s/he last occupied the dwelling; *or*
- has become a student within six weeks of leaving the dwelling.

'**Student**' has the same meaning as for council tax discount purposes (see p104). If there are joint owners of the unoccupied property, all of them must be students and at least one of them must have been solely or mainly resident there on the last day it was occupied, and the last one must have become a student within six weeks of the day it was last occupied as a sole or main residence.

Example

Josie is a single student studying in London. She left her former home in Plymouth and came to London three weeks before her course was due to start. Josie owns a flat in Plymouth, which remains unoccupied apart from when she returns for short periods during college vacations.

The flat in Plymouth is exempt because it is unoccupied and Josie became a student within six weeks of having been solely resident there. It remains exempt when Josie returns in the vacations because, during these times, although it is occupied, the sole resident is a student. If Josie decided to let the flat in Plymouth to a tenant, it would cease to be exempt because it would no longer be unoccupied. However, it would continue to be exempt if the new tenant were also a student.

Unoccupied dwelling in the possession of a mortgage lender

An unoccupied dwelling is exempt indefinitely if a mortgagee (ie, a bank, building society or finance company) is in possession under the mortgage.[27] This would arise, for example, if the lender has repossessed the property because of the borrower's failure to keep up her/his mortgage payments.

Unoccupied dwelling held by a trustee in bankruptcy

An unoccupied dwelling is exempt indefinitely if the liable owner is a trustee in bankruptcy under the Insolvency Act 1986 or other bankruptcy legislation.[28] A trustee in bankruptcy is the person appointed by a general meeting of a bankrupt person's creditors or the court, whose duty is to take over all her/his property, sell the property for cash and distribute the resulting funds among the creditors.

Unoccupied dwelling which cannot be let separately

A dwelling in England and Wales is exempt if it:

- is unoccupied; *and*
- forms part of a single property which includes another dwelling; *and*
- cannot be let separately from that other dwelling without a breach of planning control.

An example of this exemption is an empty 'granny flat'.[29]

Student halls of residence

Among the long-standing exemptions granted to dwellings liable for council tax are halls of residence, which are dwellings occupied by students. A dwelling is exempt indefinitely if it is a hall of residence provided predominantly to accommodate students who would be disregarded for the purpose of a discount (p104).[30] To qualify for the exemption, the hall must be either:

- owned or managed by a prescribed educational institution; *or*
- the subject of an agreement allowing a prescribed educational institution to nominate the majority of the people who are to occupy the accommodation.

This exemption also extends to halls of residence, predominantly for the accommodation of students, owned or managed by a body established solely for charitable purposes.[31] For example, a body set up by a university students' union to manage accommodation needs would fall within this definition. The term 'halls of residence' only applies to universities and similar institutions. It does not include boarding school houses for pupils and staff, as these are not 'halls of residence' and school children are not classed as 'students' for council tax purposes.[32]

A hall (or hostel) should be exempt even if some non-students (such as wardens, tutors or family members) live there. Any separate, self-contained flat or house provided for a non-student, such as a caretaker, is not covered by this exemption. If a hall of residence is used for more than 140 days a year for commercial purposes, such as conferences, it may be subject to non-domestic rates.

The operation of this exemption was considered straightforward until 2016 when Leicester City Council declined to award a Class M exemption to the majority of student rooms contained within three large blocks of purpose-built student accommodation operating as university halls of residence. Previously, the valuation office had banded each of the rooms as occupied by a student population.

In *Sulets v Leicester City Council*,[33] the Valuation Tribunal for England found the en-suite rooms with cooking facilities occupied by a single student to each be separate, self-contained flats and that 'in our view a separate flat for the accommodation of a single student (or, as may be, a couple sharing an intimate relationship) has no feature of a hall of residence....'. Consequently, each room attracted its own bill, with the exception of what were termed 'cluster flats', whereby rooms occupied by one that one student received a designation of a hall of residence and a Class M exemption.

As a consequence, many of the rooms were held not to fall within the exemption. While the rooms were occupied, each room received a Class N exemption (see p57) as being a dwelling occupied solely by a student. As a result, where the valuation office has elected to treat each room as a separate, chargeable dwelling, there may be a considerable administrative burden for both the billing authority and the bodies administering the student accommodation, with each formerly exempt hall of residence attracting multiple bills. In practice, different local authorities adopt different practices.

The decision in *Sulets* is likely to be challenged as a matter of interpretation.

Dwelling wholly occupied by students or 'relevant persons'

To be Class N exempt, the dwelling must be either:[34]
* occupied by one or more residents, all of whom are 'relevant persons' (see below); *or*
* occupied only by one or more 'relevant persons' as term-time accommodation.

A '**relevant person**' is a:[35]
* student disregarded for discount purposes (see p104); *or*
* student's spouse, civil partner or dependant who is not a British citizen and who is prevented by the terms of her/his leave to enter or remain in the UK from working or claiming benefits; *or*
* school or college leaver who is disregarded for discount purposes (see p103).

Students of nursing or midwifery who are studying academic courses at universities count as students.[36] If the dwelling has more than one resident, they must all meet the qualifying conditions for the exemption to apply.

A dwelling occupied by a relevant person is regarded as term-time accommodation during any vacation in which s/he:
* holds a freehold or leasehold interest in, or licence to occupy, the whole or any part of the dwelling; *and*
* has previously used, or intends to use, the dwelling as term-time accommodation.

Example

Three students rent a house as joint tenants. It is exempt from the council tax. The exemption ends when one of the students is dismissed from her course and, therefore, no longer qualifies for a status discount. The three joint tenants are now jointly liable for the council tax on the dwelling. There are three residents, but two of them are disregarded for the purpose of a discount. The bill should be reduced by 25 per cent because there is only one adult resident who is not disregarded.

The exemption is only available to full-time students.[37]

As a consequence of the decision in *Sulets v Leicester City Council* (see p56), during term-time certain student accommodation should receive an exemption as a dwelling wholly occupied by a student.

Armed forces accommodation

Dwellings, either occupied or unoccupied, are exempt indefinitely if they are:[38]
- owned by the Secretary of State for Defence; *and*
- for the purposes of armed forces accommodation.

This includes, for example, armed forces barracks and married quarters. Contributions in place of the council tax are paid by the Ministry of Defence to local authorities. These contributions should broadly match the amount which would otherwise have been payable.[39]

Visiting forces accommodation

A dwelling is exempt indefinitely if at least one person who would be liable is a member (or dependant) of a visiting force and s/he is neither a British citizen nor ordinarily resident in the UK. A dwelling is exempt under this category 'even if not all of the liable persons have a relevant association with a visiting force'. So, for instance, a dwelling in which the liable persons are a visiting serviceman and his British wife would be exempt.[40]

Unoccupied pitch and mooring

A pitch or mooring not occupied by a caravan or boat is an exempt dwelling for council tax purposes.[41]

Dwelling wholly occupied by someone under 18

A dwelling only occupied by one or more persons under 18 is exempt.[42]

Dwelling occupied by a 'severely mentally impaired' person

A dwelling is exempt if it is only occupied by a person(s) who is 'severely mentally impaired' as defined for the purposes of council tax discount (see p107).[43]

A dwelling is also exempt if it is occupied by at least one severely mentally impaired person and one or more student or 'relevant person' (see p104).[44]

People with diplomatic immunity

A dwelling is exempt if at least one liable person has diplomatic, Commonwealth or consular privilege or immunity and that person is not a permanent resident of the UK, or a British citizen, British subject or British protected person. This exemption does not apply if that person has another dwelling in the UK which is her/his main residence or if her/his main residence is in the UK.

Dwelling occupied by a dependent relative

This exemption applies to a dwelling, which is one of at least two dwellings in a single property, occupied by a dependent relative of a person living in another dwelling in the property.[45]

A relative is a **'dependant'** if s/he is 65 or over, severely mentally impaired, or substantially and permanently disabled.[46] A **'relative'** is your spouse, parent, child, grandparent, grandchild, brother, sister, uncle or aunt, nephew or niece, great-grandparent, great-grandchild, great-uncle, great-aunt, great-nephew or great-niece, great-great-grandparent, great-great-grandchild, great-great-uncle, great-great-aunt, great-great-nephew or great-great-niece. A relationship by marriage (or by living together as spouses or by civil partnership[47]) is treated as a relationship by birth and any stepchild of a person shall be treated as her/his child.

2. Exempt dwellings in Scotland

In Scotland, the classes of empty dwellings that are exempt from council tax are set out in the Council Tax (Exempt Dwellings) (Scotland) Order 1997, as amended by the Council Tax (Exempt Dwellings) (Scotland) Amendment Order 2012 and the Council Tax (Exempt Dwellings) (Scotland) Order 2018.[48]

Dwellings which were both unoccupied and unfurnished were exempt from council tax liability for a period of up to six months, subject only to a limited transitional provision until 13 May 2013.

Dwellings in Scotland which are both unoccupied and unfurnished remain exempt from council tax liability for a period of up to six months. From 1 April 2013, after six months, a second claim for the exemption is only possible after a property has been occupied for a period of at least three months. The dwelling need not have been furnished in the three months and this replaces the requirement of occupation or furnishing for a period of at least six weeks which applied for any earlier financial year.[49]

A property classed as an unoccupied dwelling is exempt if:[50]

- it is recently built and still unfurnished (see p60);
- it is undergoing, or has recently undergone, major repair work or structural alteration (see p60);
- it was last occupied by a charity (see p60);
- it is unfurnished (see p60);
- it was last occupied by, and remains the sole liability of, someone in prison or someone living elsewhere to receive or provide care (see p61);
- it is owned by someone who has died (see p61);
- it is occupied by a care leaver (see p61);
- its occupation is prohibited by law (see p61);
- it is owned by a public sector housing authority pending demolition (see p62);
- it is being kept for occupation by a minister of religion (see p62);
- it was last occupied by a student (see p62);
- it has been repossessed following a mortgage default (see p62);
- it was last occupied together with certain agricultural lands (see p62);
- it is held by a trustee in bankruptcy (see p62);

- it is part of the same premises as, or situated within the same 'curtilage' as, another dwelling and is difficult to let separately (see p62);
- the sole liable person is a student (see p63).

Exempt unoccupied dwellings

Unoccupied new dwelling

A dwelling that is unoccupied and unfurnished is exempt for up to six months if:[51]

- less than six months have elapsed since the effective date of the first entry on the valuation list; *and*
- there was no entry on the valuation list immediately before that effective date.

Unoccupied dwelling undergoing structural repair, improvement or reconstruction

An unoccupied dwelling is exempt if it cannot be lived in because, since the last occupation date, it has been undergoing, or has undergone, structural alteration or major repair work to make it habitable.[52]

The lack of occupation must be because of the work being carried out. If the dwelling is occupied, it is not exempt. The exemption may last for 12 months after the dwelling was last occupied, or (if sooner) for six months after the major repair work or alteration was substantially completed. The property may remain furnished.

The test is one of fact and the existence of an exemption will not normally justify removal of a dwelling from the valuation roll, but the possibility of cases existing 'in which the works are so extensive and so prolonged or where the essential physical characteristics of a house were lost' resulting in the property ceasing to exist as a dwelling house 'while the works are carried out' has been recognised (see Chapters 2 and 3).[53]

Unoccupied dwelling last occupied by a charity

An unoccupied dwelling last occupied by a charitable body is exempt for up to six months if it was last occupied to further the charity's objectives.[54] 'Charitable' has the same meaning as in income tax law. Any period of occupation for less than six weeks is disregarded.[55] This disregard is a device to avoid abuse of the exemption. Without the disregard, the liable person could ensure that the building is occupied for a few days near the end of the six-month period and thus trigger the exemption again for a further six months. The property may remain furnished.

Unoccupied and unfurnished dwelling

Unoccupied and unfurnished dwellings are exempt for up to six months from the end of the last period of six weeks or more during which the dwelling was occupied or furnished.[56]

Dwelling last occupied by someone in prison, or living elsewhere to receive or provide care

An unoccupied dwelling is exempt indefinitely if it was last occupied as the sole or main residence (see p72) of someone who continues to be liable for council tax, and since the last day of occupation s/he is:

- disregarded for the purpose of a council tax discount because she is in prison or detention, or is in a hospital, care home or certain care hostels in Scotland, England or Wales (see Chapter 7); or
- receiving personal care elsewhere because of her/his old age, disablement, illness, past or present alcohol or drug dependence, or past or present mental illness or disorder; or
- providing personal care elsewhere to someone who needs it because of old age, disablement, illness, past or present alcohol or drug dependence, or past or present mental illness/disorder.[57]

Any period of occupation of less than six weeks since the last day of occupation is disregarded. The property may remain furnished.

In Scotland, a care home service is one covered by Schedule 12 of the Public Services Reform (Scotland) Act 2010.[58]

Dwelling occupied by a carer leaver

From 1 April 2018, the dwelling is exempt if it is occupied exclusively by one or more care leavers.[59] You are a care leaver if you are at least 18 years old but not yet 26 years old and were previously in the care of a local authority (at age 16 or subsequently). Dwellings jointly occupied by one or more care leavers and other specified persons (including students and persons under 18) are also exempt from council tax.[60]

Dwelling owned by someone who has died

To be exempt, the dwelling must be no one's sole or main residence (see p72). Additionally, any liability to pay council tax must fall under the estate of the deceased person.[61] In such cases, the dwelling is exempt:

- indefinitely if no grant of confirmation to the estate of that person has been made; or
- for up to six months from the date such a grant is made.

The property may remain furnished.

Dwelling in which occupation is prohibited

If it is prohibited by law to occupy a dwelling, that dwelling is exempt indefinitely.[62] The property may remain furnished. The fact that such a property is actually occupied should not make it ineligible for the exemption.

It is also exempt if it is being kept unoccupied because legal action is under way to prohibit its occupation or to acquire it under a compulsory purchase order. In these circumstances, if the dwelling is actually occupied, it is not exempt. The property may remain furnished.

Unoccupied dwelling owned by a housing body pending demolition

A dwelling which is owned by a local authority or registered social landlord and is kept unoccupied pending demolition is exempt.[63] The property may remain furnished.

Dwelling held for a minister of religion

A dwelling, such as a manse, which is no one's sole or main residence (see p72), is exempt indefinitely if it is being held by, or on behalf of, any religious body to be available for occupation by a minister of religion as a residence from which to perform the duties of her/his office.[64] The property may remain furnished.

Student's unoccupied dwelling

An unoccupied dwelling which is a student's main residence and which was last occupied by a student(s) is exempt for up to four months from the last day it was occupied for a period of six weeks or more.[65] This applies, for example, to the student's term-time accommodation during vacations if the accommodation remains unoccupied during that period. The property may remain furnished.

Dwelling repossessed by a mortgage lender

A dwelling which is no one's sole or main residence (see p72) is exempt indefinitely if it has been formally repossessed by a mortgage lender.[66] The property may remain furnished.

Dwelling last occupied with agricultural lands

An unoccupied and unfurnished dwelling is exempt indefinitely if it was last used and occupied with the land on which it is situated. The land must be:[67]
- agricultural or pastoral; *or*
- woodlands, market gardens, orchards, allotments or allotment gardens; *or*
- used for the purpose of poultry farming and exceeding one-tenth of a hectare.

Dwelling held by a trustee in bankruptcy

A dwelling which is no one's sole or main residence (see p72) is exempt indefinitely if the only person who would be liable is a bankruptcy trustee.[68]

Unoccupied dwelling that is difficult to let separately

An unoccupied dwelling, such as an empty 'granny flat' or staff accommodation, is exempt indefinitely if:[69]
- it forms part of premises which include another dwelling; *or*
- it is situated within the 'curtilage' of another dwelling; *and*
- it is difficult to let separately from that other dwelling; *and*

- the person who would be liable for it has her/his sole or main residence in that other dwelling.

The property may remain furnished.

Unoccupied dwelling for which the sole liable person is a student

A dwelling which is no one's sole or main residence (see p72) is exempt indefinitely if the person who would be liable is a student for the purpose of a council tax discount (see p104).

If there are joint owners/joint tenants, they must all be students.[70] The property may remain furnished.

Exempt occupied dwellings

An occupied dwelling is exempt if it:[71]
- is only occupied by one or more students, school or college leavers or under-18-year-olds (see below);
- is occupied by a student or a student's spouse (see below);
- is a housing association 'trial' property for older people or people with disabilities (see below);
- is a students' hall of residence (see p64);
- is armed forces accommodation (see p64);
- is visiting forces accommodation (see p64);
- includes garages, carports and storage sheds (see p64);
- is occupied by a 'severely mentally impaired' person (see p64);
- is 'prescribed housing support accommodation' (see p65).

Dwelling occupied only by students or under-18-year-olds

A dwelling is exempt indefinitely if it is not the sole or main residence (see p72) of anyone other than a student for the purpose of a council tax discount (see p104) or a person under 18, and it is occupied by at least one such person.[72] Also included is a student's spouse or dependant who is not a British citizen and who is prevented by the Immigration Rules from either claiming benefits or working in the UK.[73]

Temporary dwelling for older or disabled people owned by a registered housing association

A dwelling owned by a registered housing association is exempt indefinitely if:
- it is not the sole or main residence (see p72) of any person; *and*
- it is for people over pension age or with a disability who are likely in the future to have their sole or main residences in other dwellings provided by the housing association.

This provides an exemption for trial dwellings for older or disabled people who are likely to live in other property owned by the association in the future. In practice, most local authorities do not charge council tax for the trial period while the person is still liable elsewhere.

Halls of residence

A dwelling is exempt if it is, or is part of, a hall of residence provided predominantly to accommodate students and which:[74]

- is owned and managed by a prescribed educational institution for the purpose of a council tax discount; *or*
- is the subject of an agreement allowing a prescribed educational institution to nominate the majority of the people who are to occupy the accommodation.

The fact that a student hall of residence may be used for commercial lettings between terms does not affect entitlement to an exemption providing its predominant purpose remains the accommodation of students.[75] The decision in *Sulets v Leicester City Council* (see p56) has yet to be tested in Scotland. Student halls may also be sometime classified differently under the category 'university buildings'.

Armed forces accommodation

An occupied or unoccupied dwelling is exempt indefinitely if it is:[76]

- owned by the Secretary of State for Defence; *and*
- held for the purposes of armed forces accommodation.

The local authority receives compensating payments for these dwellings.

Visiting forces accommodation

A dwelling is exempt indefinitely if a member of a visiting force or her/his dependant (but not a dependant who is a British citizen or is ordinarily resident in the UK) would be liable.[77]

Garages, carports and storage sheds

Certain garages, carports, car parking stances and premises used for storing domestic items, including cycles and similar vehicles, are considered to be dwellings (see p15). They are exempt indefinitely from council tax.[78]

Dwelling occupied by a 'severely mentally impaired' person

A dwelling is exempt if it is only occupied by a person(s) who is 'severely mentally impaired', as defined for the purposes of council tax discount (see p107).[79]

A dwelling is also exempt if it is occupied by at least one severely mentally impaired person and one or more students or relevant persons (see p104).[80]

Prescribed housing support accommodation

A dwelling is exempt if it falls into the category of 'prescribed housing support accommodation'.[81] In order to be exempt:

- the dwelling must be the residence of at least one person who is a tenant, sub-tenant or who has a licence to occupy the dwelling; *and*
- a registered prescribed housing support service must be provided to at least one licensee, tenant or subtenant of the dwelling; *and*
- all the residents must share the use of a kitchen, bathroom, shower room or toilet room, and these must also be shared with at least one other person who is not resident in the dwelling.

A dwelling is not exempt if each resident has exclusive use of a kitchen and a bathroom/shower room (either containing a toilet or if there is a separate toilet which all the residents can use).

3. How exempt dwellings are identified

Local authorities must take reasonable steps each financial year to establish whether any dwellings in their area are exempt from council tax for any period during the year.[82] Most are likely to carry out periodic postal surveys and make use of other sources of information, such as the electoral roll and their benefit records. Most local authorities also carry out regular visits to unoccupied exempt dwellings.

If the local authority has no reason to believe that a particular dwelling will be, or was, exempt, it will assume it is a chargeable dwelling for council tax billing purposes.[83] Alternatively, if it has reason to believe that a particular dwelling will be, or was, exempt for a period during the course of the year, it must make that assumption for council tax billing purposes.[84]

4. Notification of exemption

If the local authority has assumed that a dwelling is exempt, it must write to the person who would otherwise be liable.[85] The notification must be made as soon as is reasonably practicable.[86] The requirement does not apply in Scotland if:[87]

- the otherwise liable person is a housing body; *or*
- the dwelling is a separate garage, carport or storage shed.

The local authority should also supply a statement that:[88]

- shows the valuation band for the dwelling;
- summarises how to make a proposal for altering the valuation list;

- in Scotland, specifies for the financial year in question the amounts set as council tax and Scottish Water charges;
- in England and Wales, specifies the local authority's estimate of the amount of council tax (or the actual amount if the year is over) which would have been payable, disregarding any disability reduction, discount, transitional relief (in Wales) or council tax reduction that may have been awarded;
- summarises the most common classes of dwelling which are exempt;[89]
- in Scotland, summarises the individual's obligation to correct any incorrect assumptions the local authority may have made in awarding the exemption, and including the penalty which may be imposed if this obligation is not met (see below).

The above information need not be given if it was already provided when the scheme was introduced or on any bill ('demand notice').[90] If there is more than one potentially liable person, the local authority only needs to write to one of them.[91]

The duty to correct false assumptions

If you have been notified that the dwelling is, or will be, exempt, you have a duty to tell the local authority if there is reason to believe that this is not the case. The local authority should be notified in writing within 21 days.[92]

If two or more people are jointly liable to pay council tax on a dwelling, they both have a duty to notify the local authority. Only one of them, however, has to supply the information for this obligation to be met.[93]

It an offence if you obtain, through an act or ommission, a reduction under a council tax reduction scheme which you are not entitled to.

5. Penalties

The local authority has the discretion to impose a penalty of £70 (in England) or £50 (in Wales and Scotland) on a liable person who fails to notify it that her/his dwelling is no longer exempt. There are higher penalties for failing to supply information requested by the local authority for council tax purposes.[94]

Such penalties are not criminal convictions or punishments, but if unpaid can be recovered through the magistrates' court (sheriff court in Scotland) in the same way as unpaid sums of council tax.

Each time the local authority repeats the request and the person fails to supply the information, a further £280 penalty (in England) or £200 (in Wales and Scotland) can be imposed.[95]

You can appeal against the imposition of a penalty,[96] although English and Welsh local authorities have the discretion to quash the penalty beforehand.[97] In

England and Wales, you appeal directly to the valuation tribunal (see p246). In Scotland, an appeal can be made to the valuation appeal committee by writing to the local authority. The local authority should pass the appeal on to the committee. A Scottish local authority may revoke the imposition of a penalty if you have a reasonable excuse for the failure.[98] For more information about appeals, see Chapter 11.

In practice, penalties are relatively little used as they cannot be recovered through the courts while an appeal against the penalty is outstanding. As a result, few local authorities consider enforcement of penalties worth the administrative time and effort involved to recover them.

A local authority may also impose a larger penalty as an alternative to prosecution for a criminal offence of falsely supplying information under offences created following the Local Government Finance Act 2012 (see Chapter 5).[99]

6. **Appeals**

If the local authority decides that the dwelling is not exempt, you can appeal in writing to the local authority if you are an 'aggrieved person'.[100] There is no time limit for making such appeals. An **'aggrieved person'** is someone who would be liable to pay the tax if the dwelling were not exempt or s/he is the owner (if different). The appeal letter should give the reasons why the dwelling should be exempt. The local authority has two months in which to answer.[101]

Exemptions can be backdated to the date the qualifying conditions for the exemption were first met, the beginning of the scheme or when the particular exemption was first introduced, whichever is the latest. There is no requirement to show 'good cause' for the backdating.

If an exemption is not granted, or if the local authority fails to answer within two months of receiving the appeal, a further appeal can be made.[102] In theory, the local authority may commence enforcing payment of the original bill while the appeal is outstanding, but once a formal appeal has begun, the local authority ought to suspend recovery and a court may also order a stay on proceedings (see p254).

In an increasing number of cases, billing authorities have removed an exemption which has previously been awarded and recognised for more than one financial year. If this has happened to you, appeal to the tribunal.

In **England and Wales**, a further appeal can be made by writing directly to the Valuation Tribunal for England or the Valuation Tribunal for Wales. This should normally be made within two months of the date the local authority notified you of its decision, or within four months of the date when the initial written representation was made if the local authority has not responded. The president of the tribunal has the power to allow an out-of-time appeal if you have failed to meet the appropriate time limit because of reasons beyond your control.

In **Scotland**, a further appeal is made by writing again to the local authority. The local authority should pass the appeal on to the secretary of the relevant local valuation appeal committee. The appeal must be made in writing within four months of the date on which the grievance was first raised with the local authority. There is no power to consider an out-of-time appeal.

See Chapter 11 for more information about appeals.

Notes

1 **EW** s2(2)(a) LGFA 1992
  S s71(2)(a) LGFA 1992

1. Exempt dwellings in England and Wales

2 CT(ED)O
3 *Burnip v Birmingham City Council* [2013] PTSR 117; *R (Hardy) v Sandwell MBC* [2015] PTSR 1292
4 Art 2 CT(ED)(E)(A)O 2012; s11A LGFA 1992
5 Art 2 (2) CT(ED)O, as amended by CT(ED)(A)O
6 Art 2 (2) CT(ED)O, as amended by CT(ED)(A)(E)O
7 *Ealing London Borough and others v Notting Hill Housing Trust and another* [2015] All ER (D) (Feb)
8 Class B CT(ED)O, as amended by art 4(a) CT(ED)(A)O
9 *Ealing London Borough and others v Notting Hill Housing Trust and another* [2015] All ER (D) (Feb)
10 *Ealing London Borough and others v Notting Hill Housing Trust and another* [2015] All ER (D) (Feb) per Mostyn, J
11 Class C CT(ED)O
12 Class D CT(ED)O
13 s6 LGFA 1992
14 CT(ED)O, as amended by art 4(b) CT(ED)(A)O
15 Class F CT(ED)O, as amended art 4(d) CT(ED)(A)O
16 *Tew v Lewisham London Borough Council* [2018] 1 February 2018 Appeal No 5690M202173084C/4, decision of the VTE President Mr Garland

17 Valuation Tribunal Service, *Valuation in Practice,* issue No.19, November 2010
18 Class G CT(ED)O;
  E as amended by art 2(2) CT(ED)(A)(E)O
19 *Watson v Rhondda Cynon Taff Borough Council* [2001] EWHC 913 (Admin)
20 Class H CT(ED)O
21 Class H CT(ED)O
22 Class E CT(ED)O
23 Parliamentary Answer given by Dr Alan Whitehead, Under-Secretary of State for Transport, Local Government and the Regions, 24 January 2002
24 Class I CT(ED)O
25 Class J CT(ED)O
26 Class K CT(ED)O
27 Class L CT(ED)O
28 Class Q CT(ED)O, as amended by The Council Tax (Exempt Dwellings) (Amendment) Order 1993 No.150
29 Class T CT(ED)O
30 Class M CT(ED)O
31 Class M CT(ED)O
32 *Stowe School Ltd v Aylesbury Vale District Council* [2012] RA 111
33 *Sulets v Leicester City Council* [2017] Appeal No: 2465M197400/037C October 7
34 Class N CT(ED)O
35 Class N CT(ED)O
36 VOA, Council Tax Manual, Practice Note No.2, para 28
37 *Jagoo v Bristol City Council* [2017] EWHC 926 (Admin)
38 Class O CT(ED)O
39 VOA, Council Tax Manual, Practice Note No.2, para 30

40 Class P CT(ED)O
41 Class R CT(ED)O
42 Class S CT(ED)O
43 Class U CT(ED)O
44 CT(ED)O
45 Class W CT(ED)O
46 CT(ED)O
47 Class W CT(ED)(A)(E)O 2005

2. Exempt dwellings in Scotland
48 CT(ED)(S)(A)O 2012
49 Art 2 CT(ED)(S)(A)O 2012
50 CT(ED)(S)O 1997
51 Sch 1 para 1 CT(ED)(S)O 1997
52 Sch 1 para 2 CT(ED)(S)O 1997, as
    amended by Council Tax (Exempt
    Dwellings) (Scotland) Amendment
    (No.2) Order 1999 No.140
53 *Assessor Tayside Joint Valuation Board v a
    decision by the valuation appeal
    committee for Perth and Kinross* [2018]
    SC 106
54 Sch 1 para 3 CT(ED)(S)O 1997
55 Art 2 CT(ED)(S)O 1997
56 Sch 1 para 4 CT(ED)(S)O 1997
57 Sch 1 para 5 CT(ED)(S)O 1997
58 Class E CT(ED)O, as amended by art 2
    and Sch 2 para 17(a) Public Services
    Reform (Scotland) Act 2010
    (Consequential Modifications of
    Enactments) Order 2011 No.2581
59 Sch 1 para 10(a)(iii) CT(ED)(S)O, as
    amended by art 2 Council Tax (Exempt
    Dwellings) (Scotland) Amendment
    Order 2018 No.45
60 Policy note to the Council Tax (Exempt
    Dwellings) (Scotland) (Amendment)
    Order 2018 No.45
61 Sch 1 para 6 CT(ED)(S)O 1997
62 Sch 1 para 7 CT(ED)(S)O 1997
63 Sch 1 para 8 CT(ED)(S)O 1997
64 Sch 1 para 9 CT(ED)(S)O 1997
65 Sch 1 para 11 CT(ED)(S)O 1997
66 Sch 1 para 13 CT(ED)(S)O 1997
67 Sch 1 para 14 CT(ED)(S)O 1997
68 Sch 1 para 21 CT(ED)(S)O 1997
69 Sch 1 para 19 CT(ED)(S)O 1997
70 Sch 1 para 12 CT(ED)(S)O 1997
71 CT(ED)(S)(A)O
72 Sch 1 para 10(a)(iii) and (iv) CT(ED)(S)O
    1997; see also the Education (Graduate
    Endowment and Student Support)
    (Scotland) Act 2001
73 Sch 1 para 10(a)(ii) CT(ED)(S)O 1997
74 Sch 1 para 16 CT(ED)(S)O 1997
75 *Assessor for Lothian Region v Heriot-Watt
    University* [1998] SC 736
76 Sch 1 para 17 CT(ED)(S)O 1997

77 Sch 1 para 22 CT(ED)(S)O 1997
78 Sch 1 para 20 CT(ED)(S)O 1997
79 Class U CT(ED)(S)O 1997
80 CT(ED)O
81 CT(ED)(S)O 1997 was amended by the
    CT(ED)(S)(A)O 2006. Such a dwelling
    has the same meaning as
    accommodation defined by s91(8)
    Housing (Scotland) Act 2001 and the
    Housing (Scotland) Act 2001 (Housing
    Support Services) Regulations 2002,
    registered by the Scottish Commission
    for the regulation of care as a prescribed
    housing support service under the
    Regulation of Care (Scotland) Act 2001.

3. How exempt dwellings are identified
82 **EW** Reg 8 CT(AE) Regs
    S CT(ED)(S)O 1992
83 **EW** Reg 9(1) CT(AE) Regs
    S Reg 7 CT(AE)(S) Regs
84 **EW** Reg 9(2) CT(AE) Regs
    S Reg 8 CT(AE)(S) Regs

4. Notification of exemption
85 **EW** Reg 10(1) CT(AE) Regs
86 **EW** Reg 10(2) CT(AE) Regs
    S Reg 9 CT(AE)(S) Regs
87 **EW** Reg 10 CT(AE) Regs
    S Reg 9 CT(AE)(S) Regs
88 **EW** Reg 10 CT(AE) Regs
    S Reg 9 CT(AE)(S) Regs
89 **EW** Reg 10(3) CT(AE) Regs
    S Reg 9 CT(AE)(S) Regs
90 **EW** Reg 10 CT(AE) Regs
    S Reg 9 CT(AE)(S) Regs
91 **EW** Reg 10 CT(AE) Regs
    S Reg 9 CT(AE)(S) Regs
92 **EW** Reg 11 CT(AE) Regs
93 **EW** Reg 11 CT(AE) Regs
    S Reg 10 CT(AE)(S) Regs

5. Penalties
94 LGFE(SP)O
95 **EW** Sch 3 LGFA 1992; LGFE(SP)O
    S s97(4) and Sch 3 LGFA 1992
96 **EW** s14(2) and Sch 3 LGFA 1992
    S s97(4) and Sch 3 LGFA 1992
97 **EW** Sch 3 para 1 LGFA 1992
98 s97(4) and Sch 3 LGFA 1992
99 **EW** s14 LGFA 2012

6. Appeals
100 **EW** s16 LGFA 1992
101 **EW** s16 LGFA 1992
     S s81 LGFA 1992
102 **EW** s16 LGFA 1992
     S s81 LGFA 1992

Chapter 5

Liability

This chapter covers:
1. Who is liable (below)
2. Who is a resident (p72)
3. When the owner is always liable (p77)
4. Joint liability (p82)
5. Change of circumstances (p85)
6. Backdating liability (p85)
7. How the liable person is identified (p86)
8. Appeals (p88)

1. Who is liable

Council tax is payable on any dwelling which is not exempt. See Chapter 4 for more information on exemptions. Normally, the person liable to pay council tax is an adult resident of the dwelling. To be liable, the person must have her/his 'sole or main' residence in the dwelling and have a right to occupy it. To determine who is liable to pay council tax, it is necessary to consult the 'hierarchy of liability' (see p71).[1] This lists different categories of occupier, based on security of occupancy, including owners, tenants, licensees and squatters. Normally, the person(s) whose sole or main residence is in a dwelling and who has the most secure interest in it will be the liable taxpayer(s) and the person to whom the council tax bill will be sent.

Working down the list, as soon as a description is reached which applies to someone in respect of the dwelling in question, that person is the liable person.[2] This will normally be an owner-occupier or a council, housing association or private tenant. A tenant is not liable, however, if the landlord lives in the same dwelling. If no one is solely or mainly resident (see p72) in the dwelling, the non-resident owner is liable. In certain instances, however, the owner is always liable (see p77). If more than one person fits the first description that applies, they will normally be jointly liable (see p82).

For the purpose of determining the liable person on any day, the state of affairs at the end of the day is assumed to have existed throughout that day (see p72).[3]

In certain cases, the liable person may also be a person who is disregarded for the purpose of a discount (see Chapter 7). The rules on discounts are separate and do not affect liability, except in some cases where they affect 'severely mentally impaired' people and students who would otherwise be held jointly liable (see p84).

Following the death of the owner, the deceased's personal representative may become liable in her/his capacity as owner of the estate, but the dwelling is likely to be exempt until probate or letters of administration are obtained if unoccupied. See Chapter 4 for more information.

Note: you do not have to pay council tax unless a bill has been sent with your name on it or, if your name is not known, the 'council taxpayer' (see p173), unless (in Scotland) you are jointly liable with someone who has been billed.

Hierarchy of liability in England and Wales

1. A resident with a freehold interest in the whole or any part of the dwelling.

2. A resident with a leasehold interest (including an assured tenancy or assured shorthold tenancy) in the whole or any part of the dwelling which is not inferior to another such interest held by another resident.

3. A resident statutory tenant,[4] secure tenant[5] or introductory[6] tenant of the whole or any part of the dwelling.[7]

4. A resident with a contractual licence to occupy the whole or any part of the dwelling.

5. A resident (including a squatter).

6. A person who is a mortgagee in possession of the owner's interest in the dwelling. In the case of secure or introductory tenants, and a mortgagee in possession, a date for these to come into force has yet to be appointed.[8]

7. A non-resident owner – ie, the person who has the inferior (shortest) lease granted for a term of six months or more of the whole, or any part, of the dwelling. If there is no such leaseholder, the freeholder is the owner.[9]

Hierarchy of liability in Scotland[10]

1. A resident owner of the whole or any part of the dwelling.

2. A resident tenant of the whole or any part of the dwelling.

3. A resident statutory tenant,[11] resident statutory assured tenant[12] or resident secure tenant[13] of the whole or any part of the dwelling.[14]

4. A resident sub-tenant of the whole or any part of the dwelling.

5. A resident of the dwelling or:
– a sub-tenant of the whole or any part of the dwelling under a sub-lease granted for a term of six months or more;
– a tenant, under a lease granted for a term of six months or more, of any part of the dwelling which is not subject to a sub-lease granted for a term of six months or more;
– an owner of any part of the dwelling which is not subject to a lease granted for a term of six months or more.

In Scotland, in addition to council tax, Scottish Water charges are payable for any dwelling which is not exempt, except if:

- Scottish Water does not provide a supply of water to the dwelling; *or*
- the water is supplied by meter; *or*
- Scottish Water is under an obligation to provide a supply free of charge.

Caravans and boats in England and Wales

The owner of a caravan or houseboat is liable for council tax except for the days when someone other than the owner is resident and so becomes liable for those days.[15] The normal council tax definitions of 'resident' (see below) and 'owner' apply in the case of residential caravans or boats, but the definition of **'owner'** is extended to include:[16]

- the person who has possession under any hire purchase or conditional sale agreement; *or*
- the person entitled to the property apart from any mortgage or bill of sale which applies to it.

Daily liability

Liability to pay the tax arises on a daily basis. The situation at the end of the day is assumed to have existed throughout the day.[17] The amount payable for the day is the annual amount set by the local authority for that year for dwellings in the relevant valuation band, divided by the number of days in the financial year (365 or 366).

2. Who is a resident

Council tax is usually payable by someone who is resident in the dwelling. If no one is resident, the non-resident owner is liable. To count as **'resident'** you must:

- be aged 18 or over; *and*
- be solely or mainly resident in the dwelling (see below).[18]

If everyone who lives in the dwelling is aged under 18, the dwelling is exempt from the tax.

Sole or main residence

If a potentially liable person has more than one home, the local authority must decide which is her/his main residence. The concept of 'sole or main residence' is not defined in the legislation, but has been considered by the courts.

Where the taxpayer lives (England and Wales)

The Court of Appeal decision in *R (Williams) v Horsham District Council* clarifies the approach to be taken.[19] The starting point for deciding sole or main residence should be section 6(5) of the Local Government Finance Act 1992, where 'sole or main residence' refers to premises in which the taxpayer actually resides. Usually, a person's main residence would be the dwelling that 'a reasonable onlooker' with knowledge of the facts would regard as that person's home at the time. The test might not always be easy to apply and the answer would depend on the particular circumstances; it would be a matter of fact and degree.

Establishing a 'reasonable onlooker' principle sets an objective test to be applied in every case and may well differ from what a local authority would conclude. Thus, where a person *actually* lives in any financial year becomes key to determining residence, not a hypothetical question about the right to return in future years or at a period later in the same financial year.

Following this case, it is clear that the starting point for any appeal is section 6 and the question of who actually lives in the dwelling. By emphasising section 6, the Court of Appeal confirmed that resident tenants, licensees and even trespassers should normally be placed ahead of non-resident owners in terms of liability for council tax. Factors such as voter registration and registration for medical treatment have often been used by valuation tribunals to determine sole or main residence. However, the key question following the *Williams* case is: 'Where does the taxpayer actually live?' Hypothetical questions, such as where a person might move or remain in the event of job loss or serious illness or where s/he might live were tenants to move out, do not, in themselves, determine the answer to this question.

The judgment in *Williams* is particularly important if you have let your principal home to tenants or to someone who normally lives or works abroad. In the case of *Parry v Derbyshire Dales District Council*,[20] the taxpayer lived in Spain and let his cottage to tenants. The High Court held that the taxpayer was resident in Spain for local tax purposes and the fact that the tenant left did not mean that Mr Parry ceased to reside in Spain. The court followed the approach of the Court of Appeal in the *Williams* case and confirmed section 6 of the Local Government Finance Act 1992: setting out a hierarchy of liability based on who is actually resident in the dwelling rather than security of tenure is crucial to determining the liable person for council tax purposes. In some cases, it would follow that a person's home may be different to her/his sole or main residence. 'Home' has been judicially considered the place to which a person has a degree of physical and emotional attachment. The test as to whether a person occupied premises as their home is both qualitative and quantative, and a decision maker must weight all the relevant facts reasonably.[21]

Following the *Williams* case, a person letting a dwelling to tenants should ensure that the calculation of a bill should relate to when s/he actually moves out of a dwelling, not necessarily when tenants move in.

Example

Mr and Mrs Shah live in a house with their 17-year-old daughter. Mrs Shah is the joint owner of the property with her sister, who frequently comes to stay and has a bedroom of her own, but who has her main home elsewhere. The non-resident joint owner is not liable.

If the couple were to separate and Mr Shah to leave the dwelling, Mrs Shah would be liable by herself, but Mr Shah would remain jointly liable for any amount that accrued while living as a couple.

If Mrs Shah were also to leave the dwelling, leaving the daughter as the only person living there, the dwelling may be considered exempt, as it is the sole residence of someone under the age of 18. On the daughter's 18th birthday, she would become the sole liable person as the only resident of the dwelling.

Mrs Shah's sister is not liable as her main residence is elsewhere.

The fact that people may have, for whatever reason, used a dwelling for the purposes of providing a residential postal address does not, in itself, mean that such persons were actually so resident.[22]

Local authorities sometimes treat tenants as still liable if they move out of a property before the end of their tenancy.[23]

Some confusion has arisen in decisions about whether 'presumed periodic tenancies', arising under statute or by contract, may constitute qualifying leasehold tenancies of more than six months and are, therefore, classed as 'surviving' when residents move out (and also in respect of entitlement to housing benefit on a property that is no longer occupied).[24] However, no decisions to date have considered the key question of sole or main residence which is essential to any liability to tax based on residence.

The hierarchy of liability has to be considered along with the key issue of who actually has sole or main residence in the building on any particular day. In *Branwell v Valuation Office Agency*, the High Court stated:[25]

The hierarchy in section 6 shows that Parliament decided that liability should depend on residence in, and rights to reside in, a dwelling. That is an intelligible and rational legislative choice. It connects liability with actual enjoyment of the dwelling, or if no one is living in it, with the right to occupy it.

The key words are 'if no one is living in it'. Following the *Williams* case, if the former tenant no longer lives in the dwelling and actually has her/his sole or main residence elsewhere, the former tenant can no longer be said to be residing in the dwelling and ceases to be considered as liable under section 6. Once the right to occupy the dwelling is terminated, whether by giving notice and moving out, by abandonment or eviction, and the person establishes another sole or main residence in another dwelling, any liability for council tax at the former home ceases.

For instance, if a tenant vacates a property without proper notice and is settled elsewhere, the landlord becomes liable to pay the council tax during this period of non-occupancy, because the landlord has the remaining material interest and the ultimate right in law to use and occupy the home and not the former tenant or occupier.

A further important indication of 'sole or main residence' is the issue of where a person normally sleeps most or all of the time. In *Sumeghova v McMahon*,[26] the Court of Appeal ruled that the place where a person sleeps was of the most enormous importance in determining where her/his principal or only home was; while it might not be decisive, it would influence any court considerably.

Example

Ian is the tenant of a flat on an assured tenancy beginning on 1 September 2018 and pays the council tax from 1 September. He gives notice to his landlord and moves out after Christmas 2018. Ian moves in with his partner, Patricia, at her address in the same billing authority area.

The landlord does not let Ian's flat immediately and it stands empty. Applying the hierarchy under section 6, as Ian no longer has residence in the flat, he ceases to have any liability for tax at his previous address. Instead, Ian becomes jointly liable to pay council tax with Patricia at the address where they live together. The liability for council tax at Ian's former address up until 31 March 2019 falls upon the landlord unless a new tenant or occupier moves in.

If a person has never lived in a dwelling s/he cannot be considered to be resident in it, even if s/he is the owner of the dwelling or has no fixed abode.[27]

Where the taxpayer lives (Scotland)

The same approach to residence taken in the *Williams* case (see p73) has been applied in Scotland. In *Highland Council v Highland and Western Region Valuation Appeal Committee*, a taxpayer lived during the week, and some weekends, in a dwelling closer to his job rather than in the dwelling occupied by his wife and family.[28] The Court of Session ruled that the valuation appeal committee was entitled to find that the dwelling where the appellant spent most of his time during the week was his sole or main residence.

In cases where liability may fall upon the landlord, it is essential that the valuation appeal committee establish whether a property has been truly abandoned or is merely temporarily unoccupied, and is able to identify the situation from evidence.[29]

Council tax discounts and reductions

The question of sole or main residence is important when calculating the level of discounts (see Chapter 7) and disability reductions (see Chapter 6). Where there is more than one resident adult in a property, the amount of council tax support available is likely to be affected, as well as affecting entitlement to discount if only one adult is left living in the property. The local authority should be informed when a person moves in or out of the property, within 21 days, if it is the case that a change in sole or main residence (based upon the test in *Williams* – see p73) has arisen.

Merely using a property as a postal address to receive mail or keeping property does not constitute residence for council tax purposes.

Example
Doris is a pensioner with an adult son Arnie who is homeless. He comes to see her from time to time and receives post at the address, but otherwise stays in hostels or with his friends. Arnie does not have sole or main residence with Doris for council tax purposes so she is entitled to a single occupier discount.

Establishing sole or main residence

In some cases, the local authority does not accept evidence provided by the taxpayer that a person does or does not reside at a particular dwelling. If this is the case, all sorts of evidence can be used – eg, bank statements, utility bills, extracts from official registers, forms of identification and statements from neighbours and professionals who know the situation.

A local authority is expected to act reasonably when assessing evidence. For example, if proof of a tenancy agreement is supported by signatures and addresses of witnesses which are in doubt, the local authority should investigate the details and try and contact the witness, not merely ignore or dismiss the evidence as insufficient or untrustworthy.[30]

If the local authority does not accept the evidence provided, you should make an appeal to the valuation tribunal in England or Wales or to the valuation appeal committee in Scotland.

Witness statements may be used where the local authority refuses to accept evidence supplied by the taxpayer. A witness statement must give your name and address, and you can set down the relevant facts. A local authority that refuses to accept evidence in a witness statement may be liable for breach of statutory duty in civil law.

Residence in more than one place

It is possible for a person to have both a sole or main residence and also a residence in another dwelling for discount and other council tax purposes. This has been accepted by the Valuation Tribunal in an appeal against the imposition of an empty property discount under section 11B of the Local Government Finance Act 1992.[31] Since 2013, an increase in council tax can be imposed upon any dwelling in England continuously empty for two or more years, paid by the owner of the dwelling.[32]

The appellant had occupied the property from time to time for the purposes of renovation and, to a limited extent, had lived inside it. Supporting evidence included a gas bill, a bank statement, a home insurance policy letter, photographs and sundry other documents including an electoral roll form and was supported by a witness statement. Non-occupation should not be inferred simply because the appellant had other addresses for his bank accounts and did not show up on credit checks at the appeal property, or an inconsistency existed with dating in correspondence. The tribunal accepted that the legislation also uses the word 'resident' in other contexts, and from its inception, the possibility that a person may own one or more properties and pay council tax in respect of both has been a basic feature. The panel identified the correct test to be an empty property was 'simply whether the appeal property was unoccupied and unfurnished'.[33]

Further recognition of the principle that a person may have two different residences simultaneous is found in other branches of taxation law. In *Frost v Feltham*, Nourse, J ruled: 'If someone lives in two houses the question, which does he use as the principal or more important one, cannot be determined solely by reference to the way in which he divides his time between the two'.[34]

It has also been recognised that there are 'an infinity of variations of circumstances to take into account in deciding which was a man's main home. Each case would differ from the other; there might be cases where it was very difficult to decide the question.'[35]

Merely because a couple are married, and one has been ruled as having a sole main residence at one location, is not sufficient reason in itself to conclude that both spouses share the same sole or main residence.[36]

3. **When the owner is always liable**

If there are no residents in the dwelling, the non-resident owner is liable. Additionally, the Secretary of State or Welsh or Scottish ministers have power to specify circumstances in which, even if there are residents, the owner is always liable.[37] The owner (not the residents) is liable for the council tax on:
* care homes and certain hostels providing care and support (see p78);
* houses in multiple occupation (see p78);

- second homes with domestic servants (see p81);
- houses of religious communities (see p81);
- residences of ministers of religion (see p81);
- school boarding accommodation in Scotland (see p82);
- accommodation provided to an asylum seeker under section 95 of the Immigration and Asylum Act 1999 (see p82).

The owner of a house of multiple occupation is liable even if s/he has no beneficial interest in the property.[38]

Care homes and hostels

An owner is liable to pay council tax on care homes and certain hostels providing care and support that are registered in England under the Care Standards Act 2000.[39]

In Wales from 2 April 2018, the definition of an owner who is liable to pay council tax on care home is any home within the meaning of the Regulation and Inspection of Social Care (Wales) Act 2016 *or* under section 18 or 19 of the Care Act or section 35 or 36 of the Social Services and Well-being (Wales) Act 2014 *or* a hostel within the meaning of paragraph 7 of Schedule 1 of the Act.[40]

In Scotland, the owner of any building in which a care home service provides accommodation, or a private hospital which is not used wholly or mainly as the sole or main residence of a person, is liable for council tax.[41]

Houses in multiple occupation

A dwelling is classed as a house in multiple occupation if:[42]
- it was originally constructed, or subsequently adapted, for occupation by more than one household; *or*
- each person who lives in it is either:
  - a tenant or licensee able to occupy only part of the dwelling; *or*
  - a licensee liable to pay rent or a licence fee on only part of the dwelling.

Examples include some bedsits, hostels, nurses' homes and long-stay wards in hospitals classed as dwellings. In England and Wales, this class can include a dwelling occupied by only one person if the above conditions are met, provided the dwelling was originally constructed, or subsequently adapted, for occupation by multiple households.

The term 'tenant' includes a secure tenant or a statutory tenant. In England and Wales, the normal definition of an owner applies in the case of a house in multiple occupation, except if someone has a leasehold interest. In this case, it must be an interest in the whole dwelling. If this is not the case, the person who has a freehold interest in the whole or any part of the dwelling is liable.[43]

The Housing Act 2004 requires that a landlord of a house in multiple occupation in England or Wales must obtain a licence. This defines a dwelling as a house in multiple occupation if:

- it consists of one or more units of living accommodation that are not self-contained flat(s);
- the living accommodation is occupied by people who do not form a single household and as their only or main residence (or it is treated as such);
- there is no other use of the accommodation – eg, in the case of a student hall of residence or work-related accommodation;
- at least one person occupying the accommodation pays rent;
- two or more of the households who occupy the living accommodation share one or more basic amenities (eg, a kitchen or bathroom) or the living accommodation.

In Scotland, a house of multiple occupation is defined as any living accommodation occupied by three or more people who are not related who share a bathroom or toilet and kitchen.[44]

However, it is important to note that the definitions used for a house in multiple occupation which must be registered and the one for determining a multi-occupation household for council tax purposes are different, although both types of property the two definitions cover will frequently overlap. For council tax, a multi-occupation dwelling merely requires there be two or more tenants or licence holders in occupation of the premises.[45] This is so even though in other legislation a house is not registerable as a house in multiple occupation unless there are three people living in it at the same time. Courts and tribunals have to be careful not to mix up the different definitions when considering council tax issues purposes and must always follow the one that appears in the council tax regulations.[46]

A house in multiple occupation for council tax purposes could, therefore, be a self-contained flat occupied by people who do not form a single household, or a converted building containing one or more self-contained units, occupied by people who do not form a single household. The High Court held that the correct test to be applied when addressing whether a building had been constructed or adapted for use as separate living accommodation was an objective 'bricks and mortar' test which looked at the reality of what had been constructed and/or how it had been adapted.[47] The test was an objective, not a subjective, test and therefore the intention of use, whether actual or prospective, was irrelevant to the determination.

The tribunal will look for evidence of adaptation – eg, if separate locks have been fitted to the rooms of residents and they have their own keys and facilities.

Exclusive possession

When deciding the status of residents and the degree of exclusive possession (ie, whether they only occupy part of the dwelling), tribunals can look beyond the tenancy or licence agreement and examine the actual facts.[48] This is very important where the evidence and the accuracy of documents produced at the hearing are challenged – eg, parties may have used standard pre-printed tenancy forms which do not reflect the actual legal position between them. However, documents alone should not decide that a property is a house in multiple occupation simply because there are a number of tenants in the dwelling and the owner retains the use of one room – eg, for storing furniture which the tenants do not wish to use.

In the case of *R (on the application of Goremsandu) v Harrow London Borough Council*, the High Court ruled that the test to apply is whether the rent paid gives the tenants the right to occupy only part of the dwelling, or whether it related to the occupation of the house as a whole.[49] The key issue was whether, ultimately, the tenants had exclusive possession of the whole house. In this case, the owner's furniture was kept locked in the conservatory which meant the tenants could not use the conservatory. It was decided that this fact was not sufficient, since the statutory test that had to be applied was whether a tenant was a 'tenant of part only of the dwelling'. The tenants remained tenants of the conservatory even though, in fact, they were unable to use or readily gain access to it. The only items of furniture stored in the conservatory were those that the tenants were paying rent for and, since the terms of the tenancy had not been varied, they were entitled to ask for the key at any time and, if they chose to do so, they could exclude the landlord from the conservatory and also exclude her furniture from that area so long as they stored or used the furniture in another location. They were, therefore, tenants of the whole dwelling, including the conservatory.

In another case, a key issue was whether the tenants were responsible for paying rent on the dwelling as a whole.[50] The tribunal had erred in finding that they were not, contrary to what was written in the lease.

The question of what the lease or tenancy agreement says is important but it is not conclusive, in determining exclusive possession, and may not be considered binding on an individual if s/he has not signed it. The lease need not be in writing to be binding but if a written lease has not been signed, then a valuation tribunal is entitled to consider all the relevant evidence and conclude that the property constitutes a house of multiple occupation.[51] An important question may be whether the occupiers made the agreement together with the landlord or made separate arrangements. If the occupiers did not agree a lease together, the house is more likely to qualify in fact and in law as a house in multiple occupation. What a lease or rental agreement says about liability to pay council tax on a dwelling is an important factor, but does not always determine the issue. Exceptions are recognised[52] and a valuation tribunal should not just accept the view of one side on the question of a multiple occupation dwelling – eg, just the opinion of a local authority inspector.[53]

Where residents of a house in multiple occupation are wrongly held liable, evidence from the residents themselves may be crucial. In one case, the Valuation Tribunal for England (VTE) accepted a witness statement from the appellant as to his whereabouts over a disputed period of liability and his evidence that he never signed any tenancy agreement with other occupiers of a property or lived with them as part of the same household.[54] The tribunal rejected as evidence a purported rent book which contained serious discrepancies and was branded as false by the appellant who had actually been living in a different borough for two of the four years in the period of liability in dispute. The VTE accepted the evidence of the appellant given orally, and in a witness statement, as being consistent and arising from a direct knowledge of the facts and the situation of the dwelling during the material time.

Similar principles apply with the submission of evidence to valuation appeal committees in Scotland and any committee which applies the wrong tests and makes errors of fact and law may have its decision overturned by the Court of Session on appeal.[55]

Second homes with domestic servants

A dwelling fits into this category if it is:[56]
- occupied from time to time by the employer who does not live in it as her/his main residence; *and*
- all the residents are either employed in domestic service in the dwelling or are their family members.

Religious communities

For the owner to be liable, the dwelling must be inhabited by a religious community whose main occupation consists of prayer, contemplation, education, the relief of suffering or any combination of these.[57] Monasteries and convents come within this description. Members of such communities may qualify to be disregarded for the purpose of a council tax discount (see p111).

Accommodation for ministers of religion

The dwelling must be inhabited by a minister of religion (of any faith) as a residence from where s/he performs her/his duties of office. If the dwelling is owned by the minister, the minister is liable for council tax. There are exceptions to this rule for English or Welsh dwellings that are owned by a minister of the Church of England who is in receipt of a stipend. In such a case, the liability is transferred to the Diocesan Board of Finance. In Scotland, the body liable for the remuneration of the minister is liable for council tax.[58]

School boarding accommodation

In Scotland, the owner of school boarding accommodation which is specifically included in the definition of a dwelling (see p18) is liable for the council tax.[59]

Accommodation occupied by asylum seekers

Asylum seekers occupying accommodation under section 95 of the Immigration and Asylum Act 1999 are not liable for council tax. The owner is liable.[60]

4. Joint liability

If two or more people fall into the liable category (eg, joint owners, joint tenants or simply joint residents), they are jointly and severally liable, except if one is severely mentally impaired or a student (see p84).[61]

Additionally, the liable person's partner is jointly liable if s/he is:[62]

- married to or in a civil partnership with the liable person; *or*
- living with her/his partner as a married couple or as if in a civil partnership; *and*
- a resident of the dwelling.

This applies whether or not the partner has a legal interest in the dwelling. The definition of '**couple**' used to establish joint liability for council tax is similar to that applied with many social security benefits (see CPAG's *Welfare Benefits and Tax Credits Handbook*). To be a couple under the social security rules, however, both partners must reside in the same *household*. In the case of council tax, it is only necessary to show that they reside in the same *dwelling*. As it is possible for a single dwelling to contain more than one household, there will be some situations when the two definitions do not coincide. For instance, if a married couple are estranged but continue to live in the same house and have separate households, they are still classed as a jointly liable couple for council tax purposes as they remain married and continue to reside in the same dwelling. However, they are not a couple for council tax reduction (CTR) purposes because they reside in different households. This means that both partners are jointly liable, but each can make a separate claim for reductions based on an apportioned (50 per cent) share of council tax liability and her/his own individual circumstances. See Chapter 8 for more information on CTR.

In terms of joint and several liability for council tax, the meaning of provisions can be difficult to interpret as 'husband', 'wife' and 'married' are not defined in previous council tax law other than by reference to gender. There is a substantial body of social security caselaw on the various criteria that must be considered and, arguably, this will be persuasive in establishing a relationship in council tax cases. Simply because two people share accommodation, a local authority should not presume that they are sharing as the equivalent of a married couple or a couple living together as spouses, resulting in joint and several liability. Examples where the council may make erroneous inferences include cases where brothers and sisters live together and situations where two people of the same sex (whether related or not) are living at, or using, the same address.

It is difficult to see how the local authority could conclude that two unmarried people are living together as spouses unless they were members of the same household (as opposed to merely being resident in the same dwelling) without details of a sexual relationship and the roles assumed in the household. Although there is no established 'right to privacy' in domestic law, an action[63] may be taken for breach of confidence or harassment where private information is released or misused, or improperly demanded. More generally, the local authority's power to demand such information is limited in light of Article 8 of the European Convention of Human Rights, enshrining a right to privacy, and the limits placed in regulations and at law as to what information may be sought.

If the questions that you are asked by the local authority are unreasonable, you should make a formal complaint. It is a good idea to involve your Member of Parliament. Complaints may also be taken to the monitoring officer of the local authority and to the Local Government Ombudsman, and you may be able to take action through a tribunal or the civil courts in extreme cases where confidentiality is broken or improper information requested. An erroneous decision on joint and several liability may be challenged (see p88).

You cannot have joint and several liability where the facts show that you do not have sole or main residence in a dwelling with another person. A finding that you do not have sole or main residence in a dwelling will remove you from any liability for council tax altogether from the effective date you ceased to reside. In polygamous marriages, all partners resident in the dwelling are jointly liable[64] and specific provision is made in the regulations for CTR schemes (see Chapter 8).

The significance of joint liability

The local authority has the option of addressing the council tax bill to any one or more of the jointly liable people, or all of them. In Scotland, someone who is jointly liable with the person(s) named on the bill, but whose name is not included, is still liable to make the required payments. See Chapter 9 for more details. In England and Wales, a payment cannot be required from a liable person until s/he has been billed. If the local authority wants to recover the council tax from someone who is jointly liable but not named on the original bill, a fresh bill (a joint taxpayers' notice) must be issued.[65] In practice, local authorities tend to pursue the first two named persons on a bill.

To be eligible for a reduction under a CTR scheme, you have to be liable for council tax. If someone other than your partner is jointly liable, any CTR is worked out on your apportioned share, even though the local authority may be seeking to recover all of the council tax due from one person. If you are in receipt of CTR, the late identification of retrospective joint liability may mean an overpayment has been made, and could raise the possibility of a late claim for a reduction from the newly identified jointly liable person. In England and Wales, if the local authority refuses to exercise its discretion to reduce a bill in a case of late billing, you should apply for a discretionary reduction in council tax under section 13A(1) of the Local Government Finance Act 2012 (see p167) and you have a right to appeal to a valuation tribunal (see Chapter 11). For more information on CTR, see Chapter 8.

Joint liability and severe mental impairment

A person who is disregarded for discount purposes because of a 'severe mental impairment' (see p107) is not held jointly liable if there is someone else with the same status and legal interest in the property who is not severely mentally impaired.[66] However, a severely mentally impaired person is liable for the tax if:

- s/he is the only liable person; or
- s/he is the only owner, tenant or contractual licensee even if her/his partner is not severely mentally impaired; or
- all the jointly liable people are severely mentally impaired.

Dwellings in which all the occupants are severely mentally impaired are exempt (see p58).[67]

Example

Cai and Ella are a couple and are joint owners. Cai is severely mentally impaired and is disregarded for discount purposes. Normally, the couple (as joint owners and residents) would be liable, but as Cai is severely mentally impaired, Ella is liable. If she were to no longer reside in the dwelling, it would become exempt.

If someone goes into a care home, nursing home or hospital, a ruling from the Court of Protection may be required if s/he does not have the mental capacity to determine her/his place of residence.

Students

A student who is disregarded for discount purposes (see p104) is not held jointly liable if there is someone else with the same status and legal interest in the property who is not a student.

5. Change of circumstances

A change of circumstances may change council tax liability during the year – eg, a liable owner may sell the dwelling or a liable tenant may move to live elsewhere. Liability for council tax arises on a daily basis and the state of affairs at the end of the day is assumed to have lasted all that day.[68] Consequently, the liable person is liable for the first day of residence in the dwelling, but not the last.

If a liable person dies, there is no liability for any part of the day on which s/he dies. Within seven days of the registration of the death of any person aged 18 or over, the registrar of births and deaths for the district in which the person died is required to supply the billing authority with:[69]

- the name and surname of the deceased;
- the date of his/her death; *and*
- his/her usual address.

If you fail to declare a change of circumstances, you may be subject to a penalty or prosecuted for an offence in relation to any CTR claim. It is an offence not to declare a change of circumstances which you know affects your entitlement to a reduction under a local authority reduction scheme, or if you deliberately fail to give a notice of the change as required. It is also an offence to knowingly cause or allow a person to fail to give this notification. Knowledge that entitlement is affected is a requirement of the offence in England,[70] while in Wales the authority must prove dishonesty.[71] These provisions do not apply in Scotland.[72]

6. Backdating liability

Liability may be backdated to previous years. The relevant date is the day a person became liable (ie, had her/his sole or main residence in the dwelling), not the date the local authority informed the taxpayer.[73] This may lead to the local authority serving a demand on someone up to six years after s/he may have left a dwelling. However, if a local authority delays serving a demand notice, this may make the demand invalid if it causes prejudice if it seeks to enforce the demand through the magistrates' or sheriff court. See Chapters 9 and 10 for more details.

Backdating under the council tax reduction schemes varies between local authorities in England and Wales, but you may apply for a discretionary reduction in council tax under section 13A(1)(c) of the Local Government Finance Act (see p167). You may seek a discretionary reduction regardless of when the alleged liability arose.

If you want to challenge the local authority, you can appeal (see Chapter 11). It may also be worth making a complaint for delay where a local authority suddenly seeks to impose a backdated liability for previous years, and to establish why a local authority has failed to establish liability earlier or reversed an earlier decision. The Ombudsman has indicated that extensive delay in making a person aware of a liability may amount to maladministration. A judicial review of the local authority may be sought.[74]

7. How the liable person is identified

To establish liability, the local authority has a variety of powers that require people and organisations to provide information. It is also able to use its own information obtained for other purposes. If the local authority is unable to identify a liable person by name, it may serve a bill on the 'council taxpayer'. The residents of the dwelling will then need to decide who has to pay the tax.

The local authority's own information

A local authority may use information obtained under any other enactment in England and Wales, provided that it was not obtained in its role as a police authority and, in Scotland, that it is not information obtained through social work activities, unless it consists solely of names and addresses.[75]

Information from residents, owners or managing agents

The local authority has the power to write to anyone who appears to be a resident, owner or managing agent of a particular dwelling, requesting information it requires to identify the liable person or the person who would be liable if the dwelling were not exempt.[76] The rules may place a burden on officials of housing associations and those who manage accommodation for vulnerable individuals. A **'managing agent'** means any person authorised to arrange lettings of the dwelling concerned. If you receive a written enquiry, you must supply the required information within 21 days if it is in your possession or control.

Information from other public bodies

The local authority has the power to request information from:[77]
* any billing authority;
* any levying authority;
* the electoral registration officer for any area in Great Britain.

In Scotland, information may also be requested from the assessor.
Information may also be obtained from HM Revenue and Customs for the authority to:[78]
* make a council tax reduction (CTR) scheme;
* determine entitlement or continued entitlement to CTR;

- prevent, detect or secure evidence of, or prosecute the commission of, a council tax offence;
- use in valuation tribunal proceedings.

Penalties

A local authority in England has the discretion to impose a penalty of £70 on someone who fails to respond to a request for information needed to identify the liable person.[79] In Wales and Scotland, the penalty is £50. An English or Welsh authority may quash such a penalty. A Scottish authority may revoke the imposition of such a penalty if you have a reasonable excuse for failing to supply it.[80] Each time the local authority repeats the request and you fail to supply the information, another £280 penalty (£200 in Wales and Scotland) could be imposed.[81]

In Scotland, an additional set of penalties of up to £500 have been created to police claims related to the new variable charges which can be set against unoccupied long-term empty homes.[82]

Additionally, the power to impose penalties has been extended in an attempt to bring the law in line with provisions in welfare benefit security, even though local taxation law is essentially different from social security law. These regulations affect not only taxpayers but also persons who may be providing information on behalf of vulnerable people, including owners of houses in multiple occupation, managers of hostels and accommodation for other people and lawyers and advisers who may be acting on behalf of a taxpayer.

The penalty system is designed to operate in conjunction with the system of CTR schemes. Regulations make provision for powers to require information, the creation of offences and powers to impose penalties in connection with these CTR schemes.[83]

Billing authorities may authorise officers and third parties to discharge these functions for them to individuals with proper authority. These officers can act to collect information for 'detecting and securing evidence of the commission' of offences connected with an application for an award of a reduction of council tax support under a local authority scheme, including access to electronic records.[84]

It is a criminal offence to:

- intentionally delay or obstruct an authorised officer in the exercise of any power to require information;[85]
- refuse or fail (without reasonable excuse) to comply with a requirement to enter into arrangements for access to electronic records, or to fail to provide information when required to do so;[86]
- make a statement or representation which you know to be false for the purpose of obtaining a reduction under a CTR scheme;
- provide or knowingly cause or allow to be provided a document or information which you know to be false in a material particular.[87] (For the information to be material, it must actually affect the issue of whether you receive a reduction or not and not simply be any error or mistake.)

A time limit of three months from the date the authority considered evidence justifying a prosecution existed, or 12 months, is placed on bringing proceedings from the commission of the offence, whichever period last expires.[88]

An appeal may be made against the imposition of a penalty.[89] See Chapter 11 for more information about appeals.

8. Appeals

An appeal can be made against a decision on liability by writing to the local authority.[90] There is no time limit for making an appeal. To appeal, you must be an 'aggrieved person' – ie, the person considered liable to pay the tax or the owner (if different). The appeal letter should give the reasons why you believe the local authority has come to the wrong decision. The local authority has two months in which to answer.[91] In the initial appeal letter, it is advisable to refer to the right to take an appeal to the Valuation Tribunal for England (VTE), the Valuation Tribunal for Wales (VTW) or a valuation appeal committee in Scotland if the local authority does not accept the appeal.

If the local authority refuses to alter its decision or fails to answer within two months of receiving the appeal, a further appeal can be made.[92] This is done by writing to the VTE/VTW. In Scotland, a further appeal is made by writing again to the local authority. The local authority should pass the appeal to the secretary of the relevant local valuation appeal committee. If an appeal is served on the local authority, send a copy to the valuation appeal committee for it to be placed on file, in case the letter to the local authority goes astray. For more information about appeals, see Chapter 11.

The local authority may enforce payment of the original bill while the appeal is outstanding, but if recovery proceedings have been started through the magistrates' court (or a sheriff court in Scotland), you should seek an adjournment of any hearing in the magistrates' court or the sheriff court, pending the outcome of an appeal.[93]

Notes

1. Who is liable

1. **EW** s6 LGFA 1992
   S s75 LGFA 1992
2. **EW** s6(2) LGFA 1992
   S s75(2) LGFA 1992
3. **EW** s2(2)(c) LGFA 1992
   S s71(2)(c) LGFA 1992
4. Within the meaning of the Rent Act 1977 or the Rent (Agriculture) Act 1976
5. Within the meaning of Part IV of the Housing Act 1985
6. Within the meaning of Chapter I of Part V of the Housing Act 1996
7. **EW** s6(6) LGFA 1992
8. **EW** s6(5) LGFA 1992 as amended by s13(1) LGFA 2012
9. **EW** s6(5) LGFA 1992
10. s75(2) LGFA 1992
11. Within the meaning of the Rent (Scotland) Act 1984
12. Within the meaning of the Housing (Scotland) Act 1988
13. Within the meaning of Part III of the Housing (Scotland) Act 1987
14. **S** s75(5) LGFA 1992
15. **EW** ss6-7 LGFA 1992
16. **EW** ss6-7 LGFA 1992
17. **EW** s2 LGFA 1992
    S s71 LGFA 1992

2. Who is a resident

18. **EW** s6(5) LGFA 1992
    S s99(1) LGFA 1992
19. *R (Williams) v Horsham District Council* [2004] EWCA Civ 39
20. *Parry v Derbyshire Dales District Council* [2006] RA 25
21. *R (on the application of Walford) v Worcestershire County Council* [2014] 3 All ER 128
22. See Appeal no.5900M109133/084C, 30 October 2013
23. **EW** see *CT v Horsham District Council (HB)* [2013] UKUT 617 (AAC) and *MacAttram v London Borough of Camden* [2012] EWHC 1033
24. *Trustees Berwick Settlement v Shropshire Council* (3245M131738/176C) contrasting *CT v Horsham District Council (HB)* [2013] UKUT 617 (AAC)

25. *Branwell v Valuation Office Agency* [2015] All ER (D) 99 (Apr) per Mrs Judge Elisabeth Laing DBE
26. *Sumeghova v McMahon* [2002] All ER (D) 371 (Oct); [2003] RVR 8
27. *R (on the application of Bennett) v Copeland Borough Council* [2004] EWCA 672
28. *Highland Council v Highland and Western Isles Region Valuation Committee* [2008] RA 311 Sc20; *Dundee Council v Dundee Valuation Assessment Committee and Fleming Hansen* [2011] CSIH 73
29. See Appeal no.0738M144734/254C, 24 March 2015
30. See Appeal no.0738M144734/254C, 24 March 2015
31. *Khan v Burnley Borough Council* (Appeal no.2315M198655/254C/S)
32. s11A(4A) LGFA
33. *Khan v Burnley Borough Council* (Appeal no.2315M198655/254C/S), para 17
34. *Frost v Feltham* [1981] STC 115
35. *Byrne v Rowbotham* (1969) *210 Estates Gazette*, p823
36. Appeal no.0405M119713/037C, 20 May 2014

3. When the owner is always liable

37. **EW** s8(1) LGFA 1992
    S s76(1) LGFA 1992
38. *Soor and another v Mayor & Burgesses of the London Borough of Redbridge* [2013] EWHC 1239 (Admin)
39. **E** CT(LO)(A)(E) Regs
    W CT(LO)(A)(W) Regs
40. **EW** England by SI 2003/3125, reg 2 amended by SI 2012/1915, art 3 and in relation to Wales by SI 2004/2920, reg 2 amended by SI 2018/48, reg 2, Sch 1 para 5
41. Para 1 Sch 1 para 1 CT(LO)(S) Regs
42. **EW** CT(LO) Regs
    S CT(LO)(S) Regs
43. **EW** CT(LO) Regs
44. **S** s128 Housing (Scotland) Act 2006
45. *Shah v Croydon London Borough Council* [2013] EWHC 3657
46. *Shah v Croydon London Borough Council* [2013] EWHC 3657, para 43

47 *Baker (Listing Officer) v Gomperts* [2006] All ER (D) 01 (Jul)
48 *Norris and Norris v Birmingham City Council* [2001] RVR 89
49 *R (on the application of Goremsandu) v Harrow London Borough Council* [2010] EWHC 1873 (Admin)
50 *Watts v Preston City Council* [2009] EWHC 2179 (Admin)
51 *Walsh v Lonsdale* [1882] 21 ChD 9; *Soor v Mayor Burgesses of the Borough of Redbridge* [2013] EWHC 1239 (Admin)
52 *The UHU Property Trust v Lincoln City Council* [2000] unreported, per Sullivan, J cited in *Shah v Croydon London Borough Council* [2013] EWHC 3657, para 22
53 *Naz v London Borough of Redbridge* [2013] EWHC 1268 (Admin); [2013] All ER (D) 13
54 *Shaughnessy v London Borough of Hackney* [2013] VTE 13 and 20 January 2012 Appeal no.5360M70010/052C/1
55 *Dundee City Council v Dundee Valuation Appeal Committee and another* [2011] CSIH 73
56 **EW** CT(LO) Regs
   S CT(LO)(S) Regs
57 **EW** CT(LO) Regs
   S CT(LO)(S) Regs
58 **EW** CT(LO) Regs
   S CT(LO)(S) Regs
59 **S** CT(LO)(S) Regs
60 *R v Hackney LBC ex parte Adebiri and other appeals* [1997] *The Times*, 4 November 1997
   EW Reg 2 CT(LO) Regs
   S CT(LO)(S) Regs

4. Joint liability
61 **EW** s6(3)-(4) LGFA 1992, as amended by s74 LGA 2003
   S s75(3)-(4) LGFA 1992
62 **EW** s9 LGFA 1992
   S s77 LGFA 1992
63 *Wainwright v The Home Office* [2003] UKHL 53; European Court of Human Rights [2006] Application no.12350/04, 26 September 2006
64 para 20 Practice Note No.2
65 **EW** Reg 28 CT(AE) Regs 1992
66 **EW** ss6(4) and 9(2) LGFA 1992
   S ss75(4) and 77(2) LGFA 1992
67 **EW** CT(ED)O

5. Change of circumstances
68 **EW** s2 LGFA 1992
   S s71 LGFA 1992
69 **EW** Reg 5 (1)CT (AE) Regs 1992

70 **E** Reg 8(1)(c) CTRS(DFE)(E) Regs
   Shaughnessy v London Borough of Hackney [2013] VTE 13 and 20 January 2012 Appeal no.5360M70010/052C/1
71 Reg 10 CTRS(DFE)(W) Regs
72 **S** s119(3) LGFA 2012

6. Backdating liability
73 *Hammersmith and Fulham Billing Authority v Butler* [2001] RVR 197
74 *R v Lambeth Borough Council ex parte Ahijah-Sterling* [1986] RVR 27

7. How the liable person is identified
75 **EW** Reg 6 CT(AE) Regs 1992
   S Reg 5 CT(AE)(S) Regs
76 **EW** Regs 3 and 12 CT(AE) Regs 1992
   S Reg 2 CT(AE)(S) Regs
77 **EW** Reg 3 CT(AE) Regs 1992
   S Council Tax (Administration and Enforcement) (Scotland) Amendment Regulations 2012 No.338
78 Sch 2 para 15A(1)-(4) LGFA 1992
79 **EW** s14(2) and Sch 3 LGFA 1992
   S s97(4) and Sch 3 LGFA 1992
80 **EW** s14(2) and Sch 3 LGFA 1992
   S s97(4) and Sch 3 LGFA 1992
81 **EW** s14(2) and Sch 3 LGFA 1992
   S s97(4) and Sch 3 LGFA 1992
82 Sch 3 para 2(1A) LGFA 1992; s3(1)(5)(a) Local Government Finance (Unoccupied Properties etc) (Scotland) Act 2012
83 ss14A-14C LGFA 1992 inserted by s14 LGFA 2012
84 **E** Regs 4 and 5 CTRS(DFE)(E) Regs
   W Reg 5 CTRS(DFE)(W) Regs
85 **E** Reg 6 CTRS(DFE)(E) Regs
   W Reg 6 CTRS(DFE)(W) Regs
86 **E** Regs 4, 5 and 6 CTRS(DFE)(E) Regs
   W Reg 6(1)(b) CTRS(DFE)(W) Regs
87 **E** Reg 7 CTRS(DFE)(E) Regs
   W Reg 9(1) CTRS(DFE)(W) Regs
88 **E** Reg 10 CTRS(DFE)(E) Regs
   W Reg 12 CTRS(DFE)(W) Regs
89 **EW** s14(2) and Sch 3 LGFA 1992
   S s97(4) and Sch 3 LGFA 1992

8. Appeals
90 **EW** s16 LGFA 1992
   S s81 LGFA 1992
91 **EW** s16 LGFA 1992
   S s81 LGFA 1992
92 **EW** s16 LGFA 1992
   S s81 LGFA 1992
93 *R v Ealing Justices ex parte Coatsworth* [1980] 126, *Solicitors Journal* 128

Chapter 6

· ·

Disability reductions

This chapter covers:
1. What is a disability reduction (below)
2. When a disability reduction can be made (p92)
3. Getting a disability reduction (p95)
4. How the reduction is made (p95)
5. Change of circumstances (p97)
6. Appeals (p98)

1. What is a disability reduction

Disability reduction schemes apply in England and Wales,[1] and in Scotland.[2] The basic amount of the council tax and, in Scotland, Scottish Water charges,[3] may be reduced if:

- a disabled person lives in the dwelling; *and*
- the dwelling has certain features that are essential, or of major importance, to the disabled person because of her/his disability; *or*
- the disabled person uses a wheelchair in the home.

A disability reduction reduces your council tax bill to the amount payable for a home in the valuation band below yours (or by one sixth if you are in Band A). The reduction can be made on residential care or nursing homes as well as on any other dwelling.

In addition to the disability reduction scheme, the value of fixtures (such as a lift or specially designed kitchen units) designed to make the dwelling suitable for use by a physically impaired person should have been ignored in the valuation of the dwelling if they added to its value. See p28 for more details. If fixtures designed to make the dwelling suitable for use by a physically impaired person reduce the value of the dwelling, they should have been taken into account in the valuation process and will, therefore, be reflected in the dwelling's banding.[4]

It is important not to overlook the effect of any entitlement to a reduction in banding in any calculation or claim for a council tax reduction (see Chapter 8) or in any issue of disputes over monies owed in enforcement, whether by way of bankruptcy or committal to prison (see Chapter 10). Because it is possible to backdate an award of a disability reduction for up to six years or more (see p96), the amount by which your debt can be reduced can be substantial.

2. When a disability reduction can be made

The disabled person

For a reduction to be awarded, the dwelling must be the 'sole or main residence' (see p72) of at least one disabled person. No additional reduction is made if more than one disabled person lives in the dwelling.

To count as disabled for the purpose of the reduction, a person must be 'substantially and permanently disabled', whether by congenital disorder from birth, illness, injury, or otherwise. There is no general test of 'substantially and permanently disabled'. This means that someone with a learning disability, impairment or a mental health problem may qualify, as well as someone with a physical impairment. The disabled person may be an adult or a child. S/he need not be the person liable to pay council tax on the dwelling.

Social services departments in England and Wales and social work departments in Scotland have a discretion to maintain a register of, and provide various services to, people in their area who are substantially and permanently disabled. They have considerably more skills and experience in making assessments of disability than their counterparts in council tax administration. If you are on the disabled person's register, this should be sufficient to satisfy the criterion of 'substantially and permanently disabled' for the purposes of a disability reduction. However, if you are not included on the register, this does not necessarily mean you are not 'substantially and permanently disabled', as registers are not comprehensive and registering as disabled is not compulsory.

The dwelling

The dwelling must have at least one of the following features:
- a room, but not a sole bathroom, a kitchen or a lavatory, which is predominantly used by the disabled person – eg, a room used for dialysis equipment; *or*
- an additional bathroom or kitchen within the dwelling which is necessary to meet the needs of the disabled person; *or*
- sufficient floor space to permit the use of a wheelchair.

To qualify, the feature must be essential, or of major importance, to the disabled person's wellbeing because of the nature of her/his impairment.

Among the factors a local authority should consider when deciding if these conditions apply, is whether the room or feature were not available:

- the disabled person would find it physically impossible or extremely difficult to live in the dwelling; *or*
- her/his health would suffer or her/his disability would worsen.

A reduction for sufficient floor space may be available if disabled person uses a non-standard wheelchair or even a wheeled frame (see p95).[5]

The High Court has ruled that there must be an appropriate causative link between the impairment in question and the need to use the room. Relevant factors to be considered include the nature and extent of the person's impairment and whether the use of the room is essential or of major importance to her/him.[6]

A sole bathroom or kitchen, even if specially adapted, is not sufficient to qualify because everyone needs a bathroom or kitchen.[7] Similarly, simply having equipment in a room used for other purposes or merely for storing equipment used by the disabled person (eg, a heater) will not fulfil the requirement of the room being additional.[8] In an appeal in 2015,[9] the appellant had lived in a one-bedroom flat and had to use a kidney dialysis machine for several hours every day. Because of limited space, the dialysis machine had to be kept in the living room, which was used every day and night, along with chairs, sofa and a television. The application for a disability banding reduction failed because the room itself was not specifically required or set aside for meeting the needs of a disabled person. Consequently, it did not fulfil the conditions for a disability reduction set out in the regulations. However, if a local authority, or valuation tribunal, concludes that, without the room containing the equipment needed by the disabled person, it would be extremely difficult, if not impossible, for the person to live an independent life in the dwelling, then a reduction may be awarded.[10]

However, in another appeal in 2015,[11] the existence of an extra bedroom was held to attract a reduction. The council built a bedroom in a ground floor extension in addition to the previous bedroom used by the appellant which existed upstairs. The valuation tribunal rejected the argument that the appellant needed a bedroom whether disabled or not. The additional bedroom was created specifically because the nature and extent of the appellant's impairment necessitated a duplicate provision on the ground floor. As a result, the appellant was entitled to a reduction.

Similarly, in a case where a couple occupied a two-bedroom flat instead of a single-bedroom property as a consequence of the appellant's medical condition, which necessitated him sleeping separately, a reduction was granted. A causative link was established as the requirement for a separate bedroom was necessary for his condition.[12]

Major importance

The use of the room has to be of major importance to the disabled person, and a question to ask is whether the room would be being used in a particular way if the disabled person was not present.

Two High Court rulings concerning three appeals during 2006 clarified the law on rooms attracting a reduction and the meaning of 'major importance'. These were *South Gloucestershire Council v Titley and another [Clothier]*[13] and *Hanson v Middlesborough Council*.[14]

In the case of *Titley*, the taxpayer was a profoundly deaf man living alone in a two-bedroom house. His living room was fitted with a hearing loop box enabling him to hear the television and to communicate with visitors. In the case of *Clothier*, there were two bedrooms occupied by two adults with Down's syndrome who were being looked after by their parents. Both bedrooms were used for therapy and periods of relaxation, which enabled the adult children to cope with their condition. The High Court ruled that a disabled reduction should not be awarded in either case. The Court held that it was necessary to consider whether a room was specifically required for meeting the needs of a disabled person.

The Court stressed that having a disabled resident in a property was not enough. To attract the reduction, the dwelling must have a room that would not be required if the disabled person were not present.

In both of these cases, the rooms were not considered additional, since they would be essential or of major importance to almost any household. In the case of *Titley*, the taxpayer would have been using the living room if he were not deaf. Similarly, in *Clothier*, the rooms were not additional; the two adult children would still have required a bedroom if they did not have Down's syndrome.

However, in the *Hanson* case, the appellant succeeded. She was a disabled woman, registered as partially sighted. She had a bedroom converted into an en-suite bathroom in 1996, a few months after she moved into the property, and 19 months before she was registered as blind. In 2004, she became aware of the right to a disability reduction for council tax but was refused. This decision was upheld by a valuation tribunal, which rejected her appeal on the basis that the bathroom was not essential to her needs.

The High Court, however, upheld her appeal, concluding that the adaptation was of major importance to her because of her specific impairment as it reduced the risk of tripping or slipping.

Social needs of the disabled person

A room that fulfils the social needs of a disabled person may also qualify for a disability reduction. A valuation tribunal vice president addressed this in a 2014 decision.[15] The room concerned contained specialist electronic and computerised equipment for the appellant's use. It was installed to assist and allow the appellant to pursue leisure interests, work as a volunteer for the RNIB, continue with social science research and enjoy many of the pastimes that a sighted person would take for granted.

The vice president rejected arguments that room should be regarded as a 'home office', and that all of the equipment was portable and could be moved to another room. The room was of major importance to the appellant's wellbeing and quality of life. The vice president ruled that the room provided something extra that was required for meeting the needs of a disabled person. The equipment it housed was sensitive and expensive and it would be impractical for it to be moved.[16]

Taken together, the cases show that, to obtain a disability reduction, the room used or adapted for a disabled person must be:

- extra or additional to what a person would ordinarily need, whether disabled or not;
- essential or of major importance to the welfare of the disabled person; *and*
- relevant to their physical, mental and social needs.

Floor space for a wheelchair

A reduction for sufficient floor space may be available if a disabled person uses a non-standard wheelchair or even a wheeled frame.[17] When applying for a reduction, and if an appeal to the valuation tribunal becomes necessary, it is important to emphasise this point using evidence such as witness statements from carers, medical reports and evidence about any adaptations or alterations in the room to be considered.

3. **Getting a disability reduction**

Who can get a reduction

The person liable to pay council tax on the dwelling is entitled to the disability reduction. S/he may be solely liable or jointly liable. If there is joint liability, an application made by one of the liable people is treated as having been made on behalf of both of them. None of the liable people need to be disabled.

The local authority may also award a disability reduction to someone who will become liable for council tax on the dwelling – eg, following work on it to meet the needs of a disabled person.

Applications

The local authority cannot award a reduction without a written application for each financial year (April to March) from the liable person or someone acting on her/his behalf. If you are applying on behalf of someone, the local authority normally requires written authorisation or a copy of a power of attorney. There is no prescribed form, but most local authorities have a standard application form.

Backdating and repeat applications

The fact that a written application must be made for each financial year does not prevent you from making an application for previous years – ie, backdated to when the qualifying conditions were met. The year(s) in question should be identified on the application. Following the decisions in *Arca v Carlisle City Council*[18] and *HS v Leicester City Council*,[19] a disability reduction can be backdated for up to six years from the date of making an application but it is currently unclear as to whether it may be extended further as can be done with discounts. In the *Arca* case, the tribunal ruled that a taxpayer who applied for a reduction on 3 November 2011 was entitled to a disability reduction dating back to 2 November 2005, six years before the written application was made. The President of the Valuation Tribunal for England, Professor Graham Zellick QC, held that an application was permissible as a proceeding within the Limitation Act 1980 which places a six-year time limit upon civil law claims reaching the tribunal. While this is a decision of the Valuation Tribunal for England and not of the High Court, Professor Zellick stated that 'until the matter is settled by a higher court…billing authorities would be well advised not only to regard this decision as representing a correct statement of the law but also as the interpretation almost certainly to be applied by this tribunal in any future appeal raising the same issue unless fresh arguments can be made.'[20] However, in the case of discounts, in *HS v Leicester City Council*,[21] it was held that reductions by way of discount could be backdated more than six years, which conflicts with the position in *Arca*. In a future case, it seems possible that a tribunal or higher court might reach a different decision if the ruling *in HS v Leicester City Council* is also considered.

Also the Limitation Act restriction may not apply if there is a reason why evidence has not been available before as a result of fraud, concealment or mistake.[22] For example, if a disabled person was previously given wrong advice by the local authority, the Limitation Act 1980 may not apply. In Scotland, the limitation period is 20 years.[23]

Once a written application has been made, a repeat application is required each financial year. Local authorities should ideally send a repeat application form and a reminder at the appropriate time each year, but they are not required to do so. Local authorities should not generally require a full application in a second or subsequent year; it will often be sufficient to seek the liable person's confirmation that the circumstances have not changed.

Information required by the local authority

The local authority may require a supporting letter from a doctor, occupational therapist or social worker, confirming that the disabled person needs the particular qualifying feature of the dwelling because of her/his disability. There is no statutory requirement to seek such letters, however, and local authorities should consider on a case by case basis whether verification is necessary. Some local authorities also send an officer to visit the dwelling and interview residents or carers.

When considering whether or not the reduction applies, an English or Welsh local authority may make a written request for information it reasonably requires at any time and to anyone.[24] It may also require you to respond within a specified period, but must give you at least 21 days to answer.

4. How the reduction is made

If a disability reduction is awarded, the liable person's council tax bill is reduced to that of a dwelling in the valuation band immediately below the band to which the dwelling has been allocated on the valuation list.

The reduction applies for each day that the qualifying conditions are met.

The amount payable on a dwelling that qualifies for a disability reduction in Band A is reduced by the same proportion of the bill as dwellings in valuation Bands B, C and D, being equivalent to five-ninths of Band D.[25]

Example
Harry's dwelling is in Band C on the valuation list. Following the award of a disability reduction, the bill that must be paid is the same as that of a Band B dwelling.
The disability reduction does not alter the actual valuation of the dwelling or its banding on the valuation list. Harry's bill should show both the dwelling's actual band and the reduction.

The effect of the reduction on other forms of help

If you are entitled to a disability reduction, you may also be entitled to a discount or council tax reduction (CTR). These other forms of help are calculated on the basis of the council tax liability after the disability reduction has been made. Consequently, the retrospective award of a disability reduction may mean that there has been an overpayment of CTR or the former council tax benefit – seek advice if this applies to you.

5. Change of circumstances

If there is a change in circumstances (eg, if the disabled person moves to alternative accommodation), the liable person may no longer be entitled to a disability reduction. If the liable person believes that s/he has ceased to be eligible for the reduction, s/he must notify the local authority. This obligation extends to all those who are jointly liable for the tax on the dwelling in question.

---

6. **Appeals**

If the local authority refuses to award a disability reduction, an appeal can be made in writing to the local authority.[26] An appeal can be made if you are liable to pay the tax or if you are the owner of the property (if different). The appeal letter should give the reasons why you believe the local authority has come to the wrong decision. The local authority has two months in which to answer.[27] If no reduction is awarded, or if the local authority fails to answer within two months:

- in **England and Wales**, a further appeal can be made by writing to the Valuation Tribunal for England or directly to Valuation Tribunal of Wales. The appeal should normally be made within two months of the date the local authority notified you of its decision, or within four months of the date when the initial representation was made, if the local authority has not responded. An out-of-time appeal may be allowed if you have failed to meet the appropriate time limits for reasons beyond your control;[28]
- in **Scotland**, a further appeal can be made by writing again to the local authority. The local authority should pass the appeal to the secretary of the relevant local valuation appeal committee. The appeal must be made within four months of the date on which the grievance was first raised with the local authority in writing. There is no power to consider an out-of-time appeal, so you must make a fresh appeal to the local authority to begin the process again. However, if you fail to appear at a hearing, so that the appeal is dismissed, you can make representations to allow another appeal hearing. You have 14 days from being notified of the dismissal to apply in writing to request another hearing, and the appeal committee has a discretion to allow a longer period. If the appeal committee is satisfied that there was a reasonable excuse for your absence, it can recall the decision and fix a date for a further hearing.[29]

See Chapter 11 for further information about appeals.

The local authority may enforce payment of the original bill while the appeal is outstanding, but it may agree to a suspension until the matter is resolved. Alternatively, the magistrates' court (sheriff court in Scotland) may agree to an adjournment of any proceedings which may be issued if an agreement to suspend recovery is not reached and an appeal against the decision had been lodged.[30]

Notes

1. What is a disability reduction
1 **EW** s13 LGFA 1992; CT(RD) Regs and CT(RDTA)(W)(A) Regs
2 **S** s80(1)-(4) and (6)-(7) LGFA 1992; CT(RD)(S) Regs
3 **S** CT(RD)(S) Regs
4 **EW** Reg 6 CT(SVD) Regs
  S Reg 2 CT(VD)(S) Regs

2. When a disability reduction can be made
5 Appeal No.5060M73251/053C, 23 November 2011, para 25
6 *Sandwell Metropolitan District Council v Perks* [2003] RVR 317 Admin 1749 (HC)
7 **EW** Reg 6 CT(SVD) Regs
  S Reg 2 CT(VD)(S) Regs
8 *Howell Williams v Wirral Borough Council* [1981] RA 189 CA
9 Appeal No.3810M143554/084C, 2 April 2015
10 Appeal No.2235M10253/084C, 13 September 2013
11 Appeal No.5480M138614/084C, 4 March 2015
12 Appeal No.2820M165193/037C, 26 February 2016
13 *South Gloucestershire Council v Titley and another* [2006] EWHC 3117 (Admin)
14 *Hanson v Middlesborough Council* [2006] RA 320 (HC)
15 Appeal No.2710M130673/254C, 18 September 2014
16 Appeal No.2710M130673/254C, 18 September 2014
17 Appeal No.5060M73251/053C, 23 November 2011, para 25

3. Getting a disability reduction
18 *Arca v Carlisle City Council* [2013] RA 248
19 *HS v Leicester City Council* [2015] Appeal No.2465M142876/037C, 11 August 2015
20 *Arca v Carlisle City Council* [2013] RA 248; VTE 29 January and 20 March 2013, per President Professor Graham Zellick
21 *HS v Leicester City Council* [2015] Appeal No.2465M142876/037C, 11 August 2015

22 s32 Limitation Act 1980
23 s7 Prescription and Limitation (Scotland) Act 1973
24 Reg 5 CT(RD) Regs

4. How the reduction is made
25 Reg 3A(b) CT(RD) Regs

6. Appeals
26 **EW** s16 LGFA 1992
  S s81 LGFA 1992
27 **EW** s16 LGFA 1992
  S s81 LGFA 1992
28 **E** Reg 21(6) VTE(CTRA)(P) Regs
  W Reg 29(5)VTW Regs
29 Reg 31 CT(ALA)(S) Regs; reg 15 Valuation Appeal Committee (Procedure in Appeals under the Valuation Acts) (Scotland) Regulations 1995 No.572(S.41)
30 *Wiltshire Council v Piggin* [2014] CO 40116 High Court

Chapter 7

Discounts and premiums

This chapter covers:
1. 25 per cent discount for one resident (below)
2. Who counts for discount purposes (p101)
3. Who is disregarded for discount purposes (p101)
4. Getting a discount (p112)
5. Unoccupied dwellings discounts (p114)
6. Miscellaneous discounts (p116)
7. Premiums on long-term empty and second homes (p117)
8. Appeals (p120)

1. 25 per cent discount for one resident

The council tax (and Scottish Water charges in Scotland) payable on a dwelling is initially based on the assumption that there are at least two adults living in it. The bill does not increase if there are more than two, but should be reduced by 25 per cent if there is only one person solely or mainly resident in the dwelling. See p72 for what counts as 'sole or main residence'.

Certain people, however, are ignored or disregarded by local authorities when deciding how many people are solely or mainly resident in the dwelling (p101). Effectively, they are not counted as living in the dwelling for council tax purposes when calculating the bill.

For the purpose of deciding whether the council tax is subject to a discount for any day, the state of affairs at the end of the day is assumed to have existed throughout that day.[1]

Discounts and other forms of help

You can be granted a discount in addition to any disability reduction, transitional relief or council tax reduction (CTR). Local authorities are under a duty to make enquiries as to the discounts. The discount is applied to the tax after granting a disability reduction, but before calculating main CTR. Alternative CTR (known as 'second adult rebate') is worked out on the basis of the council tax liability, ignoring any discount that has been granted. This rebate is intended to compensate you if extra adults living with you cannot afford to meet the cost of losing this discount. See Chapter 8 for more details on CTR schemes.

2. Who counts for discount purposes

Only adults solely or mainly resident in the dwelling count for the purpose of working out whether or not a discount applies. People under 18 and those solely or mainly resident elsewhere are ignored.[2]

Example

Petra and her 15-year-old daughter live in a property. Thus, there is only one person aged 18 or over residing in the dwelling. A 25 per cent discount is granted.

Petra's friend Una comes to stay with her but keeps a home elsewhere. If it is decided that Una is mainly resident elsewhere, the discount should continue. If it is decided that Una is now mainly resident in Petra's house, the discount no longer applies from the day she moved in.

3. Who is disregarded for discount purposes

In addition to those who are ignored for the purposes of a discount (see above), certain categories of people are disregarded.[3] They are sometimes described as 'having a status discount', or more simply as 'invisible'. They are listed in the box on p102.

If you are disregarded for the purpose of a discount, it does not necessarily mean that the tax bill is reduced. A discount is only awarded if there are fewer than two adults in the dwelling, not counting those who are disregarded. A liable person may be disregarded for the purpose of a discount, but is still liable for the council tax. The exceptions to this last rule concern liable people who are either considered to be severely mentally impaired or students. See Chapter 5 for more details.

The discount applied is:[4]

- 25 per cent if there is one resident in the property who is not a disregarded person;
- 50 per cent if all the residents in the property are disregarded;
- if all the residents in the property are students, see p104, or 'relevant persons' the property would be 'exempt' and no council tax would be payable, see p56;

• if all the residents in the property are 'severely mentally impaired' (see p107), the property would be 'exempt' and no council tax would be payable, see (p58).

People disregarded for discount purposes

Young people:
– people aged 18 for whom child benefit is payable (see p103);
– education leavers who are under 20 (see p103);
– care leavers aged 18-25 in Scotland (see p103);
– youth trainees (see p103);
– students under the age of 20 studying up to A level, Scottish Advanced Higher or equivalent (see p104).

Full-time students attending a college or university (see p105).

Foreign language assistants who are classed as students (see p106).

A person who has diplomatic, Commonwealth or consular privilege or immunity.

Spouses or dependants of foreign students (see p106).

Student nurses (see p107).

Apprentices (see p107).

People in prison and other forms of detention (see p111).

People who are severely mentally impaired (see p107).

Certain carers (see p108).

Hospital patients (see p110).

People in care homes, private hospitals and hostels (see p110).

Members of international headquarters and defence organisations and their dependants (see p111).

Members of visiting forces (see p112).

Members of religious communities (see p111).

In England and Wales, residents in certain hostels and night shelters and other accommodation for those with no fixed abode (see p110).

Examples

Phoebe and Rachel are joint owner-occupiers. Phoebe is a full-time student and disregarded for the purpose of a discount. Rachel is in full-time work and is not disregarded. As there are only two residents and Phoebe is disregarded, a 25 per cent discount should be granted. Although they are both joint resident owners, only Rachel is liable for the reduced amount of council tax.

Mr and Mrs Donald, a couple in their fifties, are joint owner-occupiers. Their daughter, Daisy, lives with them. She is aged 20 and a full-time student. Their son, Max, aged 17, also lives with them. He is in full-time work. Daisy, as a full-time student, is disregarded for discount purposes and Max, as someone under 18, is ignored. Nevertheless, no discount is awarded because two adults (the joint owner-occupiers) live in the house and are not ignored or discounted.

Ruby and Fehed are liable joint tenants. No one else lives with them. Fehed has Alzheimer's disease and receives the care component of personal independence payment (PIP). He is considered to be severely mentally impaired. In these circumstances, a 25 per cent status discount is awarded because there are only two people solely or mainly resident in the dwelling and one of them is disregarded for discount purposes. In this instance, only Ruby is liable for the tax.

Jake, a carer, comes to live with Ruby and Fehed who provide him with free accommodation plus £50 a week. In these circumstances, Ruby and Fehed lose their discount as there are now two adults living in the dwelling who are not disregarded for discount purposes. If Jake is paid £44 a week or less (see p109 and p110), however, the discount would continue, as there would still be only one adult living in the dwelling who was not disregarded.

Young people disregarded for discount purposes

If you fall into one of the following groups a disregard applies to you.

- **18- and 19-year-olds**[5] **for whom child benefit is payable** (or would be if you were not in local authority care).[6] The conditions of entitlement to child benefit are described in CPAG's *Welfare Benefits and Tax Credits Handbook*.
- **Education leavers under 20.** If you are under the age of 20, and have left school or college on or after 1 May in any year after undertaking a qualifying course of education (ie, one no higher than A level, Scottish Advanced Higher or equivalent) or additionally, in England and Wales, full-time education, you should be disregarded for the purpose of working out a discount between 1 May and 31 October in the same year.[7] You continue to be disregarded if you go on to some other form of further or higher education.
- **Youth trainees** who are under 25 and have an approved individual training plan.[8] You are regarded as undertaking training from the day on which the course or programme begins to the day you complete, abandon or are dismissed from it.
- **Apprentices** (see p107).
- **Young people leaving care in Scotland.** You can get a discount if you:[9]
  – are at least 18 but under 26;
  – were looked after by a local authority on or after your 16th birthday;
  – are no longer looked after by a local authority.
- **Under 20 in non-advanced education.** You are regarded as a 'student' for council tax purposes if you are aged under 20 and on a non-advanced course of more than 12 hours a week (see p104).
- **Under 20 in higher education.** The rules are the same as for those aged 20 or over (see p104).

Note: if you are under 18 years old you are ignored for council tax purposes (see p101).

Students disregarded for discount purposes

You are disregarded for discount purposes if you are a student.[10] You are a student for these purposes if you study for 21 hours or more a week (see p105), are under 20 and in non-advanced education (see below), or you are a foreign language assistant (see p106).[11] Dwellings occupied only by students and certain other people are exempt (see p57).

If you are aged under 20, whether you count as a student for council tax purposes can depend on whether you are on an advanced or non-advanced course. For older students, one rule applies whatever the level of your course.

Under 20 in non-advanced education

You are regarded as a 'student' for council tax purposes if you are aged under 20 and on a non-advanced course of more than 12 hours a week.[12]

Non-advanced course

A '**non-advanced course**' is one below the level of a degree, HNC, HND or NVQ/SVQ level 4. It includes A levels, Scottish Advanced Highers, national diplomas and national certificates. The course must last more than three months. It does not include evening classes, correspondence courses, or courses taken as a result of your office or occupation.[13]

The hours that count are those required by the course rather than those you actually do, if they are different. To work out your hours, average out over term times the hours required under the course for tuition, supervised study, exams, and supervised exercises, experiments, projects and practical work.

You are treated as a student on each day from the day you start the course until the day you complete it, abandon it or are dismissed from it.[14] So you count as a student during term times, during short vacations at Christmas and Easter, and during the summer if your course continues after the summer. If your course ends in the summer and you begin a different one in the autumn, you do not count as a student in the summer between courses. However, you might be able to get a discount. In Scotland, there are limited exceptions.[15]

Example

Leo is 18 and taking three A levels at college. Including his classes, exams and supervised study, his course hours are 18 a week. He is a student for council tax purposes.

Under 20 in higher education

The rules are the same as for those aged 20 or over (see p105).

20 or over in non-advanced or higher education

You are regarded as a 'student' for council tax purposes if the course requires you to undertake periods of study, tuition or work experience for at least 21 hours a week in at least 24 weeks each academic year.[16]

If you are on a sandwich course, required periods of work experience are included.

To count as a student, you must be enrolled on a course with an educational institution. You are a student from the day you begin the course until the day you complete it, abandon it or are no longer permitted by the educational institution to undertake it.[17] So if you take time out and are not enrolled on the course during that period, you do not count as a student for council tax purposes and you may become liable for council tax. If this is the case, check whether you are eligible for council tax reduction (CTR – see Chapter 8).

If you take time out but are still enrolled on the course, you continue to count as a student, provided you have not abandoned it completely and the institution has not said you can no longer undertake the course. Because the law says you are not a student if you are 'no longer permitted by the institution to undertake [the course]', it suggests that your dismissal from the course must be final. So you could argue that if you are temporarily suspended from the course but still registered, you still count as a student. In an informal letter, written in 1996, the former Department of the Environment (then responsible for council tax) stated:[18]

In our view a period of intercalation will remain within the period of a course... and therefore, provided that the person remains enrolled at the education establishment, they will continue to fall within the definition of a full-time student.

Note: a valuation tribunal decision[19] indicates that students who are repeating a full-time course on a part-time basis may not be regarded as meeting the definition of 'full-time student' even if their normal attendance is on a full-time basis. Ensuring the institution is clear about the normal expectations of the course in any documentation is therefore of particular importance.

Your college or university determines the number of hours of your course. You may need evidence from it to prove to the local authority that you count as a student. Colleges and universities are required to provide you with a certificate if you ask for one while you are a student or for up to a year after you leave the course.[20] After that, they may still give you a certificate, but are not legally required to do so. The certificate must contain:[21]

- the name and address of the institution;
- your full name;
- your term-time address and home address (if known by the institution);

- a statement that you are (or were) a student – ie, that you are enrolled on a course requiring you to undertake periods of study, tuition or work experience of at least 21 hours a week over at least 24 weeks a year; *and*
- the date you became a student and the date your course ends.

Postgraduate students

Full-time postgraduate students are regarded as 'students' for council tax purposes in the same way as other full-time higher education students.

In the past, some local authorities have considered that research does not count as 'study' and have refused to disregard research students. This was successfully challenged in an appeal and, although it does not set a legal precedent, local authorities are obliged to have regard to this. Moreover, the regulations were amended so that the requirement is to 'undertake' the course for the prescribed periods as opposed to 'attend' it, as was previously required. This should make it easier for postgraduate students who meet the requirements to argue that they qualify.

Some postgraduate students have had difficulty in securing exemption during the thesis 'writing-up' period after the formal end of the course. While some local authorities are sympathetic and extend student status after the end of the course, others have regarded such students as liable as they are no longer 'within the period of their course'. A High Court ruling served to harden some local authorities' views (although in that case, the student was trying to claim exemption for a writing-up period lasting more than two years).[22] Indeed, the case has been used by some local authorities to suggest that PhD students are ineligible for exemption even during the formal period of the course, but this should be challenged as the ruling related only to a writing-up period.

If this affects you, seek advice from your students' union or institution's advice centre.

Note: if you have completed an undergraduate course and intend to start a postgraduate course in the following academic year, you are not exempt as you are not within the period of either course. Depending on your circumstances, however, you may be able to claim CTR (see Chapter 8) or a discount on the bill.

Foreign language assistants

You are classed as a student, and so disregarded for discount purposes, if you registered with the British Council as a foreign language assistant and have a current appointment as a foreign language assistant at a school or other educational institution in Great Britain.[23]

Spouse, civil partner or dependant of foreign students

A foreign student's spouse, civil partner or dependant who is prevented from working or claiming benefit must be disregarded for discount purposes or may be exempt.[24] To qualify, the spouse/partner/dependant must not be a British citizen and must also be someone who, under immigration rules, is not allowed either to work in the UK or claim benefit.

The decision in *Harrow London Borough Council v Ayiku*[25] clarified that the non-British spouse of a student was a 'relevant person' exempt from liability to pay council tax, although she was allowed to work in the UK. A student's spouse who has limited leave to enter the UK is prevented, as a condition of her/his leave to remain in the UK, from claiming benefits or CTR (see Chapter 8).

It is sufficient for the non-British spouse of a student to satisfy one or other of the two conditions (either being prevented from taking paid employment or prevented from claiming benefits) so as to qualify as a relevant person.

Student nurses

Although the council tax legislation includes references to 'student nurses',[26] the definition refers to traditional hospital-based courses phased out in the 1990s, and so is now redundant in practice. However, students on nursing courses in higher education are regarded as 'students' under the same definition that applies to other full-time students, as made clear in amendments to the council tax regulations in 1994.[27] If an authority seeks proof of 'student nurse' status, it should be directed to these regulations.

Apprentices disregarded for discount purposes

An apprentice is someone, of any age, who is:
* employed for the purpose of learning a trade, business, profession, office, employment or vocation;
* undertaking a programme of training leading to an accredited qualification;
* receiving a salary or allowance (or both) of no more than £195 a week before any deductions for income tax and national insurance.[28] Guidance to local authorities advises that when calculating earnings, any overtime or bonuses should be ignored.

The training must lead to an accredited qualification.[29] Before awarding a discount, most local authorities require either a copy of the apprenticeship agreement or a signed copy of an agreement between the apprentice and the employer, together with copies of wage slips.

Severely mentally impaired people disregarded for discount purposes

For council tax purposes, you are considered **'severely mentally impaired'** if you have a severe impairment of intelligence and social functioning (however caused) that appears to be permanent.[30] This includes where you are severely mentally impaired as a result of a degenerative brain disorder such as a stroke, Alzheimer's disease or other forms of dementia. To count as severely mentally impaired, you must have a certificate of confirmation from a registered medical practitioner. Certificates of severe mental impairment issued before the introduction of council tax are acceptable, provided they do not include any information that should only be used for some other purpose – eg, exemption from the community charge. Doctors must issue certificates free of charge.[31]

In addition, to qualify for the discount, you must be entitled to one of the following:[32]

- universal credit. In England and Wales, the limited capability for work/limited capability for work and work-related activity element must be included;
- employment and support allowance;
- attendance allowance (AA);
- the standard or enhanced rate of the daily living component of PIP;
- armed forces independence payment;
- the highest or middle rate care component of disability living allowance (DLA);
- incapacity benefit (IB) or severe disablement allowance;
- an increase in disablement pension for constant attendance;
- the disability element in working tax credit;
- unemployability supplement (this was abolished in 1987 but existing claimants remain entitled);
- constant attendance allowance or unemployability allowance payable under the industrial injuries or war pension schemes;
- income support including a disability premium because of incapacity for work.

If you would have been entitled to one of the above benefits except for the fact that you have reached pension age, you still qualify for the discount.[33]

You also qualify if your partner is in receipt of income-based jobseeker's allowance which includes a disability premium or higher pensioner premium because:[34]

- s/he gets the long-term rate of IB; or
- s/he was either in receipt of long-term IB up to pension age and is still alive or is entitled to AA/DLA but has been in hospital for more than 28 days.

Carers disregarded for discount purposes

You are disregarded for discount purposes as a carer if you are providing care or support (or both):[35]

- to someone in receipt of certain benefits (see below);
- to another person on behalf of a local authority or charitable body (see p109);
- to another person, are employed by her/him and were introduced by a charitable body (see p110).

Caring for someone in receipt of certain benefits

You must:

- be resident in the same dwelling as the person being cared for; and

- be providing care for at least 35 hours a week on average; *and*
- not be the partner of the person being cared for, or, if the person needing care is a child under 18, not be the child's parent; *and*
- be caring for someone entitled to:[36]
  - lower or higher rate AA; *or*
  - the middle or highest rate care component of DLA; *or*
  - the standard or enhanced rate of the daily living component of PIP; *or*
  - armed forces independence payment; *or*
  - an increase in constant attendance allowance under the industrial injuries or war pensions scheme; *or*
  - the highest rate of constant attendance allowance payable on top of full-rate disablement benefit paid for an industrial injury.

More than one person living in the same dwelling can count as a carer. You do not have to claim carer's allowance to qualify for this disregard, and your income and savings will not affect your eligibility.

Example

Ajmal and Alya have a son aged 21. He is severely mentally impaired and gets PIP at the highest rate. Both parents care for their son for at least 35 hours a week, so they both should be disregarded for discount purposes. As their son is also disregarded, their council tax bill should be reduced by 50 per cent. All three occupiers are disregarded, but cannot claim an exemption.

A dwelling left empty by a carer is exempt, whether or not you meet any of the above criteria. A dwelling left empty by someone who has moved to receive care elsewhere is also exempt (see p54).

For more information on the position of carers and council tax, see www.carersuk.org.

Carers providing care on behalf of a local authority or charitable body

You must:

- be providing the care or support on behalf of a local authority, the Court of Common Council of the City of London, the Council of the Isles of Scilly, a government department or a charitable body, and be resident in premises provided by, or on behalf of, that organisation, so that the best care can be provided; *and*
- be engaged or employed for at least 24 hours a week; *and*
- be paid no more than £44 a week.

Carers introduced by a charitable body

You must:

- be employed to provide care or support by the person who needs the care for at least 24 hours a week; *and*
- be earning no more than £44 a week from this employment; *and*
- have been introduced to the person by a charitable body; *and*
- be resident in premises provided by, or on behalf of, the person being cared for to enable the best care to be provided.

People in hospital, care homes and hostels disregarded for discount purposes

If you have a short stay in **hospital**, it has no effect on council tax liability or the amount of tax that must be paid. If you have been, or are likely to be, in a hospital for so long that you can no longer be considered to be solely or even mainly resident in your home, you should be ignored for the purpose of a discount. A dwelling left empty because you are solely or mainly resident in hospital is exempt from council tax (see p53).

Most hospitals are subject to non-domestic rates, but some types of long-stay hospitals can be considered dwellings for council tax purposes. Patients who are solely or mainly resident in such a hospital are disregarded for discount purposes.[37] In this context, and for the purpose of exemptions, a 'hospital' means:[38]

- an NHS hospital; *and*
- a military, air force or naval unit or establishment in which medical or surgical treatment is provided within the meaning of the Armed Forces Act 2006.

The owners, rather than the residents, of **care homes, independent hospitals and hostels** are liable for the council tax (see p78). The owners may be eligible for a disability reduction (see p92). If you are solely or mainly resident in such accommodation, you are disregarded for discount purposes if you are receiving care or treatment (or both) in the home, hospital or hostel.[39] If you have left your own home empty, it may be exempt from the council tax. See p53 for more details.

You are disregarded for discount purposes if you are living in a **hostel for homeless people**[40] – eg, run by the Salvation Army or Church Army. Most of the accommodation must be communal (ie, not divided into self-contained units) and most agreements to occupy the accommodation must be under licences which do not constitute tenancies. The disregard applies to resident staff as well as residents, provided the accommodation is predominantly for those with no fixed abode on the terms and conditions specified.

People in prison or other forms of detention disregarded for discount purposes

In many cases, if you are in prison or some other form of detention, you are considered no longer solely or mainly resident in a dwelling and should therefore be ignored for discount purposes. Dwellings left empty by those in detention are exempt from council tax (see p51). In certain instances, however, detention may be for such a short period that you are still considered mainly to occupy the dwelling. In this case, a disregard for discount purposes applies if you are:[41]

- detained in a prison, a hospital or any other place by a British court;
- detained under the deportation provisions of the Immigration Act 1971;
- detained under the Mental Health Act 1983 or the Mental Health (Care and Treatment) (Scotland) Act 2003 or the Criminal Procedure (Scotland) Act 1995;[42]
- imprisoned, detained or in custody (but not in custody under open arrest for the purposes of Queen's Regulations) for more than 48 hours under the Armed Forces Act 2006.[43]

If you are in police custody before your first court appearance, or are detained for non-payment of council tax in England or Wales, or non-payment of a fine in England, Wales or Scotland, you are not treated as detained for the purpose of a discount.[44] If you are on temporary release, you are treated as being detained.

Members of religious communities disregarded for discount purposes

You are a member of a religious community if:[45]

- the principal occupation of the community consists of prayer, contemplation, education, the relief of suffering, or any combination of these; *and*
- you have no income or capital of your own and are dependent on the community to provide for your material needs.

In considering whether or not you have any income, the local authority should disregard any pension(s) from former employment.

The owner, rather than the residents, is liable for the tax on a dwelling occupied by a religious community (see p81).

Members of visiting international headquarters and defence organisations disregarded for discount purposes

A member (or dependant) of certain international headquarters or defence organisations listed in section 1 of the International Headquarters and Defence Organisations Act 1964 is disregarded for discount purposes.[46]

Members of visiting forces disregarded for discount purposes

Members of visiting forces and any of their dependants who are neither British citizens nor ordinarily resident in the UK are disregarded for the purposes of a discount.[47] A dwelling is exempt from council tax if one of the liable people has a relevant association with a visiting force. See p58 for more details on exemptions. Consequently, this disregard only applies if none of the liable people have a relevant association. This would be the case, for example, if a member of a visiting force lodges with a British citizen.

4. Getting a discount

Before calculating the council tax liability of any dwelling, a local authority should take reasonable steps to establish whether any discount should be granted.[48] The failure of a billing authority to take take reasonable steps to ascertain which dwellings may be eligible to a discount may be raised in appeals about failure to award discounts, backdated claims for discounts or a refusal by billing authorities to repay any overpaid tax where discount was not awarded.[49]

Scottish local authorities are obliged to actively seek confirmation on the use of properties as second homes and long-term empty properties, now that the discount or 'variation' applied can be modified up or down (see p115).

If the local authority has reason to believe that a discount applies, this should be assumed when calculating the council tax liability for the dwelling,[50] even if it does not have conclusive evidence.

Applications

If the local authority has not granted a discount, a liable person may request one in writing. Many local authorities have paper and online claim forms for council tax discounts. Any relevant evidence supporting the request should be included. In the case of a student, a student's certificate may prove useful but is not necessary. In the case of someone who is severely mentally impaired, a certificate from a GP is required.

Backdating discounts

Authorities must grant discounts for a past period if the appropriate conditions were met, as there is no time limit on backdating discounts. Unlike the provisions for backdating most social security benefits, there is no requirement to show 'good cause' before a discount is backdated or any other restriction in the legislation. There is no time limit on how much backdating you can apply for (ie, you can apply for a discount to be backdated further than the six years imposed by the Limitation Act 1980), but in some cases the local authority may raise the decision in *Arca v Carlisle City Council*[51] and suggest that backdating can only be allowed for six years. However, in recent decisions, the President of the Valuation Tribunal for England explained that the six-year period only relates to the right to bring an appeal against a decision, rather than on legal proceedings, such as starting an appeal to the valuation tribunal. In particular, a restriction may not apply where the local authority has not taken the reasonable steps required to establish whether entitlement to discount applies.[52] Other exceptions exist to the six-year limit – eg, under section 32 Limitation Act 1980 where there relevant evidence has been concealed, where a fraud has been committed or where there has been a mistake.

If a discount should not have been granted for a past period, it may be withdrawn and you may have to appeal to the valuation tribunal.

Not only are the restrictions imposed on backdating by *Arca* much more limited than some councils suggest but this decision is only persuasive in Wales and Scotland. Moreover, the Limitation Act does not apply in Scotland where the equivalent legislation (Prescription and Limitation (Scotland) Act 1973) sets a 20-year limit.

The duty to correct false assumptions

If a discount has been granted, the local authority must inform the liable person in writing, normally on the tax bill. If that person, or any jointly liable person, has reason to believe that the discount should not have been awarded or that a smaller discount should be in place, s/he should write and advise the local authority within 21 days of first having reason to believe the discount was incorrect.[53] This obligation only arises before the end of the financial year following the financial year in respect of which the local authority's assumption about the discount was made.[54]

Penalties

The local authority has the discretion to impose a penalty of £70 (in England) and £50 (in Wales or Scotland) on a liable person who fails to notify it that a discount should not have been granted.[55] The penalty may be imposed on someone who, through negligence, fails to promptly notify the billing authority of a relevant change in circumstances or who makes an incorrect statement. An English or Welsh authority may quash such a penalty. A Scottish local authority may revoke the imposition of such a penalty if the person on whom it was imposed had a reasonable excuse for the failure.[56] Each time the local authority repeats the request and the person continues to fail to supply the information, a further £280 (England), £200 (Wales) or £500 (Scotland) can be imposed.[57]

In Scotland, the maximum fine for providing false or misleading information to obtain a reduction that is not due or to avoid a punitive 100 per cent increase if it truly is a long-term empty property has been increased to £500.[58]

An appeal against the imposition of a penalty may be made (see Chapter 11).[59] If you appeal, the penalty need not be paid until the appeal has been decided.

The billing authority may offer civil penalties as an alternative to a criminal prosecution.

5. **Unoccupied dwellings discounts**

Local authorities have a discretion to award discounts for certain classes of unoccupied dwellings – ie, in which no one has sole or main residence. The discount can be reduced ('varied' in Scotland) as the local authority sees fit.[60]

See p117 for information about long-term empty dwellings and second homes.

England and Wales

Many authorities offer no discount for such properties while others offer a short period of exemption (eg, one month) followed by full liability – or a short period of exemption, followed by a longer period of discount, followed by full liability. Contact your local authority to find out what discount, if any, it is allowing. See p49 for short-term vacant home exemptions in Wales.

After one year in Wales or two years in England, the rules for long-term empty properties apply (see p117).

Dwellings where discount cannot be changed

Local authorities cannot reduce the amount of discount applicable to some properties. These dwellings receive a discount of 50 per cent. This includes properties which consist of a pitch occupied by a caravan, a mooring occupied by a boat, job-related dwellings, and unoccupied dwellings left empty because a person is required to occupy another dwelling because of her/his job (see p115).

Scotland

Scottish local authorities can apply a variable discretionary reduction to empty dwellings and dwellings that are second homes.[61]

Unoccupied dwellings and second homes[62]

An 'unoccupied dwelling' is a dwelling which is no one's sole or main residence but is not a second home.

A 'second home' is a furnished dwelling which is no one's sole or main residence but the liable person can produce evidence to establish that it is lived in, other as a sole or main residence, for at least 25 days during any period of 12 months.

The discount is 50 per cent for every day where there is no resident in the dwelling.[63] However, the local authority may reduce the discount to any percentage not less than 10 per cent.

Where the property has been unoccupied as a sole or main residence for a continuous period exceeding 12 months, the local authority can:[64]

- apply no discount; *or*
- increase the amount of council tax payable by up to 100 per cent.

The local authority may also modify for different cases, or different classes of case, including for different areas.

From 1 April 2017, if the dwelling is a second home, no modification may be made to impose an increase in council tax liability, and:

- the discount percentage may not be greater than 50 per cent;
- the discount percentage may not be less than 10 per cent;
- the modification can impose no variation in council tax liability.[65]

Unoccupied properties being marketed for sale or for let are protected from variation where:[66]

- a property for sale is continuously unoccupied for less than two years and the liable person can provide evidence that s/he has actively marketed the property for sale on fair terms and conditions and price and that an offer to purchase on such terms would be acceptable by the owner;
- a property for let is continuously unoccupied for less than two years and the liable person can provide evidence that s/he has actively marketed the property for let on fair terms and conditions and proposed rent which is appropriate to that property and that an offer to pay such rent would be likely to lead to the creation of a tenancy.

Note that occupation as a sole or main residence of less than three months duration within any 12-month period is to be regarded as continuously unoccupied.

Purpose built holiday homes and job-related dwellings (see below) are subject to the 50 per cent discount and cannot be varied.[67]

Unoccupied dwellings undergoing or requiring major repair work to render them habitable and unoccupied dwellings undergoing structural alteration, are protected for a six-month period from the day the property was purchased by the liable person.[68]

The council cannot discriminate between private persons and social landlords solely on the grounds of ownership.

Job-related dwellings and discounts

A job-related dwelling is one provided to you or your partner because of your or her/his employment and which:[69]

- is necessary in order to do the job properly; *or*
- has been provided so that duties are performed better and where it is customary for employers to provide accommodation to employees; *or*
- is part of special security arrangements.

Job-related dwellings include any accommodation provided as a second home as part of your employment (eg, a live-in caretaker), and property owned as a second home if you are required by your employment to occupy another dwelling – eg, you are a publican who is required to live in other licensed premises as a tenant of a brewery.

If you also have a second home in England on which council tax is payable, the local authority in which the second home is situated is prevented from reducing the 50 per cent discount.

In Scotland, to be job-related, the dwelling must be owned or tenanted by someone whose sole or main residence is a different dwelling.[70]

Company directors and partnerships

If the dwelling is provided by a company and you are either a director (as defined by sections 67 and 69 of the Income Tax (Earnings and Pensions) Act 2003) of it or an associated company, the local authority may reduce the discount unless:[71]

- you are employed as a full-time director; *or*
- the company is non-profit making; *or*
- the company is established for charitable purposes.

Ministers of religion

Ministers of any religious denomination who are required to live in premises to perform their duties of office come within the definition of those with a job-related dwelling and are entitled to a discount. This discount also applies to the spouse or partner of the minister.[72] Additionally, if the minister also has a second home on which council tax is chargeable, the local authority is prohibited from reducing the council tax discount below 50 per cent.[73]

6. **Miscellaneous discounts**

Local authorities have the power to give discretionary discounts.[74] Examples include hard-to-sell property, single occupiers called up for 28 days or more as members of the reserve forces, and occupied and unoccupied property without the benefit of mains services – eg, beach chalets.[75] You should, therefore, check with your local authority whether additional discounts are available.

7. **Premiums on long-term empty and second homes**

To help tackle housing shortages, local authorities have the discretion to charge increased amounts of council tax on long-term empty properties and second homes.

Properties which have been empty for one year or more (in Wales and Scotland) or two years or more (in England) are classified as 'long-term empty properties'.[76] This includes periods where the property is empty and where it is undergoing structural repair or alteration work or is unoccupied and unfurnished, such as newly built properties. Local authorities have discretion to charge a premium on long-term empty properties – ie, to increase the amount of council tax payable. While the decision to make a determination is for billing authorities to make, the government expects that 'due consideration is given to the health of the local housing market when making determinations'.[77]

In Wales, local authorities can also charge a premium on second homes (see p118). There is no power for English and Scottish authorities to charge a premium on second homes.[78]

Properties which are vacant for shorter periods of time may be exempt (see Chapter 4) or have a discount applied (p114). Local authorities also have powers to apply discretionary reductions in cases where homes are empty due to special circumstances (see p120) – eg, hardship, flooding or fire.

Exemptions may still be claimed for previous years in some cases (see Chapter 4).

England

Local authorities can increase the amount of council tax payable by up to 50 per cent, meaning that 150 per cent council tax becomes payable.[79] In England, a dwelling is 'long term empty' if it has been continuously empty and substantially unfurnished for a period of two years. Some exceptions apply (see p119).

Future changes

It is proposed under the Rating (Property in Common Occupation) and Council Tax (Empty Dwellings) Bill 2017/19 that the premium's maximum level will increase to 100 per cent from April 2019 – ie, doubling the council tax due on the property. For homes empty for between five and 10 years, councils will be able to increase the premium by up to 200 per cent by April 2020 and, for homes empty for 10 years or more, up to 300 per cent from 2021. Local authorities will retain discretion on whether to apply a premium, and the exact rates to be charged, which will take into account local circumstances.

Example

Bella and Jake bought a property two years ago. They are majorly renovating it in their spare time and the property is unoccupied and substantially unfurnished. The monthly council tax due on the property is £225 made up of the full charge (£150) plus a premium of 50 per cent (£75).

Wales

Local authorities have discretion to charge a premium of up to 100 per cent of the standard rate of council tax on long-term empty homes[80] – ie, up to doubling the amount payable. Some exceptions apply (see p119). In Wales, a long-term empty dwelling is a dwelling which is both unoccupied and substantially unfurnished for a continuous period of at least one year.[81] The furnishing or occupation of a dwelling for one or more period of six weeks or less during the year will not affect its status as a long-term empty dwelling[82] – ie, its status as a long-term empty dwelling cannot be altered if you take up residence or install furniture for a short period.

Local authorities may specify different percentages (up to a maximum of 100 per cent) for different dwellings based on the length of time for which they have been empty, with the aim of applying stepped incremental increases over time.[83]

What factors should the local authority consider when using discretion to charge a premium?
There are a variety of factors that local authorities should consider when deciding whether to set a premium. The Welsh guidance lists the following factors to assist local authorities.[84] It is not exhaustive. While some factors are specific to either long-term empty homes or second homes, others are common to both:
 – numbers and percentages of long-term empty homes or second homes in the area;
 – distribution of long-term empty homes or second homes and other housing throughout the authority and an assessment of their impact on property values in particular areas;
 – potential impact on local economies and the tourism industry;
 – patterns of demand for, and availability of, affordable homes;
 – potential impact on local public services;
 – potential impact on the local community;
 – other measures that are available to increase housing supply;
 – other measures that are available to help bring empty properties back into use.

Local authorities in Wales have discretion to charge second home owners an additional council tax premium up to a maximum level of 100 per cent – ie, up to doubling the amount payable.[85] A second home is a dwelling which is not your sole or main home and is substantially furnished.

For a premium to apply to a second home, a billing authority must make a determination under section 12B of the Local Government Finance Act 1992 at least one year before the beginning of the financial year to which the premium relates – ie, for a premium to apply from 1 April 2019, a billing authority must make a determination before 1 April 2018.

Exceptions include job-related dwellings, seasonal holiday homes where year-round occupancy is prohibited, occupied caravan pitches and boat moorings, properties being marketed for rent or sale (for up to one year), annexes and dwellings which would be occupied if the occupier was not serving with the armed forces.

Scotland

Scottish local authorities have the discretion to vary the amount that can be charged on long-term empty properties so that a premium of up to 100 per cent of the standard council tax can be applied, unless the property qualifies for an exemption (see below).[86] The premium can be applied to homes which have been unoccupied for one year or more. An 'unoccupied dwelling' is any dwelling which is not someone's sole or main residence, but does not fall within the definition of a second home (see p114 for the definition of a second home). An unoccupied dwelling may be either furnished or unfurnished but is either not lived in at all or is lived in for less than 25 days in any 12-month period. The premium only apples to the council tax proportion of the council tax bill, not the water charge. If your property was not lived in for at least 25 days in the last 12 months, then it is required to be classified as an unoccupied property rather than as a second home.

If the local authority classes your second home as an empty property and applies a premium, you may appeal. It is for you to prove that your property is a genuine second home and you may need to provide evidence such as utility bills.

When a premium cannot be applied

A dwelling is exempt from a premium if it:[87]
- would be someone's sole or main residence if s/he was not residing in armed forces accommodation;
- is an annexe forming part of, or being treated as part of, the main dwelling; or
- is genuinely being marketed for sale or for rent. In England and Wales, this has a one-year limit starting from the date that the property is placed on the market. In Scotland, the time limit is two years.[88]

Support for owners of empty property

To help bring empty properties to back into use to meet housing demand, most local authorities have 'empty homes' or 'urban renewals' teams. Examples of the support available include:
- loans for central heating installation, boiler replacement and heating efficiency measures;
- empty homes grants to help with the costs of refurbishment;
- matching services which match empty homes with possible buyers;
- providing a letter to support VAT reduction for renovation work.

Contact your local authority to find out what is available in your area. Your local authority's council tax reduction scheme may also make provision for certain classes of dwelling.

Discretionary reductions for long-term empty and second homes

In England and Wales, local authorities can apply their discretionary powers to reduce council tax liability under section 13A Local Government Finance Act 1992 (see p167) to reduce liability in respect of a premium. If there are good reasons why your property cannot be lived in or why it cannot be sold or let, or if paying the premium is causing you hardship, apply for a discretionary reduction (see p167).

Example

Faith's unoccupied property has been for sale for 14 months. The local housing market is stagnant and, despite being reasonably priced, there has been little interest in the property. As Faith is also paying council tax on her new property, she contacts her local council to ask it to use its flexibility not to apply the 100 per cent premium as it is causing her hardship. It agrees as Faith is doing what she can to sell her property.

8. **Appeals**

If the local authority refuses to grant a discount or if you disagree about your liability to pay a premium, you can appeal in writing if you are an 'aggrieved person'.[89] There is no time limit for making such an appeal. You are an 'aggrieved person' if you are liable to pay the council tax or you are the owner (if different). The appeal letter should give the reasons why the discount should be granted. The local authority has two months in which to answer.[90] If no discount is granted, or if the local authority fails to answer within two months of receiving the appeal, you can make a further appeal to the Valuation Tribunal for England or to the Valuation Tribunal for Wales. In Scotland, a further appeal is made by writing again to the local authority. The local authority should pass the appeal to the secretary of the relevant local valuation appeal committee. See Chapter 11 for further details.[91]

If a local authority reduces the amount of discount available and you experience hardship, an application may be made to reduce the amount of council tax payable. The local authority must consider the application to reduce the sum on an individual basis.

The local authority may enforce payment of the original bill while the appeal is outstanding (see Chapter 10). The local authority may be prepared to agree to suspend recovery action while awaiting the outcome of the appeal. Alternatively, an adjournment may be sought from the magistrates' court or sheriff court if recovery proceedings are commenced.

Notes

1. **25 per cent discount for one resident**
   1 **EW** s2(2)(d) LGFA 1992
   S s71(2)(d) LGFA 1992

2. **Who counts for discount purposes**
   2 **EW** s6 LGFA 1992
   S s99(1) LGFA 1992

3. **Who is disregarded for discount purposes**
   3 **EW** s11 and Sch 1 LGFA 1992;
   CT(DD)O; CT(APDD) Regs
   S CT(D)(S)O; CT(D)(S) Regs
   4 s11 LGFA 1992
   5 Council Tax Information Letter 2/2006
   stated: 'It is our view that, under
   Schedule 7 to the Local Government
   Finance Act 1992, (these) 19 year olds
   will fall to be disregarded for CT
   purposes.'
   6 Sch 1 para 3 LGFA 1992
   7 **EW** CT(APDD) Regs
   S CT(D)(S)CAO
   8 **E** CT(DD)O
   EW Reg 3 CT(EDDD)(A)O
   S Art 8 CT(D)(S)O
   9 Sch 1 para 6 CT(D)(S) Regs
   10 Sch 1 para 4 LGFA 1992
   11 **E** W Art 4 CT (DC) O
   S Art 6 CT (D) (S) CAO
   12 **EW** Sch 1 para 5(1) CT(DD)O
   S Art 6(1)(b) and Sch 1 para 1(a)
   CT(D)(S)CAO
   13 **EW** Sch 1 para 6(1) CT(DD)O
   S Sch 1 para 2 CT(D)(S)CAO
   14 **EW** Sch 1 para 3 CT(DD)O
   S Art 2 CT(D)(S)CAO
   15 Council Tax (Discounts) (Scotland)
   Amendment Order 2014 No. 37
   16 **EW** Sch 1 para 4(1) CT(DD)O
   S Art 6(4)(c) CT(D)(S)CAO
   17 **EW** Sch 1 para 3 CT(DD)O
   S Arts 2 and 6(4)(e) CT(D)(S)CAO
   18 Council tax information letter 5, 29 April
   1996
   19 Kent Valuation Tribunal for England
   appeals 1765M88934/176C and
   1765M88933/176C
   20 Sch 1 para 5 LGFA 1992
   21 Art 5 CT(DD)O

22 *Fayad v Lewisham* [2008] EWHC 2531
   (Admin)
23 Art 4 and Sch 1 para 2 CT(DD)O
24 CT(DDED)(A)O, as amended. See also
   CT(ED)(S)(A)O 1995 and CT(D)(S)(A)
   Regs
25 *Harrow London Borough Council v Ayiku*
   [2012] EWHC 1200
26 Sch 1 para 7 CT(DD)O
27 Council Tax (Discount Disregards)
   (Amendment) Order 1994 No.543
28 **E** Amended by art 2(2) CT(DD)(A)(E)O
   W Amended by CT(DD)(A)(W)O
   S CT(D)(S)CAO
29 **EW** Art 4(b)(i) and b(ii) CT(DD)O; art
   2(3) and Sch 3 Deregulation Act 2015
   Consequential Order 2015 No.971
30 Sch 1 para 2 LGFA 1992
31 In Scotland from 19 Feb 2018, see reg
   25 and Sch 4 National Health Service
   (General Medical Services Contracts)
   (Scotland) Regulations 2018 No.66
32 **EW** Art 3 CT(DD)O
   S Art 4(2) CT(S)(D)CAO
33 **EW** CT(DD)O
   S Art 4(3) CT(S)(D)CAO
34 **EW** CT(DD)O **S** CT(D)(S)O
35 **E** CT(APDD) Regs, amended by The
   Council Tax and Non-Domestic Rating
   (Amendment) (England) Regulations
   2006 No.3395
   W Council Tax (Additional Provisions for
   Discount Disregards) (Amendment)
   (Wales) Regulations 2007 No.581
   S Reg 2 CT(D)(S) Regs 1992
36 **EW** Art 3 (2) CT(DD)O
   S Art 4 (2) CT(D)(S)CAO
37 Sch 1 para 6 LGFA 1992
38 Sch 1 para 6 LGFA 1992; National
   Health Service Act 2006; National
   Health Service (Wales) Act 2006; s108
   National Health Service (Scotland) Act
   1978
39 Sch 1 paras 7-8 LGFA 1992
40 Sch 1 para 10 LGFA 1992
41 Sch 1 para 1 LGFA 1992
   EW CT(DD)O
   S Reg 3 CT(D)(S)CAO
42 **S** Sch 1 para 1(c)-(d) LGFA 1992
43 s300 Armed Forces Act 2006

44 Sch 1 para 1 LGFA 1992; art 9 SI 2010
No.813EW CT(DD)O
45 **EW** CT(APDD) Regs
S CT(D)(S) Regs
46 Sch 1 para 11 LGFA 1992; The European
Union Military Staff (Immunities and
Privileges) Order 2009 No.887; The
International Organisations (Immunities
and Privileges) (Scotland) Order 2009
No.44E
WCT(APDD) Regs
S CT(D)(S) Regs
47 **EW** CT(APDD)(A) RegsS CT(D)(S)(A)
Regs
See also The Visiting Forces and
International Headquarters (Application
of Law) (Amendment) Order 2009
No.705 and The European Union
Military Staff (Immunities and Privileges)
Order 2009 No.887

4. Getting a discount
48 **EW** Reg 14 CT(AE) Regs 1992
S Reg 12 CT(AE)(S) Regs
49 *Singh v Leicester City Council*, VTE Appeal
number: 2465M142876/037C, 11
August 2015
50 **EW** Reg 15 CT(AE) Regs 1992
S Reg 13 CT(AE)(S) Regs
51 *Arca v Carlisle City Council* [2013] RA
248; VTE 29 January and 20 March
2013, per Graham Zellick QC, President
52 *HS v Leicester City Council* Appeal No:
2465M142876/037C, 11 August 2015;
Holdsworth et al v City of Bradford MDC,
Appeal No: 2465M142876/037C, 6 July
2015
53 **EW** Reg 16 CT(AE) Regs 1992
S Reg 15 CT(AE)(S) Regs
54 **EW** Reg 16 CT(AE) Regs 1992
S Reg 15 CT(AE)(S) Regs
55 **EW** s14(2) and Sch 3 LGFA 1992
S s97(4) and Sch 3 LGFA 1992
56 **EW** s14(2) and Sch 3 LGFA 1992
S s97(4) and Sch 3 LGFA 1992
57 **EW** s14(2) and Sch 3 LGFA 1992
S s97(4) and Sch 3 LGFA 1992
58 Sch 3 para 2(1A) LGFA 1992
59 **EW** s14(2) and Sch 3 LGFA 1992
S s97(4) and Sch 3 LGFA 1992

5. Unoccupied dwellings discounts
60 **E** s11A LGFA 1992
W s12 LGFA 1992
S Schs 1 and 2 CT(VUD)(S) Regs
61 CT(VUD)(S) Regs
62 Reg 2 CT(VUD)(S) Regs
63 Reg 3 CT(VUD)(S) Regs

64 Regs 4-6 CT(VUD)(S) Regs
65 Reg 6(1A) CT(VUD)(S) Regs
66 Sch 2 CT(VUD)(S) Regs
67 Sch 1 CT(VUD)(S) Regs
68 Reg 5 CT(VUD)(S) Regs
69 **E** Sch 1 CT(PCD)(E) Regs
W Sch 1 CT(VUD)(W) Regs
S Sch1 para 2 CT(VUD)(S) Regs
70 **S** Sch 1 paras 2(1) CT(VUD)(S) Regs
71 Sch 1 paras 2 and 3 CT(PCD)(E) Regs
S Sch 1 paras 2(6)-(7) CT(VUD)(S) Regs
72 **E** Sch 1 CT(PCD)(E) Regs
W Sch 1 para 3 CT(VUD)(W) Regs
S Sch 1 paras 2(5)-(7) CT(VUD)(S) Regs
73 **E** Regs 2 and 6 CT(PCD)(E) Regs
W Reg 10 CT(VUD)(W) Regs
S Reg 3 CT(VUD)(S) Regs

6. Miscellaneous discounts
74 s13A LGFA 1992
75 Parliamentary Answer given in the
House of Commons by John Healy,
Minister for Local Government, 2
February 2009

**7. Premiums on long-term empty and
second homes**
76 **E** s11B(1)(b) LGFA 1992
W ss112A and 112B LGFA 1992 as
inserted by s139 Housing (Wales) Act
2014
S Reg 6 CT(VUD)(S) Regs
77 Department for Communities and Local
Government, *Council tax empty homes
premium: guidance for properties for sale
and Letting*, May 2013, para 5
78 Scottish Government, *Guidance on
second homes and long-term empty
properties*, 21 May 2013 (updated 9
April 2018)
79 s11B(1)(b) LGFA
80 ss112A and 112B LGFA 1992 as inserted
by s139 Housing (Wales) Act 2014
81 Welsh Government, *Guidance on the
Implementation of the Council Tax
Premiums on Long-Term Empty Homes
and Second Homes in Wales*, January
2016
82 s11B(9) LGFA 1992
83 Welsh Government, *Exemptions to the
Council Tax premium on Long-Term
Empty Homes in Wales*, 13 March 2015;
s12A LGFA 1992
84 Welsh Government, *Guidance on the
Implementation of the Council Tax
Premiums on Long-Term Empty Homes
and Second Homes in Wales*, January
2016

85 s112B LGFA 1992 as inserted by s139
    Housing (Wales) Act 2014
86 Reg 6 CT(VUD)(S) Regs
87 **E** Council Tax (Prescribed Classes of
    Dwellings) (England) Regulations 2003
    W Council Tax (Exceptions to Higher
    Amounts) (Wales) Regulations 2015
    S Sch 2 para 2 CT(VUD)(S) Regs
88 Sch 2 para 1 CT(VUD)(S) Regs

8. Appeals
89 **EW** s16 LGFA 1992
    S s81 LGFA 1992
90 **EW** s16 LGFA 1992
    S s81 LGFA 1992
91 **EW** s16 LGFA 1992
    S s81 LGFA 1992

Chapter 8

Council tax reduction schemes

This chapter covers:
1. What is a council tax reduction (below)
2. How council tax reduction schemes work (p128)
3. Council tax reduction schemes for pensioners (p131)
4. Council tax reduction schemes in England (p133)
5. Council tax reduction schemes in Wales (p137)
6. Council tax reduction schemes in Scotland (p137)
7. Alternative maximum council tax reduction ('second adult rebate') (p138)
8. How council tax reduction entitlement is calculated (p141)
9. Applying for council tax reduction (p161)
10. If you disagree with a council tax reduction decision (p165)
11. Discretionary reductions (p167)
12. Future changes (p168)

Key facts
- Council tax reduction (CTR) reduces the sum of the weekly amount of council tax payable on your dwelling. It is not a cash payment.
- In **England and Wales**, local authorities may devise their own local schemes which must meet minimum 'prescribed' requirements.
- One CTR scheme applies throughout **Scotland**, with no local variations.
- There are separate rules for people of working age and pensioners.
- Entitlement to CTR is based on your income and capital and the circumstances of the people living with you.
- Any non-dependants (see p147) are normally expected to contribute to the council tax.
- You have a right of appeal against decisions made by the local authority about your CTR.

1. **What is a council tax reduction**

If you have a low income, you might be able to get a council tax reduction (CTR). The level of reduction that can be awarded depends on where you live and your age. Different rules apply in England, Wales and Scotland.

CTR may be referred to in your local authority area as council tax 'benefit', 'support' or 'rebate'. The regulations throughout Britain refer to making 'an application' for CTR and to people who receive it as 'applicants'. These are the terms used throughout this chapter. However, most local authorities administer CTR alongside the housing benefit (HB) scheme and so your local authority may issue a 'claim form' and refer to you as a 'claimant' if you make an application.

National rules

Local CTR schemes must apply a means test controlled by different rules in each nation. In England and Wales, authorities have discretion to vary the tests for working-age applicants.[1] If you are a pensioner, your local authority should provide support which mirrors that previously available under council tax benefit (CTB) until April 2013. CTR reduces the sum of the weekly amount payable on the property, but not necessarily the complete amount. Full CTR, equal to 100 per cent of the tax due, can be awarded to low-income pensioners who have capital under £16,000 or who receive pension credit guarantee credit. 'Pensioner' has a specific meaning in CTR regulations (see p132). This chapter refers to people within this group as 'pensioners' and everyone else as 'working-age' applicants, whatever your actual age.

CTR schemes in England, Wales and Scotland

	England	Wales	Scotland
If you are a pensioner	You can get CTR on up to 100 per cent of your bill, depending on your circumstances. See sections 2, 3 and 4. You can get CTR on up to 25 per cent of your bill, based on the income of a 'second adult'. See sections 2 and 7.	You can get CTR on up to 100 per cent of your bill, depending on your circumstances. See sections 2, 3 and 5. There is no help based on the income of a 'second adult' available in Wales.	You can get CTR on up to 100 per cent of your bill, depending on your circumstances. See sections 2, 3 and 6. You can get CTR on up to 25 per cent of your bill, based on the income of a 'second adult'. See sections 2 and 7.
If you are of working age	You can get CTR on a percentage of your bill, which varies from local authority to local authority, subject to a means test. See sections 2 and 4.	You can get CTR on up to 100 per cent of your bill, subject to a means test. See sections 2 and 5.	You can get CTR on up to 100 per cent of your bill, depending on your circumstances. See sections 2 and 6.

You may get CTR on up to 25 per cent of your bill, based on the income of a 'second adult' in some local authority areas. See sections 2 and 7.	There is no help based on the income of a 'second adult' available in Wales.	You can get CTR on up to 25 per cent of your bill, based on the income of a 'second adult.' See sections 2 and 7.

In **England and Wales**, local authorities may devise their own local schemes which must meet minimum 'prescribed' requirements (see p127).[2] As a result, in England, there could be as many as 326 different local systems of support, each with its own rules, and 22 in Wales. Local schemes vary between areas; the reduction that you receive may be different to that given in the next borough. Crucially, **English** local authorities may set a percentage of the council tax bill which all working-age applicants must pay, whether or not they are on any benefit. A person of working age may be required in some boroughs to pay up to 45 per cent of the annual council tax bill, which was previously covered by full CTB. It is estimated that over two million low-income families in England have been adversely affected by the change from CTB. On average, they had to pay £191 more council tax in 2017/18 than they did under the CTB system.[3]

If you are of working age in **England and Wales**, you need to check the details of the scheme operated by your local authority. To determine how much support may be available to you, contact your local authority and make an application as soon as possible. Many local authorities use the same application form as for HB, and have online calculators you can use to see if you might qualify. Always apply if your income is low, or you are having difficulty paying your council tax bill. Making an application for CTR is an essential step for receiving it (see p161).

One CTR scheme applies throughout **Scotland**, with no local variations. The Scottish government has absorbed the cost of the abolition of CTB, so if you were previously entitled to CTB you should, normally, be awarded CTR.[4] The entitlement criteria, wherever possible, are identical to those used under the previous CTB scheme.

There are separate rules for people of working age and pensioners. If you are a pensioner but you or your partner claim universal credit (UC), income support (IS), income-based jobseeker's allowance (JSA) or income-related employment and support allowance (ESA), you are assessed under the scheme for working-age applicants.

In **England**, there are two types of CTR:
- **main CTR**, based on your council tax liability and your (and any partner's and dependants') needs and resources; *and*
- **alternative maximum CTR**, known as 'second adult rebate', to help you if you share your home with anyone on a low income, and lose your 'single

occupier discount' as a result. This is not based on your needs or resources, but on the circumstances of certain other adults ('second adults') living with you (see p138).

Second adult rebate can be paid instead of, but not in addition to, main CTR. If you are eligible for both, you are paid whichever is the higher.

In **Wales**, there is no second adult rebate, only main CTR.

In **Scotland**, as well as main CTR and second adult rebate, there is a third additional type of CTR: **'Band E–H CTR'** which helps low- and medium-income applicants to meet the additional cost of changes to the multiplier used in calculating council tax in these higher bands (see p137).

If you are entitled to maximum UC, IS, income-based JSA or income-related ESA, you may qualify for maximum main CTR. Otherwise, your CTR is calculated using a special formula (see p141).

Prescribed requirements and default schemes (in England and Wales only)

In England and Wales, certain key requirements which every local authority scheme must include for each financial year are laid down in regulations. These are known as the 'prescribed requirements'.[5] Otherwise, local authorities are free to set the particular details of their CTR schemes. If a local authority in Wales does not produce a scheme, a default scheme prepared by the Welsh government applies.

CTR schemes must state the classes of person entitled to a reduction.[6] The classes may be determined by assessing the income or capital of any person liable to pay council tax.[7] The English prescribed requirements only specify that low income pensioners are entitled to a 100 per cent reduction (as existed with CTB).[8] All local authorities in England and Wales are required to consult on, and create, schemes for people 'in financial need'.[9] However, especially in England, the size of any reduction varies from area to area, and there is no fixed definition in the legislation of how the local authority is to determine 'financial need', although the phrase has been considered in some court decisions by the higher courts (see p167).

A local authority scheme must also set out the procedure for applying for a reduction,[10] together with details of the right of appeal.

In addition to CTR schemes, a local authority in England and Wales also has discretionary powers to reduce a sum in council tax (see p167). This does not apply in Scotland.[11]

How council tax reduction is applied to your bill

The reduction available under a local CTR scheme is applied after the banding and the amount of tax on a dwelling, and the person(s) liable to pay it, have been established (see Chapters 3, 4 and 5).

CTR schemes take into account any disability reduction (see Chapter 6) or discount (see Chapter 7). The reduction is applied to the amount of council tax after either or both have been awarded.

In England and Wales, CTR may be awarded in a number of ways:[12]

- as a discount on the dwelling, calculated as a percentage of the bill payable on the dwelling;
- as a discount of an amount set out in your council's scheme, or to be calculated in accordance with provisions laid down in your council's scheme;
- as a part reduction in the council tax bill payable on your property;
- as a reduction of the entire council tax bill payable on the property (so that the amount payable is nil).

In most cases, CTR is awarded as a part reduction on the weekly amount payable on the dwelling.

2. How council tax reduction schemes work

Who is eligible for council tax reduction

If you are liable to pay council tax (see Chapter 5), your entitlement to council tax reduction (CTR) is based on your and, if you have a partner, your partner's income and capital and the circumstances of the people living with you.

A means test is applied to establish whether you have sufficient resources to pay your bill after making set allowances for your daily living costs. These are referred to as your 'applicable amount' (see p142). The resources taken into account include the savings, pensions and income of your spouse or partner. Your applicable amount depends on the number of people in your family and your personal circumstances.

Your CTR can also be affected by any other adults who live with you, other than your partner.

Who is not eligible for council tax reduction

You are excluded from CTR if you:

- have over £16,000 capital (see p158);[13]
- are subject to immigration control;[14]
- are not habitually resident in the UK.[15]

See CPAG's *Welfare Benefits and Tax Credits Handbook* for more about who is a person subject to immigration control and who is habitually resident.

Who is your family

For the purposes of a CTR scheme, your 'family' means:[16]
- your partner – ie, anyone with whom you live as 'a couple'; *and*
- any children or young people for whom you or your partner are responsible who are members of your household (see below).

Definitions

A **'child'** or **'young person'** includes anyone under 20 for whom child benefit is payable. It does not include a young person on income support or jobseeker's allowance or to whom section 6 of the Children (Leaving Care) Act 2000 (exclusion from benefits) applies. For more about this definition, see CPAG's *Welfare Benefits and Tax Credits Handbook*.[17]

A **'couple'** means:[18]

– two people who are married to each other or in a civil partnership and who are members of the same household; *or*

– two people who are not married to each other or in a civil partnership but are living together as if they were married or in a civil partnership.

There is a substantial body of benefits caselaw establshing when two people should be treated 'as if they were married' or 'as civil partners'. You can argue that local authorities should take the same approach when making decisions on CTR. See CPAG's *Welfare Rights and Tax Credits Handbook*.

Provision is also made in the regulations for polygamous marriages, but this is not explained in detail in this *Handbook*. Seek advice if this applies to you.[19]

Who is included your household

CTR schemes consider you partner and dependent children to be part of your **'household'** if they live with you.[20] The temporary absence of a child or young person does not affect her/his position as part of your household.

Your local authority must treat a child or young person who is in social services care as a member of your household in any reduction week where:
- s/he lives with you for part or all of that reduction week; *and*
- the authority considers that it is reasonable to do so, taking into account the nature and frequency of her/his visits to you.[21]

You are treated as being responsible for a child or young person who normally lives with you. Where a child or young person spends equal amounts of time in different households, or where there is a question as to which household s/he is living in, s/he is treated as normally living with the person who is receiving child benefit for her/him.[22]

A child or young person is not usually treated as a member of your household if s/he is being fostered by you or your partner, or s/he is placed or boarded with you prior to adoption.

Joint liability

Where you are jointly liable for council tax with one or more other people who are not part of your household, the amount of maximum CTR is divided by the number of liable people.[23] The entitlement of each liable person is then calculated based on the applicable amount and resources appropriate to her/him (and her/his household if s/he has one).

Where you are resident

For CTR purposes, you are resident in the home where you live – ie, your normal 'sole or main residence' (see p72).[24]

If you are not yet liable for the council tax on the property (eg, because you have not yet moved in) but are likely to be eligible for CTR when you become liable, you can make your application in advance and the authority is required to treat it as having been made on the date you become liable. You can apply up to eight weeks in advance in England and 13 weeks in advance in Wales and Scotland.[25]

Owners not resident in a dwelling, or those whose main residence is elsewhere, are not entitled to CTR for that dwelling – ie, for a second home.

Temporary absence from home

Where you are entitled to CTR, a property can count as your sole or main residence even if you spend substantial periods of time away from it, if you consider it to be the main place where you live. The rules below do not necessarily apply to working-age applicants in England or Wales. You will need to check how you will be treated under your local authority's scheme. You can argue that you count as temporarily absent from home even if you have not yet stayed there – eg, you move your furniture and belongings in but then have to go into hospital.[26]

You can get CTR for up to **13 weeks** for your normal home while you are away, whatever the reason, provided you have not let or sublet your dwelling to someone else.[27] You must be unlikely to be away for longer than this.

You can get CTR for up to **52 weeks** providing you intend to return to the dwelling (normally within 52 weeks but, exceptionally, if you are unlikely to be absent for substantially longer), have not let or sublet it and fulfil certain conditions.

The circumstances in which you can remain eligible for up to 52 weeks include:
- you are detained in custody on remand pending trial or sentence;
- you are on bail and required, as a condition of bail, to stay in a bail hostel or in premises approved under section 13 of the Offender Management Act 2007;

- you are a patient in a hospital or similar institution;
- you, your partner or a dependent child under 16 is undergoing, in the UK or elsewhere, medical treatment, or medically approved convalescence, in accommodation other than residential accommodation;
- you are on (in the UK or elsewhere) a training course which will help you secure employment;
- you are undertaking medically approved care of a person residing in the UK or elsewhere;
- you are undertaking the care of a child whose parent or guardian is temporarily absent from the dwelling normally occupied by that parent or guardian for the purpose of receiving medically approved care or medical treatment;
- you are in the UK or elsewhere, receiving medically approved care provided in accommodation other than residential accommodation;
- you are a student;
- you are away from home as a result of a fear of violence;
- you are in residential accommodation for a trial period and intend to return home if it is not suitable. You can only get a reduction for 13 weeks in any one trial period. If the accommodation is not suitable, you may have further trial periods, as long as they do not exceed 52 weeks.[28]

Note: the rules in England restrict absences outside the UK. In most cases, you can only be absent for four weeks at a time. This can be extended for a further four weeks in limited cases. You can be absent from the UK for up to 26 weeks at a time if your absence is for one of the reasons which would permit you to be absent for up to 52 weeks from Wales or Scotland. If you are a working-age applicant in England or Wales, your local authority can set its own rules. In this, and all other respects, these are unlikely to be more generous than those for pensioners in your nation, but could be more restrictive.

3. **Council tax reduction schemes for pensioners**

All council tax reduction (CTR) schemes in England, Wales and Scotland give reductions to all pensioners on low incomes, provided their capital or savings are not too high. Pensioners who have capital or savings above £16,000 are excluded from CTR and must not be included in the local authority's scheme, unless they receive the guarantee credit of pension credit (PC), in which case all their capital and income is disregarded.[29]

Who is a pensioner

You are a pensioner for CTR purposes if:[30]
- you have 'attained the qualifying age for PC', in this *Handbook* this is referred to as 'pension age' (see below); *and*
- you or your partner are not in receipt of universal credit (UC), income support, income-based jobseeker's allowance (JSA) or income-related employment and support allowance (ESA).

Pension age

The pension age for a woman is the minimum age she can receive state retirement pension. The pension age for a man is the minimum age a woman born on the same day as him can receive state retirement pension.
– If your date of birth is before 6 April 1950, your pension age is 60.
– If your date of birth is between 6 April 1950 and 5 December 1953 inclusive, your pension age will be between 60 and 65.
– If your date of birth is after 5 December 1953, your qualifying age will be 65 or over. The qualifying age for men and women is rising steadily to 66 (by 2020) and will eventually go up to 68.
To check your pension age, see www.gov.uk/state-pension-age.

How council tax reduction for pensioners is calculated

In England, pensioners are divided into three groups: Class A, Class B and Class C (some local authorities refer to them as Class 1, Class 2 and Class 3). The Welsh regulations recognise Class A and Class B but do not have an equivalent to Class C. The Scottish regulations do not categorise pensioners in the same way; however, your entitlement can still be understood using these categories.[31]

With all three classes, you must make an application to receive a reduction (see p161). The class into which you are placed is determined by your income and applicable amount.

Income is no greater than your applicable amount

If your weekly income is equal to or less than your applicable amount (see p146), you qualify for 100 per cent CTR, less any non-dependant deductions (see p147).[32] In England and Wales, this means that you are in 'Class A'.

If you are in Class A and get the guarantee credit of PC, your income and capital are disregarded. This means that your income is automatically less than your applicable amount and you automatically qualify for your maximum CTR wherever you live.[33]

Income is greater than applicable amount

In England and Wales, you are in Class B if your weekly income is greater than your applicable amount (see p146).[34] If your total net income exceeds your applicable amount, your CTR is reduced by 20 pence for every £1 you receive above the applicable amount. The same calculation applies in Scotland. See p157 for more about this calculation.

Entitled to second adult rebate

In England and Scotland, you may be entitled to alternative maximum CTR, usually known as 'second adult rebate', where you are liable to pay council tax in respect of a dwelling which is shared with one or more adults on a low income who are not your spouse or partner and who do not pay rent to you.[35] These people are referred to as 'second adults' (see p139). There is no second adult rebate in Wales. In England, pensioners who receive second adult rebate form 'Class C' under the regulations.

It is the income of the second adult that determines what level of reduction is awarded. The reduction awarded can be 7.5, 15, 25 or 100 per cent (see p140 for an explanation of the calculation).

Applicable amounts for pensioners

The applicable amount (see p142) for a pensioner is made up of:[36]
- a personal allowance for you, and you partner if you have one;
- extra allowances for any child or young person who is a member of your family;
- any premiums which may be applicable. See p142 for the amounts of premiums and personal allowances.

Example
John, 70, lives alone and has a council tax liability of £18.50 a week. His weekly income is £125.95 state pension and £51.97 private pension, totaling £177.92. His applicable amount in 2018/19 is £176.40 (his personal allowance). John does not qualify for any premiums.
Total income £177.92 *minus* £176.40 applicable amount = £1.52
20% of £1.52 excess income = £0.30
£18.50 – £0.30 = £18.20 CTR
John is entitled to £18.20 CTR on his weekly council tax liability.

4. Council tax reduction schemes in England

Pensioners have their entitlement assessed under rules common to all three nations (see p131). Those not defined as pensioners are by default defined as 'working age'. See p132 for who is defined as a pensioner.[37] It is left to each English local authority to decide which classes of working-age adults are eligible to receive council tax reduction (CTR) and how much help is provided. Local authorities are entitled to set a lower level of CTR for people of working age than existed until 1 April 2013 under council tax benefit (CTB). In 2017/18, 289 out of 326 local authorities did so.

Levels of reduction for working-age applicants

If you are of working age, are over 18 years of age and receive universal credit, income support, income-based jobseeker's allowance (JSA) or income-related employment and support allowance (ESA) (known as 'passporting' benefits), you are eligible to receive CTR on the maximum council tax payable under your local scheme (see p142). If you have a low income, even if you are employed or self-employed, the local authority will carry out its own means test (see p128) to see if your income and capital are low enough.

Check the details of the scheme for your area.

The amount of CTR is calculated using a maximum figure and the percentage of support given by the local authority.

See the table on p136 for examples of the percentages different authorities expect applicants to pay.

Example

George, 45, is single and gets income-based JSA. He lives in a local authority area where the maximum CTR allowed for people of working age is 80 per cent.

Annual council tax bill on the property	£854.10
Less single occupancy discount of 25%	£640.57
Divided by 52 weeks = council tax weekly liability	£12.32
Maximum eligible CTR (80% x £12.32)	£9.86

George is required to pay council tax of £2.46 in each week he qualifies for CTR.

Reducing local council tax reduction for working-age applicants

Local authorities may adopt the following measures to reduce the support given by a CTR scheme to working-age applicants. See the table on p136 for examples of how particular authorities have done this.

- **Introducing a property banding cap.** Some authorities may limit the CTR they give people living in properties the higher bands. This may be done by imposing a banding cap whereby properties higher than Band D do not receive any CTR. Alternatively, applicants in higher banded properties may receive a reduction but their entitlement is limited to that which would be received on a property in lower bands.
- **Limiting the amount of maximum CTR.** Some authorities have a policy of only granting a reduction above a minimum figure, such as £2, £4 or £5 a week. If your CTR would be below this figure, no CTR is paid.

- **Minimum payments.** Some CTR schemes may require you to pay at least some council tax each month if you are of working age. This can be set either by limiting your maximum CTR to a percentage of your council tax (minus any non-dependant deductions) or as an across-the-board cut to your actual entitlement.
- **Lowering the savings cap.** Pensioners with savings equal to or below £16,000 are eligible to apply for help. However, with working-age adults, the savings cap can be lowered. Some local authorities place their savings cap as low as £6,000. If your savings fall below this level because you pay your council tax or other essential bills, you may be able to apply for CTR.
- **Changing the income taper.** For pensioners, the amount of CTR that you receive falls by 20 per cent or 20 pence for every extra £1 of income above your applicable amount. For working-age applicants, some local authorities increase this – eg, to 25 pence or 30 pence for each £1 of excess income.
- **Disregarding earnings for certain groups.** Some schemes disregard more of the earnings for applicants who find it harder to work. These include lone parents with pre-school-aged children, disabled people and their carers, and those who receive disability living allowance (DLA), attendance allowance or ESA.
- **Disregarding additional income.** In calculating income for CTR for pensioners, certain benefits and other forms of income are disregarded. However, local authorities may change these amounts if you are of working age. For example, some authorities may give more CTR to households with children by disregarding amounts of income or certain forms of benefit.
- **Removal or reduction of the second adult rebate.** If you are of working age and share your home with someone on a low income, the entitlement to second adult rebate may be changed.
- **Changing non-dependant deductions.** The deductions made for other adults living in your property could be increased or decreased.

Example

Albert and Victoria are in their 50s and live in a Band D property. Victoria works part time, earning £120 a week and receives £64.60 carer's allowance. Albert receives the middle rate of the care component of DLA and £110.75 ESA. They have savings of £9,000. The table on p136 shows how much relief they would receive on (notional) council tax of £30 a week in each of five different local authorities.

	Adur, West Sussex*	Tameside, Greater Manchester	Waltham Forest, London	South Tyneside	Mid Sussex, West Sussex
Income taper rate	20%	20%	25%	20%	15%
Minimum payment	0%	25% reduction in maximum entitlement	24% reduction in maximum entitlement	30% cut across the board (15% if you receive disability/ severe disability premium or have a child under five)	39 % cut across the board unless you receive certain disability benefits or are the lone parent of a child under five
Capital limit	£16,000	£16,000	£6,000	£16,000	£16,000
Band restriction	None	Restricted to Band A (£21.16)	None	None	None
Minimum CTR	None	None	£1 a week	None	None
Albert and Victoria's CTR	£20.21	£6.08 (due to band restriction and payment limit)	Nil (excluded by capital limit)	£17.18 (15% cut across the board)	£22.66 (due to taper, exempt from cut across the board because Albert is in the support group for ESA)
Annual loss or gain compared to CTB	Nil	£736.78 loss	£1,053.81 loss	£126.71 loss	£127.75 gain

*Adur is one of the 37 local authorities whose scheme still retains the level of support provided under CTB before 2013.

5. Council tax reduction schemes in Wales

Pensioners have their entitlement assessed under rules common to all three nations (see p131). Those not defined as pensioners are by default defined as 'working age'. In theory, each Welsh local authority is free to devise a council tax reduction (CTR) scheme for working-age applicants. However, the 'prescribed requirements' include many provisions which mirror the relief provided under council tax benefit before 2013 and local authorities do not have as much discretion as their English counterparts.[38] The gap between Westminster funding and the cost of maintaining pre-2013 levels of benefit will be met from the Welsh government's budget until at least April 2019. The extra costs include a commitment to increase all personal allowances and premiums in line with inflation, even where the equivalent allowances in UK-wide social security payments have been frozen. This means that when calculating your entitlement in Wales, you should use the allowances given in the second column in the table on p142.

There is no alternative maximum CTR scheme ('second adult rebate') in Wales (see p138). This means that both pensioners and working-age applicants can only have their council tax reduced as a result of the financial circumstances of their own household.

6. Council tax reduction schemes in Scotland

The council tax reduction (CTR) schemes in Scotland are national schemes governed by separate regulations for working-age and pensioner claimants. They are intended to preserve the levels of entitlement from the council tax benefit scheme before 2013.[39] All personal allowances and premiums rise in line with inflation, even where the equivalent allowances in UK-wide social security payments have been frozen, and the personal allowances for children and young people are even more generous. This means that when calculating your entitlement in Scotland, you should use the allowances given in the third column in the table on p142.

Band E–H council tax reduction

In 2017/18, the Scottish government increased the multipliers used to set the council tax for properties in bands above D (see p44). A new class of CTR was introduced, designed to compensate 'low- to middle-income households' affected by this change. If your home is in any of these bands, you will receive full CTR for any part of this increase which is not met by any other class of CTR if your income is less than a 'median income' figure established by the Scottish government. This will be the case if:

- you are a single applicant and your income is less than £321 a week;
- you are a member of a couple or polygamous marriage, or a single parent, and have an income of less than £479 a week; *or*
- you or your partner receive income support, income-based jobseeker's allowance, income-related employment and support allowance or pension credit (however, these would usually passport you to full CTR under the main scheme).

If your income is more than this level, then a taper of 20 per cent is applied to the excess. Your income and capital is assessed in exactly the same way as for other classes of CTR (see p158 for capital and p152 if you are working age, or p151 if you are a pensioner, for the income rules) and other rules such as 'non-dependant deductions' (see p147) apply. All the other qualifying conditions and exclusions, such as the capital limits, are the same as for other classes of CTR.[40]

Example
James and Shona are in their fifties and live in a Band G property in Aberdeen. Their council tax increased by £358.86 (£6.88 a week) as a result of the multiplier change. This is their maximum entitlement to Band E–H CTR. Their combined income after disregards is £507.80. This £28.80 more than the median income figure so a 20 per cent taper is applied to this excess: £28.80 x 20 per cent = £5.79. They expected to pay this amount towards the multiplier increase and Band E–H CTR will pay the remaining £1.09 (£56.68 per annum).

As James and Shona have provided full information about their income and other circumstances in support of their CTR application, the local authority would also compare their income against their applicable amount (see p142) and pay them under the main CTR scheme if this would result in a higher award.

---

7. **Alternative maximum council tax reduction ('second adult rebate')**

In **England and Scotland**, 'alternative maximum council tax reduction', known as 'second adult rebate', is designed to help you if you if you share your home with anyone on a low income who does not share liability for council tax with you or pay rent to you (referred to as a 'second adult').[41]

Second adult rebate is an alternative type of council tax reduction (CTR) that can be received instead of, but not as well as, main CTR. When you apply for CTR, the local authority must assess you for both types and award whichever is the higher – sometimes referred to as the 'best buy'.[42]

The second adult rebate rules:

- apply to all eligible pensioners in England and Scotland;[43]
- apply to working-age adults in Scotland;[44]
- vary for working-age adults in England, with some local authorities choosing not to award a second adult rebate. In 2017/18, 214 English authorities either provided no second adult rebate or restricted its provision;
- do not apply in Wales.

You qualify for a second adult rebate if:[45]
- you are liable for council tax in respect of the home where you are 'resident' (see p70); *and*
- you are the only person liable for the council tax on the home (with certain exceptions – see p70); *and*
- no one living in your home is liable to pay you rent; *and*
- you have one or more 'second adult(s)' living with you who are on a low income (see the income figures on p140); *and*
- you satisfy the 'right to reside test' and the 'habitual residence test' and are not a 'person subject to immigration control' for benefit purposes (see CPAG's *Welfare Benefits and Tax Credits Handbook*).

Note: second adult rebate is based on the circumstances of the 'second adult(s)' living with you. The whole of *your* income and capital is ignored. Therefore, you can get second adult rebate even if you have a high income and/or capital worth more than £16,000, or if you are student who is liable to pay council tax.

Example
Nita owns her own home and earns £40,000 a year. She is liable for council tax of £750 a year after her single occupier discount, and her income is too high for her to qualify for main CTR. Nita's adult son, Zac, who receives income support (IS), moves in with her. Nita loses her 25 per cent single person's discount and her council tax liability is now £1,000. Zac is a second adult. Nita is entitled to a second adult rebate of £250.

Who counts as a second adult

You must have at least one 'second adult' residing with you to qualify for alternative maximum CTR. In practice, those classified as second adults are mainly the same people as those treated as non-dependants (see p147).

Who does not count as a second adult

Someone residing with you does not count as a second adult if s/he is:
- aged under 18;[46] *or*
- disregarded for council tax purposes (see p101);[47] *or*
- your partner with whom you are jointly liable for council tax;[48] *or*

- jointly liable to pay the council tax on the dwelling with you – eg, because s/he is a joint owner or tenant.[49] Although you cannot get second adult rebate for her/him, s/he may be able to apply for main CTR for her/his own share of the bill (see p130).

Examples

Jason owns his home. His mother lives with him and receives pension credit (PC) guarantee credit. Jason is liable for council tax and can apply for alternative maximum CTR, as his mother is a second adult.

Dorinda lives with her partner, who is a full-time student and is disregarded for the purpose of a council tax discount. Their 20-year-old daughter and 25-year-old son live with them. The daughter is unemployed and in receipt of income-based jobseeker's allowance (JSA). The son is in low-paid employment. Dorinda may apply for the alternative maximum CTR, as the adult daughter and son are second adults.

Penny is a lone parent who lives with her two children aged 10 and 14. She is not entitled to alternative maximum CTR as there are no second adults in the dwelling. However, she is entitled to a single occupier discount.

You cannot qualify for alternative maximum CTR if a second adult who lives with you is liable to pay you rent for occupying your home.

It is important to check that the local authority has not confused a 'non-dependant deduction' situation with a case where a 'second adult reduction' should be applied.

Calculating alternative maximum council tax reduction

The amount of second adult rebate you get is a percentage of your council tax liability based on the gross income of the second adult.[50] If there is more than one second adult, their combined gross income is used. If the second adult receives universal credit (UC), you are not automatically 'passported' to entitlement. Her/his UC is added to her/his other income in the calculation instead.

Income of second adult(s)	Second adult rebate
Second adult(s) on IS/income-based JSA/income-related employment and support allowance (ESA)/PC	25 per cent
Second adult(s) total gross weekly income:	
Below £193	15 per cent
£187–£249.99	7.5 per cent
£250 and over	Nil

Student dwellings:
All occupiers are either students excluded from   100 per cent
entitlement to main CTR or on IS/income-based
JSA/income-related ESA/PC. At least one must be a
student and at least one on IS/income-based JSA/
income-related ESA/PC.

For the 100 per cent rebate, someone counts as a student excluded from entitlement to main CTR if s/he would be excluded if s/he were under the qualifying age for PC (see p132).

Unless you qualify for a 100 per cent rebate, the maximum second adult rebate you can get is always 25 per cent of your council tax liability, even if you would have received a 50 per cent council tax discount, or would have been exempt from council tax altogether, were it not for the presence of two or more second adults in your home.

Examples

Liam is a student who lives alone in a home he owns, so he is exempt from paying council tax. His friend Brian, who is on income-related ESA, comes to lodge with him, so Liam is now liable for council tax. Liam applies for second adult rebate. This is 100 per cent of his council tax liability. If, however, Brian received the same amount of contributory ESA or UC, Liam would not be eligible for 100 per cent rebate and Liam would have to pay at least 85 per cent of the assessed tax for the property.

Ravi is the tenant of his flat. He is in a well-paid job so lets his friend Carl stay with him without charging him rent. Carl earns £190 a week. Ravi's second adult rebate is 7.5 per cent of his council tax liability.

8. **How council tax reduction entitlement is calculated**

The amount of council tax reduction (CTR) you get may depend on:
- whether you are a pensioner or an adult of working age; *and*
- your 'maximum CTR' under your local scheme (see p142); *and*
- your 'applicable amount' (see p142). This is made up of personal allowances, as well as premiums and components for any special needs; *and*
- how much income and capital you and your partner have (see p150 and p158); *and*

- how many people live with you in the dwelling, their circumstances and income.

If you get the guarantee credit of pension credit (PC), you are automatically passported to maximum CTR (once you have applied for it). You do not, therefore, need to work out applicable amounts, income or capital. In England and Wales, the rules for working-age applicants vary considerably. Contact your local authority for information about the scheme in your area.

Online calculators

Most local authorities have an online benefit calculator on their websites. If you cannot use the internet yourself, you can ask another person to do this for you.[51] The calculator should enable you to put in your details and those of your partner to determine the amount of support for the property which you occupy.

Maximum council tax reductions and eligible council tax

Maximum CTR is your council tax liability, minus any non-dependant deductions (see p147).[52] Until you reach pension age, you may not be entitled to 100 per cent CTR (see p132).

All pensioners whose income and capital are low enough will receive maximum CTR. In England, if you are working age, your maximum CTR may be based on a percentage of your council tax liability minus non-dependant deductions.

Example
Edward, 37, lives in a Bnd B property in Bath and North East Somerset. He receives a single occupier discount. His daily council tax bill is £2.59. However, in Bath and North East Somerset most working-age applicants are expected to pay at least 22 per cent of their council tax liability. Edward is only eligible to receive CTR on the remaining 78 per cent: £2.02 a day, or £14.15 a week. Therefore, Edward's maximum CTR is 78 per cent of his council tax liability.

Applicable amounts

CTR is usually calculated with reference to your applicable amount, a notional figure you are expected to live on, and whether your income is below or above this amount. This will always be the case in Scotland and Wales and if you are a pensioner. Most local authorities in England use an applicable amount when assessing whether you have a 'low income', but there is no requirement that they must do so. You should check whether your local scheme uses all the amounts and qualifying rules set out below.

Your applicable amount is made up of:[53]

- a personal allowance (which is based on whether you are single or part of a couple);
- extra personal allowances for at least the first two dependent children you are responsible for; *and*
- any 'premiums' or 'components' which you or other members of your family (see p129) qualify for because of your circumstances, or the benefits you receive.

This table outlines the most common qualifying circumstances. See the table on p146 for the amounts.

Summary of qualifying conditions for personal allowances, components and premiums

Allowance, component or premium	Condition of entitlement
Personal allowance (claimant and partner)	Paid for you and your partner if you have one. The level paid depends on your age.
Personal allowance (child or young person)	Paid for each child or young person that you or your partner have responsibility for. If you apply in England after 1 April 2018, you will only receive personal allowances for a maximum of two children or young people, unless you are entitled to child tax credit (CTC) for the extra children. The same restriction applies to new children or young people joining your household.
Work-related activity component*	Paid if you or your partner receive this component with your employment and support allowance (ESA)
Support component*	Paid if you or your partner receive this component with your ESA.
Family premium	Paid if your application includes a personal allowance for a child or a young person. **Note:** this is not included for applications made after 1 May 2016.

Disability premium	Paid if you are: – a working-age applicant; *and* – not assessed or treated as having limited capability for work; *and* – you, or your partner, are: – 'long-term sick' since before 27 October 2008; *or* – receiving disability living allowance (DLA), personal independence payment (PIP), the disability or severe disability element of working tax credit (WTC) or another specified disability benefit. For a full list of disability benefits, the meaning of limited capability for work and the transitional rules which allow you to keep the premium after transferring to ESA, see CPAG's *Welfare Benefits and Tax Credits Handbook*.
Disabled child premium	Paid for each child or young person you are responsible for who: – is (or has recently ceased to be) registered blind or severely sight impaired; *or* – receives PIP; *or* – receives DLA.
Enhanced disability premium (sometimes called the 'disability income guarantee')	Paid if you are a working-age applicant and you or your partner (provided s/he is below pension age): – receive enhanced rate of the daily living component of PIP; *or* – receive highest rate of the care component of DLA; *or* – if you are the CTR applicant, have limited capability for work-related activity (ie, have been placed in the 'support group'). This premium is paid at a single and couple rate. Only one member of the couple needs to qualify in order for you to be paid the couple rate. An enhanced disability premium is also paid (at the single rate) for each child or young person you are responsible for who receives PIP or DLA at the rates listed above.

Severe disability premium**	If you are **single**, this premium is paid if: – you receive one of the following benefits: daily living component of PIP; middle or highest rate of the care component of DLA; attendance allowance (AA); or an equivalent benefit (see CPAG's *Welfare Benefits and Tax Credits Handbook*); *and* – you do not have a non-dependant living with you (see CPAG's *Welfare Benefits and Tax Credits Handbook* for the exceptions to this rule); *and* – no one is paid carer's allowance (CA) or the carer element of universal credit (UC) for looking after you. For **couples**, the rules are more complicated. If both of you satisfy all three conditions above, you are paid two premiums. If one of you satisfies all three conditions and the other satisfies the first two, you are paid one premium. If you, as the applicant, satisfy all three conditions and your partner does not but is registered blind or severely sight impaired, you are paid one premium. If this applies to you and your partner is the applicant, consider changing who makes the application.
Carer premium**	Paid if you or your partner are entitled to CA, or were entitled to it during the last eight weeks.

*These components are normally paid whichever partner qualifies. However, each claim only includes one of these premiums. If you and your partner both receive ESA, with different components, your CTR calculation will only include the component paid to the claimant. If the claimant receives the work-related activity component, you should consider swapping the claim.

One of the conditions of entitlement to the severe disability premium is that no one should receive CA in respect of you. If a carer claims, and **is paid, CA, the disabled person for whom s/he cares could lose entitlement to the severe disability premium. Always consider who will be 'better off' in this situation and seek advice if necessary.

See CPAG's *Welfare Benefits and Tax Credits Handbook* for more information about the applicable amounts. Normally the rules for calculating applicable amounts for CTR are the same as those used in calculating housing benefit (HB).

Applicable amounts for 2018/19[54]

Personal allowances		England	Wales	Scotland
Single	Under 25	£57.90	£60.25	£57.90
	Under 25 (on main phase ESA)	£73.10	£76.10	£73.10
	25 or over	£73.10	£76.10	£73.10
Lone parent	18 or over	£73.10	£76.10	£73.10
Couple	One or both 18 or over	£114.85	£119.50	£114.85
Dependent child/ young person	Under 20	£66.90	£66.90	£83.63
Pensioners	Single, under 65	£163.00	£163.00	£163.00
	Single, 65 or over	£176.40	£176.40	££176.40
	Couples, both under 65	£248.80	£248.80	£248.80
	Couple, one or both 65 or over	£263.80	£263.80	£263.80
Components				
Work-related activity		£29.05	£29.05	£29.05
Support		£37.65	£37.65	£37.65
Premiums				
Carer		£36.00	£36.00	£36.00
Disability	Single	£33.55	£33.55	£33.55
	Couple	£47.80	£47.80	£47.80
Disabled child		£62.86	£62.86	£62.86
Enhanced disability	Single	£16.40	£16.40	£16.40
	Couple	£23.55	£23.55	£23.55
	Child	£25.48	£24.48	£25.48
Severe disability	One qualifies	£64.30	£64.30	£64.30
	Two qualify	£128.60	£128.60	£128.60
Family*	Ordinary rate	£17.45	£17.45	£17.45
	Some lone parents	£22.20	£22.20	£22.20

* Not included in new applications after 1 May 2016.

In calculating your entitlement to CTR, the local authority will compare your applicable amount to your income. See p150 for what counts as income.

Income less than or equal to applicable amount

If you are a pensioner and your income is equal to, or less than, your applicable amount, 100 per cent of your maximum council tax liability can be covered by CTR (see p142). If you get the guarantee credit of PC, your income and capital are counted as zero.

If you are working age and your income in any week is equal to, or less than, your applicable amount, it does not preclude you from being liable for some of the council tax in England, although certain groups may receive a 100 per cent reduction under a local scheme. In Scotland and Wales, you should receive CTR equal to your maximum CTR.

Income is greater than the applicable amount

Where your income is greater than your applicable amount, work out the difference. Your CTR equals you maximum CTR minus a set percentage of this figure (known as the 'taper'). For all pensioners and working-age applicants in Wales and Scotland, this 'taper' is always applied at the rate of 20 per cent.

In many areas of England, a higher taper is applied by the local authority under its scheme. English local authorities may also set a lower taper, and some do.

Non-dependant deductions

If other people normally live with you in your home who are not part of your 'family' (see p129) and are not also liable for council tax (called 'non-dependants'), a set deduction may be made from the amount of your council tax when calculating your maximum CTR. These are non-liable adults who are expected to help you to pay the council tax bill but do not come within the hierarchy of liability imposed by section 6 of the Local Government Finance Act 1992 (see p71). It is assumed that the non-dependant makes a contribution towards your outgoings, whether or not s/he does so in practice. Examples of non-dependants are adult sons or daughters, or older relatives who share your home. You may therefore need to ask your non-dependant(s) for a contribution. A person can only be treated as living with you if s/he shares some accommodation with you. A person does not normally live with you if s/he has not been there long enough to regard your home as her/his normal home.

Students and partners do not count as non-dependants, nor does anyone disregarded for the purposes of discount (see p101).

A 'non-dependant' is any person who normally resides with you. Certain people are not non dependants. These include:
- a member of your family (see p129);
- a child or young person who is living with you but is not a member of your household (see p129);
- a person who makes payments of rent on a commercial basis to you or your partner. **Note:** although no non-dependant deduction can be made for him/ her, the rent s/he pays can count as your income;
- certain live-in carers;
- a person who is jointly and severally liable for council tax with you.

Example

Sara, 72, gets PC guarantee credit. Her non-dependent son, who is in receipt of contribution-based JSA, lives with her.

Weekly council tax liability	£23.36
Less non-dependant deductions	£3.90
Maximum CTR	£19.46

Sara is awarded £19.46 CTR and her son is expected to pay £3.90 a week towards her council tax liability.

Exceptions to rules on non-dependant deductions

Even if a non-dependant lives with you, no deduction is made in the circumstances detailed below. These exceptions always apply if you are a pensioner, and for working-age claimants in Wales and Scotland. Local authorities in England have discretion to vary the rules. Check with your local authority to see which rules apply in your area.

No non-dependant deduction is to be made **if you or (in England and Scotland) your partner** are:[55]

- receiving AA;
- receiving the care component of DLA;
- receiving the daily living component of PIP;
- receiving an armed forces independence payment;
- blind, severely partially sighted, or treated as blind (this also applies in Wales if you partner qualifies).

No deduction is made **for a non-dependant** who:[56]

- although s/he resides with you, has her/his normal home elsewhere (see p72 and p130);
- is on UC and does not have any earned income (in England and Wales only);
- is on income support (IS), PC, income-based jobseeker's allowance (JSA) or income-related ESA;
- is receiving a training allowance paid for doing youth training;
- is a full-time student;
- has been in hospital for more than 52 weeks. Separate stays which are not more than 28 days apart are added together when calculating the 52 weeks;
- is a member of the armed forces or reserve forces and is absent on operations (this only applies in England and Scotland); *or*
- is disregarded for the purposes of a council tax discount (see p101).

Amount of non-dependant deduction

The amount of non-dependant deduction to be applied each week is set out in regulations. In England, your local authority can chose to set different amounts in its scheme for working-age applicants. The deduction reduces the amount of CTR you are awarded.[57]

England

If the non-dependant is:	Deduction
Working 16 hours a week with an average weekly gross income of:	
Below £202.85	£3.90
£202.85 to £351.64	£7.90
£351.65 to £436.89	£9.95
£436.90 or above	£11.90
Not working or working less than 16 hours a week.	£3.90

Wales

If the non-dependant is:	Deduction
Working 16 hours a week with an average weekly gross income of:	
Below £205.00	£4.25
£205.00 to £354.99	£8.70
£355.00 to £439.99	£10.95
£440.00 or above	£13.10
Not working or working less than 16 hours a week.	£4.25

Scotland

If the non-dependant is:	Deduction
Working 16 hours a week with an average weekly gross income of:	
Below £204.00	£4.05
£204.00 to £353.99	£8.10
£354.00 to £438.99	£10.25
£439.00 or above	£12.29
Not working or working less than 16 hours a week.	£4.05

Certain sums may be disregarded when calculating the income of a non-dependant. AA, DLA, PIP and armed forces independence payment are disregarded from the non-dependant's weekly gross income. However, English local authorities are not required to make these disregards for working-age applicants. Certain charitable funds (eg, to compensate for medical injuries and acts of terror) are also disregarded.[58]

8

Example

Geraldine, 70, is single and claims guarantee credit of PC. She lives alone in a Band D property in England. Her son, Ben, comes to live with her. He works 30 hours a week and has a gross income of £410 a week. Her CTR calculation is:

Before Ben moves in:

Weekly council tax	£28.88
Minus 25 per cent single occupier discount	£7.22
Net liability	£21.66
Weekly CTR	£21.66

So Geraldine does not have to pay any council tax

After Ben moves in:

Weekly council tax	£28.88
No discount so:	
Net liability	£28.88
Minus non-dependant deduction	£9.95
Maximum CTR (paid in full)	£18.93

So Geraldine is required to pay £9.95 council tax

Shortly after Ben moved in, however, Geraldine was awarded AA. In consequence, no non-dependant deduction was made. She then received CTR on the full weekly liability of £28.88.

Calculation of income

Income is calculated on a weekly basis.[59] The local authority will include earned and unearned income which you and you partner have. This includes:

- wages;
- earnings from self-employment;
- social security benefits; *and*
- payments from a trust or a charity.

'Tariff income' is also included. This is the presumed income you are deemed to obtain from savings or other capital assets. Your actual income from these sources is ignored (see p157).

If you a pensioner (see p132), the regulations lay down what counts as your income. Any monies not specified in the regulations are ignored when calculating your income. Some income is 'disregarded' either in full or in part.[60]

If you are of working age in Wales, Scotland and under most English local schemes, all income is taken into account unless it is specifically 'disregarded', either by the national regulations or by your local council's scheme, as the case may be. In most cases, the amount of your income will be quite clear. The rules for calculating your income from work or self-employment can be more complex (see p154). Consult the regulations or see CPAG's *Welfare Benefits and Tax Credits Handbook* to help you interpret them. The rules for CTR usually mirror those for HB.

If you get pension credit: income rules for pensioners

If you or your partner get the **guarantee credit** of PC, the whole of your income and capital is disregarded and you automatically qualify for maximum CTR. Remember, however, that you may have non-dependant deductions (see p147).[61]

If you get the **savings credit** of PC but not the guarantee credit, the local authority uses the Pension Service's assessment of your income and capital to calculate your CTR, and counts your savings credit as income. However, it may 'disregard' more of your earned income (under the rules on p155).

If you do not get pension credit: income rules for pensioners

If you are a pensioner but do not get PC, your income is assessed by the local authority. Your income is compared to your applicable amount (see p142) to determine how much CTR you get. **Note**: if you have capital of more than £16,000, you are not entitled to CTR.

The following are counted as income – however, often all or some of the payment is disregarded in the calculation:[62]

- earned income from employment or self-employment (see p154 for how this is calculated and p155 for how much is disregarded). **Note**: statutory sick pay (SSP) and statutory maternity/adoption/paternity/shared parental pay are treated as earnings;
- tax credits. CTC is disregarded in full. If deductions are being made from your tax credits to recover an overpayment, the amount counted towards income is the amount you are paid after deductions;
- retirement pension income;
- income from annuities (the capital value of the annuity itself is ignored);
- war pensions. Any disability increases are disregarded in full, but local authorities only need to disregard £10 of the war pension itself although they have discretion to disregard more. Check your council's policy;
- AA, DLA, PIP and armed forces independence payment (disregarded in full);
- child benefit and guardian's allowance (disregarded in full);
- social fund payments (disregarded in full);
- Christmas bonus (disregarded);
- HB (disregarded);
- widow's pension and bereavement support payment (however, the first £15 of the latter is disregarded);
- certain other payments.

As well as the benefits identified above, certain other forms of income are disregarded.[63] Common cases are listed below. For more details, consult the regulations or CPAG's *Welfare Benefits and Tax Credits Handbook* (the rules for CTR mirror the HB rules for people over PC age).

- £15 of any maintenance payments paid for you or your partner by someone to whom you or your partner are, or were, married or had/have a civil partnership with. In Wales, this only applies if a family premium is included in your applicable amount. Maintenance paid for a child or young person is disregarded in full.
- In certain circumstances, income from an annuity purchased with a loan secured on your home (a 'home income plan') which is used to pay the interest on that loan.
- Certain contributions paid to your son or daughter aged under 25 while in education.
- Payments from a discretionary trust. However, if these are used to pay essential bills, there is a weekly limit on the amount of the disregard.
- Compensation for personal injury. In some cases, this is extends to payments to compensate for 'accident...or disease'.[64]
- The first £20 of income from a tenant or boarder who shares your premises is always disregarded. If you provide board and lodgings, 50 per cent of the remaining income is disregarded as well.

Note: the disregards for maintenance and contributions to students listed above are subject to an overall limit of £20.

Income rules for working-age applicants

In Wales and Scotland, all of your income is counted unless it is specifically disregarded under the national scheme. If you receive IS, income-based JSA or income-related ESA, your actual income and capital are disregarded and you are automatically entitled to your maximum CTR (see p142).

If you receive UC, your local authority usually uses the Department for Work and Pension's (DWP's) assessment of your income and capital, to which it adds your UC entitlement, to calculate your CTR. Anything else is disregarded. However, local authorities in England have discretion to treat your income differently. In Scotland, your local authority can estimate an average where your UC and other payments fluctuate from one assessed income period to another.

In all other cases, the local authority makes its own assessment of your income. See p154 for how your earned income is calculated, and below for the rules about income other than earnings. The rules set out below apply throughout Scotland and, with minor variations, which are indicated, in Wales. Local authorities in England have discretion to assess some forms of income differently. You will need to check with your council about the rules in your area, but the general framework will usually still apply.

Benefits and tax credits

The following benefits are disregarded **in full:**[65]
- HB;
- DLA, PIP, AA and constant attendance allowance paid with industrial injuries benefit;
- armed forces independence payments (in England and Wales but not in Scotland);
- child benefit and guardian's allowance;
- social fund payments;
- Christmas bonus;
- bereavement support payment is treated as capital and, in Scotland, is ignored for 52 weeks from payment;
- constant attendance allowance or mobility supplement paid with a war pension. In Scotland, the whole of the war pension is disregarded.

There are **partial disregards** of the following benefits:
- the first £15 of a widowed parent's allowance is disregarded;
- if deductions are being made from your tax credits to recover an overpayment from a previous year, the amount counted towards your income is the amount of WTC or CTC awarded **less** the amount of that deduction;[66]
- the first £10 of a war disablement pension. However, local authorities in England and Wales have discretion to disregard more.

Other income

A number of other forms unearned income are disregarded.[67] Common examples are listed below. For more details, consult the regulations or CPAG's *Welfare Benefits and Tax Credits Handbook* (the rules for CTR usually mirror the HB rules in this regard).
- Maintenance payments for children included in your family are disregarded in full, provided they are made by a 'liable relative'. A liable relative is the child's parent or step-parent or someone whom it is reasonable to treat as the child's father because he is making payments. £15 of maintenance payments to you or your partner can be disregarded. In Wales, this applies only if you are entitled to a family premium. The payments must always be made by the recipient's former partner.[68]
- Compensation for personal injury. In some cases, this is extends to payments to compensate for 'accident... disease'.
- The first £20 of income from a tenant or boarder who shares your premises is always disregarded. If you provide board and lodgings, 50 per cent of the remaining income is disregarded as well.
- If you let property other than your own home, the capital value of which is disregarded, any rent used to pay the mortgage payments, council tax and water charges on the property are disregarded for the period covered by the

rent, but the remaining rent you receive counts as income, whether or not you have any other letting costs.

- If you let property and its capital value is not disregarded, all letting costs can be deducted and the net rent counts as capital, not as income. You will still, however, be deemed to receive 'tariff income' on the capital valuation of the property. In most cases, the capital value of the property itself is likely to exceed £16,000 (or your local authority's capital limit, if that is lower) and so you are not entitled to any CTR. However, in some circumstances (eg, if you have sitting tenant or there is 'planning blight'), you may be able to argue that the likely resale value is so low that the council should ignore it.

- Any regular voluntary payments from charities or individuals (such as friends and family) are disregarded. One-off or irregular payments count as capital.

- Certain payments from public bodies, including local authority welfare provision, discretionary housing payments, social services payments and payments from trusts set up by central government to compensate the victims of medical accidents and disasters, are also disregarded.

Note: the disregards for maintenance and bereavement payments listed above are subject to an overall limit of £20.

Earned income

The rules below apply to pensioners and to working-age applicants in Wales and Scotland. English local authorities can set their own rules for working-age applicants but they are often very similar. Earnings are income from employment, self-employment or any office or position you hold. This includes all bonuses and commissions, payments in lieu of notice where employment ends, holiday pay and retainers. SSP and statutory maternity/adoption/paternity/shared parental pay are also treated as earnings. [69]

Self-employed average weekly earnings are based on either a yearly amount if your business is established or a different period if you have recently started your business. If there is a change in the pattern of the business, the period can be adjusted to provide the weekly amount which most accurately reflects your income.[70]

Expenses counted as earnings

Any expenses you receive that are not wholly incurred for the performance of a job, including traveling expenses between your home and place of employment, count as income.

Amounts not included as earnings from employment

The following amounts are *not* included as income from employment for CTR purposes:[71]

- any payment in kind – eg, a free meal;

- payments in respect of expenses wholly, exclusively and necessarily incurred in the performance of your job or employment;
- redundancy payments;
- occupational pensions;
- any lump-sum payment made under the Iron and Steel Employees Re-adaptation Benefits Scheme;
- compensation awarded by an employment tribunal for unfair dismissal or unlawful discrimination;
- any payment of expenses arising from being involved with a service user group – eg, a group consulted by a health board or public authority;
- some non-cash vouchers.

Your earnings are considered net of tax and national insurance (NI).

Sums disregarded from earnings

The following sums may be disregarded from earnings. If you and your partner both work, your earnings are aggregated and the highest disregard for which you qualify is used, plus the £17.10 disregard if you qualify for that.[72]

£25 disregard	You are a lone parent (unless claiming IS, income-based JSA or income-related ESA).
£20 disregard	You or your partner qualify for a disability premium, severe disability premium, carer premium or the work-related activity or support component.
	You or you partner are employed as a part-time firefighter, lifeboat crew, auxiliary coastguard or a member of any territorial or reserve force.
	You or your partner get main phase ESA, long-term incapacity benefit, severe disablement allowance (SDA), AA, DLA, PIP, armed forces independence payment or the disability or severe disability element of WTC.
£17.10 disregard	You or your partner get the 30-hour element of WTC.
	You or your partner are aged over 25 and work 30 hours a week or more.
	You or your partner work 16 hours a week or more and get the disability premium, work-related activity component, support component or (in Wales only) family premium. **Note:** like the childcare disregard (see p156), this disregard can be applied in full or part to your WTC if your earnings are less than the disregards you qualify for.
£10 disregard	None of the above apply and you are a member of a couple.
£5 disregard	None of the above apply and you are single.

Note: if you are doing 'permitted work' while claiming UC or ESA (or NI credits on the basis of limited capability for work), all of your earnings from permitted work are disregarded. See CPAG's *Welfare Benefits and Tax Credits Handbook* for an explanation of 'permitted work'.

These disregards apply to pensioners in England, Wales and Scotland. They also apply for to working-age applicants in Wales and Scotland. Local authorities in England have discretion to use higher or lower disregards for working-age applicants or not to apply a disregard at all – check the rules applied under your council's scheme.

Childcare disregard

If you have earned income, in some circumstances the amount you pay for certain kinds of childcare can also be disregarded from your earnings subject to a weekly maximum. These are applied to any earned income which you and your partner have left after the disregards on p155. If your eligible childcare costs are greater than the remaining earned income, the remainder can be disregarded from any WTC you receive.

What childcare costs are eligible and who qualifies

Eligible childcare costs are any that you pay to a registered childcare provider, an after school club or another provider specified in the regulations.[73] To be eligible, you must be:

- a lone parent working 16 hours or more a week; *or*
- a member of a couple, both of whom work 16 hours a week or more; *or*
- a member of a couple, one of whom works 16 hours a week or more, provided that the other partner is:
  - incapacitated – ie, s/he is aged over 80 or s/he receives main phase ESA or another sickness or disability benefit prescribed in the regulations;
  - a hospital inpatient; *or*
  - in prison.

In some circumstances, you can be treated as working 16 hours a week – eg, if you are getting SSP or ESA and were working at least 16 hours a week immediately before.

How much in childcare costs can be disregarded

If you are a pensioner, or a working-age applicant in Wales or Scotland, your eligible childcare costs can be disregarded up to the following weekly maximums:

- £175 for one child;
- £300 for two or more children.

If you are a working-age applicant in England, there is no requirement for your authority to disregard a set, or any, amount.

Tariff income from capital

The local authority will add to your actual income a notional figure for the income which you are 'deemed' to derive from any capital you have that is not disregarded. This 'tariff income' is worked out in the following way.[74]

- If you are a pensioner: the first £10,000 of your capital is ignored and you are assumed to earn £1 from each £500 of capital or part thereof above that level.
- If you are a working-age applicant in Wales or Scotland, the first £6,000 of your capital is ignored and you are assumed to earn £1 for each £250 of capital or part thereof above that level. In England, the capital limits and tariff income rules will be set by your local authority.

The income taper

The amount of CTR you are entitled to is subject to an income taper which applies if your income goes above the applicable amount. The threshold, set by the regulations for pensioners in England and all applicants in Wales and Scotland, reduces the amount of CTR by 20 pence for every extra £1 of income that is received.[75]

If you are of working age in England, the taper varies between local authorities and can be greater than 20 per cent.

Example
Ivana and Franek are pensioners aged 64 years and they do not qualify for any premiums. Their applicable amount is £248.80 and their occupational pensions total £307.65 a week. Their entitlement is worked out in the following way.

The difference between their income and their applicable amount is £307.65 − £248.80 = £58.85.

The taper is applied to this 'difference figure' at the rate of 20 pence in the pound (£58.85 × 20% = £11.77).

£11.77 is deducted from Ivana and Franek's maximum CTR of £22.63. This means that they will receive £10.86 CTR.

Calculating income

All income figures are calculated on a weekly basis, so your earnings and other income have to be converted into a weekly amount if necessary.[76]

- In a case where the payment is for a calendar month, multiply the amount of the payment by 12 and divide the total by 52. If you are on UC, your council will use the DWP assessment of your income and use this method to convert this to a weekly figure.

- In a case where the payment is for three months, multiply the amount of the payment by four and divide the total by 52.
- In a case where the payment is for is a year, divide the amount of the payment by 52.
- In any other case, divide the amount of the payment by the number of days in the period in respect of which it is made and multiply the result by seven.

Example

Marcia and Themba both work. They are paid £83.60 tax credits every Tuesday, including the childcare element. Their actual childcare costs are £48 a week for an after-school scheme. Themba's employers pay his wages monthly. He takes home £864 after tax and NI. Marcia, who works shifts, is paid weekly. She takes home £79.50 most weeks, and is paid £39.70 extra one week in four when she works nights. Marcia is paid £137.60 child benefit every four weeks. Their weekly income is as follows.

Tax credits		£83.60
Themba's wages	(£864 x 12 = £10,368 ÷ 52)	£199.38
Marcia's wages	(averaged over her 'recognisable cycle' of four weeks: £79.50 x 4 + £39.70 = £357.70)	
	(£357.70 ÷ 28 = £12.775 x 7)	£89.43
Child benefit	(£137.60 ÷ 28 x 7)	£34.40
Total income		£406.81

£10 of their earnings is disregarded because they are a couple. The further £17.10 is disregarded because they satisfy the qualifying criteria (see p155), as are their childcare costs. So the actual income used to calculate their CTR is £334.71.

Calculation of capital

CTR is only available to people with capital below certain fixed limits. The capital limit for a pensioner is £16,000 and any pensioner who has capital above this is not entitled to CTR, unless s/he receives the guarantee credit of PC. The same limit applies to all working-age applicants in Wales and Scotland.[77] Local authorities in England can set any capital limit for their working-age local schemes.

Where capital cannot accurately be determined, the local authority may estimate a figure.

What counts as capital

The term 'capital' is not defined. In general, it means lump-sum or one-off payments rather than a series of payments – eg, it includes savings, property and statutory redundancy payments.

The capital rules for a reduction are set out in detail in the regulations and must be the whole of your capital and include any arrears of benefit owed from an earlier claim.

Where you have two accounts with the same bank, one of which is in credit and the other is overdrawn, the amount of the overdraft should be deducted from the account in credit to determine the actual figure of capital.[78]

Disregarded capital

Some capital receipts are disregarded for a fixed period, others indefinitely. Disregarded capital includes:[79]
- any personal possessions;
- the value of the home you live in (but not more than one home);
- amounts paid under an insurance policy for loss or damage to your home and to your personal possessions, for one year;
- assets from a former business which are in the process of being disposed of;
- any premises acquired which you intend to occupy as your home within 26 weeks of the date of acquisition (or longer period if reasonable);
- any premises which you intend to occupy as your home but which need essential repairs or alterations to render them fit for such occupation, for a period of 26 weeks from the date you first take steps to carry out the repairs, or as long as is needed for them to be completed;
- any premises occupied in whole or in part by a relative who has reached the qualifying age for PC (see p132) or who is incapacitated;
- premises occupied by a former partner as her/his home, in specified circumstances;
- any case where you are taking 'reasonable steps' to dispose of an interest in capital – eg, selling your home to pay for care costs or entering sheltered accommodation, for 26 weeks or longer if reasonable;
- certain business assets.

Rules differentiate between capital in the UK and outside it. Consult the regulations and CPAG's *Welfare Benefits and Tax Credits Handbook* for more information. The rules usually mirror those for HB.

Notional capital

In certain circumstances, you may be treated as having capital that you do not actually have. You are treated as possessing capital of which you have deprived yourself for the purpose of securing entitlement to CTR or increasing the amount of CTR you receive. Cases where this occurs are likely to be rare, and the local authority should have evidence for such a claim. However, some authorities have been known to decide that applicants have done this simply because their savings have been reduced prior to an application.

The regulations specify for pensioners, and you can argue if you are working-age, that you should not treated as depriving yourself of capital, if you dispose of it as a means of:

- reducing or paying debts you owe; *or*
- purchasing goods or services, if the expenditure is reasonable in the circumstances.

For example, if you spend your savings to have special medical treatment, this would be reasonable.[80]

Where you hold capital jointly with another person, it may be presumed that you have equal shares, unless you provide evidence to contrary.[81]

Extended reduction on entering work

If you have been continuously getting IS, income-based JSA, income-related or contributory ESA, incapacity benefit or SDA for 26 weeks and it stops because you or your partner start work or your hours or earnings in your existing job increase, you may be entitled to an 'extended reduction' of your CTR for four weeks.[82] The change must be expected to last for at least five weeks. If you qualify, you receive the same amount in CTR as you did before you started work or increased your hours or pay.

Local authorities in England and Wales can vary the conditions for extended reduction payments, but these are minimum requirements in Wales and for pensioners in England.[83] Contact your local authority to report the change in your circumstances and it will assess whether you are entitled to an extended reduction.

After the extended reduction period, you may still qualify for CTR but your entitlement is reassessed on the basis of your new circumstances – check with your local authority.

Example
Deanna, 34, has been getting income-related ESA for 32 weeks. She starts a full-time job on 5 November 2018. She receives an extended reduction for four weeks to 3 December 2018. From 4 December 2018, if she still qualifies for CTR under her local authority's scheme, Deanna is entitled to a new award of CTR. She does not need to make a new application, but does need to provide the information the local authority needs to calculate her new CTR.

Continuing reduction on claiming pension credit

To avoid problems caused by delays in reassessing your CTR when you move from UC, IS, income-based JSA or income-related ESA onto PC, provided you otherwise continue to qualify for CTR, you continue to receive it, normally at the same rate as before this happened.[84] You qualify for continuing payments if:

- your partner has claimed PC and the DWP has certified this; *or*
- your UC, IS, income-based JSA or income-related ESA ceased because you reached pension age (see p132) or, if you were getting income-based JSA or income-related ESA beyond that age, this ceased because you turned 65. The DWP must certify this and that you are required to claim or have claimed PC (or are treated as having done so).

You get continuing payments for four weeks.

9. Applying for council tax reduction

You should apply for council tax reduction (CTR) as soon as you think you might be entitled.

If you are not eligible, you may still apply for a discretionary reduction (see p167).

Making an application

An application for CTR may be made:[85]

- in writing on a properly completed application form. Forms are available from your local authority, or you may be able to download one from its website;
- online (Scottish councils do not need to make this means available); *or*
- by telephone, if the local authority has published a number for this purpose.

A written application must be made to your local authority's 'designated office'. You must provide any information and evidence required. You can claim in some other written form (eg, by letter), as long as the written information and evidence you provide is sufficient. An application made on a form provided by a local authority is properly completed if it is completed in accordance with the instructions on the form, including providing information and evidence.[86]

Check with the local authority that any application you make has been received. If you are applying for CTR in writing, keep a copy of your application and proof of posting or receipt in case queries arise.

Applying in advance

Unless you are living abroad, you can apply in advance if you think you are going to become eligible in the future – eg, because you know that you are going to have a drop in income. Your application can be made up to 13 weeks before you become eligible.[87]

In England and Scotland, you can make an advance application up to 17 weeks before you become eligible if you are a pensioner and in the 17 weeks before you, or you partner, reach pension age (see p132). If you are going to become liable to pay council tax for the first time, the local authority must assess your application, but you may not be able to do this so far in advance. Although the local authority does not have to accept your application, it should not refuse to do so unreasonably.

Supply of further information

Where possible, your application should be accompanied by all the information and evidence needed to assess it, but you should not delay your claim just because you do not have all the evidence ready to send. Even if you provide all the information required with your application, the local authority might ask you for further evidence or information. If the local authority requests further information, you must supply it within one month of a request being made, or such longer time as the local authority considers reasonable.[88]

If you think the local authority has made a wrong decision, you can appeal (see p165 and Chapter 11) and also make a formal complaint to the council.

Applications by couples

If you are part of a couple (see p129), your application for CTR is to be made by you or your partner, as agreed between yourselves. If you do not agree between yourselves, the local authority may pick the person who is required to make the application.[89] In some cases, how much CTR you are paid can change depending on who makes the application – eg, an enhanced disability premium is only paid if the applicant has limited capability for work-related activity (see p142).

Amending and withdrawing applications

Your application may be amended at any time before a decision has been made on it. This gives an opportunity to include new information or changes in circumstances or to correct any errors. Any amendments are treated as if they were included in your original application.

You may withdraw your application at any time before a decision has been made on it. A notice of withdrawal has effect from when it is received by the local authority. Where you amend or withdraw by telephone, you may be required to confirm in writing.

Notification of decisions

In **England and Wales**, your local authority must make its decision within 14 days, or as soon as reasonably practicable thereafter. It must notify you, and any other person affected, of the decision in writing.[90]

When your entitlement begins and ends

In **Scotland and for pensioners in England**, the general rule is that your first day of entitlement to CTR is the Monday following your date of application (or the date on which your application is treated as having been made).[91] If that is a Monday, you have to wait until the following Monday to be paid. In **Wales**, your first day of entitlement is the exact date that you apply.[92]

In **Scotland and for pensioners in England**, if you become liable for the first time for a dwelling in which you are resident, you are entitled from that reduction week.[93] This may arise where the circumstances of the liable person changes – eg, where s/he ceases to be a student.

You do not have to reapply for CTR. Your award continues indefinitely. However, your entitlement to CTR ends if your circumstances change in a way that means you no longer satisfy the rules described in this chapter. **Note:** if you stop claiming income support, income-based jobseeker's allowance or income-related employment and support allowance, your entitlement to CTR continues without your having to make a fresh application, but your new circumstances could affect the amount of CTR you get. You need to provide any evidence required by your council.

Backdating

Working age applicants usually have to show 'continuous good cause' for backdating. For more about what constitutes 'good cause', see CPAG's *Welfare Benefits and Tax Credits Handbook*.

- In **England**, backdating for working-age applicants is limited to that provided in your local authority's scheme, although many allow up to six months backdating for good cause.
- The **Welsh** regulations allow backdating for up to three months if you show continuous good cause; however, local authorities are permitted to extend this limit and may also set more generous criteria for allowing backdating.[94]
- In **Scotland**, you can request backdating for up to six months.[95]

If you are a **pensioner**, CTR can be backdated for up to three months from the date you applied, so long as you were entitled throughout. There is no need to show 'good cause'.[96] This can be extended where you have made a claim for the guarantee credit of pension credit (PC) and apply for CTR within one month of this claim being awarded, but your award of CTR cannot begin more than three months before your claim for PC was made.[97]

Reporting changes in circumstances

It is your duty to report any change in your circumstances which you might reasonably be expected to know might affect your right to, or the amount of, CTR.[98] You, or a person acting on your behalf, must notify the authority of any changes between the making of an application and a decision being made on it. Similarly, changes must be reported after the decision is made, including at any time you are in receipt of a reduction.

Examples of changes that you must inform the local authority about
Whenever you have a change of address.
Whenever any person joins or leaves your household.
Whenever the income or capital of anyone in the property changes so as to affect your CTR.
Changes in the amount of tax credits or benefits received.
Whenever anyone in the property starts or finishes employment.
Whenever there is a change of ownership of the property in which you live.

In **England and Wales**, you must report the change within 21 days of the change occurring, or if later, as soon as reasonably practicable after the change occurs.[99] In **Scotland**, there is no set time limit to report changes. Do this promptly to the office handling your application. You can do this in writing, or by telephone if your local authority has published a number for that purpose. If your local authority authorises it, you can also report changes by electronic means, such as email or an online form. However, it is always best to report a change in writing and to keep a copy in case of a dispute in the future.

There is also a special service called 'Tell Us Once' for births and deaths. You can report these changes to the local authority (and, in England, to a county council) office. Check with your local authority (at the register office) to see if it provides this service, or visit the 'Tell Us Once' page on the gov.uk website for a list of the local authorities which offer this service.

If you fail to report a change in circumstances, your CTR may be ended and you become liable to pay the tax for the period concerned. If you are considered to have deliberately acted falsely or dishonestly, you may also be guilty of an offence.

If you move to a new local authority area, report this change to your old authority and apply for CTR in your new local authority.

Note: what is reasonable may vary from person to person and from area to area, in the same way that CTR schemes vary between different local authorities. For instance, it may not always be reasonable to expect you to report changes promptly if English or Welsh is not your first language. Similarly, disabled people may be prevented by their physical or mental impairments from reporting changes as quickly as other people. However, if you could get help from another person to report a change but do not do so, any delay is less likely to be considered reasonable.

10. **If you disagree with a council tax reduction decision**

Challenging a decision about your council tax reduction

England and Wales

You have a right of appeal against decisions made by the local authority about your council tax reduction (CTR). Your local authority scheme should contain details of your right of appeal, and the decision notification the local authority issues you about your CTR award should explain how to appeal.[100]

You can appeal decisions about your entitlement or the amount of reduction awarded.[101] This includes decisions about your entitlement to, or the amount of, a discretionary council tax reduction (see p167).[102]

Before you can appeal a decision, you must first challenge the council's decision. This is referred to as a 'notice of appeal'. The notice must be in writing and should explain why you disagree with the local authority's decision – eg, because the council has established the wrong facts or did not apply the regulations properly. The authority must consider the matters raised in your notice of appeal and inform you in writing either that it does not feel that your challenge is well founded, and give its reasons, or state the steps it will take to resolve the issue – eg, look at the matter again, or award the reduction to which you are entitled.[103]

- In **England,** because CTR and housing benefit (HB) are administered together, if your appeal is challenging a decision that affects both benefits, it makes sense to lodge it within one month of the decision (the time limit to ask the authority to revise its HB decision). In other cases, it is advisable to appeal within a month, but you can issue a notice of appeal at any time.
- In **Wales,** you must start your appeal within one month of the decision or of the written explanation of that decision.[104]

Correspondence with the local authority
It is advisable to refer to the right of appeal in the initial letter you send to the local authority. In the case of a dispute over entitlement to CTR, a calculation or the amount of CTR you are entitled to, a letter can, for example, include the following line: 'In the event that you cannot change your decision, please treat this letter as notice of appeal established under section 16 of the Local Government Finance Act 1992.'

If you are not satisfied with the response of the local authority, or if it fails to respond within two months, you may appeal to the Valuation Tribunal for England (VTE) or the Valuation Tribunal for Wales (VTW). You should do this within a further two months (see Chapter 11).[105] Contact details can be found at www.valuationtribunal.gov.uk or www.valuation-tribunals-wales.org.uk.

If you do not start your appeal within this time limit, unless there are reasons beyond your control which prevented you from doing so, the valuation tribunal may strike out your appeal.[106]

In exceptional circumstances, the High Court may also consider applications for judicial review concerning the failure of local authorities to properly consider and review applications (see p292).[107]

Scotland

If you disagree with the local authority's decision on your CTR application, you can request that the local authority review its decision on your CTR application in the same way as described above for England and Wales. You must make the request within two months of the decision on your request, stating what you disagree with.[108]

The local authority must considered the matter and inform you in writing within two months of its decision.[109]

If you are still dissatisfied with the local authority's decision following its review, you have a further right of review by the Council Tax Reduction Review Panel (CTRRP) within 42 days of the date of the local authority's notification.[110]

Review panel members are normally solicitors or legally qualified individuals of at least five years' or more standing.[111]

A further review of a determination on an application is normally heard by one member of the panel. It is an oral hearing unless you, the local authority and the member of the panel undertaking the review agree that the review is to be dealt with by written representations.[112]

An application for a review before a panel must:
- be made in writing;
- include a copy of your CTR decision letter;
- give your reasons for the request of the review;
- be signed by you, unless a court has appointed someone else to act on your behalf;
- be received within 42 days of the local authority review decision notification.

An application form can be downloaded from the CTRRP website (http://counciltaxreductionreview.scotland.gov.uk) and is a good way to include all of the information required. This includes details of any representative helping you, and whether you want an oral hearing of your review or not.

Challenging the local authority's scheme

If you want to challenge the local authority's CTR scheme itself (eg, because you think it is unlawful), you can only do so by way of judicial review.[113] For more information on judicial reviews, see p292.

11. **Discretionary reductions**

In addition to reductions under its CTR scheme, each local authority in **England and Wales** has a discretionary power to reduce a bill.[114]

Even if your local authority has a scheme which does entitle you to support, it still has a discretion to grant you a reduction. Local authorities can reduce sums payable in individual cases to prevent financial hardship and in groups of cases[115] – eg, to victims of flooding or persons in receipt of particular benefits or in respect of personal circumstances such as pregnancy.

Councils have been given wide scope to reduce bills. The power to apply a discretionary reduction includes the power to reduce the bill to zero.[116] A reduction may be awarded to cover any liability regardless of when the liability arose,[117] so a discretionary reduction can be used to clear arrears of council tax from an earlier year or years – ie, at any time before the CTR schemes came into force.[118]

Each scheme must explain how a discretionary reduction can be applied for.[119] You should apply for a discretionary reduction in writing and provide supporting evidence. When making an application, it is advisable to include a full income and expenditure breakdown, together with that of any other household members.

Meaning of financial hardship

The term 'financial need' is not defined but it should be given a wide interpretation, in accordance with existing caselaw.

It has been held by the courts: 'To need is not the same as want. "Need" is a lack of what is essential for the ordinary business of living.'[120] Financial need may be distinguished from such terms as 'hardship' and 'poverty'. Poverty has been considered as usually involving 'extreme financial stringency such that the applicant has some difficulty in meeting the conventional necessities of life.'[121] Accordingly, the term 'financial need' can cover persons not in a state described as poverty but who nonetheless may be, or who are, experiencing difficulty in meeting ordinary bills and household expenses in the course of the financial year unless support is given. The term 'financial need' is a lower threshold or test than poverty or hardship and may also include persons who are, or who will be, in debt unless support is given. Note that a person is not required to be without any money or assets, with certain amounts and types of savings being allowed.

This can cover persons the authority considers to be in financial need on an individual basis, or classes of persons whom the authority decides are in general need, such as certain groups of employees.[122]

A local authority is expected to behave reasonably when deciding whether to grant a discretionary reduction. An important decision clarifying the scope and range of matters to be considered by a local authority when deciding whether to grant a reduction was decided by the president of the Valuation Tribunal for England (VTE) in *SC and CW v East Riding of Yorkshire Council* (see p247).[123]

If you disagree with the council's decision, you can appeal against it (see p247).

12. **Future changes**

Each financial year, in England and Wales a local authority must consider whether to revise or to replace its scheme.[124] It must consult with any major precepting authorities such as police and fire and rescue authorities. The authority is also required to publish a draft scheme and consult with such 'other persons as the authority considers to be likely to have an interest in the operation of the scheme'.

If a reduction is to be reduced or removed, the billing authority must make such transitional provisions as it thinks fit.

Review of council tax support by the Secretary of State

An independent review of all local reduction schemes in England and Wales was carried out for the Secretary of State and reported in March 2016.[125] The report noted that council tax collection rates had fallen in the first three years of the scheme, but nonetheless recommended that it should remain a localised scheme and that council tax reduction should remain separate from universal credit. This recommendation was accepted in the government's response published in January 2018.[126]

Notes

1. What is a council tax reduction
1 s13A LGFA 1992
  E CTRS(PR)E Regs
  W CTRSPR(W) Regs
  S CTR(S) Regs; CTR(SPC)(S) Regs
2 **E** CTRS(PR)(E) Regs
  W CTRS(DS)(W) Regs; CTRSPR(W) Regs
3 Research for Joseph Rowntree Foundation by New Policy Institute, at www.npi.org.uk/publications/council-tax/key-changes-council-tax-support-201718

4 Statement by the Scottish government; CTR(S) Regs
5 **E** CTRS(PR)(E) Regs
  W CTRSPR(W) Regs
6 **E** Reg 14 and Sch 1 paras 1-4 CTRS(PR)(E) Regs
  W Regs 21-23 CTRS(PR)(W) Regs
7 **E** Sch 1A para 2(2) LGFA 1992
  W Sch 1B para 3 LGFA 1992
8 **E** Reg 14 and Sch 1 paras 1-4 CTRS(PR)(E) Regs
9 **E** s13A (2)(a) and (b) LGFA 1992
  W s13A(i)(c) LGFA 1992

10 **E** Sch 1A para 2(5) LGFA 1992
   W Sch 1B para 5(1)(a) LGFA 1992
11 s13A(i)(c) LGFA 1992
12 Sch 1A para 2(4) and Sch 1B para 4 (5)
   LGFA 1992

2. How council tax reduction schemes work

13 **E** Reg 11(2) CTRS(PR)(E) Regs
   W Reg 30 CTRSPR(W) Regs
   S Reg 42 CTR(S) Regs; reg 40
   CTR(SPC)(S) Regs
14 **E** Reg 13 CTRS(PR)(E) Regs
   W Reg 29 CTRSPR(W) Regs
   S Reg 19 CTR(S) Regs; reg 19
   CTR(SPC)(S) Regs
15 **E** Reg 12 CTRS(PR)(E) Regs
   W Reg 28 CTRSPR(W) Regs
   S Reg 16 CTR(S) Regs; reg 16
   CTR(SPC)(S) Regs
16 **E** Reg 6 CTRS(PR)(E) Regs
   W Reg 6 CTRSPR(W) Regs
   S Regs 2, 9 and 11 CTR(S) Regs; regs 2, 9
   and 11 CTR(SPC)(S) Regs
17 **E** Reg 2 and 6 CTRS(PR)(E) Regs
   W Reg 2 and 6 CTRSPR(W) Regs
   S Regs 2 and 4 CTR(S) Regs; regs 2 and 4
   CTR(SPC)(S) Regs
18 **E** Reg 4 CTRS(PR)(E) Regs
   W Reg 4 CTRSPR(W) Regs
   S Reg 2 CTR(S) Regs; reg 2 CTR(SPC)(S)
   Regs
19 **E** Reg 5 and Sch 1 paras 4, 8 and 11
   CTRS(PR)(E) Regs
   W Regs 5 and 9 and Schs 1 and 6
   CTRSPR(W) Regs
   S Regs 8, 24 and 67 CTR(S) Regs; regs 8,
   21 and 48 CTR(SPC)(S) Regs
20 **E** Reg 8 CTRS(PR)(E) Regs
   W Reg 8 CTRSPR(W) Regs
   S Reg 11 CTR(S) Regs; reg 11
   CTR(SPC)(S) Regs
21 **E** Reg 8(4) CTRS(PR)(E) Regs
   W Reg 8(4) CTRSPR(W) Regs
   S Reg 11(4) CTR(S) Regs; reg 11(4)
   CTR(SPC)(S) Regs
22 **E** Reg 7 CTRS(PR)(E) Regs
   W Reg 7 CTRSPR(W) Regs
   S Reg 10 CTR(S) Regs; reg 10
   CTR(SPC)(S) Regs
23 **E** Sch 1 para 7(3)-(5) CTRS(PR)(E) Regs
   W Sch 1 para 2(3)-(5) and Sch 6 para
   4(3)-(5) CTRSPR(W) Regs
   S Reg 66(2) and (3) CTR(S) Regs; reg
   47(2) and (3) CTR(SPC)(S) Regs
24 *R (on the application of Williams) v
   Horsham District Council* [2004] *The
   Times*, 29 January

25 **E** Sch 8 para 5(6) CTRS(PR)(E) Regs
   W Sch 13 para 2(6) CTRSPR(W) Regs
   S Reg 85(3) CTR(S) Regs; reg 65(2)
   CTR(SPC)(S) Regs
26 R(H) 9/05
27 **E** Sch 1 para 5 CTRS(PR)(E) Regs
   W Reg 26 CTRSPR(W) Regs
   S Reg 5(13) CTR(S) Regs; reg 5(13)
   CTR(SPC)(S) Regs
28 **E** Sch 1 para 5(2) and (3)(i) CTRS(PR)(E)
   Regs
   W Reg 26(2)(a) and (3)(i) CTRSPR(W)
   Regs
   S Reg 15 CTR(S) Regs; reg 15
   CTR(SPC)(S) Regs

3. Council tax reduction schemes for pensioners

29 **E** Sch 1 para 13 CTRS(PR)(E) Regs
   W Sch 1 para 7 CTRSPR(W) Regs
   S Reg 24 CTR(SPC)(S) Regs
30 **E** Reg 3 CTRS(PR)(E) Regs
   W Reg 3 CTRSPR(W) Regs
   S Reg 12 CTR(S) Regs; reg 12
   CTR(SPC)(S) Regs
31 **E** Sch 1 paras 1-4 CTRS(PR)(E) Regs
   W Regs 21-23 CTRSPR(W) Regs
   S Reg 14 CTR(SPC)(S) Regs
32 **E** Sch 1 para 2 CTRS(PR)(E) Regs
   W Reg 22 CTRSPR(W) Regs
   S Reg 14(5)(a) CTR(SPC)(S) Regs
33 **E** Sch 1 para 13 CTRS(PR)(E) Regs
   W Sch 1 para 7 CTRSPR(W) Regs
   S Reg 24 CTR(SPC)(S) Regs
34 **E** Sch 1 para 3 CTRS(PR)(E) Regs
   W Reg 23 CTRSPR(W) Regs
   S Reg 14(5)(b) CTR(SPC)(S) Regs
35 **E** Sch 1 para 4 CTRS(PR)(E) Regs
   S Reg 56 and Sch 5 CTR(SPC)(S) Regs
36 **E** Sch 1 para 6(1) CTRS(PR)(E) Regs
   W Sch 1 para 1 CTRSPR(W) Regs
   S Reg 20 CTR (SPC)(S) Regs

4. Council tax reduction schemes in England

37 Reg 3 CTRS(PR)(E) Regs

5. Council tax reduction schemes in Wales

38 CTRSPR(W) Regs

6. Council tax reduction schemes in Scotland

39 CTR(S) Regs; CTR(SPC)(S) Regs
40 Reg 14A CTR(S) Regs; reg 14A
   CTR(SPC)(S) Regs

7. Alternative maximum council tax reduction ('second adult rebate')

41 **E** Sch 1 para 4 and (PR)(E) Regs
   S Reg 14(6) and (7) Regs; reg 15(6) and (7) CTR(SPC)(S) Regs
42 CH/48/2006
43 **E** Sch 3 CTRS(PR)(E) Regs
   S Reg 56 CTR(SPC)(S) Regs
44 Reg 78 CTR(S) Regs
45 **E** Sch 1 para 4 CTRS(PR)(E) Regs
   S Reg 14 CTR(S)Regs; reg 14 CTR(SPC)(S) Regs
46 s6(5) LGFA 1992
47 Sch 1 LGFA 1992
   E Sch 1 para 4(3)(a) CTRS(PR)(E) Regs
   S Reg 14(7)(a) CTR(S) Regs; reg 14(7)(a) CTR(SPC)(S) Regs
48 **E** Sch 1 para 9 CTRS(PR)(E) Regs
   S Reg 78 CTR(S) Regs; reg 56 CTR(SPC)(S) Regs
49 **E** Sch 1 para 4(3) CTRS(PR)(E) Regs
   S Reg 79 CTR(S) Regs; reg 57 CTR(SPC)(S) Regs
50 **E** Sch 3 CTRS(PR)(E) Regs
   S Sch 5 CTR (S) Regs; Sch 2 CTR(SPC)(S) Regs

8. How council tax reduction entitlement is calculated

51 **E** Sch 8 para 4(3) CTRS(PR)(E) Regs; reg 109(3)
   W Sch 13 para 1(3) CTRSPR(W) Regs; reg 107(3) CTRS(DS)(W) Regs
52 **E** Sch 1 para 7 CTRS(PR)(E) Regs
   W Sch 1 para 2 and Sch 6 para 4 CTRSPR(W) Regs; reg 27(1) CTRS(DS)(W) Regs
   S Reg 66 CTR(S) Regs; reg 47 CTR(SPC)(S) Regs
53 **E** Sch 1 para 6 CTRS(PR)(E) Regs
   W Sch 1 para 1 and Sch 6 paras 1-3 CTRSPR(W) Regs; regs 23-25 CTRS(DS)(W) Regs
   S Regs 21-23 CTR(S) Regs; reg 20 CTR(SPC)(S) Regs
54 **E** Sch 2 CTRS(PR)(E) Regs
   W Sch 2 CTRSPR(W) Regs; Sch 3 CTRS(DS)(W) Regs
   S Sch 1 CTR(S) Regs; Sch 1 CTR(SPC)(S) Regs
55 **E** Sch 1 para 8 CTRS(PR)(E) Regs
   W Sch 1 para 3 CTRSPR(W) Regs
   S Reg 66(2) CTR(S) Regs; reg 48(6) CTR(SPC)(S) Regs
56 **E** Sch 1 paras 7 and 8 CTRS(PR)(E) Regs
   W Sch 1 Pare 3(7) and (8) and Sch 6 para 5(8) CTRSPR(W) Regs
   S Reg 67(6) and (8) CTR(S) Regs; reg 48(7) and (8) CTR(SPC)(S) Regs
57 **E** Sch 1 para 8 CTRS(PR)(E) Regs
   W Sch 1 paras 3 and Sch 6 para 5 CTRSPR(W) Regs
   S Reg 67(9) CTR(S) Regs; reg 48(9) CTRS(SPC)(S) Regs
58 **E** Sch 1 para 8 CRTRS(PR)(E) Regs
   W Sch 1 para 3(9) and Sch 6 para 5(9) CTRSPR(W) Regs; reg 28(9) CTRS(DS)(W) Regs
   S Reg 67(9) CTR(S) Regs; reg 48(9) CTR(SPC)(S) Regs
59 **E** Sch 1 para 17 CTRS(PR)(E) Regs
   W Sch 1 paras 11 and18 and Sch 6 para 20 CTRSPR(W) Regs
   S Reg 27 CTR(S) Regs; reg 28 CTR(SPC)(S) Regs
60 **E** Sch 1 para 16(3) CTRS(PR)(E) Regs
   W Sch 1 CTRSPR(W) Regs
   S Regs 27-33 CTR(SPC)(S) Regs
61 **E** Sch 1 para 13 CTRS(PR)(E) Regs
   W Sch 1 para 7 CTRSPR(W) Regs
   S Reg 24 CTR(SPC)(S) Regs
62 **E** Sch 5 CTRS(PR)(E) Regs
   W Sch 4 CTRSPR(W) Regs
   S Sch 3 CTR(SPC)(S) Regs
63 **E** Sch 5 CTRS(PR)(E) Regs
   W Sch 4 CTRSPR(W) Regs
   S Sch 3 CTR(SPC)(S) Regs
64 **E** Sch 5 paras 14 and 15 CTRS(PR)(E) Regs
   W Sch 4 paras 14 and 15 CTRSPR(W) Regs
   S Sch3 paras 13 and 14 CTR(SPC)(S) Regs
65 **W** Sch 6 para Reg 17(2) and Sch 9 CTRSPR(W) Regs
   S Reg 31(1) and Sch 4 CTR(S) Regs
66 **W** Sch 6 para 17(d) CTRSPR(W) Regs; reg 51(5) CTRS(DS)(W) Regs
   S Reg 39(5) CTR(S) Regs
67 **W** Sch 9 CTRSPR(W) Regs
   S Sch 4 CTR(S) Regs
68 **W** Sch 8 para 49 CTRSPR(W) Regs
   S Sch 4 para 49 CTR(S) Regs
69 **E** Sch 1 paras 18 and 23 CTRS(PR)(E) Regs
   W Sch 1 para 12 and Sch 6 para 14 CTRSPR(W) Regs
   S Reg 34 CTR(S) Regs; reg 32 CTR(SPC)(S) Regs

70 **E** Sch 1 para 20 CTRS(PR)(E) Regs
   W Sch 1 para 14 and Sch 6 para 11
   CTRSPR(W) Regs
   S Reg 30 CTR (S) Regs; reg 34
   CTR(SPC)(S) Regs
71 **E** Sch 1 para 18(1)(b) and (2)
   CTRS(PR)(E) Regs
   W Sch 1 para 12(1)(b) and (2) and Sch 6
   para 14(1)(b) and (2) CTRSPR(W) Regs
   S Reg 34(1)(b) and (2) CTR(S) Regs; reg
   32 (1)(b) and (2) CTR(SPC)(S) Regs
72 **E** Sch 4 CTRS(PR)(E) Regs
   W Schs 3 and 8 CTRSPR(W) Regs
   S Sch 3 CTR(S) Regs; Sch 2 CTR(SPC)(S)
   Regs
73 **E** Sch 1 para 25 CTRS(PR)(E) Regs
   W Sch 1 para 19 and Sch 6 para 21
   CTRSPR(W) Regs
   S Reg 28 CTR(S) Regs; reg 29
   CTR(SPC)(S) Regs
74 **E** Sch 1 para 37 CTRS(PR)(E) Regs
   W Sch 1 para 31 and Sch 6 para 33
   CTRSPR(W) Regs
   S Reg 51 CTR(S) Regs; reg 27(2)
   CTR(SPC)(S) Regs
75 **E** Sch 1 para 3 CTRS(PR)(E) Regs
   W Regs 23 and 25 CTRSPR(W) Regs
   S Reg 14(5)(b) CTR(S) Regs; reg
   14(5)(b) CTR(SPC)(S) Regs
76 **E** Sch 1 para 17(1) CTRS(PR)(E) Regs
   W Sch 1 para 11(1) and Sch 6 para
   13(1) CTRSPR(W) Regs
   S Reg 33(1) CTR(S) Regs; reg 31(1)
   CTR(SPC)(S) Regs
77 **E** Reg 11(2) and Sch 1 paras 31-37
   CTRS(PR)(E) Regs
   W Reg 30 and Sch 1 paras 25-31 and
   Sch 6 paras 26-33 CTRSPR(W) Regs
   S Regs 42-51 CTR(S) Regs; regs 40-46
   CTR(SPC)(S) Regs
78 *JRL v Secretary of State for Work and
   Pensions (JSA)* [2011] UKUT 63 (AAC)
79 **E** Sch 6 Part 1 CTRS(PR)(E) Regs
   W Schs 5 and 10 CTRSPR(W) Regs
   S Sch 5 CTR(S) Regs; Sch 4 CTR(SPC)(S)
   Regs
80 **E** Sch 1 para 34 CTRS(PR)(E) Regs
   W Sch 1 para 28 and Sch 6 para 30
   CTRSPR(W) Regs
   S Reg 48 CRT(S) Regs; reg 44
   CTR(SPC)(S) Regs
81 **E** Sch 1 para 36 CTRS(PR)(E) Regs
   W Sch 1 para 30 and Sch 6 para 32
   CTRSPR(W) Regs
   S Reg 50 CTR(S) Regs; reg 46
   CTR(SPC)(S) Regs

82 **E** Sch 1 para 38 CTRS(PR)(E) Regs
   W Sch 1 para 32 and Sch 6 para 34 and
   39 CTRSPR(W) Regs
   S Regs 68 and 73 CTR(S) Regs; reg 49
   CTR(SPC)(S) Regs
83 **W** Reg 31(3) CTRSPR(W) Regs
84 **E** Sch 1 para 43 CTRS(PR)(E) Regs
   W Sch 1 para 37 CTRSPR(W) Regs
   S Reg 55 CTR(SPC)(S) Regs

9. Applying for council tax reduction

85 **E** Sch 7 paras 2-3 CTRS(PR)(E) Regs; Sch
   1 paras 2-3 CTRS(DS)(E) Regs
   W Sch 12 paras 2-3 CTRSPR(W) Regs;
   Sch 1 paras 2-3 CTRS(DS)(W) Regs
   S Regs 83 and 84 CTR(S) Regs; regs 63
   and 64 CTR(SPC)(S) Regs
86 **E** Sch 7 para 4 CTRS(PR)(E) Regs
   W Sch 12 para 4 CTRSPR(W) Regs; Sch 1
   para 4 CTRS(DS)(W) Regs
   S Reg 83(6) CTR(S) Regs; reg 63(6)
   CTR(SPC)(S) Regs
87 **E** Sch 8 para 5(6)-(7) CTRS(PR)(E) Regs
   W Sch 13 para 2(6)-(7) CTRSPR(W)
   Regs; reg 108(6) and (7) CTRS(DS)(W)
   Regs
   S Reg 85(3), (5) and (6) CTR(S) Regs;
   reg 65(2) and (3) CTR(SPC)(S) Regs
88 **E** Sch 8 para 5(5)(c) CTRS(PR)(E) Regs
   W Sch 13 paras 2(4) and (5)(c) and 5(4)
   CTRSPR(W) Regs; reg 111(4)
   CTRS(DS)(W) Regs
   S Reg 86(1) CTR(S) Regs; reg 66(1)
   CTR(SPC)(S) Regs
89 **E** Sch 8 para 4(1) CTRS(PR)(E) Regs
   W Sch 13 para 1 CTRSPR(W) Regs; reg
   107(1) CTRS(DS)(W) Regs
   S Reg 82 CTR(S) Regs; reg 61
   CTR(SPC)(S) Regs
90 **E** Sch 8 paras 11 and 12 CTRS(PR)(E)
   Regs
   W Sch 13 paras 8 and 9 CTRSPR(W)
   Regs; reg 114 CTRS(DS)(W) Regs
91 **E** Sch 1 para 45(1) CTRS(PR)(E) Regs
   S Reg 80(1) CTR(S) Regs; reg 58(1)
   CTR(SPC)(S) Regs
92 **W** Sch 1 para 39 and Sch 6 para 45
   CTRSPR(W) Regs; Sch para 104
   CTRS(DS)(W) Regs
93 **E** Sch 1 para 45(2) CTRS(PR)(E) Regs
   S Reg 80(2) CTR(S) Regs; reg 58(2)
   CTR(SPC)(S) Regs
94 **W** Sch 13 para 4 CTRSPR(W) Regs
95 **S** Reg 85(7) and (8) CTR(S) Regs
96 **E** Sch 8 para 6(2) CTRS(PR)(E) Regs
   W Sch 13 para 3(1) CTRSPR(W) Regs
   S Reg 62(1) CTR(SPC)(S) Regs

97 **E** Sch 8 Reg 6(3) CTRS(PR)(E) Regs
W Sch 13 para 3(2) CTRSPR(W) Regs
S Reg 62(2) CTR(SPC)(S) Regs
98 **E** Sch 8 para 9 CTRS(PR)(E) Regs
W Sch 13 para 7 CTRSPR(W) Regs
S Reg 89 CTR(S) Regs; reg 69
CTR(SPC)(S) Regs
99 **E** Sch 8 para 9(2) CTRS(PR)(E) Regs
W Sch 13 para 7(2) CTRSPR(W) Regs

**10. If you disagree with a council tax
reduction decision**
100 **E** Sch 1A para 2(6) LGFA 1992; Sch 8
para 12(4) CTRS(PR)(E) Regs
W Sch B para 5(1)(b) LGFA 1992; Sch
14 para 3 CTRSPR(W) Regs; Sch 10 para
3 CTRS(DS)(W) Regs
101 **EW** s16 LGFA 1992
E Sch 7 para 8(1) CTRS(PR)(E) Regs
W Sch 12 para 8 CTRSPR(W) Regs; Sch 1
para 8 CTRS(DS)(W) Regs
102 *SC and CW v East Riding of Yorkshire
Council*, Appeals 2001M113393 and
2001M117503, 27 May 2014
103 **E** Sch 7 para 8(2) CTRS(PR)(E) Regs
W Sch 12 para 9 CTRSPR(W) Regs
104 Sch 12 para 8(2) CTRSPR(W) Regs; Sch 1
para 8(2) CTRS(DS)(W) Regs
105 **E** Sch 7 para 8(3) CTRS(PR)(E) Regs
W Sch 12 para 10 CTRSPR(W) Regs
106 **E** Reg 21 VTE(CTRA)(P) Regs
W Reg 29 VTW Regs
107 *Norman and another v East Dorset District
Council* [2012] EWHC 3696 (Admin)
108 Reg 90A(3) CTR(S) Regs; reg 70A(2)
CTR(SPC)(S) Regs
109 Reg 90A(4) CTR(S) Regs; reg 70A(4)
CTR(SPC)(S) Regs
110 Reg 90B(1) CTR(S) Regs; reg 70B(1)
CTR(SPC)(S) Regs
111 Reg 90C(2) CTR(S) Regs; reg 70C(1)
CTR(SPC)(S) Regs
112 Regs 90D(1) and (2) CTR(S) Regs; regs
70C(1) and (2) CTR(SPC)(S) Regs
113 s66 (2) (ba) LGFA 1992

11. Discretionary reductions
114 s13A(1)(c) LGFA 1992
115 1s13A(7) LGFA B1991
116 Sch A para 2(7) and 1B para 5(1)(c)
LGFA 1992
117 *Morgan v Warwick District Council* [2015]
RVR 224 VTE per President Professor
Graham Zellick
118 *Morgan v Warwick District Council* [2015]
RVR 224
119 s13A(1)(c) LGFA 1992

120 *R v Gloucestershire County Council and
another ex parte Barry* [1997] 2 All ER 1
HL
121 *Windsor Securities Ltd v Liverpool City
Council* [1978] LGR 502, Court of
Appeal, per Cumings-Bruce LJ
122 s13A(2) LGFA 1992
123 *SC and CW v East Riding of Yorkshire
Council* [2014] VTE per President
Professor Graham Zellick

12. Future changes
124 **E** Sch 1A para 5(1) LGFA 1992
W Reg 18 CTRSPR(W) Regs
125 s9(1) and (2) LGFA 2012; www.gov.uk/
government/publications/local-council-
tax-support-schemes-an-independent-
review
126 www.gov.uk/government/publications/
independent-review-of-local-council-
tax-support-schemes-government-
response

Chapter 9: Bills and payments

Chapter 9

Bills and payments

This chapter covers:
1. Who must pay the bill (below)
2. When bills should be issued (p174)
3. How the bill is calculated (p176)
4. How bills are served (p179)
5. Information the bill should contain (p180)
6. Payment arrangements (p183)
7. Penalties (p189)
8. Appeals against the amount of the bill (p191)

1. Who must pay the bill

Chapter 5 identified the people who are liable for council tax, but in most cases no one need actually pay the tax until a bill has been issued.[1] As council tax is a tax on property, the individual is not under a duty to inform the local authority if s/he is or may be a liable person, but the expectation is on the local authority to serve bills. If the name of a liable person cannot be established after reasonable enquiries have been made by the local authority, the bill may be addressed to the 'council taxpayer'.[2] Bills may be issued to both individual taxpayers and a company if it is liable – eg, as an owner of a dwelling.

Local authorities may serve bills, certain notices and information required for council tax by electronic means. You must agree for the bill to be served electronically.[3]

Local authorities should ensure that their computer systems do not issue bills in the name of taxpayers who have died. These should normally be sent to the 'personal representatives of deceased' or the 'executors of the deceased'.

The liable person's spouse or partner, and anyone who has the same degree of legal interest in the dwelling, is jointly liable for the bill (see p82). In Scotland, but not England and Wales, someone who is jointly liable with the person(s) named on the bill but whose name is not included on the bill is still liable to make any payments required.[4]

In England and Wales, no payment can be required of someone who is jointly liable who has not previously been included on a bill until a 'joint taxpayers' bill' has been issued.[5] This must be served within six years of the first day of the financial year to which it relates. The liable people themselves must determine how exactly they share the responsibility for the bill.

Joint liability means that both or all jointly liable taxpayers can be held individually or collectively liable to pay the whole amount. A decision on 'joint and several liability' can be appealed (see Chapter 11).

In Scotland, a bill need not be issued if the only liable person is a housing body (eg, a local council) or an owner who has agreed with the local authority that a bill need not be served.[6]

2. When bills should be issued

The local authority should serve a council tax bill on each chargeable dwelling each financial year. In England and Wales, this should be done 'as soon as practicable' after the local authority first sets a council tax for the year.[7] In Scotland, a local authority should serve the bill as soon as practicable after it has first set a council tax and knows the water charge for the year.[8]

Separate bills must be sent for different financial years and for different dwellings, even if the same person is liable for both.[9] This rule is sometimes breached by outsourced companies acting for local authorities who may issue repeated bills for the same periods, each with differing amounts. In such a case, problems may arise at the enforcement stage, as it can be unclear which bill is to be treated as valid and difficult for the local authority to show it has complied with the rules on billing. In England and Wales, however, one council tax bill may also cover the current and preceding financial years if it is for the same dwelling.[10]

Local authorities will want to ensure that bills are produced promptly to maximise their cash flows. Most local authorities aim to send out council tax bills in mid-March, with the payment falling due from 1 April. If you pay by direct debit, you may be given several dates in April on which to make your first payment.

Late bills

A local authority must issue a bill (or 'demand notice') 'as soon as reasonably practicable'.[11] If there has been a long delay, the local authority may not be able to recover the money if it has been in breach of this requirement. In one case concerning non-domestic rates, the local authority delayed seven years before serving demand notices.[12] When the ratepayers failed to pay, the local authority obtained liability orders. The High Court, however, quashed the liability orders as the delay in serving the demand notices was 'inexcusable'.

The High Court has indicated, however, that late bills may be valid, even if they are sent several years after the tax fell due, but invalid if they cause 'prejudice' to the taxpayer. In three cases involving North Somerset District Council, the High Court considered the effect that serving a bill late had on validity.[13] Ordinarily, mere delay is not sufficient to invalidate a notice. The High Court ruled that the test was to look at the length of the delay and the impact on the taxpayer. The key test is whether 'prejudice' has been caused. **'Prejudice'** is different from inconvenience and must be substantial and can be caused in a number of ways. The court also said that there was also a public interest in ensuring that local taxes were collected, which had to be weighed in the balance. In all three cases, the defendants were found to have suffered prejudice and liability orders should not have been issued.

Prejudice caused by late billing

Prejudice could arise for an individual on a low income who is sent council tax bills for previous financial years that do not take into account any past entitlement to council tax reduction (CTR) or to council tax benefit (CTB) that might have existed at the time. Indeed, any application for CTR or CTB for earlier financial years will be thwarted by the benefit backdating rules. Arguably, prejudice is caused to anyone who effectively loses a right to claim CTR or CTB which might have covered the total liability for the year concerned. Similarly, if you have been unable to claim under a CTR scheme since 1 April 2013 because of failure to supply a demand notice in time, it would be possible to challenge the bill as invalid as it has caused prejudice – ie, the loss of the opportunity to apply for CTR. Prejudice may also arise from the failure to be provided, as soon as practicable, with the information accompanying the demand notice (see p181). Prejudice may arise from not being able to make provision from a limited income for paying the bill or from the loss of the right to pay instalments or loss of an appeal right. The longer the delay that is involved in the serving of a demand notice, the greater the risk that you will be able to show prejudice.[14]

Challenging late issue of a bill

If you want to challenge the late issue of a bill, do so before a liability order is issued by a magistrates' court.[15] In theory, this should also be the case before the sheriff court in Scotland, but the difficulty is the Scottish summary procedure does not give notice to the council taxpayer (see Chapter 10).

Another remedy might be to lodge an appeal with the valuation tribunal or valuation appeal committee in Scotland under section 16 (section 81 in Scotland) of the Local Government Finance Act 1992, which allows appeals on 'any calculation' in respect of a sum of council tax (see p243). The right to appeal arises as soon as you become aware of the bill.

Reducing council tax if a bill is late

In England and Wales, a local authority has the power to reduce an individual council tax bill (see p167). If a bill is served late, perhaps years after the original liability arose, you can apply to the local authority to reduce the sum concerned by way of a discretionary reduction. A discretionary reduction may be granted for any liability to council tax, no matter when it arose.[16]

Late service of a bill may amount to maladministration (see p273) and cause hardship. Although a bill being served late does not automatically make it invalid, a local authority is expected to act sympathetically and reasonably if you are prejudiced through official error, including not giving you enough time to pay. A failure to respond properly if a late bill causes hardship to a vulnerable person may amount to maladministration. If a council has an anti-poverty strategy, it is expected to act in accordance with it.

Making a complaint

If you are a victim of late billing for which you are not responsible, make a formal complaint to the local authority. Experience suggests that some billing authorities will make a decision to withdraw a late bill rather than face a formal complaint investigation. You should also be prepared to lodge an appeal either to the valuation tribunal or valuation appeal committee in Scotland if there is a question of CTR entitlement (see Chapters 8 and 11) or the First-tier Tribunal (Social Security and Child Support) if the alleged bill concerns a matter of CTB entitlement for a period before 1 April 2013 (see CPAG's *Welfare Credits and Tax Credits Handbook*). It is important to consider the time limits and you should not delay.

A complaint will examine the reasons for the delay and find out why, and by whom, a decision was made to retrospectively reopen an account from an earlier financial year which had been considered closed.

The Ombudsman will investigate late billing cases as a form of maladministration (see p272).[17]

3. **How the bill is calculated**

Liability for council tax is calculated on a daily basis. Council tax is payable for each day a dwelling is a chargeable dwelling which is the sole or main residence of the taxpayer, with the taxpayer being liable for each day s/he lives in the dwelling. As soon as you cease to have sole or main residence, liability to pay tax ends, unless the dwelling is unoccupied and not exempt. In some cases, you may be able to get a discount on a vacant dwelling or be subject to a premium (see Chapter 7).[18] However, the bill issued at the beginning of the financial year is for the full year. The local authority is required to use certain assumptions to estimate what it thinks the council tax will be for the whole year and correct it later, if necessary (see p178).

The local authority must estimate the 'chargeable amount' by taking the relevant amount of council tax for that dwelling (depending on its valuation band), and then make the following assumptions.

- The person will be liable for every day.
- The dwelling's valuation band will not change and it will remain a chargeable dwelling throughout the year.
- Any reduction under the disability reduction scheme has been properly calculated and applies throughout the year.
- The bill is either eligible or not eligible for a discount throughout the year.
- Any council tax reduction (CTR) which applies does so throughout the year.[19]
- Liability for Scottish Water charges applies throughout the year.[20]

If more than one reduction applies to the council tax for the band, they should be applied in the following order:
- disability reduction;
- discount;
- any reduction under a CTR scheme and/or any discretionary reduction.

The local authority must ensure that if 100 per cent CTR is awarded, this is equal to your liability.

The bill can also take into account any credits from past periods, penalties due and any alleged overpayment of council tax benefit (CTB) pre-2013 or tax which remains unpaid as a result of the removal of a council tax reduction after it is awarded. It should be noted that it is not possible to overpay an amount of CTR as it takes effect as a reduction in tax – ie, the amount of your council tax liablity is reduced.

The question of whether an amount of excess CTB from more than one year earlier may be subject to recovery action through the magistrates' court and should be challenged. When CTB was in existence, the system operated in tandem with the housing benefit system, with excess payments recoverable as a civil debt through the county court.

Special rules apply if a bill is for a period earlier in the financial year, and if, on the day it is issued, you are no longer liable for council tax at that address. The bill will either:
- require payment of the amount due up to the last day of liability (calculated as described above but based on the actual, not estimated, circumstances); or
- if you are due a credit, require the amount payable (if any) after the credit has been offset against the chargeable amount.[21] This could apply, for example, following a delay in recalculating a reduction or, in theory, where a referendum over the level of council tax is held.

If a bill is issued after the end of the year to which it relates, it must require payment of the amount due for the year, calculated as described above, but based on the actual circumstances and after taking into account any credits carried over from earlier years. Such payments are usually requested as a lump sum.

If the estimated amount has been based on incorrect assumptions

It may become clear during the course of a year that an estimated amount has been based on an incorrect assumption – eg, your entitlement to a discount may change part way through the year. If so, the local authority should now calculate the appropriate amount that appears due for the year.[22] If:

- the new amount is **greater than** the estimated amount, the local authority should bill you and give you at least 14 days to make the interim payment;
- the new amount is **less than** the estimated amount, the local authority should notify you accordingly and make an interim repayment (but see below).

Further rules apply about changes in the tax payable as a consequence of any local referendum (see p182).[23]

In England and Wales, if an overpayment of council tax has occurred because you are no longer liable to make payments on one dwelling but become immediately liable to make payments to the same local authority on another dwelling, the local authority may credit the overpayment against your new liability, rather than make a repayment to you. This is likely to be done unless you specify otherwise to the authority. If you overpaid a lump-sum payment, the local authority should make an interim repayment in the usual way.[24]

If you have made payments under the statutory instalment scheme or, in England and Wales, the council tenant instalment scheme, see p186 and p187.

In Scotland, if an overpayment of council tax has occurred because you are no longer liable to make payments, you can request the local authority to refund the amount to you. The council may retain the overpayment until it receives such a request, and may seek to offset the overpayment against any subsequent balance due.[25]

Incorrect payments

The actual amount owed to the local authority will be known for certain only at the end of the financial year or when your liability ends. Another bill is therefore required if a previous bill was issued for a financial year (or part of a financial year), and the payment(s) required was, in fact, more or less than the actual liability and there has been no appropriate adjustment. The local authority should, as soon as practicable after the end of the year (or the part of a year), serve a new bill on you as the liable person. This should state the actual amount due and adjust the amount(s) required to be paid under the previous bill.[26]

If the amount stated in the new notice is greater than the amount previously required, you must pay the difference within a period specified by the local authority. This period must be at least 14 days following the issue of the new bill.[27]

If there has been an overpayment of council tax and you require a refund, this must be given. In any other case, the local authority may decide either to repay the amount in question to you or credit it against any future council tax liability.[28] However, if the overpayment has arisen because you are no longer liable to make payments on one dwelling, but are immediately liable to make payments to the same local authority on another dwelling and you have not made a lump-sum payment, the local authority may require the amount of any overpayment to be credited against the new liability.[29]

In England and Wales, if the local authority is required to repay a sum but does not do so, you can take recovery action using the civil debt procedure in the county court.[30] The small claims procedure of the county court can be used for sums of up to £5,000 and £10,000. A similar procedure exists in Scotland for sums of up to £3,000. Complaints may also be taken to the Ombudsman (see p272).

See also excessive amounts of council tax on p182.

4. How bills are served

Before you are required to pay council tax, a bill must be served. This does not mean that you actually received the bill, only that the local authority has served it in such a way that you could be expected to know about it. Bills may be served by:[31]

- post; *or*
- being delivered to the liable person at her/his usual or last known address; *or*
- being delivered to some other person at the chargeable dwelling; *or*
- being fixed to some conspicuous part of the dwelling; *or*
- email, by special arrangement.

If a bill has been served in one of the above ways, the date of issue is the date the bill was sent or left at the address. In all other cases, it is the actual service of the notice – eg, where the notice is delivered by hand. The bill should include the date of issue, which determines such matters as when payments become due.[32] Local authorities should ensure that when a bill is sent by post, the first instalment due is payable at least 14 days after the day on which it is delivered to a post office. Local authorities should maintain records of the days on which bills are posted so that they can present evidence of the date of issue for any particular bill. If the bill has not arrived at the appropriate address, the local authority must serve it again if it wishes to start enforcement proceedings (see Chapter 10). If the bill is formally returned as undelivered by the post office (known as 'returned, gone away'), the local authority should make investigations as to who should now be liable. Ignoring such returns may give rise to late bill appeals.

A document is deemed served two days after it is sent by first-class post.[33] Some local authorities use outsourced providers who organise specially arranged deliveries with the post office. In such a case, the local authority must still be able to provide evidence that demands have been served correctly (see Chapter 10). Service of notices by social media is not permitted, as this is outside the scope of the legislation and will not have been intended by parliament when the relevant law was made.[34]

5. Information the bill should contain

The bill must contain certain prescribed information. There are minor variations between England, Wales and Scotland. Local authorities can decide the exact wording and how the information appears on the bill.

Information provided on council tax bills[35]
- The name of the person to whom the bill is addressed. If not known, the bill may be addressed to the 'council taxpayer'.
- The date of issue.
- The period covered by the bill.
- The address of the chargeable dwelling.
- The dwelling's valuation band.
- The amount of council tax (and Scottish Water charges in Scotland) per chargeable dwelling for the relevant valuation band for each tier of local government (eg, district and county council) including, where applicable, a specified amount to cover parish or community council expenditure.
- In England, details about the amount of adult social care expenditure by the authority.[36]
- In England and Wales, a reference to the billing authority's discretionary power to reduce bills under section 13A(1) of the Local Government Finance Act.[37]
- How the amount of the council tax (and Scottish Water charges in Scotland) payable has been calculated, showing separate amounts of any disability reduction, discount and variation of discount or council tax reduction (CTR) under the local authority scheme and the period they cover.
- In England, the percentage change in council tax from the previous year, expressed to one decimal place.
- The gross expenditure of each billing and precepting authority for the year and the previous year, and the reasons for any difference between the figures for the previous and current year.
- The opinions of the billing authority and precepting authority of the effect that its gross expenditure has on the level of council tax set for the relevant year.[38]

- Details of any discount, reduction or premium and the reason for it a statement of your duty to inform the local authority of anything that affects entitlement to a discount and the fact that if you do not comply with this duty, without a reasonable excuse, the local authority may impose a financial penalties.[39]
- The amount (if any) to be credited against the amount of council tax which would otherwise be payable for the relevant year.
- The amount of any penalty. (Scottish civil penalties are usually issued as a separate bill.)
- Council tax arrears from the preceding year(s), but only to the extent that they have not already been billed for. (In Scotland, arrears are usually issued as a separate bill.)
- The amount of council tax payable and how it should be paid.
- The address, telephone number and email to which enquiries may be made.
- A statement on any CTR applicable, explaining the amount of CTR and the reasons for it.[40]
- An explanation of the duty to report changes of circumstances[41] and the possible consequences of failing to notify relevant changes in circumstances.
- In Scotland, the average Scottish council tax charge (excluding water charges) for a Band D property for the current year and for a Band D property in the previous year (excluding water charges).

Bills served after the end of the year in question, or with another bill for another period, are not required to contain all of the above information.[42]

Explanatory notes and accompanying information

The bill should be accompanied by a set of explanatory notes that provide key points of information on: valuation and banding, exempt dwellings, disability reductions, discounts, appeals and the local CTR scheme. The billing regulations distinguish between information which a demand notice is required to contain and information which it is required to supply with a demand notice.[43]

Additionally, in England and Wales, the bill, if issued before the end of the financial year to which it relates, must be accompanied by information explaining the local authority's income and expenditure. Bills that are served after the end of the financial year concerned or with another bill are not required to contain all the specified information.[44]

A local authority may publish the information on its website rather than including the information with a demand notice.[45] The website address must be provided in the demand notice's explanatory notes. It must also be stated that there is a right to request, in writing, a printed copy of that information free of charge and that the authority must supply it as soon as reasonably practicable.[46]

Local authorities are also required to include information about the annual percentage changes in council tax between the previous year and the relevant year. In England if the valuation band of a dwelling has changed, the bill must show the percentage difference between the amounts calculated in the relevant year and the previous year.[47]

Invalid bills

A bill is invalid if it does not contain all the required information. Nevertheless, if the failure to comply with these requirements arose because of a mistake and the amount to be paid is demanded correctly, the bill is treated as valid. The local authority must issue a correction and a statement of the matter omitted from the bill as soon as practicable after the mistake has been found and send it to you.[48] However, there may be situations where the details contained in the bill are confusing or contradicted by amounts stated in other demands. It may be that the bill is a nullity and should be treated as invalid. If the amount stated in the bill is incorrect, it should be challenged immediately with the local authority and an appeal commenced (see Chapter 11).[49] If the local authority or an outsourced company acting on its behalf does not respond, make a formal complaint and ensure that it is acknowledged.

Excessive amounts of council tax and referendums

In England, if an authority's relevant basic amount of council tax is excessive, the local authority is required to include details as a footnote and give notice that a referendum will be held with further information to be supplied in due course. The demand notice continues to be valid in spite of the inclusion of the additional amount identified as excessive but, importantly, the local authority cannot take recovery action in respect of the additional amount until a referendum is held.

No liability order may be issued and no enforcement action (eg, an attachment of earnings order) may be taken for an additional amount, unless it is approved by a referendum. The 'additional amount' is the difference between the amount on the bill and the capped amount and/or any substituted amount which is applicable following a referendum.[50]

If the excessive amount is not approved in a referendum, a referendum is held to be void, or if no referendum is held, a substitute non-excessive amount takes effect, and a local authority may issue a further revised demand notice.[51] No recovery action can be taken in respect of the amount on a demand that has been declared excessive following a referendum.[52]

If you request that a fresh bill be issued, the local authority must provide it. This also appears to have consequences for enforcement as, if the local authority does not issue a fresh bill, the sum cannot be enforced as the local authority will be unable to prove it has followed the rules on billing that are essential for applying for a liability order (see Chapter 10).[53]

Where an authority's excessive relevant basic amount is not approved in a referendum, its substitute calculations have effect.

Where the result of the referendum is to approve the level of council tax originally set by the local authority, the original demand notice is enforceable.[54]

Any demand notices originally issued for the excessive amount continue to have effect, and have effect as if they include the difference between the excessive amount and the substituted amount.[55]

6. **Payment arrangements**

Most taxpayers have a right to pay by instalments. The 'normal' method of payment is by 10 monthly instalments between April and January (see below).[56] In England, this can be spread over 12 instalments if you inform the local authority before 15 April, or over as many months of the year as remain up until 31 March. The local authority may, however, adopt a variety of different payment arrangements, including:
- in England and Wales, the council tenant instalment scheme (see p186). In Scotland, the local authority may establish an agency arrangement with a housing body which then establishes its own payment arrangements;[57]
- special arrangements (see p188);
- discounted lump-sum payments (see p188);
- discounts for non cash payments (see p188).

Instalments

In England and Wales, if the bill is issued:[58]
- on or before 30 April in the relevant year, payments under the statutory scheme are made in 10 monthly instalments;
- from 1 May onwards, the monthly instalments must equal one less than the number of whole months remaining in the financial year (see below);
- between 1 January and 31 March in the relevant year, the total amount due is payable in a single instalment on the day specified on the bill.

The instalments must be made in consecutive months, but the local authority may choose the month in which to start and state this on the bill.[59]

Number of instalments

Month in which demand notice is issued	Number of instalments
April (or before)	10
May	9
June	8
July	7
August	6
September	5

October	4
November	3
December	2
January	1
February	1
March	1

In England, you also have a legal right to request to pay your council tax bill in 12 monthly payments, rather than a maximum of 10, in the course of the year.[60] Information on how to arrange this should be given with the explanatory notes which accompany the demand notice sent at the beginning of the financial year.[61] Where your request to arrange payment in 12 monthly instalments is made between 1 January and 15 April in the year in which the financial year begins, the number of instalments is 12. If your request is made on or after 16 April of the year in question, the number of monthly instalments is the number of whole months remaining in the relevant year after the issue of the notice.[62] Effectively, in any case arising after 16 April, you are able to spread the remaining year's liability over as many months as remain, which also means treating February and March as instalment months.

Example
Eliza wants to pay in 12 monthly instalments in 2018/19. She must request this from the local authority between 1 January and 15 April 2018.
However, if Eliza does not make her request until 6 June, she will have nine instalments to pay (July to March).

In England, where the total amount is calculated by reference to a determination involving a discount which varies during the course of the year (eg, where the Secretary of State or the local authority changes the classification of dwelling entitled to discount), the monthly instalments do not need to be equal amounts but shall be as specified in the notice.[63]

In Scotland, a local authority cannot demand the first instalment in the same month as the bill was issued. If the bill is issued:[64]

- before 1 April in the relevant year, the local authority determines when the first of the 10 instalments is due – this can be either in April or May;
- from 1 April onwards, the monthly instalments must equal one less than the number of whole months remaining in the financial year (see p185);
- between 1 December and 31 March in the relevant year, the total amount due is payable in a single instalment on the day specified on the bill.

Some Scottish councils allow 12 monthly instalments at their own discretion if you pay by direct debit.

Amount of the instalments

The amount of the instalments is worked out by dividing the total amount of the bill by the number of instalments. If this gives an amount which is a multiple of a pound, the instalments will be of that amount.[65]

Example

Craig's council tax is £900 and payments are to be by 10 instalments. The amount of each instalment is £90.

If the total amount due, divided by the number of instalments, does not give an amount which is a multiple of a pound, the amount payable is divided by the number of instalments and rounded to the nearest pound. Amounts ending in 50p should be rounded up. This amount is the amount of the instalments other than the first. This first amount is multiplied by the number of instalments less one, and the resulting amount is subtracted from the total amount payable. The amount remaining is the amount of the first instalment.[66]

Example

Holly's council tax is £500 and payments are to be by nine instalments.
The amount of all but the first instalment is £56.
(ie, £500 ÷ 9 = £55.5555)
The first instalment is £52.
(ie, £500 – (£56 x 8 instalments))

If you only have a small amount of council tax to pay, the instalment method is an expensive way for the local authority to collect it. Consequently, local authorities have the power not to accept any instalment for less than £5. If the calculation of instalments would produce an instalment of less than £5, the local authority may require that the second instalment be added to the first and that the number of instalments be reduced by one. If the total amount payable is less than £10, the local authority may request payment of that amount in a single instalment. If the total amount payable is £10 or more, the local authority may reduce the number of instalments to the greatest number that allows individual instalments of at least £5.[67]

Where the annual amount is divided into 12 instalments, the annual amount is payable over 12 months unless otherwise specified or agreed. The onus is on you to begin the process by requesting this from the local authority. Your request may be made either before or after a demand notice is issued and may be made in relation to the relevant year, or the year following the relevant year.

If you make a request during the financial year, the local authority must issue an instalment notice 'as soon as reasonably practicable'.[68]

Instalment scheme for council tenants

In England and Wales, a local authority may have an instalment scheme for its council tenants to pay their council tax on the same day as they pay their rent, but these have become increasingly rare. This means that if you pay your rent weekly, for example, the local authority may also allow you to pay your council tax weekly.[69] The scheme may also continue to apply during any period in the year in which rent is not payable, provided such a period follows a period in which rent was payable. Check with your local authority whether the scheme operates in your area.

In Scotland, the local authority may establish an agency arrangement with a housing body. It is then for that housing body to establish appropriate payment arrangements.[70]

Instalments when liability ends

No further instalments under either the statutory schemes or, in England and Wales, the council tenant's scheme are due once you are no longer liable for council tax (and for Scottish Water charges in Scotland). If more than one person is jointly liable, whether named on the original bill or not, this only applies if both or all of them are no longer liable. In England and Wales, if the only person(s) who is liable is someone not named on the original bill, the local authority must issue a joint taxpayers' notice on her/him.[71]

If the original liable person(s) is no longer liable, the local authority must serve a notice on the former liable person or, if there was joint liability, on at least one of the jointly liable people. The notice should state the actual amount due up to the day liability ended. This should be done as soon as practicable after liability ends.[72]

If the amount due is less than the total amount paid, the liable person may require the local authority to repay the overpayment. If no request is made, the local authority may decide either to repay it or to credit it against a subsequent council tax debt on another property for which the same person is liable.[73] It cannot be used to meet any other debt recoverable by the local authority, such as an overpayment of housing benefit.

If the amount due is greater than the total amount paid, the local authority will issue a bill requiring the liable person to pay the outstanding amount to the local authority. The local authority must allow at least 14 days from issuing the bill for this amount to be paid.[74]

If the former liable person becomes, once again, liable for the tax to the local authority in the same financial year, the matter is dealt with afresh. Any previous overpayment of tax by the liable person may, however, be credited against the subsequent liability.

Instalments when liability changes

The instalment schemes are based on the assumption that your circumstances will remain the same throughout the year. Liability may change, however, because:[75]

- there is a change to a joint liability or from a joint liability to sole liability; *or*
- the dwelling becomes exempt (see Chapter 4); *or*
- the dwelling's valuation band changes (see Chapter 3); *or*
- entitlement to a discount/variation changes (see Chapter 7); *or*
- entitlement to a disability reduction changes (see Chapter 6); *or*
- entitlement to a council tax reduction (CTR) changes (see Chapter 8); *or*
- a premium is imposed (see p117); *or*
- liability to pay Scottish Water charges in Scotland changes.

The local authority must adjust the remaining instalments (if any) as soon as practicable after the change of circumstances.[76] As many adjustments may be made as the circumstances require. The local authority must also serve a revised bill (an adjustment notice) each time an adjustment is made. This should state the:

- revised estimated liability for the relevant year, assuming no further changes; *and*
- amount of any instalments that remain 14 or more days after the issue of the notice.

In England and Wales, if instalments are payable under the statutory scheme and additional amounts are now due as a result of a change, the payments must be fixed in accordance with the rules for that scheme (see p183). In Scotland, the local authority has the discretion to set the amount of each remaining instalment. If no further instalments are due, the additional amount must be paid as a lump sum within a period set by the local authority. The local authority must give you at least 14 days from the date the bill was issued to pay the amount owing. In Scotland, at least two instalments must fall to be paid under the demand notice concerned in accordance with the statutory instalment scheme or any agreement with the council.[77]

If the revised amount is less than the combined amounts of the instalments payable before the change, you should request that the overpayment be refunded. If you do not make such a request, the local authority may decide either to repay it or credit it against your subsequent liability.[78]

If a local authority revises its estimate of your council tax liability, when adjusting the remaining instalments it must take into account any amounts paid before the day on which the adjustment takes effect which were due to be paid after that day.[79]

Special payment arrangements

A local authority may agree that you can pay your council tax in a particular manner.[80] These special payment arrangements may be entered into either before or after a bill has been issued, although in England and Wales if there is joint liability, the arrangement can only be entered into with someone named on the bill. Special payment arrangements may prove useful if you are facing financial problems. These may allow payments to be ended or adjusted. They may also allow for a fresh estimate to be made if the original estimate turns out to be wrong. If the special arrangement is entered into after the bill has been issued, it may make provision for dealing with any sums paid by instalments.

A bill issued under a special arrangement requires payment of the amount concerned:

- within a set period of not less than 14 days after the day the bill is issued; *or*
- by instalments and payable at intervals and on days as specified on the bill.

The normal enforcement procedures (see Chapter 10) do not apply to special agreements. Procedures to be followed in the event of non-payment should be set out.

Discounts for lump-sum payments

The local authority may decide to encourage payment of council tax by lump sums as this improves its cash flow and reduces its collection costs. The benefits and costs of such an arrangement, not only to the local authority but to all taxpayers, need to be considered carefully. To encourage lump-sum payments, the local authority can offer a discount.[81] Contact your local authority to find out if it offers a discount.

Discounts for non-cash payments

Various methods are available to pay the council tax, but some are more cost-effective for local authorities than others. From the local authority's point of view, direct debit has the most advantages, and direct debit mandate forms are often sent with demand notices to encourage the use of this payment method. In addition, the local authority is able to offer a discount to taxpayers if they use such non-cash methods of payment.[82]

The local authority should consider the costs and benefits of such arrangements. The size of the discount and when non-cash payments are to be accepted must be decided by the local authority on or before the day it first sets the council tax for the year.

If an adjustment is needed to the amount paid and the amount has been paid by a discounted non-cash payment, the instalment or other payment on which the discounted amount was accepted must be treated as having been paid in full.

Any sum to be repaid, or credited against any subsequent liability, however, is reduced by the same proportion as was allowed for the discount.

If you have debts from previous years

If you make a payment to a local authority when you have an existing debt (eg, if you have a council tax liability for a previous year), you should specify the period of liability that the payment is to cover. You must do this, even if the local authority has suddenly issued a bill for an earlier period of liability. If you are paying towards this earlier period, clearly indicate this when making your payment, to avoid the local authority only using your payment for the current year. If you pay by cheque, mark the back of the cheque with details of the year for which payment is made and also enclose a written note. If you do not, you could face enforcement action, as most council tax computer systems are not programmed to recognise such overpayments and, as a default, the total payment may be allocated to the current year while the older bill remains uncredited. If you owe council tax for a previous year and want to repay it by instalments, the local authority may agree to this.

The software default in Scotland is that payments made from 1 April to 31 March are for the current financial year, unless a specific council tax payment reference number, which has a year reference number built in, is quoted with the payment. Some Scottish taxpayers have, upon receiving a new council tax bill in February, started to make payments in March which cause the payment to be defaulted to the terminating financial year. The new tax year reference numbers are not 'live' until 1 April.

If liability orders have been obtained in earlier years, the local authority is likely to include sums in costs. You should challenge the sums in costs as it is unclear on what basis a local authority will have calculated or imposed these and whether they are reasonable (see p208).

If the local authority repeatedly allocates payments to different years so as to create or allow indebtness to continue, make a complaint as this is likely to be maladministration (see p273).

7. Penalties

In certain circumstances, a civil penalty may be imposed by the local authority if you:
* fail to respond to a request for information to identify the liable person (see Chapter 5);
* fail to notify the local authority that a dwelling is no longer entitled to an exemption (see Chapter 4);

- fail to notify the local authority that you are no longer entitled to the same level of discount or premium (Chapter 7);
- fail to timeously advise the local authority that an assumption made that awards a discount/variation received is erroneous; *or*
- knowingly make a false declaration as to the non-occupation of a dwelling in order to benefit from a discount/variation or avoid an increase in council tax liability.

A penalty may be collected by the local authority by including it on your council tax bill (see p180) or sending a separate bill.[83]

If the local authority sends a separate bill, it must allow at least 14 days for it to be paid. If the imposition of a penalty is subject to an appeal or, in England and Wales, arbitration:[84]

- no bill can be issued for the recovery of a penalty;
- no amount is payable in respect of the penalty.

You may not be liable to a penalty if you have a reasonable excuse for not notifying the local authority. Each case will depend on its facts and the individual circumstances of the taxpayer. What is reasonable depends upon the facts and a tribunal will not readily infer that you should be subject to a penalty in circumstances where there is no criminal intent, wilfulness or recklessness. The words 'reasonable excuse' should be given their plain and ordinary meaning without unnecessary embellishment and include whether there are circumstances beyond your control or not.[85] Tax avoidance aimed at reducing liability should not be confused with tax evasion and the fact that a billing authority does not believe you does not amount to proof of factual wrongdoing.[86]

The proportions of the instalments on the bill attributable to the penalty are not payable until the appeal or arbitration is finally disposed of, abandoned or fails for non-prosecution.[87]

If a penalty is paid and is later quashed either by the local authority or following an appeal, the local authority must repay it. This can be done by deducting an amount from any other penalty, council tax and, in Scotland, Scottish Water charges that are owed to the local authority and repaying any balance.[88] In deciding to impose a penalty, the local authority is expected to act reasonably and proportionally. If the penalty is excessive compared with the matter complained of, or unreasonable in the circumstances (eg, if you are terminally ill or have mental health issues), you should appeal to the valuation tribunal or valuation appeal committee in Scotland.

The local authority is expected to act reasonably when imposing a penalty.[89] A complaint can also be made to the Ombudsman who may make an award of compensation.

8. Appeals against the amount of the bill

If you do not agree with the calculation of the amount you are liable to pay, you should write to the local authority. This includes both actual and estimated amounts.[90] Explain which decision you believe to be incorrect and why – eg, because a disability reduction, discount or council tax reduction has not been awarded.

The local authority has two months in which to consider the representations made. If it fails to respond in writing within the two-month period, or if you are still dissatisfied with the response, an appeal can be made to the valuation tribunal or via the local authority to a valuation appeal committee in Scotland. This should normally be done within four months of the date the grievance was first raised with the local authority.

An appeal cannot be made on the basis that any assumption the local authority is required to make about the future may prove to be inaccurate.[91]

The council tax bill should normally still be paid while the appeal is outstanding, subject to any agreement made with the local authority. However, if the local authority has applied for a liability order in the magistrates' court, apply for an adjournment of the liability order hearing if a formal appeal is underway.[92]

Notes

1. Who must pay the bill
1 **EW** Reg 22 CT(AE) Regs; *R (on the application of London Borough of Waltham Forest) v Waltham Forest Magistrates' Court* [2008] EWHC 3579 (Admin); CO/2347/2007
S Reg 18 CT(AE)(S) Regs
2 **EW** Reg 2(3) CT(AE) Regs
S Reg 19(2) CT(AE)(S) Regs
3 **EW** Reg 2(4) CT(AE) Regs
4 **S** Reg 18 CT(AE)(S) Regs
5 **EW** Reg 28 CT(AE) Regs
6 **S** Reg 17 CT(AE)(S) Regs

2. When bills should be issued
7 **EW** Reg 19 CT(AE) Regs
8 **S** Reg 17 CT(AE)(S) Regs
9 **EW** Reg 18 CT(AE) Regs
S Reg 19 CT(AE)(S) Regs

10 **EW** Reg 18 CT(AE) Regs
11 **EW** Reg 19 CT(AE) Regs
12 *Encon Insulation Ltd v Nottingham City Council* [1999] RA 382
13 *North Somerset District Council v Honda Motor Europe Ltd; North Somerset District Council v Chevrolet United Kingdom Ltd; North Somerset District Council v Martin Graham* [2010] EWHC 1505 (QB)
14 *R (on the application of London Borough of Waltham Forest) v Waltham Forest Magistrates' Court* [2008] EWHC 3579 (Admin); CO/2347/2007
15 *Regentford Ltd v Thanet District Council* [2004] EWHC 246 (Admin, [2004] RA 113 (QBD)

16 *Morgan v Warwick District Council* [2015]
   RVR 224
17 Ombudsman Report 13019622, Derby
   City Council, 30 October 2014

3. How the bill is calculated
18 **E** Reg 14 CT(AE) Regs
   W Council Tax (Administration and
   Enforcement) (Amendment) (Wales)
   Regulations 2017 No.41
19 **EW** Reg 20 CT(AE) Regs
   S Reg 20 CT(AE)(S) Regs
20 **S** Reg 20 CT(AE)(S) Regs
21 **EW** Reg 20 CT(AE) Regs
   S Reg 20 CT(AE)(S) Regs
22 **EW** Regs 24 and 25 CT(AE) Regs
   S Regs 23 and 24 CT(AE)(S) Regs
23 **E** Regs 21A and 21b CT(AE) Regs
24 **EW** Reg 24 CT(AE) Regs 1992
25 Reg 27(4) CT(AE)(S) Regs
26 **EW** Regs 24, 25 and 31 CT(AE) Regs
   S Regs 23, 24 and 27 CT(AE)(S) Regs
27 **EW** Regs 24, 25 and 31 CT(AE) Regs
   S Regs 23, 24 and 27 CT(AE)(S) Regs
28 **EW** Regs 24, 25 and 31 CT(AE) Regs
   S Regs 23, 24 and 27 CT(AE)(S) Regs
29 **EW** Reg 24 CT(AE) Regs
   S Reg 23 CT(AE)(S) Regs
30 **EW** Reg 55 CT(AE) Regs

4. How bills are served
31 **EW** Reg 2 CT(AE) Regs
   S s192 Local Government Scotland Act;
   regs 1(3) and 20 CT(AE)(S) Regs
32 **EW** Reg 17(4) CT(AE) Regs
33 s7 Interpretation Act 1978
34 *Sharpe v Wakefield* [1888] 22 QBD at
   239

5. Information the bill should contain
35 Schs 1 and 2 CT(DN)(E) Regs
36 Council Tax (Demand Notices)
   (England) (Amendment) Regulations
   2016 No.188, as amended by the
   Council Tax (Demand Notices)
   (England) (Amendment) Regulations
   2017 No.13
37 Sch 1 para 18 CT(DN)(E) Regs 2011
38 Sch 2 paras 2-6 CT(DN)(E) Regs
39 **E** Sch 2 CT(DN)(E) Regs
   W CT(DN)(W) Regs
40 **E** Reg 19(1)(a) CT(DN)(E) Regs 2011
   W CT(DN)(W) Regs
41 **E** Reg 19A CT(DN)(E) Regs 2011
   W Sch 1 para 8A CT(DN)(W) Regs
42 Reg 5 and 6 CT(DN)(E) Regs 2011
43 Schs 1 and 2 CT(DN)(E) Regs 2011
44 Reg 5(2) CT(DN)(E) Regs 2011

45 Reg 2(4)A CT(AE) Regs
46 Reg 2(4C) CT(AE) Regs
47 Sch 1 paras 13 and 14 CT(DN)(E) Regs
48 Reg 7 CT(DN)(E) Regs 2011
49 s16 LGFA 1992
   E Reg 4C CTNDR(DN)(E) Regs
   W Reg 5 CT(DN)(W) Regs
   S Reg 29 CT(AE)(S) Regs
50 Reg 21A(5) CT(AE) Regs
51 Reg 21A(3)(a) CT(AE) Regs
52 Reg 21A(2) CT(AE) Regs
53 Reg 21A(3)(b) CT(AE) Regs
54 s52ZH LGFA 1992
55 Reg 21 CT(AE) Regs

6. Payment arrangements
56 **EW** Reg 21 and Sch 1 Part I CT(AE) Regs
   S Reg 21 and Sch 1 CT(AE)(S) Regs
57 **S** Sch 2 para 19 LGFA 1992
58 **EW** Sch 1 Part I CT(AE) Regs
59 **EW** Sch 1 Part I CT(AE) Regs
   S Sch 1 CT(AE)(S) Regs
60 Reg 21(1A) CT(AE) Regs
61 Sch 1 para 27 LGFA 1992
62 s11A LGFA 1992; para 2(3A) and Sch 1
   CT(AE) Regs
63 Sch 1 para 2(3B) CT(AE) Regs, as
   inserted by reg 2(14) CT(AE)(A)(No2)(E)
   Regs
64 Sch 1 Part I CT(AE)(S) Regs
65 **EW** Sch 1 Part I CT(AE) Regs
   S Sch 1 Part I CT(AE)(S) Regs
66 **EW** Sch 1 Part I CT(AE) Regs
   S Sch 1 Part 1 CT(AE)(S) Regs
67 **EW** Sch 1 CT(AE) Regs
68 **E** Reg 21(1C) CT(AE) Regs
69 **EW** Sch 1 Part II LGFA 1992
70 Sch 2 para 19 LGFA 1992
71 **EW** Reg 28 CT(AE) Regs
72 **EW** Sch 1 Part III CT(AE) Regs
   S Sch 1 Part II CT(AE)(S) Regs
73 **EW** Sch 1 Part III CT(AE) Regs
   S Sch 1 Part II CT(AE)(S) Regs
74 **EW** Sch 1 Part III CT(AE) Regs
   S Sch 1 Part II CT(AE)(S) Regs
75 **EW** Sch 1 Part III CT(AE) Regs
   S Sch 1 Part II CT(AE)(S) Regs
76 **EW** Sch 1 Part III CT(AE) Regs
   S Sch 1 Part II CT(AE)(S) Regs
77 **S** Reg 24 CT(AE)(S) Regs
78 **EW** Sch 1 Part III CT(AE) Regs
   S Sch 1 Part II CT(AE)(S) Regs
79 **EW** Sch 1 Part III CT(AE) Regs
80 **EW** Reg 21 CT(AE) Regs
   S Reg 21 CT(AE)(S) Regs

81 **EW** Reg 25 CT(AE) Regs
   S Reg 24 CT(AE)(S) Regs
82 **EW** Reg 26 CT(AE) Regs
   S Reg 25 CT(AE)(S) Regs

7. Penalties
83 **EW** Reg 29 CT(AE) Regs
   S Reg 26 CT(AE)(S) Regs
84 **EW** Reg 29 CT(AE) Regs
   S Reg 26 CT(AE)(S) Regs
85 *World of Enterprise Ltd v Revenue and Customs* UKFTT 719(TC)
86 Appeal nos. 0665M130018/254C and 0665M132093/254C, 16 October 2014
87 **EW** Reg 29 CT(AE) Regs
   S Reg 26 CT(AE)(S) Regs
88 **EW** Reg 29 CT(AE) Regs
   S Reg 26 CT(AE)(S) Regs
89 *Associated Provincial Picture Houses v Wednesbury Corporation* [1948] 1 KB 223

8. Appeals against the amount of the bill
90 **EW** s16 LGFA 1992
   S s81 LGFA 1992
91 **EW** Reg 30 CT(AE) Regs
92 *Wiltshire Council v Piggin* [2014] EWHC 4386 (Admin)

Chapter 10

Enforcement

This chapter covers:
1. Introduction (below)
2. Statutory enforcement in England and Wales (p195)
3. Liability orders (England and Wales) (p198)
4. Recovery methods (England and Wales) (p210)
5. Statutory enforcement in Scotland (p229)

1. Introduction

This chapter describes the statutory enforcement process. This is the way in which the local authority can recover unpaid amounts of council tax. The process in Scotland is different from the one in England and Wales. Some elements, however, such as the ability to make deductions from certain benefits, are common to both systems.

The local authority can agree a special payment arrangement with you (see p188). The rescheduling of payments under such an arrangement may often be the most appropriate response if you are in arrears. Non-payment of any amount due under a special payment arrangement is also covered by the statutory enforcement procedure. **Note:** if you do not keep to the agreement, the local authority can commence recovery.

Certain enforcement functions can be performed on behalf of the local authority by an outsourced subcontractor but not the power to make applications to commit a debtor to prison. This can only be done by the local authority.[1]

Note: at any point in the enforcement process, recovery action must stop if the outstanding amount (including costs) is paid.

2. Statutory enforcement in England and Wales

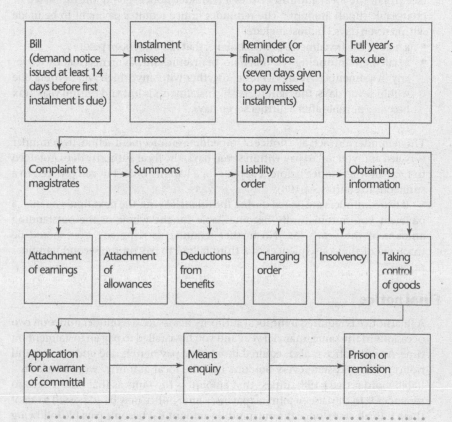

Council tax collection protocol and local authority enforcement policies

Launched in 2009 and revised in June 2017, a protocol on council tax collection was jointly issued by the Local Government Association and Citizens Advice.[2] This aims to promote good practice in the recovery of council tax and co-operation between billing authorities and advice agencies, including the use of civil enforcement agents, but does not refer to other enforcement methods such as bankruptcy and charging orders. The full protocol can be found at www.citizensadvice.org.uk.

Local authorities should also have their own written debt collection policies which they should publish and are expected to adhere to.[3] Failure to have a written policy on the use of bankruptcy is maladministration.[4] A local authority is at fault if it states it has, or will, suspend enforcement action but continues it.[5] In some cases, this may arise because enforcement functions have been delegated to outsourced contractors.

Reminder notice

If the council tax bill has been correctly issued but you fail to pay an instalment (see p183), the local authority issues a reminder notice, giving the estimated or chargeable (final) amount.[6] The reminder notice requires payment to be made within seven days.[7] It must include:

- a note of the instalment, or instalments, that have not been paid;
- a statement informing you that if no, or insufficient, payment is made to cover any instalments that are overdue, together with any which will become due within seven days, the right to pay by instalments is lost and the full year's tax becomes payable after a further seven days.

This reminder also acts as a notice of impending enforcement action. If a reminder is issued and you fail to pay within seven days, the local authority does not need to issue another notice before it applies for a liability order but can proceed to a summons to court (see p198).

If two reminders are issued during the financial year, the next time you miss a payment you automatically become liable for the whole of the outstanding amount of the year's tax. No further reminder is required.[8] You should be informed of the consequences of a third failure to pay on the second reminder notice.[9]

Final notice

A final notice is required if the local authority has issued a reminder notice on two occasions in the same financial year and you have failed to pay an instalment on time. A final notice is also required if only one payment is due under a demand notice. It should state every amount that the local authority would seek on a liability order (see p198), unless that amount is the same as that on the second reminder.[10] In the case of joint taxpayers, a final notice may be addressed to all of them.[11] In all cases, once the outstanding amount has become payable following a reminder, or after seven days following a final notice, the local authority may seek a liability order from the magistrates' court (see p198).[12]

Joint liability

If a bill has been issued in joint names, the local authority can seek to recover the unpaid amount from anyone who is jointly liable. If a joint bill has not been issued, the authority must send a notice to those who are jointly liable but who have not previously been issued with a bill before any recovery action can be taken against them. The jointly liable person must be given at least 14 days in which to pay the bill. If s/he does not then make a payment, a reminder must be served on her/him. If payment is not received after seven days, an application may be made to a magistrates' court for the issue of a summons for a liability order and a further 14 days must be given between any summons and hearing where a liability order may be granted (see p198).

It is possible to apply for a liability order solely against the person to whom the bill was originally sent (even if a joint bill has not been sent), or against both that person and another person(s) who is (or are) jointly and severally liable with that person. It is not, however, possible for a summons to cover more than one person – separate summonses are needed.

Write-offs and payments

While local authorities normally pursue debts until they are recovered, in certain instances it may be appropriate for a local authority to consider writing off a debt which is not cost effective to pursue or in a case of particular financial hardship. It may, for instance, be appropriate to write off liability if a person dies soon after the start of the financial year and so only had a small liability.

Some local authorities may deny they have any power to write off a council tax debt, but section 13A(1)(c) of the Local Government Finance Act 1992 allows an authority to reduce a sum that may be owed in council tax as it thinks fit. This power can be used where a reduction has already been awarded under the local authority's council tax reduction scheme.[13] The reduction may be granted regardless of when the liability arose.[14] A wider power also exists which would allow the write-off of any sum under the general financial powers of a local authority in law.[15]

Outstanding liabilities on death

Liabilities owed by a person who has died may be recovered from her/his estate.[16] The billing authority is required to serve a notice requiring payment of the sum in respect of the alleged liability. Such a sum is enforceable in the administration of the estate as a debt of the deceased person and no liability order need be sought. The executor or personal representative may challenge the alleged liability in an appeal to the valuation tribunal or to another court if proceedings are commenced in respect of the debt. Overpayments of council tax may be recovered by the executor.[17]

The executor or administrator cannot be liable her/himself for the debt, nor may any other relative or beneficiary of the deceased be pursued. No liability to pay arises unless the executor or administrator is first served with a demand.

If the billing authority is unaware that the person has died, enforcement action may have been commenced in the usual way (see p195). In this situation, court and other costs incurred after the death are not enforceable. The imposition of any costs should be challenged.[18]

3. Liability orders (England and Wales)

A liability order issued by a magistrates' court provides a local authority with a variety of options to recover the amount of council tax owed (see p210). It is not a judgment debt for the purposes of the Civil Procedure Rules or the Magistrates' Court Act 1980. This means it cannot be enforced as a judgment debt in the county court or High Court.[19]

A local authority must follow the rules on billing, as an order cannot be obtained if it has not issued a reminder or final notice, as described on p196. Before seeking a liability order, the local authority should, as a matter of good practice, carry out checks to see whether you:

- are entitled to a reduction under its council tax reduction (CTR) scheme (see Chapter 8);
- have made a claim for CTR which has yet to be processed (see p199);
- have appealed or are seeking a review (see Chapter 11);
- are owed a refund for previous period;
- have made a claim for a discretionary reduction (see p167).

Some local authorities, however, fail to carry out sufficient checks and there are frequently failures by local authorities to communicate adequately between the council tax department and the section handling CTR. The problem is particularly acute where council taxpayers who move in and out of low-paid jobs, rely on benefits during periods of unemployment. Delays in awarding discounts or CTR and delays by the Department for Work and Pensions in awarding social security benefits, can all result in many people being wrongly recorded as council tax debtors. Because the enforcement process is effectively governed by a computer program, a failure to award CTR or an exemption – however caused – results in the automatic commencement of enforcement proceedings and costs and penalties being added to bills.

If any of the above circumstances apply, the local authority may suspend recovery action until benefit entitlement has been determined or an appeal decided and should consider refunding these charges.

Considerable effort may be needed to persuade relevant officers of the local authority (or the employees of any company employed by the billing authority if outsourcing collection) to suspend recovery proceedings. Where possible you should consider appealing (see Chapter 11), although it can take time to obtain a hearing. The local authority may be willing to make an alternative payment arrangement with you in return for withdrawing proceedings. Many local authorities will still wish to obtain a full liability order, however, as this gives them the ability to enforce payment if the arrangements are broken. If the local authority does not act reasonably and a summons is issued, go into the court and tell the magistrates what has happened.

If your council tax reduction has yet to be determined

If you receive a summons before your application for CTR has been determined, apply to the magistrates' court for an adjournment of the hearing (see p204).

Under the previous council tax benefit (CTB) system, the view of some local authorities was that a person was liable for the full amount of the council tax demanded by the local authority, and a magistrates' court can order payment. In a community charge (or poll tax) case, it was decided that the magistrates' court could grant a liability order, despite the fact that a claim for community charge benefit had been made and despite the fact that the local authority had failed to determine the claim within the statutory period. In court, local authorities often seek to rely on this case.[20]

The decision to seek a liability order, however, is a discretionary one.[21] Consequently, the local authority must consider the relevant facts of the individual case and not act in an unreasonable manner.[22] A magistrates' court may decline to issue the order if the local authority has not determined a reduction either under the authority's scheme or an application for a discretionary reduction for persons in financial need (see p167).

The decision to issue a summons is also a discretionary matter which has to be exercised reasonably; even though the process is controlled by computer programs, it remains a legal decision, not a technical operation. If a local authority seeks a liability order knowing that a CTR claim is pending, it is possible to argue that this constitutes an unreasonable exercise of the local authority's discretionary power. Furthermore, pensioners on low incomes should have up to 100 per cent of their liability covered by CTR, and some help should be given to others on low incomes. So, it is arguable that parliament did not envisage that such support systems should be undermined by making liability orders in the magistrates' courts with the imposition of costs. Such a case can clearly be made in the case of pensioners – eg, a pensioner who is entitled to the guarantee credit of pension credit. Arguably, the function of the local support system is to provide support for local taxpayers, not to create debt.

A test of 'substantial prejudice' to the taxpayer caused by delays on the part of the local authority has been applied in cases of bills and summons which are issued late.[23] Arguably, substantial prejudice may arise to a council taxpayer where a summons is sent early, before CTR has been determined, as well as when a bill and summons have been sent out late and it is no longer possible to apply for any CTR. Loss of CTR because of the rules preventing backdating, which would otherwise have been payable, is also an example of prejudice. Other examples of prejudice include losing a right of appeal or having to move home or being unable to meet other payment demands.

It may also be possible to use human rights law to object to a liability order if a sum has yet to be calculated. The European Court of Human Rights considers that there must be clarity in orders and judgments issued by courts.[24] If a liability order is made, but CTR entitlement is still to be determined for the year ahead, the amount ultimately due is uncertain, and may be revised. However, the matter has yet to be tested.

Readjusted bills

It is often unclear on what basis a readjusted bill has been issued, particularly if it is several years after the initial period of liability. This may cause particular problems for people who may have been entitled to CTB before April 2013 or who are entitled to CTR but whose circumstances change.

If a readjusted bill is served, request an explanation for the readjustment. Experience suggests this may cause the local authority to re-examine the amount being claimed. Be prepared to take an appeal to a valuation tribunal to challenge any readjustment, particularly if CTR has already been awarded.

If a discretionary reduction is refused, or there is no lawful basis for a bill which the local authority persists in trying to enforce, you should attend court and challenge the bill before the magistrate and argue that either you have paid your liability for the year in question or you have been caused prejudice.

Have you been caused prejudice?

The issue of a late bill which has caused prejudice is a defence to an application to make a liability order. In *North Somerset District Council v (1) Honda Motor Europe Ltd and (2) Chevrolet United Kingdom Ltd and (3) Martin Graham,*[25] the local authority delayed sending out bills for local taxes payable between 2002 and 2007. The High Court accepted the argument that the failure to serve the business rates as soon as practicable after 1 April in the relevant financial year rendered the notices invalid.

The court held that no duty existed on the taxpayer to pay the rates until a correct demand notice was served. Relevant factors to be considered are the length of the delay and the prejudice to the taxpayer which could arise in any number of ways.

Prejudice is considered different from inconvenience and must be 'substantial' and certainly not technical or contrived. There was also countervailing public interest in the collection of taxes, the interests of other taxpayers and the revenues of the local authority concerned which had to be examined by the court.

The judgment shows that the courts will look beyond the simple failures to serve notices and consider both the overall conduct of the local authority and the impact that defects in procedure may have on taxpayers.

Significantly, the court recognises (paragraph 34) that the defendants are entitled to raise an issue of invalidity by way of defence at both the magistrates' court and as an administrative decision: 'Had the Council sought to enforce the notices by way of complaint in the Magistrates' Court the same defence could have been raised.'[26] This means that an objection should be made before the magistrates' court.

Time limits

An application for a liability order from the magistrates' court must be made within six years from the date the bill was issued.

Once a liability order has been made, there is no time limit on how long the local authority may take to enforce it. In *Bolsover District Council and another v Ashfield Nominees Ltd and another*, a local authority was allowed to use insolvency proceedings against a company where a liability order had been obtained more than six years earlier. However, it is possible that an attempt to enforce a liability order that is more than six years old might be considered an abuse of process and unreasonable in law if the taxpayer is an individual.

If a local authority is seeking to enforce liability from an earlier year, the Valuation Tribunal for England (VTE) or the Valuation Tribunal for Wales (VTW) still has jurisdiction to determine the matter. If there have been extensive delays, this may be considered maladministration and you can complain to the Ombudsman (see p272). If bills and reminder notices are served late, liability order proceedings based on them may be dismissed by the magistrates' court if prejudice can be shown (see p174). A discretionary reduction under section 13A of the Local Government Finance Act 1992 might be used to cover a late claim of liability where other benefits or reductions are not available (see p167).

The Ombudsman has ruled that delay was not acceptable where a local authority claimed a liability order for a debt but could not prove it because it had lost the relevant paperwork.[27] The Ombudsman considered that if a debt is properly owed, there is no injustice resulting from delays in recovering that debt, but the case was different because the council was unable to provide documents in support of its claim.

That there exists a limit, in the interests of justice, as to how long delay may be tolerated is shown by a decision under the old rating system.[28] The Court of Appeal held it was unjust for a local authority to have delayed for 12 years before pursuing a local tax demand, with the liable person entitled to bring judicial review proceedings in the High Court.

Obtaining a liability order

To obtain a liability order, the local authority must apply to the magistrates' court for a summons to be issued to you. In practice, this is issued by computer and endorsed with a facsimile signature of a justice of the peace. The decision to seek a summons must be in accordance with the regulations and be a reasonable one.[29]

Regulations state that a summons may be addressed to two or more joint taxpayers in joint names, but natural justice would require that separate summonses should be issued against each defendant, in order to give each person notice of the hearing. If a single reminder is issued to two or more people who are jointly and severally liable, the local authority should produce separate summonses for each person against whom a liability order is to be sought.

The summons instructs you to attend the court to show why you have not paid.[30] No warrant may be issued for your arrest if you do not appear. In practice, most people who have been summonsed do not attend and the 'hearing' takes place in their absence. You should have reasonable notice of the hearing as there must be at least 14 days between serving the summons and the hearing at which the liability order is made.[31]

The summons is not a prescribed form, but should set out the amount outstanding. It may also include the costs reasonably incurred.

The costs for issuing a liability order

In England, the cost of issuing the summons is £3.[32] However, costs vary dramatically for what is essentially an identical and almost fully automated procedure.[33] This is likely to be in breach of the intention of the regulations, which allow only permitted costs which are 'reasonable'. For costs to be reasonable, an explanation as to how they have been calculated should be available. The inflated sums being charged are further likely to be a breach of the legal and constitutional requirement that statutes must precisely set out the basis for charging any sum or amount. It has been held that a local authority must not attempt to raise revenue in the absence of a statutory authority to do so.[34]

In many cases there may be an arguable case that costs being claimed by the local authority may be unlawful.

The costs of the application are divided into two stages: those reasonably incurred before and after a hearing. If you pay before the hearing, these costs are separate to those which are reasonably incurred after the hearing and the making of an order and they should be lower.[35]

You should query other amounts included in the costs on a summons and with making the application to establish why they have been incurred. The costs claimed by a local authority on a summons can sometimes be up to £125 or more, and the legal basis of these costs is unclear. You should demand to know the legal basis of, and calculation of, any costs above £3. You can do this before the hearing, and if the local authority does not agree to reduce or drop the costs, the matter may be raised in court. The authority is required to provide a breakdown of costs claimed in seeking the liability order if requested in court.[36]

The magistrates have a discretion to award costs and may reduce them if they consider they are unreasonable. If you are successful in the magistrates' court, a limitation may be imposed upon an award of costs against the local authority, which means you may not be able to successfully recover the money incurred in defending the claim.

In Wales, the maximum that may be charged in costs when seeking a liability order is £70.[37]

Challenging the costs of a liability order

The costs of applying for a liability order may be challenged if they are unreasonable. The magistrates must be satisfied that the costs are reasonable and properly incurred and cannot simply grant any sum the local authority is asking for.[38]

In *Nicolson v Tottenham Magistrates' Court*, it was held that the debtor was entitled to know the basis on which costs had been awarded and an explanation of the sums. The question of costs is a mixture of fact and law. Magistrates may only award costs where they are satisfied that:[39]

- the local authority has actually incurred those costs;
- the costs were incurred in obtaining your liability order; *and*
- it was reasonable for the local authority to incur them.

The court ruled:

It is clear that there must be a sufficient link between the costs in question and the process of obtaining the liability order. It would obviously be impermissible (for example) to include in the costs claimed any element referable to the costs of executing the order *after* it was obtained, or to the overall administration of council tax in the area concerned.

This means that only the essential costs of obtaining the liability order in the court are recoverable. Simply because a local authority claims an item on a document described as a 'bill of costs', it does not mean it can be included as costs incurred in obtaining a liability order.

Items on any costs bill should be examined closely, distinguishing between costs which arise for administration (eg, computers, offices, wages of staff or sending out bills and reminders) and those which are actually required in making the application to court before the magistrates. There has to be a sufficient link between the costs and the application to be recoverable.[40] The legal costs must also relate to the actual legal steps for the liability order, not to any other type of legal proceedings – eg, the cost of obtaining warrants against debtors in committal proceedings which have fixed-cost schemes of their own.

If a local authority offers an estimated sum in costs, based upon figures in previous years and divided up among debtors, it should submit the information to the clerk and court and also make it available to you.[41] Having demonstrated a causal link, the council must show that costs were reasonably incurred. For magistrates to reach a proper judgment, it is necessary for the council to provide sufficient information as to how the figure was arrived at, and what 'costs' it represents; and it is necessary for the court to have enough information with which it can be satisfied that the costs were incurred in obtaining the order and not for anything else.

Serving the summons

A summons may be served, giving at least 14 days' notice, by:[42]
- posting it to your usual or last-known place of abode;
- delivering it to you;
- leaving it at your usual or last-known address;
- in the case of a company, leaving it at, or posting it to, its registered office;
- leaving it at, or posting it to, an address given by you as an address at which service will be accepted.

If you do not receive a summons for a liability order hearing and the magistrates' court makes the order in your absence, the order may be quashed by the High Court on judicial review.[43] If a summons is not served, any liability order purportedly based upon it is invalid.[44]

Withdrawal of the summons

A summons can only be withdrawn by the court. The power to withdraw a summons is inherent in the powers of the court, and a summons, once issued, cannot be withdrawn by the local authority which is a party to the case.[45] A summons may be withdrawn by the justices' clerk if both you and the council agree. If a party does not agree to the withdrawal, it can only be withdrawn by a magistrate after both parties have been heard in court.

Payment of the outstanding amount

If the outstanding amount, plus costs, is paid, the local authority cannot continue with the application for a liability order.[46] If the amount outstanding has been paid or CTR awarded but the costs have not, a liability order can still be made for the costs alone, although the local authority may be prepared to forego these.[47] If the delay has arisen through the action or inaction of the local authority, the authority may be prepared to waive the costs.

Payment of liabilities for previous years

If you have existing liabilities (eg, you owe money for several years), always specify the year for which you are making the payment, and include a letter or cheque endorsed with the relevant financial year. This will avoid the problem of the local authority applying the sum to different years and leaving outstanding debts.

Adjournments

You can apply to the court for an adjournment if, for instance, you have an arguable case that you should be exempt, if you should be receiving CTR or if there is a matter that should go as an appeal to a valuation tribunal (see p242). This is done by writing to the justices' clerk.

In some courts, the task of listing and adjourning proceedings is carried out by the local authority for reasons of administrative convenience. This raises questions of natural justice, since there is no power in law to delegate the functions and duties of the court to a party to the case.

The grant or refusal of an adjournment is a judicial act and should be exercised fairly.[48] If a court fails to consider an application for an adjournment, any decision may be quashed by judicial review to the High Court.[49] A complaint should also be lodged with the court concerned, and it is advisable to contact your MP.

A sample letter for applying for an adjournment can be found in Appendix 3.

If you do not receive a reply from the magistrates' court, telephone the listing department of the court to enquire about what is being done. You can also go to the court to make an application to the court.

Attending court

If the matter cannot be adjourned, you will have to attend court. Before this, however, the local authority may try to reach an agreement or settlement with you. In some cases, the local authority will agree to withdraw the application, but it is more common for it to insist on getting a liability order to rely on if the agreement is not kept. This also enables the local authority to obtain more in costs.

Most local authorities normally send officials to court to negotiate with taxpayers outside the court room. This can provide an opportunity to discuss any problems that have arisen and to negotiate and reach a solution. In some cases, the local authority may agree to withdraw the liability order application, but any agreement should be in writing. It may be advisable to go into the court room following such an agreement to ensure that this is done formally with notice given to the court. You will be in a stronger position to negotiate if you have already applied for an adjournment in writing to the court. In some cases, the local authority will agree to withdraw the sum in costs, though it may insist on obtaining a liability order. You should ask for an explanation of the costs if they exceed £3, and the authority should provide a breakdown (see p202).

Often the local authority will agree to suspend the liability order application on terms that require you to repay the money or agree an adjournment if there is a matter being appealed to the valuation tribunal. This agreement should be obtained in writing.

The hearing

If it is not possible to reach a settlement, or you wish to challenge the basis of the local authority's case, there must be a hearing.

You are entitled to be present and hear the case against you and to speak in your defence. The burden of proof is on the local authority to demonstrate that it has complied with the rules of billing, not upon you to show why you have not paid. If you are prevented from either addressing the court or seeing the evidence, the hearing will be a breach of natural justice and you are entitled to appeal as the hearing was not fair.

The procedure for the hearing follows rule 14 of the Magistrates' Courts Rules 1981. You should be allowed an opportunity to examine all the evidence produced by the local authority and ask questions in cross-examination. The court normally must comprise two justices of the peace or a single magistrate, now known as a district judge.[50] You may make a submission of 'no case to answer' if the local authority has failed to prove an essential part of its case. If the submission of 'no case to answer' succeeds, the local authority is not entitled to a liability order.

Representatives

You can represent yourself without a legal representative. In addition, you have the right to have the assistance of a friend – eg, an adviser who is not a lawyer.[51] Such a person can sit with you in court and help by taking notes, prompting and giving you advice on the conduct of the case. S/he is known as a 'McKenzie friend'. It is sensible to mention to the court that such an adviser is present at the earliest opportunity. Anyone considering attending court as a McKenzie friend should read the practice guidelines available at www.judicary.gov.uk. The court may also exercise a discretion to allow a non-lawyer to represent an otherwise unrepresented person, but only if it is in the interests of justice.[52]

Grounds for granting a liability order

An order must be made if the magistrates are satisfied that:[53]
- the sum is payable by the person concerned; *and*
- it has not been paid.

The local authority must satisfy the court that:
- the council tax has been fixed by the local authority;
- the sums have been demanded in accordance with the regulations;
- full payment of the amount due has not been made by the required date;
- a reminder, second reminder or a final notice has been issued;
- the sum has not been paid within seven days of the reminder or final notice being issued and the full amount has become payable;
- the summons has been served for the amount outstanding at least seven days after the reminder or final notice; *and*
- the full sum claimed has not been paid.

The defences available to you include:

- the amount has not been demanded in accordance with the regulations – eg, the local authority failed to follow the correct time periods in serving bills and reminders;
- the authority has issued two bills for the same amount;
- bills have been issued late (see p200 and Chapter 9);
- instalments have not been calculated in accordance with the regulations (see Chapter 9);
- the amount has been paid;
- you are not the person named on the summons;
- the level of council tax is not in accordance with the sum set by the local authority;
- the hearing is being held less than 14 days following the issue of the summons;
- you have properly requested to pay by instalments in accordance with the statutory scheme but the local authority has failed to comply with requirements and issued a summons.[54]

An appeal to a valuation tribunal (see p243) may be raised in liability order proceedings – eg:[55]
- whether or not you are a liable person;
- whether or not the dwelling is a chargeable dwelling;
- with regard to entitlement to a disability reduction;
- with regard to entitlement to a discount or exemption.

However, there are two High Court conflicting decisions on this point, suggesting that the jurisdiction of the magistrates' court may not be wholly excluded from consideration by the magistrates' court, and the High Court may decide to follow which it prefers.[56] Practices can vary greatly between courts, but if there is evidence of a serious objection to liability, many courts will adjourn the proceedings. A local authority which acts unreasonably in refusing payment at the liability order stage may be penalised in costs if an appeal has to go to the High Court.[57]

The case for an adjournment may be strengthened if you have lodged an appeal with the VTE/VTW.[58] Unless agreed in advance, an application for an adjournment must be made in the courtroom directly to the bench on the 'return day' of the summons. Wherever possible, contact the court in writing to seek an adjournment, and also inform the local authority.

Evidence
The local authority can use any statement contained in a document, including a computer-generated statement, provided:[59]
- the document forms part of a record compiled by the authority;
- direct oral evidence of any fact stated in it would have been admissible;

- if the document has been produced by a computer, it is accompanied by a signed certificate validating that the computer was operating properly.

The local authority officer presenting the case should be asked to produce the certificate for inspection. Failure to do so will make the computer evidence inadmissible and the local authority will be unable to prove its case in court.[60]

Your direct evidence, given as a witness, is admissible, together with any other documents or statements.[61] Notice of any document used or any other hearsay statement[62] (ie, a statement made by any person not called as a witness in court) must be given to the clerk and the local authority. These rules are complicated and place you at a disadvantage, as they require notice to be given to the clerk at least 21 days before a hearing, whereas you may only receive 14 days' notice of a summons. However, one possible way around this problem is to serve copies of any documents on the local authority so that they become records held by the local authority (which are acceptable). Alternatively, in many cases the local authority will have had notice of the documentary evidence more than 21 days before a hearing – eg, where correspondence has been ongoing over CTR. If there has been a history of maladministration of billing and reminder notices by the local authority, the magistrates' court may order staff from the billing authority to explain what has happened. In exceptional circumstances, the High Court may also order the local authority to reconsider a benefit application from an earlier year on judicial review.[63]

The liability order

The court may make a liability order for one person for one amount. It can also make one liability order for more than one person and more than one amount in the form of a schedule.[64]

Note: the form (Form A) originally provided to draw up liability orders was removed from law from 10 July 2003 in Wales and 1 October 2003 in England and no form has been substituted in its place.[65] Without any written record of its order or judgment being issued by the court, an order from a magistrates' court may be invalid.[66] This point has begun to be raised in proceedings at various magistrates' courts since August 2015 and has yet to be resolved. The failure by parliament to create the necessary form is a serious flaw in the legislation which potentially compromises the making of all orders and enforcement activity. It is clear that parliament envisaged magistrates making a physical liability order as the basis for taking of any further enforcement action, including any further steps in the court which have to be based upon a judgment or order – eg, bankruptcy.

A liability order is meant to identify the aggregate amount that can be recovered, including the costs, but it is unclear how this can be achieved if a magistrates' court does not make a liability order in writing and only purports to issue the liability order orally. If the full sum claimed has been reduced (eg, because CTR has been awarded), the liability order will be for a greater sum than the amount payable. In such cases, the order remains in force and the excess amount should be treated as paid. If, following the issue of an order, you owe more than the amount specified, the local authority can only enforce up to the limit stated in the order. It must seek a new order to enforce the outstanding balance. However, if no proper stamped and sealed order is drawn up and issued by the court, then effectively the local authority may not be able to establish that any such order exists or existed at any stage, nor show that the magistrates were ever satisfied that the local authority had proved all the matters it is required to prove.

In practice, the courts seldom issue individual liability orders; the judge or chair of the magistrates normally just signs a certificate attached to the list of non-payers, but in a form that does not comply with the regulations – without the stamp or seal of the court or any form laid down in regulations since 2003 (see p208).

This is a serious flaw in proceedings identified by the Court of Appeal.[67] Until 2012, many courts did not keep any proper record of liability order hearings or the orders issued, leaving local authorities to maintain records which could be wrong and incapable of independent verification. This has also been identified as a serious omission in enforcement by the High Court.[68]

The lack of an adequate and independent record may be a breach of the human rights of the debtor under Article 6 of the European Convention on Human Rights, regarding the process of determining the civil rights and obligations of a citizen.[69]

Setting aside a liability order

It is possible for a liability order to be 'set aside' – ie, the court quashes or cancels the order and the local authority cannot take enforcement action. A local authority can apply to a magistrates' court to have a liability order quashed, on the basis that it should not have been made.[70] If the court decides that it would have granted an order for a lesser sum, it may make a liability order for a lesser sum together with the costs reasonably incurred in obtaining the order. The local authority must issue a summons for a new amount within six years.

One potential drawback for the council taxpayer is that the right to quash the order is wholly reliant on the local authority's being willing to make the application. Unreasonable refusals to quash liability orders could be challenged by judicial review. A complaint of maladministration may also be made (see p272). In the meantime, you remain subject to the order.

If the magistrates' court has acted 'in excess of jurisdiction' (ie, if it has made an order that it had no power to make), you can ask it to set aside the order.[71] For example, the High Court ruled that magistrates were wrong not to have quashed three liability orders made between 1996 and 1998 against an applicant who was unaware of the proceedings until January 2004.[72]

The High Court ruled that the following apply when deciding to set aside a liability order.[73]
- There must be a genuine and arguable dispute about the liability to pay.
- There must have been substantial procedural error, defect or mishap for the liability order to have been made.
- The application to set aside was made promptly after the defendant had notice of its existence.

There is no prescribed form for making an application to set aside a liability order but a letter can be sent to the court's clerk identifying the liability order and requesting a hearing to consider setting it aside.[74] This is crucial if a local authority is seeking to enforce a liability order through bankruptcy proceedings unless the matter is also being challenged through the valuation tribunal (see p223). Therefore, it may also be necessary in order to lodge an appeal with the VTE/VTW. See Chapter 11 for more information on appeals. Costs may be awarded to the successful party if a set-aside application is contested.[75]

4. Recovery methods (England and Wales)

The liability order gives the local authority the power to:
- obtain information about your financial circumstances and thus assess the best course of recovery action (see p211);
- make an attachment of earnings order (see p211);
- make an attachment order on an elected member's allowances (see p214);
- apply to the Department for Work and Pensions (DWP) for deductions to be made from your universal credit (UC), income support (IS), jobseeker's allowance (JSA), employment and support allowance (ESA) or pension credit (PC) (see p214);[76]
- use enforcement agents (previously known as bailiffs) to take control of your goods (see p215);
- apply for a charging order against the dwelling in respect of which your liability arose (see p222);
- apply to bankrupt you (see p223).

The local authority may decide which recovery method it wishes to use in each case, and may use it more than once, but it may not pursue more than one method at any one time.[77] In the case of joint liability, it may pursue only one person at a time.[78] So if, for example, one of the joint taxpayers is the subject of an attachment of earnings order (see p211), the local authority cannot take control of the goods of the other.

Providing information

Once the liability order has been made and for as long as the amount in question remains unpaid,[79] the local authority may request you to provide the following information:

- the name and address of your employer;
- your earnings or expected earnings;
- statutory deductions from pay (these must be disregarded when calculating the amount to be deducted under an attachment of earnings order);
- your payroll number;
- details of existing attachment of earnings orders;
- details of other sources of income – eg, occupational pension, benefits;
- whether there is anyone jointly liable for the whole, or any part, of the amount for which the order was made.[80]

You do not have to supply the information if the request is not made in writing, or if the information is not in your possession or control.[81] Similarly, you are not required to provide any information which is not prescribed by the regulations – eg, the number plate of a vehicle you may own. Otherwise, you must provide the information within 14 days of the request being made.[82] You do not, however, have to advise the local authority of a change of circumstances unless it makes a fresh request for the relevant information, but you do have to inform it about any change in your circumstances as regards your ongoing liability (see Chapter 5) and entitlement to council tax reduction (CTR – see Chapter 8). If a liability order has been granted against people who are jointly liable, the local authority can require this information from any, or all, of them. If you fail, without a reasonable excuse, to supply the requested information, you are guilty of a criminal offence and may be fined by the magistrates' court up to a maximum of level 2 (£500).[83] If you 'knowingly or recklessly' supply false information, you could be found guilty of a criminal offence and fined up to a maximum of level 3 (£1,000).[84]

Attachment of earnings order

An attachment of earnings order requires an employer who is paying wages, statutory sick pay or an occupational pension to deduct some of it and make payments to the court to meet a debt. A local authority with a liability order against you may arrange to have standard deductions made from your earnings in this way.[85] Certain costs arising from unsuccessful enforcement activity may also be recovered by an attachment of earnings order.

Attachment of earnings orders are a practical and, in many cases, preferable alternative to taking control of goods (see p215). The decision to use this method of recovery, however, is a discretionary one and the local authority must consider all the relevant factors before deciding to adopt this method. Normally, the local authority offers you the opportunity to pay by instalments before using an attachment of earnings order.

A local authority cannot have more than two council tax attachment of earnings orders against a person at one time.[86]

In addition to each amount deducted under the attachment of earnings order, the employer can deduct a further £1 towards administration costs each time a deduction is made.

The order

The attachment of earnings order must specify:

- the fact that a liability order has been obtained against you, and the outstanding sum;
- the rate at which deductions are to be made from net earnings (see p213);
- the period within which each deduction made is to be paid to the local authority – ie, within 19 days of the end of the month in which the deduction is made.

The order must be signed by the proper officer at the local authority. A facsimile signature is acceptable.

Once an attachment of earnings order has been made, it remains in force until:

- the whole amount to which it relates has been paid; *or*
- it is cancelled by the issuing authority.[87]

The local authority may cancel the order on its own initiative or following an application by you or your employer.[88]

Notifying employment changes

While an attachment of earnings order is in force, you must notify the local authority in writing if you leave a job or become employed or re-employed.[89] This notification must be given within 14 days of the day on which you leave, start or recommence the employment, or (if later) the day on which you are informed by the local authority that the order has been made.[90] If you do not comply, without a reasonable excuse, you commit an offence and may be fined.[91] If you make a statement which you know to be false, you may also be found guilty of an offence.[92]

Complaints about attachment of earnings orders

The Ombudsman does not usually investigate the decision to apply for an attachment of earnings order, but may investigate maladministration in the way in which the order is carried out and errors which may arise in seeking or applying the order. An error may arise, for example, where the use of an attachment of earnings order would be considered 'disproportionate and heavy handed'.[93]

A council is not at fault for seeking an attachment of earnings order without your permission if you have been given the opportunity to make a settlement arrangement but have not done so.[94] However, a council is at fault if it gives wrong advice on which you rely and you are denied the opportunity to make a reasonable payment offer.[95]

The deductions to be made

The deductions under an attachment of earnings order are made from your net earnings.[96] The amount deducted depends on the payment period. If you are not paid weekly or monthly, or are paid on an irregular basis, a daily rate is used. Special rules cover more unusual payment arrangements. You can agree with the local authority and your employer a lower deduction than the statutory amount. Your employer should alter the deductions if your earnings change.

'**Earnings**' include any fees, bonus, commission, overtime pay or other emoluments payable in addition to wages or salary, or payable under a contract of service. They also include statutory sick pay.[97] The following are not treated as earnings:[98]

- social security benefits (including UC) and tax credits;
- allowances payable for disablement or disability;
- sums payable by any public department of the government of Northern Ireland or of a territory outside the UK;
- pay or allowances payable to a member of the armed forces;
- wages paid to a seaman, other than of a fishing boat.

'**Net earnings**' are defined as the gross earnings minus:[99]

- income tax;
- class 1 national insurance (NI) contributions;
- amounts deducted towards a superannuation scheme; *and*
- tax credits.

Deductions from weekly net earnings[100]

Monthly	Weekly	Daily	Deduction rate
Up to £300	Up to £75	Up to £11	0%
£300.01 to £550	£75.01 to £135	£11.01 to £20	3%
£550.01 to £740	£135.01 to £185	£20.01 to £27	5%
£740.01 to £900	£185.01 to £225	£27.01 to £33	7%
£900.01 to £1,420	£225.01 to £355	£33.01 to £52	12%
£1,420.01 to £2,020	£355.01 to £505	£52.01 to £72	17%
£2,020.01 and over	£505.01 and over	£72.01 and over	17% of this threshold and 50% of the remainder

Priority of attachment of earnings orders

There is a priority for attachment of earnings orders if more than one has been made against you.[101] Council tax attachment of earnings orders should be dealt with one at a time and in the order in which they are made. If an order is already in force (eg, for child support arrears), a council tax order is applied to the balance of pay remaining after the other deductions have been made. If an order for council tax is in effect when another order is made, the council tax order should continue to be met and the balance considered attachable for the other order.

Councillors' allowances

If you are a local authority councillor (but not a member of the Court of Common Council of the City of London or the Receiver for the Metropolitan Police District), the local authority can make an order to deduct 40 per cent from your allowances – eg, for attending meetings and for special responsibilities. The decision to use this method of recovery is a discretionary one. The local authority must consider all the relevant factors before deciding to adopt this method.

Note: where an elected member fails to pay an amount of council tax within two months of the due date, s/he cannot vote on any matter which influences the setting of the local authority's council tax.[102]

Deductions from benefits

In England, Wales and Scotland, if a liability order (in Scotland, a summary warrant or decree from the sheriff court) has been obtained, the local authority may apply for deductions to be made from your UC, IS, JSA, ESA or PC.[103] The decision to use this method of recovery is a discretionary one. The local authority must take all the circumstances of the case into account before deciding to pursue it.

The maximum weekly amount that can be deducted from your benefits for council tax arrears is £3.70. There are also restrictions if deductions are being made for other debts. See CPAG's *Welfare Benefits and Tax Credits Handbook* for details about the rules.

Deductions from UC/IS/JSA/ESA/PC can only be made in respect of one application from the local authority at any given time. If a second application is made before the sum specified in the first application has been fully recovered, the second has to wait until the first has been cleared.[104]

As far as is practicable, you and the local authority should be notified of the decision in writing within 14 days. You should also be notified of your right to appeal against the decision.

When the debt has been paid, the local authority must notify the local Jobcentre Plus office within 21 days, or as soon as practicable after that.[105]

The DWP must notify you in writing of the total amount deducted under any application if:[106]

- you request this information in writing; *or*
- the deduction ends.

Taking control of goods

The seizure of goods and their sale at auction to pay off a debt is a remedy that local authorities have long used in local taxation.

From April 2014, Schedule 12 of the Tribunals, Courts and Enforcement Act 2007 and the Taking of Control of Goods Regulations 2013 set the rules about the taking control of goods and what enforcement agents can and cannot do. These rules govern council tax enforcement against goods.[107] The previous process of 'distress' has been abolished and a new procedure of 'taking control of goods' applies to the recovery of debts. Because of their broadened powers, the government now prefers to refer to bailiffs as 'enforcement agents' but the term 'bailiff' remains in common use, including by bailiffs themselves.

There are several different types of enforcement agent operating in England and Wales. Some are employed as public servants and some are private agents. They all enforce liabilities by taking control of goods.

The billing authority may employ its own enforcement agents, but many use private companies of bailiffs to take control of goods as part of the range of enforcement services.

It is good practice for local authorities to consider other methods (such as attachment of earnings orders or deductions from benefits) in preference to taking control of goods as an initial enforcement option. If some other method of recovery is in force, the local authority has no power to take control of goods.[108]

The local authority cannot attempt to take control of goods unless you have been sent a written notice giving you a minimum of 'seven clear days' notice that a visit will take place to take control of goods.[109] Sundays, bank holidays, Good Friday and Christmas Day do not count in calculating the seven-day period.[110]

The written notice must mention the following specified matters:[111]

- your name and address;
- the reference number(s);
- the date of notice;
- details of the liability order;
- the amount of any enforcement costs incurred up to the date of notice;
- the possible additional costs of enforcement if the sum outstanding should remain unpaid;
- how, and between which hours and on which days, payment of the sum outstanding may be made;
- a contact telephone number and address at which, and the days on which and the hours between which, the enforcement agent or the enforcement agent's office may be contacted;
- sufficient details of the debt to enable the debtor to identify the debt correctly;

- the amount of the debt including any interest due as at the date of the notice; *and*
- the date and time by which the sum outstanding must be paid to prevent goods of the debtor being taken control of and sold and the debtor incurring additional costs.

The seven-day notice may be served by post, fax or electronic measures, or be hand delivered through the letter box or (where there is no letter box) by affixing it to the property or the place where it is likely to come to your attention.[112]

Codes of practice

The local authority is responsible for ensuring that its enforcement agents are properly authorised and comply with the law.[113] As well as *Taking Control of Goods: national standards* issued by the Ministry of Justice, local authorities may also have their own codes of practice, setting out rules for taking control of goods to which they are expected to adhere. If a local authority fails to observe its code of practice, this may amount to maladministration and may be grounds for a complaint to the Ombudsman (see p272).[114]

Vulnerable households

Care should be taken with vulnerable households. The regulations restrict the steps that enforcement agents may take when encountering individuals who may be classed as vulnerable. The legislation does not define 'vulnerability'. However, *Taking Control of Goods: national standards* provides some detailed guidance on this. It considers you vulnerable if, because of your age, health or disability, you are unable to safeguard your personal welfare or that of other members of your household.[115] See p299 for examples of groups who could be considered vulnerable.[116] Vulnerability may be a temporary phase – eg, if you have a serious short-term illness or injury. The enforcement officer must assess the situation s/he finds at the property and make a decision on whether or not to proceed.

Note: taking control of goods cannot take place where a child or vulnerable person is the only person present in the dwelling where the goods are located.

Goods

An enforcement agent can only take control of goods which belong to you[117] on premises which s/he has power to enter (see p217) or which are on the highway.[118] If goods are jointly owned, the enforcement agent must obtain full details of the co-owner and s/he must be included in subsequent proceedings and be paid her/his share of the proceeds of any sale.

Exempt goods

The following are exempt and cannot be taken into control:[119]

- your only or principal home. This can include a houseboat, tent, caravan and mobile home if it is your home;[120]

- items or equipment (eg, tools, books, telephones, computers and vehicles) which you need for your employment, business, trade, profession, study or education. The total value of these items must not exceed more than £1,350;
- clothing, bedding, furniture, household equipment, items and provisions that are reasonably required to satisfy your basic domestic needs and those of every member of your household. These include:
  - a cooker or microwave, but not both;
  - a refrigerator;
  - a washing machine;
  - a dining table, large enough, and enough dining chairs, to seat all members of the household;
  - beds and bedding sufficient for every member the household;
  - one landline telephone, or if there is no landline telephone at the premises, a mobile or internet telephone;
  - any item or equipment reasonably required for the medical care of any member of the household, or for safety or security – eg, an alarm system;
  - sufficient lamps or stoves, or other lighting and heating appliances to satisfy the basic heating and lighting needs of household;
- any item or equipment reasonably required for the care of a person under the age of 18, a disabled person or an older person;
- assistance dogs (including guide dogs, hearing dogs and dogs for disabled persons), sheep dogs, guard dogs and domestic pets;
- a vehicle used by a disabled person on which a valid disabled person's badge is displayed;
- fixtures – ie, things which are attached to the property, including anything which is plumbed in or forms part of the property. This includes light and electrical fittings, baths, hobs, stoves, shelves and built-in wardrobes;
- goods which are in use and their seizure would be likely to result in a breach of the peace.[121]

Goods belonging to children cannot be taken. Nor can items exclusively used by children, even if they may be your property.[122]

Lawful entry to premises

Time
In general, entry should only take place between 6am and 9pm on any day of the week.[123]

Place
An enforcement agent can only enter a 'relevant premise' if s/he believes that it is the place, or one of the places, where you usually live, or carry out a trade or business – ie, if you are self-employed. In practice, this means the dwelling on which council tax is paid, or your principal home if you have a second home. It

also means that the enforcement agent cannot enter other premises owned by relatives or neighbours unless you either reside in them or carry out a business from them.[124] **Note:** 'premises' can include vehicles, vessels and tents or other moveable structures. However, there is no automatic right to take control of goods on private land – eg, car parks. This can only be done with a prior court order. This means that clamping cars other than on your own drive or on the highway is not lawful.

Method of entry

The enforcement agent must enter a property peacefully through an unlocked door or other usual entrance.[125] S/he should be clear as to why s/he is seeking entry to the premises. Enforcement agents cannot obtain a court order to gain entry to any property for council tax, nor can an occupier be sent to prison merely for refusing to entry. You are entitled to use reasonable force in resisting agents who try unlawfully to push their way in.[126]

Identification

The enforcement agent must show evidence of her/his identity and authority to enter the premises. This can be requested before s/he enters the premises or while s/he is there.[127]

Ways of taking control

To take control of goods, an enforcement officer must do *one* of the following:[128]
- enter into a 'controlled goods agreement'; *or*
- secure the goods on the premises; *or*
- secure the goods on the highway; *or*
- remove the goods and secure them elsewhere.

Controlled goods agreements

A '**controlled goods agreement**' is an agreement under which you retain custody of the goods, but which acknowledges that the enforcement agent has taken control of them. You must not remove or dispose of the goods, nor permit anyone else to do so, before the debt is paid.

The enforcement agent may not enter into a controlled goods agreement if you appear not to understand the effect of such an agreement – eg, because of language difficulties, mental disability or mental illness.[129]

The agreement must be in writing and signed by you (or someone permitted to sign on your behalf) and the enforcement agent,[130] and must contain:
- your name and address;
- the reference number or numbers and the date of the agreement;
- the names of the persons entering into the agreement;
- a contact telephone number and address and the hours available for the enforcement agent or her/his office;

- a list of the goods and their description, including;
  - the manufacturer, model and serial number of the goods;
  - in the case of a vehicle, the manufacturer, model, colour and registration mark of the vehicle; *and*
  - the material, colour and usage, and (where appropriate) any other identifying characteristic, of the goods; *and*
- the terms of the arrangement entered into for the repayment of the debt.

A copy of the signed agreement must be given to the person who signed it – and to you, if someone signed on your behalf. Where it is signed by a person authorised by you, a copy must also be provided to you by either leaving it on the premises, delivering it to your address or delivering it to any relevant premises, in a sealed envelope addressed to you.[131]

Securing the goods
Goods may be secured on the premises – eg, in a cupboard, room, garage or outbuilding.[132] Vehicles may be immobilised, and separate rules and notice provisions apply to take goods from the highway.[133] The enforcement agent is responsible for keeping goods in 'a similar condition to that which the enforcement agent found them' and the storage must be secure and the conditions of that storage must prevent damage to or deterioration of the goods for so long as they remain in the enforcement agent's control.[134]

Having taken control of the goods, the enforcement agent cannot be refused entry if s/he has to return to remove them at a later date. The enforcement agent is entitled to force entry under these circumstances, but a form notifying you should be given before any forcible entry to remove the goods is made.[135]

The form may be served in the same ways as an initial notice at the beginning of enforcement with the exception of the post, and the notice must be given by the enforcement agent her/himself.[136]

Removing the goods
Additional information and notice and an inventory are issued if goods are removed,[137] including a notice giving the date of removal of the goods to storage or for sale, the daily and weekly charges and the procedure for collection by, or on behalf of, the debtor.[138] However, removal of goods is rare because the prices which goods fetch at auction seldom cover enforcement or auction fees and leave the debt outstanding. Rather, enforcement agents usually prefer to obtain payment or get a controlled goods agreement.

Selling goods
The purpose of taking control of goods is to provide valuable security that can be realised if you fail to pay. Seizure and sale of goods, however, is rare.

Enforcement officers have a general duty to sell the goods for the best price that can reasonably be obtained. A valuation must be obtained by the enforcement officer and you (or a co-owner) should be given the opportunity to get an independent valuation if desired.

The enforcement officer must then give you written notice of the date, time and place of the sale. The minimum notice period is seven clear days before the date of sale and it must be given within 12 months. This period can be extended (repeatedly, if necessary). This gives you an opportunity to make instalment payments to discharge the debt.

Note: a sale cannot be completed if a third-party claim to ownership is outstanding.[139]

After the sale

Immediately after the sale, the enforcement officer must provide you and any co-owner with a statement detailing the items sold and the sum received for each. It must also state how the proceeds of the sale are applied to the costs and to your debt. Any recoverable expenses incurred by the enforcement officer should be listed.

Fees

Fees

Compliance stage fee: £75
Upon receipt of an instruction from the authority, the enforcement agent must send a 'notice of enforcement' giving you a minimum of seven clear days' notice that a visit will take place to take control of goods.
This fee is payable for each liability order/warrant of control.
Enforcement stage fee: £235 (plus 7.5 per cent of the value of any council tax debt that exceeds £1,500)
This fee becomes chargeable when the debt is not paid during the compliance stage or where a payment arrangement is broken and an enforcement agent visits the property to remove goods.
Sale stage fee: £11 (plus 7.5 per cent of the value of the debt that exceeds £1,500)[140]
This fee is charged when an enforcement agent attends the premises to remove goods and arrange for the sale of goods. Additional charges may be applied relating to the removal. These include storage and locksmith's fees.

As soon as one of the above stages has started, the fee is likely to be demanded, even though all the activities covered by the stage may not have been carried out or completed. Fees should only br charged for steps actually taken.

In practice, the sums raised at auction seldom even cover the enforcement agent and auctioneer's fees or any of these charges.

Where a liability order has been made against more than one person in respect of an amount, only one compliance fee is payable and no additional charge may be imposed against the other persons. A single charge for the compliance stage is treated as the charge covering the others as well as the first named person.[141]

Where you fall into a vulnerable category (see p216), the enforcement agent is required to give you 'an adequate opportunity to obtain assistance and advice prior to removal of the goods'. If the enforcement agent does not do this, the enforcement stage fee is not recoverable.[142]

Enforcement agents can only impose the charges on p220, plus the outstanding amount due under the liability order. The enforcement agent and the local authority cannot charge for other matters, such as writing letters or making arrangements to pay.

Any spurious charges should be challenged, first with the enforcement agents concerned and, if that fails, with the local authority, if necessary using the local authority's formal complaints procedure. If neither succeeds, a complaint may be made to the Ombudsman who may investigate (see p272) and order a refund of any overcharged fees.[143] For example, where an arrangement is made with the enforcement agent and no goods taken, there is no charge for the removal of goods.[144]

Fees are recoverable from the proceeds of sale of the seized goods or may be paid by the local authority.[145] Legislation states that fees may be recovered from you but no mechanism is clearly set out to enforce payment; the legislation envisages that the sums claimed are only payable where the steps for which they are levied are actually taken. No second liability order may be sought in respect of fees alone.

You can take any dispute over the fees to the civil courts.[146] If you think you have been overcharged, an application may also be made in the small claims court.

Return of the council tax debt to the local authority

Some local authority finance departments claim that, once an enforcement agent is instructed, it is not possible to return the debt to the local authority. This is wrong in law as the enforcement agents are the servants of the local authority and subject to its direction, since the liability order grants a range of options to be pursued. The only powers of enforcement agents set down in the legislation are to take control of goods, not to make binding financial decisions on behalf of the authority. Furthermore, the enforcement regulations previously made it clear that money may be paid to the local authority at any time, and there is no restriction in any regulations which prevents you paying direct, to the authority.[147] The Ombudsman has indicated that local authorities must act appropriately and in a proportionate way when enforcing debts. If a local authority refuses to consider taking back a particular debt from its enforcement agents, this can be challenged by a complaint to the district auditor. Informing the local authority that the matter will be sent to the auditor for investigation invariably results in the local authority reconsidering its policy and action.

Remedies against wrongful enforcement

You and any third party (eg, your landlord or a relative) may take legal action in cases of wrongful enforcement against goods. The most common ground of action is when enforcement agents have taken control of the wrong person's goods, such as those belonging to a non-liable person.[148]

You, a creditor or co-owner of any goods are entitled to make an application to court. In a dispute about the amount of proceeds payable to the co-owner of the goods, the matter is determined by the court.[149]

You may take proceedings in the county court or High Court for a remedy. The court may order:

* the goods to be returned to you;
* payment of damages to you;[150]
* any other remedy available to the court[151] – eg, an injunction.

Individual enforcement agents may have a defence to a claim if they have a reasonable belief that what was done was not in breach of Schedule 12 or the liability order was not defective.[152]

If harm or damage caused by an enforcement agent is valued below £10,000, a claim may be pursued through the small claims court. For example, if you are owed money or should be paid compensation, a claim can be commenced through the county court using Form N1, with the amount limited to a maximum of £10,000. The action may proceed against the enforcement agent individually, the company employing the enforcement agent or the local authority.[153] The small claims court is a more attractive option, as neither side can claim for legal costs.

Leaflets explaining how to bring a claim in the county court can be obtained from your local county court or at http://hmctsformfinder.justice.gov.uk.

Charging orders

A charging order effectively 'mortgages' the property with the debt. This method of recovery is available if you are the owner or part-owner of the dwelling. It cannot be used if you are a tenant or licensee. If the local authority has obtained one or more liability orders and the total debt outstanding is at least £1,000, it can apply to the county court for a charging order against the dwelling, provided it is the one that gave rise to the council tax arrears.[154] **Note:** a charging order cannot be used against any other property owned or occupied by you. The decision to use this method of recovery is a discretionary one. In practice, local authorities are more likely to use a charging order if you have £5,000 or more in council tax arrears. The local authority must consider all the relevant factors before deciding to adopt this method, and a local authority is likely to attract criticism if it seeks to obtain a charging order for a relatively small amount.

In deciding whether to grant a charging order, the county court must consider all the circumstances of the case, including:[155]

- your personal circumstances; *and*
- whether any other person would be 'unduly prejudiced' if an order were granted.

If the debt remains unpaid, the local authority may apply to the court for the property to be sold to pay the debt. In practice, the court rarely orders the property to be sold. Obtaining a charging order does mean, however, that if the property is sold or remortgaged, the local authority is potentially entitled to receive the outstanding amount from the proceeds of the sale. This is only the case, however, if there are sufficient funds remaining after any charge with a higher priority, such as a mortgage, has been met. If you have negative equity with an existing mortgage lender, the use of a charging order will not result in any recovery.

Bankruptcy proceedings

If a liability order has been obtained, the (outstanding) amount on it is a debt for the purposes of bankruptcy and the local authority can apply to bankrupt you. The local authority can commence proceedings where you owe at least £5,000 (the local authority can combine all the debts you owe it – eg, rent and council tax). Before 1 October 2015, the amount for a bankruptcy debt was £750.[156]

The official receiver or an insolvency practitioner is appointed to handle your financial affairs. This person is known as the 'trustee in bankruptcy'. Bankruptcy can be requested by you or by the local authority. Bankruptcy generally lasts for 12 months, after which time you are discharged from your debt.

The only advantage to a bankruptcy order being made against you is that no other enforcement measure can be used thereafter, including imprisonment,[157] and it will clear other debts.

If you are facing bankruptcy proceedings, you should obtain professional advice as quickly as possible. The implications for homeowners are serious because bankruptcy can result in the loss of your home. The bankruptcy process also adds heavy legal costs which will be added to the money owed. However, bankruptcy proceedings provide a last chance to dispute council tax liability or local authority calculations. It is possible that the claim is based on an error or miscalculation – eg, if an exemption on the dwelling should have been awarded or you were not liable or you were not awarded any CTR to which you are entitled. It is useful to consider whether there are grounds for an appeal to a valuation tribunal (see Chapter 11). While a formal appeal is outstanding, the local authority should not pursue recovery action and bankruptcy proceedings should not be used.

A useful guide to bankruptcy, produced by the Insolvency Service, is available at www.gov.uk/government/organisations/insolvency-service. See also CPAG's *Debt Advice Handbook* for detailed information.

The Local Government snd Social Care Ombudsman has repeatedly highlighted flaws in the way councils pursue bankruptcy for council tax debts,[158] and concern about the practice has also been raised by the higher courts.[159]

Proving the bankruptcy debt

It is essential that the local authority be required to produce a copy of the liability order or prove that it exists. The High Court has indicated that it is prepared to look at whether the debt can be proved, and this may be the only option for the debtor in many cases. The problem for the local authority is that liability orders are often not properly recorded by the magistrates' court and no properly signed or sealed judgment is available (see p209). If a liability order is being relied on, the local authority must be able to prove its existence to the satisfaction of the court.[160]

Often the computerised bulk summonsing procedures used by local authorities may not actually result in a hard copy of an individual order against a debtor being signed or endorsed by a court. If you have had no notice of liability order proceedings, request that the local authority produces the liability order.[161] If no liability order can be produced in a correct form which is endorsed by a signature of a justice of the peace or other court stamp, the application may fail on the grounds that the order was not properly obtained from the magistrates' court.

Paying the debt

You can avoid bankruptcy by paying the debt at the stage of the final bankruptcy order, and the court may adjourn proceedings if there is a realistic chance of your raising the money – eg, by borrowing it from other sources. However, repeated adjournments are unlikely, and you may still be liable for the costs of the bankruptcy proceedings even if the council tax is paid.

The bankruptcy hearing

It is essential to attend any hearing, otherwise you risk being made bankrupt in your absence. You are entitled to representation at such a hearing, and evidence should be given by witness statement. You may raise arguments in law against being made bankrupt but, unfortunately, legal aid can be very hard to obtain until a person is already made bankrupt. The local authority evidence can be tested and cross-examined. The court may dismiss the bankruptcy petition. The county court may dismiss the petition if it is satisfied that you are able to pay all your debts or is satisfied:[162]

that you have made an offer to secure or compound the amount and that the acceptance of the offer would have required the dismissal of the petition, *and* the offer has been unreasonably refused by the council. An example might be where a relative or friend might lend you the money to cover the council tax debt but the council refuses it. In determining for the purposes of this subsection the court will consider your means and liabilities.

By the time the bankruptcy petition reaches court, it is often too late to challenge the liability order by applying to the magistrates' court or the High Court. However, there are circumstances in which the court may look at issues regarding liability for, or the amount of, council tax.[163] You should also try to raise reasonable arguments previously put forward at a hearing to set aside a statutory demand, although the court may limit or not entertain these unless they are raising matters amounting 'to fraud, collusion or possibly some glaring miscarriage of justice'.[164]

If a statutory demand has failed to refer to the right to have it set aside, arguments may still be raised at the bankruptcy petition stage.[165]

You may raise any arguments as to why you consider the liability order to be wrong in law if you have not raised them at the statutory demand stage or if you raised them in the statutory demand set-aside application and they were rejected. The High Court has stated that if a bona fide appeal had been lodged with the valuation tribunal, 'it is extremely unlikely that an order will be made. Normally either the petition will be dismissed on the basis that there is a disputed debt, or at least, and perhaps more usually, the court will await the outcome of the appeal.'[166]

An adjournment might be obtained if there is a bona fide appeal that can be taken to the valuation tribunal. Such an appeal should be begun as soon as possible. An adjournment is much more likely to be granted where the taxpayer has appealed in time and a decision of the tribunal can be expected reasonably soon than if you made an out-of-time appeal.[167]

An adjournment may also be granted as a realistic prospect of settling the debt and should not be unreasonably refused if you have evidence of making payments or attempts at making payment. Factors that may be taken into account include a lack of legal advice or knowledge and the confusion on what may be required.[168]

If the court is satisfied that the appeal has no real prospect of success, then the court should make a bankruptcy order. Otherwise, the court may either adjourn the petition or dismiss it depending on the circumstances.[169]

Appeals on a point of law against a bankruptcy order

Where a bankruptcy order is made by the county court which involves an error of law, an application must be made to the High Court.[170] A notice of appeal must be served on the High Court at the Royal Courts of Justice in London within 14 days of the bankruptcy judgment. A practice direction about bankruptcy proceedings is available at www.justice.gov.uk/courts/procedure-rules/civil/rules/insolvency_pd.

You have to provide details of the county court which made the order, as well as details of the local authority and a copy of any judgment. You are required to obtain a transcript of the hearing and a skeleton argument and chronology (the requirement to serve these with the notice of appeal may be waived if you are unrepresented, although you will be required to do this later).[171]

The High Court may grant a stay on the bankruptcy proceedings until your appeal is heard. If you have already been made bankrupt in the county court and your home is at risk, you may be eligible for legal aid assistance. The appeal should provide grounds of appeal, explaining where the county court judge erred in law by granting the bankruptcy petition. Grounds of appeal may include that the local authority could not produce a valid liability order or the evidence is not probative or there has been a material irregularity during the proceedings.

Annulment and rescission of bankruptcy orders

Once the bankruptcy order has been made, you may apply to have it annulled – ie, cancelled by the court if relevant grounds exist. A right to apply for an annulment of an existing bankruptcy order exists under the Insolvency Act 1986.

The law in this area is a grey area, with the higher courts expressing concern that the Civil Procedure Rules, which apply in other civil courts, do not apply in magistrates' courts where liability orders are issued.[172] Annulment may be justified where:[173]

- the local authority cannot provide a proper account;
- the local authority has failed to follow its own criteria;
- the local authority could have pursued other recovery methods;
- it is disproportionate in the circumstances;[174]
- the amount of the debt has been paid.[175]

The application goes to the court that made the order, and the official receiver must be sent a copy. An alternative remedy may be the rescission of the bankruptcy order.[176] Specialist advice should be sought on these issues.

Imprisonment

England and Wales remain the only countries in Europe in which a person can be sent to prison for not paying a local tax. There is no imprisonment for failure to pay council tax in Scotland.

In certain circumstances, English or Welsh local authorities can apply to the magistrates' court for a warrant committing a debtor to prison.[177] This is a coercive measure designed to extract payment from someone who has the means to pay the debt. It is not a punishment for failure to pay or imposed as a deterrent.[178]

A warrant of commitment may only be sought where the local authority has been informed that an attempt to recover the debt by way of enforcement agents seeking to seize has been unsuccessful. If it appears to the authority that (for whatever reason) no or insufficient sums can be recovered, the local authority may proceed to seek committal. If there has been no attempt to seize goods, imprisonment is not available.

Where a local authority employs a subcontractor to undertake any of its functions in collecting and enforcing council tax, it must issue a notice to the subcontractor stating all relevant functions being performed for the authority are to cease and no other enforcement steps should be taken.[179]

The maximum period of imprisonment is three months,[180] but this should be reserved for only the most extreme cases, such as deliberate non-payment.[181]

If you are unable to pay and are threatened with imprisonment, contact the local authority immediately in writing, setting out the financial problems which you are experiencing, and ask the local authority to use its power under section 13A(1)(c) of the Local Government Finance Act 1992 to reduce or remit the debt where there is financial hardship (see p167).

Means inquiry

The court must examine your means before issuing a warrant to commit you to prison (a 'means inquiry'). This involves questioning you about your circumstances, income, outgoings, debts and savings to discover the reason for your failure to pay. To enable such an inquiry to take place, you may be summoned to appear before a magistrates' court.[182]

A warrant to commit you to prison is only issued if the court is satisfied that failure to pay is due to:
* your wilful refusal; *or*
* your culpable neglect;[183] *and*
* you have the means on the day of the hearing to pay the debt.[184]

If magistrates do not hold a proper means inquiry, the proceedings are unlawful and any order committing you to imprisonment may be quashed on appeal to the High Court. Magistrates are expected to properly assess your means and not to make unreasonable or irrational assumptions. If you are in receipt of means-tested benefits, point out that your financial circumstances have already been assessed and found to be limited.

There have yet to be any decisions in relation to UC in the context of committal, but previous caselaw indicates that deductions from benefits should be considered as an alternative.

A typical error of many means inquiries is to fail to ask the debtor if s/he has any savings or capital. A lack of accessible savings or capital is likely to mean that you lack the ability to pay the sum immediately. If you cannot actually pay on the day because you simply do not have enough money, the warrant should not be issued[185] as the purpose of committal is coercive and not intended as a punishment or as a deterrent to other non-payers.[186] This principle also applies to any decision to issue a warrant which has previously been suspended on terms. Magistrates should not simply assume that a failure to keep to an order is a result of wilful refusal.[187]

Only a failure by you to pay council tax which is 'blameworthy' is considered to be wilful refusal or culpable neglect. If you are unable to pay council tax because you are too poor, or the failure arose through illness, job loss, a domestic disaster such as a fire or flood, unexpected pregnancy, being forced from a property as a result of domestic violence, or a failure to pay benefit, you should not be at risk of imprisonment. In such cases, an application should be made by the court to remit the debt (see below).

If wilful refusal or culpable neglect is found, the decision to issue a warrant must still be a reasonable one. A debtor is often asked to make an offer of payment. If a viable offer has been made, magistrates should accept it and not issue the warrant.[188]

- -

Mothers with young children

The provisions of the Human Rights Act 1998 apply to imprisonment for debts recoverable in magistrates' courts. In *R (Stokes) v Gwent Magistrates' Court*, the High Court held that the decision to jail a young mother for 12 days for owing £455 was an infringement of Article 8 of the European Convention on Human Rights (right to family life).[189] Magistrates' courts, therefore, have to consider whether the proposed interference with the rights of the children is in proportion to the amount of debt involved.

Committal proceedings for default on local taxes have often involved mothers with young children and the disproportionate nature of imprisonment has been expressed in other cases. Arguably, in every case where someone could be imprisoned, the effect on family life must be considered. There would seem to be very few cases where a warrant of commitment would be justified or proportional, particularly with the availability of deductions from benefit and attachment of earnings orders.[190] The courts have also indicated that imprisonment is inappropriate where the amounts concerned are small.[191]

- -

Remission of the debt

If you are unable to pay or the debts are very old, the magistrates' court can remit the debt, in part or in full.[192] The council tax debt is extinguished for the financial year in question, but liability remains for subsequent years.

Magistrates should remit part of the debt if an order to pay instalments would result in an unreasonably long repayment period.[193] Any period in excess of three years is considered unreasonable.[194] However, the court may choose to postpone the warrant to a specific date (if it appears that the payment level will not achieve payment within three years) and conduct a review at that time to see if repayment should be increased or reduced.

Once the magistrates have set a term of imprisonment, however, there is no power to remit. Therefore, if your circumstances deteriorate and you can no longer pay the amounts ordered, you should tell the court, which can simply postpone the issue of the warrant indefinitely, without any payments being ordered. Alternatively, a warrant may be quashed by the High Court if the means enquiry has been defective so that a warrant based on it is invalid.[195]

Challenging a decision to imprison

A decision to imprison can be challenged by appealing (within 21 days) or by judicial review (within three months). In practice, if the warrant of commitment has been issued and you are already in prison, judicial review is the preferred route of appeal, as the High Court can grant immediate bail to an imprisoned debtor, pending the full appeal hearing.

---

5. **Statutory enforcement in Scotland**

The enforcement system for local taxes in Scotland varies greatly from that in England and Wales. Enforcement in Scotland has been subject to far less scrutiny and clarification by the higher courts and council tax debtors have suffered a wide range of difficulties.

Individuals may be unaware that local tax debts are owed and are suddenly faced with large bills with no apparent warning.

Unlike in England and Wales where a six-year limitation applies,[196] the limitation in Scotland is 20 years, but some local authorities may adopt a policy not to pursue debts for this length of time. **Note:** all liabilities under the former community charge have been extinguished.[197] Scottish authorities can only pursue once a bill has been issued or acknowledged. A bill must be served for a sum to be enforceable, and this can only be done retrospectively if you have either given false information or deliberately evaded payment.[198]

Reminders and losing the right to pay by instalments

If an instalment under the statutory instalment scheme or any special agreement has not been paid by the due date, the local authority must serve a reminder notice on the liable person. The reminder notice requires payment to be made within seven days.[199] It must include a:

- note of the instalment(s) required to be paid and the remainder to be paid for the year;
- statement that if no, or insufficient, payment is made to cover any instalments that are, or will become, due within seven days of the issue of the reminder, the right to pay by instalments is lost and the remaining balance for the year becomes payable after a further seven days.

If two reminders have been issued during the financial year, even if you pay what you owe, you become liable for the whole of the outstanding amount following a third failure to pay, without the need for another reminder.[200] On the second reminder notice, you should be informed of the consequences of a third failure to pay.[201]

The local authority may take recovery action if any sum, including the 10 per cent statutory surcharge and civil penalties, which has become payable to the local authority has not been paid.[202] Additionally, if an elected member of a local authority is in at least two months' arrears, there are restrictions on her/his ability to vote on specific matters (see p214).[203]

Summary warrant or decree

If council tax, Scottish Water charges or a civil penalty are owed, the local authority can apply to the sheriff court for a 'summary warrant' or seek a 'decree' for payment. The summary warrant allows for a special accelerated enforcement procedure.

The sheriff must grant a summary warrant if the local authority provides a certificate.[204] The certificate must contain the following statements:
- that the person(s) specified in the application have not paid the sums due;
- that the local authority has served a reminder notice on the person(s) requiring the amount due to be paid within 14 days from the day on which the notice was served;
- that this period has expired without full payment;
- that, in respect of each person on the application, either:
  – a period of 14 days has passed without her/him initiating an appeal because s/he disagrees with the local authority's decision that the dwelling is a chargeable dwelling, or that s/he is liable to pay the tax, or with the calculation of the amount which must be paid, including her/his entitlement to a disability reduction or a discount; *or*
  – the local authority has notified that it believes the grievance is not well founded, or steps have been taken to deal with the grievance, or two months have passed since the service of the aggrieved person's notice;
- the amount unpaid by each person.[205]

If two or more people are jointly liable, the local authority may seek a warrant which shows them as jointly or individually liable for the outstanding sum.[206]

There is no requirement for the council or the sheriff court to give notice to you or allow an opportunity for you or any other person to make representations.

A number of legal opinions consider that the summary warrant procedure may be in breach of human rights law and open to challenge under the Human Rights Act 1998.[207] Article 6 of the European Convention on Human Rights guarantees a fair and impartial tribunal and the right to be represented in courts and tribunals in the determination of civil rights and obligations,[208] but no opportunity is given to the debtor to be heard in a summary warrant application.

In a summary warrant application, you are prevented from any opportunity to present evidence that may show the rules on billing have not been followed, that the sum has been paid or to make any application to postpone proceedings where an appeal may lie to a valuation committee (see Chapter 11).

Providing information

If a summary warrant or decree for payment has been granted, you must provide specified information required by the local authority.[209] The obligation lasts for as long as any part of the relevant amount remains unpaid. You must provide:

- the name of your employer;
- the address of the employer's premises where you work – if there are no such premises in Scotland, the address of any one place of the employer's business in Scotland;
- your national insurance number;
- details of your bank account;
- the name and address of any other person(s) who is jointly liable to pay the whole or any part of the amount in respect of which the warrant or decree was granted.

The information must be supplied in writing within 14 days of the day on which the request is made by the local authority.[210] Failure to comply could result in a civil penalty being imposed.[211]

Recovery methods

The summary warrant or decree of payment authorises the local authority to recover the unpaid council tax, Scottish Water charges and civil penalties, plus a surcharge of 10 per cent of the amount owed (see p234), by either:

- an earnings arrestment (see p232); *or*
- deductions from benefits (see p214); *or*
- an arrestment and action of furthcoming and sale (see p233);[212] *or*
- sequestration of the debtor's assets where the debt exceeds £3,000. For more information, see www.aib.gov.uk; *or*
- attachment and exceptional attachment orders. **Note:** special permission is needed from the sheriff for a special attachment to seize goods.

The summary warrant is enforced by sheriff officers or messengers at arms. Their fees and expenses in connection with the warrant are charged to you.[213]

Most councils have arranged for sheriff officers to deliver a formal 'debt advice and information package' (DAIP) when they first communicate with the debtor. Attachment is competent only where a summary warrant has been granted and, before taking any steps to execute an attachment, a DAIP has been issued to you. The DAIP is a document or bundle of documents containing information such as where to get debt and money advice from locally.[214]

The DAIP provides specific legal information and if it is not sent/received, the formal recovery process will be affected. For more information, see www.aib.gov.uk/debt/deal-debt/debt-advice-and-information-package.

When sheriff officers serve a document by leaving it at a household or place of business, it must be in such a way that it is likely to come to the attention of that person. It must be appropriately addressed and placed in a sealed envelope and bearing the notice: 'This envelope contains a citation or intimation from [the specific sheriff court] and sealed by the sheriff officer.'[215]

Note: sheriff officers cannot demand entry to your home unless a court order, known as an 'exceptional attachment order', has been obtained. Forced entry cannot take place unless there is a person present who is at least 16 and is not, because of her/his age, knowledge of English, mental illness, mental or physical disability or otherwise, unable to understand the consequence of the procedure being carried out.

Challenging liability

If you dispute your liability to or the amount the authority is asking for, challenge this as soon as possible by appealing to the appeal committee under section 81 of the Local Government Finance Act 1992 (see Chapter 11). This is particularly important where you are facing, or likely to face, enforcement action. Merely writing, or communicating with, the sheriff officers acting for a local authority about a dispute has been ruled insufficient to be a valid notice of appeal to the valuation appeal committee.[216]

Representation at hearings

If you cannot afford a lawyer, you are entitled to be represented by another person, who need not be legally qualified.[217] A lay representative (eg, a debt adviser) can appear in the Court of Session but the closed petition process nature of the summary warrant does not provide an opportunity for your case to be argued in the sheriff court. However, if a normal decree is applied for by the local authority, the opportunity to argue the case in the court will arise. The lay person must first complete a formal application to the court to obtain the appropriate approval to be heard.[218]

The right to a McKenzie friend does not exist in Scotland.

Earnings arrestment

A sheriff officer serves an 'earnings arrestment' schedule on your employer. This requires the employer to deduct a prescribed amount from your net earnings on every payday. The arrestment remains in force until either the debt has been paid in full or you stop working for the employer.

The amounts that can be seized by way of a diligence against earnings are similar to those for an attachment of earnings order in England and Wales. The amounts are set out on p233.[219] These figures do not apply to any existing diligence made before 6 April 2013, unless an employer chooses to apply them after being informed about them.[220]

Net monthly earnings	Deduction
Not exceeding £494.01	Nil
Exceeding £494.01 but not exceeding £1,785.61	£15.00 or 19% of earnings exceeding £494.01, whichever is the greater
Exceeding £1,785.61 but not exceeding £2,684.51	£245.40 plus 23% of earnings exceeding £1,785.61
Exceeding £2,684.51	£452.15 plus 50% of earnings exceeding £2,684.51

Net weekly earnings	Deduction
Not exceeding £113.68	Nil
Exceeding £113.68 but not exceeding £410.90	£4 or 19% of earnings exceeding £113.68, whichever is the greater
Exceeding £410.90 but not exceeding £617.82	£56.47 plus 23% of earnings exceeding £410.90
Exceeding £617.82	£104.06 plus 50% of earnings exceeding £617.82

Net daily earnings	Deduction
Not exceeding £16.24	Nil
Exceeding £16.24 but not exceeding £58.70	£0.50 or 19% of earnings exceeding £16.24, whichever is the greater
Exceeding £58.70 but not exceeding £88.26	£8.07 plus 23% of earnings exceeding £58.70
Exceeding £88.26	£14.87 plus 50% of earnings exceeding £88.26

The regulations make very specific provision for calculating percentages of both monthly and weekly earnings which should be followed to the letter.[221]

An arrestment and action of furthcoming or sale

'Arrestment' is the process by which money or goods held by a third party for a debtor may be frozen. It could be applied, for example, to money held in your bank account. If your bank account details are unknown, usually bank arrestments are initiated by serving letters on the main banks. If money is identified as being held by a third party, an arrestment is served by an officer of the court in the presence of one witness and it freezes the funds. They cannot be withdrawn until the debt has been settled. Usually, you are asked to sign a mandate authorising the release of funds equal to the arrears and costs to the local authority. Any money that remains in the account is released. If a mandate is not signed, the local authority must raise an action of **'furthcoming'** to allow arrested funds to be transferred. You cannot defend the action by disputing the debt, but you can defend it by showing that the arrestment was invalid, procedurally irregular or gained nothing.

Time to pay orders

You can apply to a sheriff court for a **'time to pay order'**.[222] If granted, the local authority cannot seek to enforce a council tax debt while the order is in force.

The court must grant the order if it is satisfied that it is reasonable in all the circumstances to do so. It must take into account:

- the nature of, and reasons for, the debt;
- any action taken by the local authority to assist you in paying the debt;
- your financial circumstances;
- the reasonableness of your proposal;
- the reasonableness of any refusal or any objection from the local authority.

Enforcement costs

The amount added to the debt is 10 per cent of the outstanding balance. The sheriff officer's fees set by the court, together with costs incurred in connection with the execution of a summary warrant, can also be charged to you once formal recovery proceedings begin through a summary warrant.

Notes

1. **Introduction**
    1 Local Authorities (Contracting Out of Tax Billing, Collection and Enforcement Functions) Order 1996 No.1880

2. **Statutory enforcement in England and Wales**
    2 Citizens Advice and the Local Government Association, *Collection of Council Tax Arrears Good Practice Protocol*, October 2013
    3 Ombudsman Report 13004696, Plymouth City Council, 13 January 2014
    4 Ombudsman Report 07B10432, Manchester City Council, 22 September 2009

    5 Ombudsman Report 14000871, Sandwell Metropolitan Borough, 18 December 2014
    6 Reg 23 CT(AE) Regs as amended by reg 4 CT(AE)(A) Regs
    7 Reg 23 CT(AE) Regs
    8 Reg 23(2) CT(AE) Regs
    9 Reg 23 CT(AE) Regs
    10 Reg 33 CT(AE) Regs
    11 Reg 54 CT(AE) Regs
    12 Reg 34 CT(AE) Regs
    13 s13A(1)(c) LGFA 1992 inserted by s10 LGFA 2012
    14 *Morgan v Warwick District Council* [2015] RVR 224
    15 s151 Local Government Act 1972

16 Reg 58 CT(AE) Regs
17 Reg 58(4) CT(AE) Regs
18 See reg 58(2)(b) CT(AE) Regs

3. Liability orders (England and Wales)

19 *Powys County Council v Hurst* [2018] EWHC 1684 (Admin) 4 July 2018, per Hickinbottom J
20 *R v Bristol Magistrates' Court ex parte Willsman and Young* [1991] RA
21 Reg 34 CT(AE) Regs
22 *Associated Provincial Picture Houses Ltd v Wednesbury Corporation* [1948] 1 KB 223
23 *North Somerset District Council v (1) Honda Motor Europe Ltd and (2) Chevrolet United Kingdom Ltd and (3) Martin Graham* [2010] EWHC 1505 (QB)
24 *Hadjianastassiou v Greece* [1992] European Court Application No.12945/87, 16 December
25 *North Somerset District Council v (1) Honda Motor Europe Ltd and (2) Chevrolet United Kingdom Ltd and (3) Martin Graham* [2010] EWHC 1505 (QB)
26 *North Somerset District Council v (1) Honda Motor Europe Ltd and (2) Chevrolet United Kingdom Ltd and (3) Martin Graham* [2010] EWHC 1505 (QB)
27 Ombudsman Report 13019622, Derby City Council, 30 October 2014
28 *R v Lambeth London Borough Council ex parte Ahijah Sterling* [1986] RVR 27
29 *Ratford and Haywards (Receivers and Managers) v Northavon District Council* [1986] RA 137
30 *Ratford and Haywards (Receivers and Managers) v Northavon District Council* [1986] RA 137
31 Reg 35(2A) CT(AE) Regs
32 Magistrates' Courts Fees (Amendment) Order 2013 No.1409
33 Study by Zacchaeus 2000 Trust and Nucleus Legal Advice
34 *Attfield v the London Borough of Barnet* [2013] EWHC 2089 (Admin)
35 Reg 34(5) and (7) CT(AE) Regs; *R (on the application of Reverend Nicolson) v Tottenham Magistrates* [2015] EWHC 1252 (Admin)
36 *R (on the Application of Reverend Nicolson) v Tottenham Magistrates* [2015] EWHC 1252 (Admin)
37 Reg 3 the Council Tax and Non-Domestic Rating (Amendment) (Wales) Regulations 2011 No.528
38 Magistrates' Courts Fees (Amendment) Order 2013 No.1409

39 *Reg 34(7) CT(AE) Regs; R (on the application of Reverend Nicolson) v Tottenham Magistrates* [2015] EWHC 1252 (Admin), Mrs Justice Andrews
40 *R (on the application of Reverend Nicolson) v Tottenham Magistrates* [2015] EWHC 1252 (Admin), Mrs Justice Andrews paras 35-44
41 *R (on the application of Reverend Nicolson) v Tottenham Magistrates* [2015] EWHC 1252 (Admin), Mrs Justice Andrews paras 44-end
42 Reg 35 CT(AE) Regs
43 In *R (on the application of Clark-Darby) v Highbury Corner Magistrates' Court* [2001] All.ER (D) 229, the High Court quashed a liability order where the person had not received the notice of the hearing, as it was unjust to allow the order to stand.
44 *Chowdhury v Westminster City Council* [2013] EWHC 1921
45 *DPP v Porthouse* [1988] 153 JP 57
46 Reg 34 CT(AE) Regs
47 Reg 34 CT(AE) Regs
48 *R v Kingston upon Thames Court ex parte Peter Martin* [1994] Imm AR 172
49 *Liverpool City Council v Pleroma Distribution Ltd* [2002] All ER (D) 302
50 Reg 2 CCCTNR(E)(MC) Regs
51 *R v Leicester City Justices ex parte Barrow and another* [1991] 3 All ER 935; Practice Guidance: McKenzie friends, issued by Lord Neuberger, Master of the Rolls, 12 July 2010
52 *O'Toole v Scott* [1965] UKFC 14; [1965] AC 939
53 Reg 34 CT(AE) Regs
54 *Evans v Caterham and Warlingham UDC* [1974] *The Times*, 29 January
55 Reg 57 CT(AE) Regs
56 *R (on the application of John Stuart Salmon) v Feltham Magistrates' Court* [2008] EWHC 3507 (Admin); *Mahendra Shah v London Borough of Croydon* [2013] EWHC 3657 (Admin); *Wiltshire Council v Piggin* [2014] EWHC 4386 (Admin)
57 See *Wiltshire Council v Piggin* [2014] EWHC 4386 (Admin)
58 See *Wiltshire Council v Piggin* [2014] EWHC 4386 (Admin)
59 Reg 53(4) CT(AE) Regs
60 *Sutton v Islington London Borough Council* [1997] CO/1784/94, 17 October 1997, unreported
61 Magistrates' Courts (Hearsay Evidence in Civil Proceedings) Rules 1999 No.681

62 rr3-6 Magistrates' Courts (Hearsay
Evidence in Civil Proceedings) Rules
1999 No.681

63 *Norman and another v East Dorset District
Council* [2013] All ER (D) 153

64 Regs 35 and 48 and Sch 2 Forms A and B
CT(AE) Regs

65 **E** Reg 3 Council Tax (Administration and
Enforcement) (Amendment) (No.2)
(England) Regulations 2003 No.2211
W Reg 3 Council Tax (Administration
and Enforcement) (Amendment No.2)
(Wales) Regulations 2003 No.1715

66 *R v H Sherman Ltd* [1949] 2 All ER 210
per Lord Goddard

67 *R (on the application of Mathialagan) v
London Borough of Southwark and
another* [2005] RA 43

68 See *London Borough of Lambeth v Simon*
[2007] BPIR 1629, 6 June 2007

69 Art 6 ECHR; see also *Rommelfanger v
Germany* (1989) 62 DR 151 and *Diennert
v France* (1996) 21 EHRR 554

70 s82 LGA 2003

71 *Liverpool City Council v Pleroma
Distribution Ltd* [2002] All ER (D) 302

72 *R (on the application of Tull) v Camberwell
Green Magistrates' Court and another*
[2005] RA 30

73 *R (on the application of Newham London
Borough Council) v Stratford Magistrates'
Court* [2008] All ER (D) 17

74 *R (on the Application of Khan) v Feltham
Magistrates' Court* [2017] EWHC 3042
(Admin) Cockerhill, J

75 s64 of the Magistrates' Court Act 1980;
*R (on the Application of Khan v Feltham
Magistrates' Court* [2017] n.68

4. Recovery methods (England and Wales)

76 Reg 56 Universal Credit (Consequential,
Supplementary, Incidental and
Miscellaneous Provisions) Regulations
2013 No.630

77 Reg 52 CT(AE) Regs
78 Reg 54 CT(AE) Regs
79 Reg 36 CT(AE) Regs
80 Reg 36 CT(AE) Regs
81 Reg 36 CT(AE) Regs
82 Reg 36 CT(AE) Regs
83 Reg 56 CT(AE) Regs
84 Reg 56 CT(AE) Regs
85 Reg 37 CT(AE) Regs
86 Reg 37(4) CT(AE) Regs
87 Reg 37a(2) CT(AE) Regs
88 Reg 41 CT(AE) Regs
89 Reg 40 CT(AE) Regs

90 Reg 40 CT(AE) Regs
91 Reg 56 CT(AE) Regs
92 Reg 56 CT(AE) Regs
93 Complaint against Birmingham City
Council, Ombudsman Report
13016986, 3 June 2014
94 Ombudsman Report 14006007,
Ashford Borough Council, 7 November
2014; Ombudsman Report 008317,
Manchester City Council, November
2013
95 Ombudsman Report 14006452,
Sandwell Metropolitan Borough
Council, 19 November 2014
96 Reg 38 and Sch 4 CT(AE) Regs
97 Reg 32 CT(AE) Regs
98 Reg 32 CT(AE) Regs
99 Reg 32(1) CT(AE) Regs; CT(AE)(A)(E)
Regs
100 Sch 4 CT(AE) Regs; CT(AE)(A)(W) Regs
101 Reg 42 CT(AE) Regs
102 s106 LGFA 1992
103 CT(DIS) Regs as amended by the Fines,
Council Tax and Community Charges
(Deductions from Universal Credit and
Other Benefits) Regs 2013 No.612
104 Reg 8(4) CT(DIS) Regs
105 Reg 8(6) CT(DIS) Regs
106 Reg 8(7) CT(DIS) Regs
107 Tribunals, Courts and Enforcement Act
2007 (Commencement No.11) Order
2014 No.768
108 Reg 52 CT(AE) Regs
109 Reg 6 TCG Regs
110 Reg 6(2) TCG Regs
111 Reg 7 TCG Regs
112 Reg 8 TCG Regs
113 Part 3 TCEA 2007
114 Local Government Ombudsman Report,
96/A/3626
115 Ministry of Justice, *Taking Control of
Goods: national standards*, 6 April 2014,
para 74
116 Ministry of Justice, *Taking Control of
Goods: national standards*, 6 April 2014,
para 77
117 Reg 45 CT(AE) Regs as amended by art 7
Tribunals, Courts and Enforcement Act
2007 (Consequential, Transitional and
Saving Provision) Order 2014 No.600
118 Sch 12 para 9(a)-(b) TCEA 2007
119 Reg 4 TCG Regs
120 Reg 5(1) TCG Regs
121 Reg 10 TCG Regs
122 Ministry of Justice, *Taking Control of
Goods: national standards*, 6 April 2014,
para 64
123 Reg 22 TCG Regs

124 Sch 12 para 14(6) TCEA 2007
125 Ministry of Justice, *Taking Control of Goods: national standards*, 6 April 2014, paras 57-61
126 *Vaughan v McKenzie* [1969] 1 QB 557
127 Sch 12 para 26 TCEA 2007
128 Sch 12 para 13 TCEA 2007
129 Reg 14(2) TCG Regs
130 Reg 15(3) TCG Regs
131 Reg 15 TCG Regs
132 Reg 16 TCG Regs
133 Reg 30 TCG Regs
134 Reg 34(1)(a) and (c) TCG Regs
135 Reg 26 TCG Regs; *Khazanachi v Faircharm Investments Ltd and others and McLeod v Butterwick* [1998] EWCA Civ 471
136 Reg 27 TCG Regs
137 Regs 32 and 38 TCG Regs
138 Reg 32(1)(c)-(e) TCG Regs
139 *Celador Radio Ltd v Rancho Steak House Ltd* and *Riaz v Designer Collection Europ Ltd* [2018] EWHC 219 (QB)
140 Regs 4 and 5 and Table 1 TCG(F) Regs
141 Tribunals, Courts and Enforcement Act 2007 (Consequential, Transitional and Saving Provision) Order 2014 No.600
142 Reg 12 TCG(F) Regs
143 Ombudsman Report 13012969, London Borough of Haringey, 14 January 2014
144 Ombudsman Report 13011264, Hyndburn Borough Council, 24 September 2014
145 Reg 4(2) TCG(F) Regs
146 Reg 16 TCG(F) Regs
147 Reg 45 CT(AE) Regs
148 Reg 45(1) CT(AE) Regs.
149 Sch 12 para 50(6)(a) TCEA 2007
150 Sch 12 para 66(5) TCEA 2007
151 Sch 12 para 66(7) TCEA 2007
152 Sch 12 para 66(8)(a) and (b) TCEA 2007
153 Sch 12 para 66(6) TCEA 2007
154 Reg 50(1)-(3) CT(AE) Regs
155 Reg 51(1) CT(AE) Regs
156 Insolvency Act 1986, as amended by Insolvency Act 1986 (Amendment) Order 2015 No.922
157 *Re: Smith (a bankrupt) ex parte Braintree District Council* [1990] 2 AC 215
158 Local Government Ombudsman press release, 6 October 2011
159 *Lonegran v Gedling Borough Council* [2009] EWCA Civ 745; *Yang v Official Receiver* [2017] EWCA Civ 1465
160 *London Borough of Lambeth v Simon* [2007] BPIR 1629

161 *Smolen v Tower Hamlets LBC* [2006] RVR 296
162 s271 Insolvency Act 1986
163 *Mohammed v Southwark Borough Council* [2006] RVR 124; see also *HMRC v Chamberlain* [2011] EWCA Civ 271, para 20 per Sir Andrew Morritt
164 *Lam v Inland Revenue* [2005] BPIR 301
165 *Clarke and another v Cognita Schools Ltd (trading as Hydesville Tower School)* [2015] EWHC 932 (Ch)
166 *London Borough of Waltham Forest v Zafar* [2014] EWHC 791 (Ch)
167 *Vieira v Revenue and Customs Commissioners* [2017] EWHC 936 (Ch)
168 *Patterson v Lewisham Bankruptcy* [2017] EWHC 632 (Ch)
169 *Vieira v Revenue and Customs Commissioners* [2017] EWHC 936 (Ch), para 84
170 r52.4 Civil Procedure Rules 1998
171 Civil Procedure Rules 1998; Practice Direction – Insolvency Proceedings, para 17.22(7B)
172 Insolvency Proceedings practice direction, PD 2012 13.4.3; *London Borough of Waltham Forest v Zafar* [2014] EWHC 791 (Ch), para 5
173 *Parveen v Manchester City Council and Helland*, 24 September 2007, Manchester County Court, District Judge Khan, unreported
174 *Parveen v Manchester City Council and Helland*, 24 September 2007, Manchester County Court, District Judge Khan, unreported
175 *Adetula (Claimant) v Barking and Dagenham London Borough Council* [2016] HC/2015/004349 [2017] EWHC 2279 (Ch)
176 s375 Insolvency Act 1986
177 Reg 47(1) CT(AE) Regs
178 *Stevenson v Southwark Borough Council* [1993] RA 113
179 Reg 73 Local Authorities (Contracting Out of Tax Billing, Collection and Enforcement Functions) Order 1996 No.1880
180 Reg 47(7) CT(AE) Regs
181 *R v Highbury Corner Magistrates' Court ex parte Uchendu* [1994] 158 JP 409
182 Reg 48(5) CT(AE) Regs
183 Reg 47(2) CT(AE) Regs
184 *R v Poole Justices ex parte Benham* [1992] 156 JP 157
185 *R v Poole Justices ex parte Benham* [1992] 156 JP 157

186 *Re Smith (a bankrupt) ex parte Braintree District Council* [1990] 2 AC 215
187 *R v Poole Justices ex parte Fleet* [1983] 1 WLR 973; *R v Horseferry Road Magistrates' Court ex parte Collins* [1986] CO/324/86; *R v Lewes and Crowborough Magistrates' Court ex parte Mackleden* [2002] RVR 363, para 15
188 *R v Alfreton Justices ex parte Gratton, The Times*, 8 December 1993
189 *R (on the application of Stokes) v Gwent Magistrates' Court* [2001] All ER (D) 125
190 *R v Highbury Corner Magistrates' Court ex parte Edis* [1994] Lexis citation 2788 CO/789/92, 31 January 1991
191 *R v Worthing Justices ex parte Waller* [1988] COD 69
192 Reg 48(2) CT(AE) Regs
193 *R v Newcastle-Upon-Tyne Justices ex parte Devine* [1998] RA 97
194 *R v Newcastle-Upon-Tyne Justices ex parte Devine* [1998] RA 97
195 See *R (on the application of Wandless) v Halifax Magistrates' Court and Calderdale Metropolitan Borough Council* [2009] EWHC 1857 (Admin) QBD, [2010] RVR 6

5. **Statutory enforcement in Scotland**
196 Reg CT(AE) Regs; *China v Harrow UDC* [1954] 1 QB 178
197 Community Charge Debt (Scotland) Act 2015
198 s8 Prescription and Limitation (Scotland) Act 1973
199 Reg 22 CT(AE)(S) Regs
200 Reg 22 CT(AE)(S) Regs
201 Reg 22 CT(AE)(S) Regs
202 s97 and Sch 8 para 1 LGFA 1992
203 s112 LGFA 1992
204 Sch 8 para 2 LGFA 1992
205 Reg 30 CT(AE)(S) Regs
206 Reg 30 CT(AE)(S) Regs
207 Consumer Focus Scotland response to the consultation document on the proposal for the Enforcement of Local Tax Arrears (Scotland) Bill, June 2010
208 *Rommelfanger v Germany* (1989) 62 DR 151; *Diennert v France* (1996) 21 EHRR 554
209 Reg 31 CT(AE)(S) Regs
210 Reg 31 CT(AE)(S) Regs
211 Sch 8 para 5 LGFA 1992; reg 31 CT(AE) Regs
212 Sch 8 para 2 LGFA 1992
213 Sch 8 para 4 LGFA 1992
214 s10 Debt Arrangement and Attachment (Scotland) Act 2002
215 Act of Sederunt (Sheriff Court Rules) (Miscellaneous Amendments) (No.2) 2011 No.289
216 See *Polley v (1) West Lothian Council and (2) the Accountant in Bankruptcy* [2015] CSIH 19
217 s5A Court of Session Act 1988; s32A Sheriff Courts (Scotland) Act 1971
218 Act of Sederunt (Sheriff Court Rules) (Lay Representation) 2013 No.91
219 Sch Diligence Against Earnings (Variation) (Scotland) Regulations 2015 No.370
220 Explanatory Note, The Diligence Against Earnings (Variation) (Scotland) Regs 2012 No.308
221 Sch Diligence Against Earnings (Variation) (Scotland) Regulations 2015 No.370
222 Part 1 Debtors (Scotland) Act 1987

Chapter 11

Appeals

This chapter covers:
1. Valuation tribunals and valuation appeal committees (below)
2. Matters that can be appealed (p241)
3. How to appeal (p249)
4. How appeals are dealt with (p250)
5. Appeal hearings (p255)
6. Reviews of tribunal and committee decisions (p266)

1. Valuation tribunals and valuation appeal committees

In England and Wales, appeals are dealt with by valuation tribunals. In England, appeals are heard by the Valuation Tribunal for England (VTE), and in Wales, by the Valuation Tribunal for Wales (VTW). In Scotland, appeals are heard by valuation appeal committees.

The tribunals provide a free service and cannot award costs against you. However, you do have to meet your own expenses in going to the tribunal hearing. See p241 for the matters which can be appealed.

Disputes over entitlement to a council tax reduction (CTR) in England and Wales may also be taken on appeal to the valuation tribunals. Scottish appeals about CTR do not go to committees but are heard by a separate panel, the Council Tax Reduction Review Panel.[1]

Both tribunals and appeal committees should conduct themselves in a more informal and less intimidating way than a court of law, and provide a mechanism to review and correct any erroneous decisions affecting taxpayers. They are designed to be independent of both the local authority and the Valuation Office Agency (VOA).

In England and Wales, a tribunal is usually made up of two or three members, with one of them chairing the tribunal. Tribunal members are local people serving in a voluntary capacity.[2] Members do not necessarily have any particular professional qualifications, but judges from the First-tier Tribunal (Social Security and Child Support) have sat in the past with the chairs of tribunals to hear appeals which involve CTR.[3] The administration of the tribunal is done by Valuation Tribunal Service staff from centralised offices. Tribunals in England and Wales sometimes sit at an administrative centre, but more often may sit in a local authority building or in rooms or suites booked at hotels, conference centres and church halls. Owing to reductions in staffing and funding, members of valuation panels are now expected to cover a wider geographical area than in the past, which may result in a decline in specifically local expertise.

In Scotland, a valuation appeal committee is made up of local people appointed by the appropriate sheriff principal. A committee consists of a chairperson and three to six ordinary members. Members are unpaid and independent of the assessor and the local authority. The committee is assisted by a paid secretary who is usually a lawyer. Tribunals and committees are advised on matters of law and procedure by clerks, employed by the tribunal or committee. The clerk is your point of contact and should be able to respond to requests for advice on procedures in advance of the hearing. S/he cannot, however, advise on the substance or merits of the appeal.

Useful information and guidance

Information on valuation matters and appeals can be found at the VOA website (www.voa.gov.uk).

More information about appeals in England is available at www.valuationtribunal.gov.uk. This is regularly updated, with summaries given in recent valuation tribunal decisions. The practice statements can be found here.

The Valuation Tribunal for Wales produces guidance notes and best practice protocols that provide in-depth guidance on the procedures that will be followed during the appeal process. These are available at www.valuation-tribunals-wales.org.uk.

The procedure for appealing council tax in Scotland is available at www.gov.scot.

It is important to distinguish between appeals to the VTE/VTW and appeals that go to the First-tier Tribunal for other social security benefits, such as Department for Work and Pensions benefits, and for decisions about entitlement and calculations which were made for the council tax benefit (CTB) system before 1 April 2013.

The overriding objective

The overriding objective of the tribunal is to deal with cases fairly and justly. To further the objective the tribunal must:[4]

- exercise any power given it by law;
- apply any practice statement or direction;
- interpret any rule or practice direction to ensure that appeals proceed with due expedition.

---

2. **Matters that can be appealed**

Appeals can be on:
- valuations (see below);
- liability (see p243);
- discounts (see p243);
- disability reductions (see p243);
- exemption (see p243);
- calculations on the amount of tax (apart from council tax reduction (CTR) decisions – see p243);
- completion notices (see p245);
- penalties (see p246);
- discretionary reductions (see p247);
- CTR decisions in Scotland (p245);
- incorrect amounts payable, including attempts to impose liability for past periods.

A number of matters are excluded, including those for which there is some other route of appeal – eg, to the First-tier Tribunal, the magistrates' court or the High Court.

In England and Wales, some matters can only be dealt with by the High Court – eg, the classes of dwellings that qualify for an exemption and the setting of the council tax.

If an appeal raises any topic which is outside of the jurisdiction of the tribunal, it will be struck out.[5]

Valuations

Chapter 3 describes the way in which you can make a proposal to the listing officer/assessor to alter the valuation list – eg, to put your home in a lower band.

England and Wales

If you make a valid proposal to the Valuation Office Agency (VOA), the listing officer has four months to decide whether or not to alter the list and to issue you with a decision notice. During this four-month period, you can negotiate and reach an amicable solution on the banding. The listing officer should discuss the proposal with you and any interested parties before issuing a decision notice. The notice states either that the listing officer agrees to alter the valuation list or that s/he rejects the proposal and no alteration is made. A letter is sent with the notice, explaining that you and any interested party have a right of appeal. This must be done within three months of the date of the decision letter.

You and any interested party have three months from being notified of the listing officer's decision to appeal to the Valuation Tribunal for England (VTE)/

Valuation Tribunal for Wales (VTW).[6] If you fail to commence an appeal within three months, the tribunal president has the discretion to allow the appeal if satisfied that the delay arose because of circumstances beyond or your control.[7]

The tribunal should aim to list the appeal within six months of receiving the appeal notice and give you not less than four weeks' notice of the hearing.

If you decide to appeal, the listing officer prepares a presentation pack. This typically includes background information relating to the case, accompanied by evidence of comparable property values. You can also present your valuation evidence.

If a listing officer believes that a proposal has not been validly made and serves an 'invalidity notice' (see p37) on you, you can appeal against the invalidity notice (within four weeks) directly to the VTE/VTW. You must serve a notice of appeal to the clerk of the tribunal with a copy of the notice. The notice must include a written statement of the following if they are not included on the invalidity notice:[8]

- the address of the dwelling;
- the reasons for the appeal against the invalidity notice;
- the names and addresses of the proposer and the listing officer.

If the listing officer reconsiders the matter and withdraws an invalidity notice after an appeal has been started, s/he must inform the tribunal.[9]

If the listing officer agrees to the proposal or decides to alter the list, whether or not an agreement has been reached, the list will be altered within six weeks.[10]

Scotland

In Scotland, the regional assessor must refer appeals to the valuation appeal committee.

Deciding which valuation applies

When determining a council tax banding, the VTE, VTW or valuation appeal committee in Scotland applies the same valuation assumptions that were applied in the original valuation (see p27). The High Court has ruled that the statutory assumptions have to be applied regardless of whether a dwelling is in single or shared ownership.[11]

Example

Virat and Jamila live in a shared-ownership flat which is part of a block with 25 years remaining on the lease. The tribunal must ignore any lower value of shared-ownership properties and presume that there are 99 years left to run the lease.

Once the valuation assumptions have been applied, you must show that, on applying the correct valuation assumptions to your dwelling, a different sale price to that which the listing officer or assessor reached would be obtained. An appeal is only likely to succeed, therefore, if you can show that:

- a mistake was made in the way the assumptions were originally applied to the individual dwelling, indicating that a different value should have been reached; *and*
- the difference in value is sufficient to justify moving the dwelling into another valuation band.

The mistake may include, for instance, an error about the number of rooms in a property, or the size of its garden or the existence of something in the locality which would have an effect on the valuation of a property – eg, it is next door to an industrial building, the nature of which is likely to bring down the value of a neighbouring property.

The VTE/VTW or valuation appeal committee is bound to follow the valuation assumptions and cannot consider whether they are wrong in law or that the regulations themselves are defective.

If your appeal covers a particularly complex, novel or contentious point of law (including principles of valuation), the case may be listed for hearing by the president or a vice-president of the tribunal.

Liability, exemptions, reductions, discounts and amounts

You can appeal if you disagree with the local authority's decision that:

- someone is, or is not, a liable person, including if it is the owner of the dwelling who should be paying the tax (Chapter 5);
- a dwelling is not exempt (Chapter 4);
- a disability reduction should not be granted (Chapter 6);
- a discount should not be granted (Chapter 7);
- whether you should or should not be entitled to CTR or the amount of CTR awarded (see Chapter 8);
- the amount payable is correct;
- an existing exemption should be removed.

There are two stages to appeals on liability and calculation issues. The first stage involves writing to the local authority.[12] The letter should state the decision that is in dispute and the reason(s) for the disagreement. For example, it may be that you have been deemed a liable person for council tax when the property in which you live is actually a house of multiple occupation where the owner should be paying the council tax. The local authority has two months in which to consider these matters and may ask for additional information. A further appeal may be made to the VTE/VTW or valuation appeal committee if the local authority:[13]

- rejects the appeal;
- makes some changes, but fails to satisfy you; *or*
- fails to make a decision within the two-month period.

The local authority should normally inform you directly or publish information on its website of the right to take an appeal to the VTE/VTW or valuation appeal committee, but local authorities do not always do this.

Tactically, it is advantageous to mention your right of appeal in the early stages of correspondence. In the case of a dispute over liability, a calculation or an exemption, a letter can, for example, include the following line: 'If you have not resolved this matter to my satisfaction by (two months), I intent to appeal to the valuation tribunal under section 16 of the Local Government Finance Act 1992.'

As a precaution against the loss of relevant correspondence by the local authority, it may also be advisable to send a copy to the relevant tribunal or committee, with an accompanying letter stating that you wish an appeal to be listed in the event that a negotiated settlement cannot be reached with the local authority. Such a copy should be marked 'For information' and dated clearly. In the event that the local authority loses the appeal letter or it is not forwarded for some reason, this will provide a record to establish it was made within the time limits. Alternatively, the correspondence can be sent electronically to the local authority which will create an automatic receipt.

If you do not get a reply or acknowledgement from the local authority, proceed with your appeal by contacting the VTE/VTW or valuation appeal committee direct. Copies of appeal forms can be obtained from the Valuation Tribunal Service website. Also send copies of all documents you intend to use to the local authority, even though it does not reply. You can make also make a formal complaint about the failure of the authority to respond.

Example

Zoe is a single student on a four-year course which she started two years ago. Her flat has been exempt from council tax since she started her course. During the third year of her course, the local authority removed the exemption. She writes to the local authority providing evidence of her status as a student. The local authority does not respond within two months so Zoe appeals to the valuation tribunal.

England and Wales

An appeal to the VTE/VTW must normally be made:[14]

- within two months of the date the local authority notified you of its decision;
  or
- within four months of the date when the initial representation was made, if the local authority has not responded.

The tribunal president has the discretion to allow an out-of-time appeal if you have failed to meet the time limit because of reasons beyond your control.[15]

It is important to distinguish between appeals to the VTE/VTW and appeals that go to the First-tier Tribunal for other social security benefits, such as

Department for Work and Pensions benefits, and for decisions about entitlement and calculations which were made for the council tax benefit (CTB) system before 1 April 2013.

Scotland

Liability and exemption appeals

In Scotland, an appeal to the valuation appeal committee must normally be made within:[16]

- two months of the date the local authority notified you of its decision; *or*
- four months of the date when the initial representation was made, if the local authority has not responded.

The local authority will forward your appeal to the valuation appeal committee.

Council tax reduction appeals in Scotland

To appeal a determination by a local authority about an amount of CTR, you must first seek a review by the local authority that made the determination. You should write directly to the local authority to request an internal review within two months of the determination.[17]

If you are still dissatisfied with the decision following a review, you have a further right of appeal to the Council Tax Reduction Review Panel (CTRRP) within 42 days of the date of the local authority notification.[18] You may also request a further review of a determination on an application, where your local authority has not notified you of a decision on your first request for review and more than two months have gone by.[19]

See p166 for more details about the CTRRP.

Completion notices

In England and Wales, the local authority and, in Scotland, the assessor may issue a completion notice that states the date on which a newly erected or structurally altered property is considered to be a dwelling. While the matter can be discussed with the local authority or the assessor, an appeal can be made to the VTE/VTW or valuation appeal committee.

England and Wales

An appeal on a completion notice must normally be made within four weeks of the notice being sent.[20] An out-of-time appeal may be allowed if you have failed to meet this time limit for reasons beyond your control.[21]

You, or someone on your behalf, should write directly to the clerk of the relevant tribunal.[22] The letter should:

- state the reasons for the appeal; *and*
- be accompanied by a copy of the completion notice.

Appeal forms on which the information is requested are available from the relevant tribunal office. In England, you can register an appeal online at the Valuation Tribunal Service website. The clerk should notify you within two weeks that the appeal request has been received. The clerk should also acknowledge it and send a copy of the appeal letter or form to the local authority.[23]

Scotland

An appeal to the valuation appeal committee must be made in writing to the assessor within 21 days of receiving the completion notice.[24] There is no power to consider out-of-time appeals. The letter should state the reasons for the appeal and be accompanied by a copy of the completion notice.[25] The assessor must pass the appeal to the secretary of the relevant valuation appeal committee.[26]

Penalties

The local authority has the power to impose a penalty in certain instances if you are required to provide information but fail to do so, or you provide information which you know to be false. While the matter may be discussed with the local authority, and it has the power to withdraw the penalty, an appeal can be made to the VTE/VTW or a valuation appeal committee in Scotland. For more on penalties, see p189. Grounds on which a penalty may be quashed include where:
- the local authority already has the information;
- you have valid reasons for withholding the information – eg, on grounds of confidentiality;
- the amount of information being sought is excessive or the demand is impossible to comply with;
- the information is irrelevant or it is not within the remit of the local authority to seek.

England and Wales

An appeal must normally be made within two months of the penalty being imposed.[27] The tribunal president has the discretion to allow an out-of-time appeal if you have failed to meet the time limit for reasons beyond your control.[28] The appeal is made by you, or someone acting on your behalf, by writing directly to the clerk of the relevant tribunal. The letter should state:[29]
- the reasons for the appeal; *and*
- the date, if any, you were notified by the local authority of the penalty.

Appeal forms on which the required information is requested are available from the relevant tribunal office. In England, you can register an appeal online at the Valuation Tribunal Service website. The clerk should notify you within two weeks that the appeal request has been received. The clerk should also send a copy of the appeal letter or form and any accompanying documents to the local authority.[30]

Scotland

An appeal to a valuation appeal committee must be made by writing to the local authority within two months of the penalty being imposed.[31] There is no power to consider out-of-time appeals. The letter should state:

- the reasons for the appeal; *and*
- the date, if any, you were notified by the local authority of the penalty.[32]

The local authority must pass the appeal to the secretary of the relevant valuation appeal committee.[33]

Discretionary reductions

You have a right of appeal against the billing authority's discretionary decision to refuse a reduction, or in respect of the amount awarded.[34] The right of appeal against a refusal arises regardless of whenever the actual liability to the sum arose.[35]

The tribunal will not simply substitute its decision for that of the local authority but will consider whether the local authority has used its powers correctly and lawfully when deciding whether to grant a discretionary reduction. However, following the decision in *SC and CW v East Riding of Yorkshire Council*,[36] the tribunal may look at the actual facts of your appeal (eg, your financial circumstances) and substitute its own decision if it is satisfied the authority made the wrong decision. The tribunal applies principles which are similar, but wider, to those which operate in judicial review hearings in the High Court, and considers whether the local authority has made an error of law, which means its decision should be quashed.

> ### *SC and CW v East Riding of Yorkshire Council*
>
> **Mr and Mrs W**
>
> Mr and Mrs W, an unemployed couple with no savings, applied for a discretionary reduction. The council refused it. The couple had no surplus income and, by the local authority's own calculations, there was a shortfall of £72.34 in their income to meet existing liabilities and outgoings.
>
> In the view of tribunal, the simple fact was that there was no surplus income to meet a council tax bill and that: 'It is difficult to imagine a clearer case for discretionary assistance'. It found that Mr and Mrs W were entitled to discretionary relief and there was no plausible or rational basis for limiting that relief to 12 weeks or any other period and 'that only full remission of the residual council tax for the year makes any sense in view of the absence of any funds to meet their liability.'[42]
>
> **Mr and Mrs C**
>
> Mr and Mrs C were also a couple in a difficult financial position who applied for a discretionary reduction. The council refused it. Mrs C was disabled and her husband was her carer. They had one dependent child, but although they were 'a household existing at

the very margins of viability' and 'in extremely hard-pressed financial circumstances', there was nonetheless a very small surplus of income over expenditure, which allowed very little latitude for contingencies or emergencies. However, because there was such a surplus, there was no basis in law for interfering with the council's decision to reject the application for discretionary relief, and their appeal was dismissed.

Principles of law by which the tribunal may quash a decision to refuse a discretionary reduction include the following.

- The authority has got the facts wrong. This applies where the authority has made fundamental mistakes of fact that completely alter the nature of the decision and the way it approached the question of using its discretion.
- The authority fails to follow due process – eg, it failed to follow proper procedures determining a discretionary reduction or to look at the application properly. The authority also is expected to follow its own rules and guidance on discretionary reductions.
- The authority fails to consider the hardship test properly. The discretionary reduction is meant to include tackling hardship, and a local authority errs when it fails to give sufficient weight to this purpose.
- The authority fails to make an individual decision on your case. The local authority should look at individual circumstances and not simply apply a general policy.
- The authority fails to follow its own guidance, which will usually mean a different decision will be made.[37]
- The authority has acted unreasonably.[38] An authority may act unreasonably by:
  - failing to consider relevant facts;
  - considering irrelevant facts;
  - acting perversely or irrationally.

Failing to consider relevant facts occurs where the authority has ignored matters it should have considered when looking at your application. For example, the local authority may fail to consider your income properly or fail to apply a means test or ignore the effect on any disability.

Taking irrelevant facts into consideration may occur where an authority refuses you a reduction over an irrelevant issue, such as your having just moved into a property, that you are unemployed or have been bankrupt, or you have rent arrears.

The authority has acted irrationally and perversely where it has refused an application for a discretionary amount and has made a decision that no authority, properly directing itself would have reached. An example where an authority might act unreasonably in refusing a discretionary reduction is where the authority has created a liability by its own failure to award you a reduction at the correct stage, due to its own errors.

The tribunal may remit the matter to the billing authority to be reconsidered.

The tribunal cannot hear an appeal if it amounts to a challenge to the legality of the local authority's discretionary reduction scheme. This can only be done by an application for judicial review in the High Court. The right of appeal does not extend to decisions by a billing authority on a person's application for funding or financial support unrelated to the discretionary scheme.[39]

3. **How to appeal**

England and Wales

Your appeal must be in writing. You, or someone on your behalf, must write directly to the clerk of the relevant tribunal. In England, you can register an appeal online at the Valuation Tribunal Service website. However you appeal, you should state a number of prescribed matters, including:[40]
- the reasons for the appeal;
- the date on which the first letter about the matter was served on the local authority;
- the date, if any, when you were notified by the local authority of its decision.

If your appeal arises under section 16 of the Local Government Finance Act 1992 regarding liability, exemption or discount or from a decision about your entitlement to council tax reduction (CTR), it must include the following:
- your full name and address;
- the address of the property (if different to your home address);
- the name of your local authority and the date you first wrote to it;
- the date on which the authority refused your appeal (if it replied);
- brief reasons why you consider the decision or calculation to be wrong;
- details of any other appeal relating to council tax benefit (pre-1 April 2013) or housing benefit, which arises from the same facts and which you made to the First-tier Tribunal for social security matters.[41]

If you fail to supply the information, you are requested to provide it. If you do not supply the information within the time specified, your appeal will not be admitted.

If it is discovered at the hearing that you have omitted information which should have been supplied, the tribunal can apply a 'common sense test' so the appeal is not struck out. The appeal should not be struck out if the error or omission is merely technical or the result of a clerical error and no difficulty or prejudice has been caused to the billing authority. If the appeal is struck out, you may start a new appeal.

Directions to parties

Instructions of how to proceed with your appeal, known as 'standard directions', are sent to both sides when the notice of an appeal hearing is issued. If you do not follow the steps laid down in the direction, your submission may be excluded.[42] The valuation officer and the local authority are also expected to follow directions. It is important to read the directions and comply with them as fully as possible, including any time limits.

A failure by the billing authority to comply with the standard directions in the specified time will result in its evidence being excluded and in its being barred from any further participation in the proceedings, with a notice being issued to the authority.[43]

Where the billing authority has been barred for failure to provide the material specified in the standard directions, the appeal is automatically allowed by default, without any consideration of the merits of the appeal. However, the tribunal's order will be delayed for 28 days in such a case. This is to allow the billing authority an opportunity to apply to the tribunal (which it must do within 14 days) for the appeal to be relisted for hearing on the grounds that it did not receive the notice of hearing, or alternatively, that it did comply with the standard directions or for some other exceptional and compelling reason that provides an excuse for failure to comply.

Scotland

An appeal to a valuation appeal committee must be made by writing to the local authority within four months of the date on which the grievance was first raised with it in writing.[44] There is no power to consider out-of-time appeals. The letter should state:[45]

- the reasons for the appeal; *and*
- the date on which the first letter disputing the matter(s) was served on the local authority.

The local authority must pass the appeal to the secretary of the relevant valuation appeal committee.[46]

4. **How appeals are dealt with**

While there are many similarities in the way in which the Scottish valuation appeal committee and the English and Welsh valuation tribunals deal with appeals, different rules apply in Scotland from those which apply in England and Wales.[47]

An appeal is normally dealt with by an oral hearing (see p255) but, if all the parties agree, it can be dealt with by written representation (see p252).[48] In most cases, it is advisable to request an oral hearing.

There is likely to be a wait of some months between the acknowledgment of your appeal and the actual hearing. Use this time to prepare for the hearing. The Valuation Tribunal Service's customer charter aims to list council tax liability and banding appeals within four months of registration.

In an appeal under section 16 of the Local Government Finance Act 1992 on liability, exemptions, discount or any calculation, the tribunal normally contacts you about two weeks before the hearing, and you must make sure you send copies of any documents you intend to use at the hearing well in advance to the tribunal and other parties to the appeal.

Appeal management powers – Valuation Tribunal for England

The Valuation Tribunal for England (VTE) enjoys the power to regulate its own procedures,[49] including extending, amending, suspending or setting aside an earlier direction[50] and case management powers to:

– extend or shorten the time for complying with any regulation or directions;
– consolidate or hear together two or more sets of proceedings or parts of proceedings raising common issues, or treat an appeal as a lead appeal;
– permit or require a party to amend a document;
– permit or require a party or another person to provide documents, evidence, information, or submissions to the VTE or a party;
– deal with an issue in proceedings as a preliminary issue;
– hold a hearing to consider any matter, including a case management issue;
– decide the form of any hearing;
– adjourn or postpone a hearing;
– require a party to produce a bundle of documents for a hearing;
– stay proceedings; or
– suspend the effect of its own decision pending the determination by the Upper Tribunal or a court of an application for permission to appeal against, and any appeal against or review of, that decision.

Pre-appeal agreement

In England, the parties may reach an agreement before the appeal hearing (see p255) or before written representations are considered (see p252). The agreement includes how the valuation list is to be altered and the listing officer must serve a copy of this on the VTE and on all the parties to the agreement. The appeal is treated as withdrawn and there is no need for you to do anything further. The alteration to the list must take place within six weeks.[51] In Wales, an appeal can be settled and disposed of on the basis of written representations if all the parties have given their consent in writing.[52]

Written representations

Written representations are a relatively quick and effective procedure for resolving straightforward appeals. For an appeal to be dealt with in this way, all the parties (normally you, the listing officer/assessor and the local authority) must give their written agreement.[53]

There is no maximum time limit in which the tribunal or committee must determine the appeal on the basis of written representations. Once it is agreed that the appeal is to be dealt with in this way, the clerk must serve notice on the parties, and they have four weeks in which to send their written representations. Copies are sent to the other parties. There is then a further four-week period in which comments may be made. At the end of this last period, the clerk or secretary sends the available material to the tribunal or committee within four weeks. The tribunal or committee may:[54]

- require any party to provide additional material;
- order that the appeal be dealt with by a hearing; or
- proceed to reach a decision.

If additional information is required, copies of that material must be provided to all the other parties. Each party may, within four weeks of receiving the additional material, supply a further statement in response.[55]

In Scotland, permission to deal with the appeal by written representation can be withdrawn by any of the parties at any time before a decision is reached. This might happen, for example, if the other party's arguments are not as expected. If permission has been withdrawn, the appeal must be dealt with by an oral hearing.[56]

Pre-hearing review

In England and Wales, a tribunal chair may order a pre-hearing review to clarify the issues to be dealt with at the hearing, such as the procedure to be followed, evidence and time limits.[57] This may be done either at the request of you, any other party, or on the chair's own initiative. At least four weeks' notice must be given of a pre-hearing.

Extension of time limits

If you cannot meet a time limit in any of the steps of an appeal, ask for it to be extended. Time limits can be extended in appeals about liability, completion notices, penalties and council tax valuation bands.[58]

A request for an extension of time should be made to the president using the prescribed form.

An appeal can be pursued out of time if the president is satisfied that you were unable to appeal by the normal deadline because of circumstances beyond your control. You must therefore provide a reason for why you need an extension.

More information may be requested from you and other parties to the appeal in order for a decision to be made. In some cases, a hearing may be held.

The president considers the following when deciding whether an extension should be granted:[59]

- when the notice was actually received;
- whether you were informed of the right of appeal and the 28-day limit;
- whether you have acted with all reasonable speed in the circumstances;
- your reasons (and any proof) for the delay, such as illness, absence from home or bereavement;
- whether it would be contrary to the interests of justice not to permit the appeal to be heard, or heard fairly.

A decision is sent to you, with copies sent to all other parties (or potential parties). There is normally no further right of appeal against the decision to reject an application to extend time limits. A further application may be made only on the basis of completely new information that was not available or known at the time of the earlier application.[60]

If you are dealing with administration staff at an early stage of a liability appeal where no reply has been received from the billing authority, it may be advisable to refer to section 16 of the Local Government Finance Act 1992 if staff are reluctant to register the appeal. You are not required to produce a reply from the local authority where none has been issued and more than eight weeks have elapsed since first writing to the authority.

Lead cases

If appeals are made to the tribunal by more than one person about the same issues of fact or law (eg, a number of appeals about valuations in the same block of new flats), the tribunal can specify one or more of the appeals as a 'lead case' and postpone making a decision on all other related appeals. The result of the lead appeal can apply to (and be binding on) the postponed appeals.[61] You must be sent a copy of the decision. If your appeal is not the lead case, you can apply in writing to the tribunal within one month for a direction that the decision does not apply to, and is not binding on, your appeal.[62]

Withdrawing an appeal

In England and Wales, you may withdraw an appeal on a valuation matter by either sending or delivering a notice to the VTE/VTW.[63] The tribunal must notify each party in writing that an appeal has been withdrawn.

In England, you can orally give notice to withdraw the appeal at the hearing. The tribunal must give its formal consent. In Wales, your appeal may be withdrawn at the hearing itself by the appeal panel after considering written representations.[64]

In Scotland, an appeal may be withdrawn by writing to the secretary of the valuation appeal committee, or at the hearing by asking the permission of the committee. If the assessor decides, after the appeal has been initiated, to agree to the original proposal or the local authority decides not to contest the appeal, it is considered to be withdrawn.[65]

Reinstatement of an appeal

In England, it is possible to apply to reinstate an appeal after you have given notice to withdraw it. This might be appropriate, for instance, if an appeal has been withdrawn by mistake, if new advice or evidence has been obtained or if a ruling of another tribunal or the High Court might affect the position.

An application must be made in writing to the VTE and within one month of either the date:[66]

- on which the VTE received the withdrawal notice; *or*
- of the hearing at which the appeal was withdrawn.

You should provide any supporting documentation and give your reasons.

Paying council tax while an appeal is pending

A person who has been served a bill must make the payments required by either the bill or by any subsequent special agreement reached with the local authority. The fact that an appeal has been made does not affect this obligation, though some local authorities are willing to suspend recovery action until an appeal has been dealt with. If an appeal is upheld, any overpayment of tax should be refunded or credited against future liability.

In England and Wales, if the local authority seeks a liability order, the magistrates' court may also agree to an adjournment if an appeal about liability has started. An adjournment should always be granted if there is the prospect of a successful appeal in a case in which a local authority is seeking a committal order against a debtor (see p226). This approach has been approved by the High Court.[67]

If, however, the authority has obtained a liability order through the magistrates' court or a summary warrant or decree in Scotland, it should suspend recovery action until the appeal has been determined. In such a case, the local authority should suspend recovery action until the appeal has been determined.

A further exception is if an appeal has been made against a penalty imposed by the local authority (see p246). In such cases, the penalty does not have to be paid until the appeal has been decided. If a sum in council tax relates to a previous year, it could also be argued that the matter should wait for a determination by the VTE/VTW or a valuation appeal committee in Scotland.

If, following the initiation of an appeal against the imposition of a council tax penalty, the local authority decides to remit the penalty, it notifies the VTE/VTW or valuation appeal committee and the appeal is treated as withdrawn on the date on which the notice is served.[68]

Appealing as an interested person

An interested party is anyone who is affected by the appeal. It includes:[69]
- the property's owner;
- a person who may be jointly or severally liable to pay council tax;
- a person other than an owner who would be liable to pay council tax if the dwelling were not an exempt dwelling or where the amount so set were other than nil;
- any other person who is a taxpayer in respect of the dwelling.

---

5. **Appeal hearings**

The president of the Valuation Tribunal for England (VTE) has issued a consolidated practice statement for the conduct of proceedings. The Valuation Tribunal for Wales' (VTW) best practice protocols cover the same areas. These help interpret the procedural regulations and the steps which must be taken when appealing, and give an idea of the approach of the tribunal in specific situations. The practice statements apply whenever problems arise and are worth consulting when making an appeal.

Practice statements in England and Wales
The president of the VTE's consolidated practice statement is available at www.valuationtribunal.gov.uk/preparing-for-the-hearing/practice-statements/.
The Valuation Tribunal for Wales' (VTW) best practice protocols are available at www.valuation-tribunals-wales.org.uk/best-practice-protocols.html.

You should read the information in the practice statement/best practice protocol which provides key details of how appeals should be prepared, particularly if you are a professional representative or acting in an official capacity. However, taxpayers acting by themselves are not necessarily expected to follow all the preferred steps in the practice directions, but are required to provide material to the best of their ability so that the other parties and the tribunal are able to deal properly and fairly with the case. A higher standard may be expected of professional representatives and local authorities. Most valuation tribunal hearings are open to the public and, if possible, it is a good idea to watch the tribunal in action to learn how proceedings operate.

Postponements

In some cases it may be necessary to postpone a hearing.

Postponements are handled initially by staff of the valuation tribunal before any hearing has commenced, and, although 'administrative', must be handled in accordance with judicial practice and procedural principles.[70]

Either party may apply for a postponement in advance of the hearing date. You must supply reasons and these must be given and the other party or parties notified, with the application made in writing as soon as possible. The application and should indicate the reasons behind it and whether the other parties agree. In cases of urgency, the application for a postponement may be made over the telephone.

The presumption is against the granting of postponements. The valuation tribunal states that postponements will not therefore be granted automatically but only if there are (exceptional) good and sufficient reasons for doing so, and it is in the interests of justice to do so.

What are considered 'good reasons' for granting a postponement may include the following:[71]
- the ill health of a party or representative. If a representative has a long-term illness, it is expected that alternative arrangements for representation will be made. If possible, an application for reasons of ill-health should be supported with medical evidence;[72]
- an unexpected or unforeseen event which makes it impossible to attend the arranged day of the hearing – eg, significant IT problems;
- new evidence or caselaw that requires consideration;
- material or notices sent to an incorrect email address resulting in delay in reaching the correct recipient.

The following examples do not constitute good reasons:
- holiday commitments;
- the fact that the parties have failed to enter into meaningful negotiations or negotiations are under way but incomplete and are expected to continue beyond the hearing date.

Where you have a good reason for postponement, it should normally be granted unless either the other party presents a stronger argument to the contrary or the interests of justice require the application to be rejected.[73] Similar principles to those applied with granting adjournments may be expected to apply in law (see p204).

All parties are advised in writing (normally within three working days) of the decision, together with the reasons, provided that there is sufficient time prior to the hearing.[74]

Notice of the hearing

In England, the VTE must give each party 'reasonable notice' of the date and time of the hearing.[75] This normally means 14 days, unless parties consent or there are urgent or exceptional circumstances. In Wales, the clerk to the tribunal must give at least four weeks' written notice of the date, time and place of the hearing.[76] In Scotland, the secretary to the valuation appeal committee must give at least 35 days' written notice.[77]

There is no maximum time limit in which the tribunal or committee must hear the appeal.

In Wales, the clerk must advertise the date, time and place of the hearing:[78]
- at the tribunal's office; *and*
- outside an office earmarked by the local authority for this purpose; *or*
- in another place within the local authority's area.

In Scotland, the secretary must advertise the details at a local authority office and the place at which the hearing will be, if different.[79]

In all cases, the advert must name a place where a list of the appeals to be heard may be inspected by members of the public.[80]

Representatives

On the day of the hearing, any party may:[81]
- represent her/himself; *or*
- be represented by a lawyer; *or*
- be represented by anyone else.

In England and Wales, where you are representing yourself, you may have the assistance of someone else – eg, a friend, a relative or an adviser.[82] In Scotland, you may be represented by another person, whether legally qualified or not. However, if there are good and sufficient reasons for doing so, the committee may refuse to permit a particular person to represent a party at a hearing.[83]

How the hearing is conducted

In England and Wales, the appeal is heard by two members, one of whom must be the chair and who must preside. The president, vice presidents and nominated senior members may sit alone as the tribunal. If all parties who attend the hearing agree, the appeal may be decided by two members in the absence of a chair.[84]

A council tax reduction (CTR) appeal must have a First-tier Tribunal judge as one of the panel if it involves:[85]
- an assessment of income or capital;
- a right of residence (whether you are from the UK or not, so far as it is relevant).

Putting documentary evidence to the tribunal

Written statements are encouraged from appellants, and you should produce relevant documents concerning your appeal. The Valuation Tribunal Service states in the booklet *Council Tax Valuation: your appeal and preparing for your valuation tribunal hearing*: 'You should make sure that your case explains the issues that you and the VOA disagree about and the decision you want from the tribunal. Set out your arguments that support your case (including any legislation or case law) and enclose any evidence that you have to support this.' This is good advice because, although the tribunal allows you to give oral evidence to establish the facts, it often wants whatever you say to be confirmed by documentary evidence.

Serving documents on the local authority or listing officer

At least six weeks before the hearing, you should receive the other party's full case in response to the appeal, including arguments, evidence, legislation, caselaw and documents.

If you wish to provide evidence for the appeal, you should submit copies to the other party at least four weeks before the hearing. This may include caselaw or references to the legislation.

Anything sent to after the four-week deadline may not be considered by the tribunal unless you can demonstrate reasons why the evidence was not available at the time.

Unless your case is postponed or settled by agreement or withdrawal, it is expected that you (or your representative) will attend the hearing to present the appeal. You may request that the hearing proceed without you being there by contacting the tribunal at least 24 hours before the hearing day.

Evidence that has been served earlier in the appeal need not be submitted again, but it should be made clear which evidence or argument will be relied upon.[86]

At least two weeks before the hearing, a billing authority may be required to electronically submit to the tribunal and by either email or post to the appellant, a bundle of documents including any documents provided under any directions.

A failure to do so may lead to evidence being excluded or a party being barred from taking further part in proceedings.

The VTE advises that you should aim to bring five copies of any written documents that you want to present in evidence (a copy for each of the two or three members, and one each for the clerk and the other party as well as your own).

It is very important that the local authority or listing officer be sent the copies of any evidence in advance, even if these are not read. At the very least, the opportunity to read the evidence in advance should be given.

In an appeal about CTR, send the local authority copies of any documents you want the tribunal to consider at least 14 days in advance of the hearing.

In an appeal about liability, a discount, an exemption or any calculation, you should also send copies of the written evidence and documents in advance to the local authority. Ideally, this should be at least one month before the hearing, subject to any directions before the hearing, or otherwise there may have to be a postponement of the case. However, in the case of documents that may become available at a late stage, the tribunal has the discretion to admit or exclude such evidence.[87] In Wales, the VTW expects parties to have discussed and exchanged evidence at least two weeks before the hearing day.[88]

The tribunal may give directions to produce what is known as a 'bundle'[89] and this is often the best way to present your evidence, whether the tribunal gives a direction or not.

Bundle

A **'bundle'** is a collection of all the documents attached together, with each page given a number. The simplest way to produce a bundle is to put the documents together in date order, although there is no specific rule that documents have to be in this order. You can also add your own statement or witness statement to the documents, which you can place at the beginning of the bundle. You should add a front page to the bundle. This should be marked 'In the Valuation Tribunal for England' (or Welsh or Scottish equivalent) and give the appeal number, the address of the property and your name as the appellant and that of the local authority or listing officer as the respondent. The purpose of the bundle is to help the tribunal pinpoint the key evidence, and speeds up the tribunal process where all parties have copies of the documents in the same order.

Other evidence that may be difficult to copy, such as photographs and large plans, can be shared on the day, but you should let the other parties know in advance.

You can send copies of information by electronic means, as well as providing physical copies.

Public hearing

The hearing normally takes place in public (this gives you an opportunity to attend another hearing as an observer to see how a tribunal works). However, in England and Wales, a tribunal can decide to hold the hearing in private if any of the parties request it and the tribunal considers that the interests of that party would be prejudicially affected if the hearing were held in public.[90] In this case, the panel decides who should be present.[91] Someone who might disrupt a hearing or who is likely to prevent another person giving evidence may be excluded.

In Scotland, the committee may, if it has reasonable cause, hold the hearing in private.[92]

Extraordinary hearing venues

In exceptional cases, it is possible to hold a tribunal at a place other than that normally used for hearings.[93] This could include your home in exceptional circumstances (eg, due to serious illness) or in a place where you are staying if you are unable to attend any other venue. Such venues are known as 'extraordinary venues'. In such a case, the requirement that a hearing be open to the public may be waived. Applications for extraordinary venues should be made in writing to the tribunal or committee.

Failure to appear and striking out of appeals

In England and Wales, if you (or in Scotland, you or your representative) fail to appear at the hearing, the appeal may be dismissed or struck out, including where a party fails to follow a direction from the tribunal.[94] In England and Wales, an appeal on a valuation matter may also be struck out if any party other than the listing officer fails to attend. The VTW may also strike out an appeal or part of an appeal related to CTR where the reduction awarded is the maximum that the authority can award under its scheme. If the appeal relates to more than one issue, only that part which relates to the reduction can be struck out by the tribunal under this power, although the tribunal must give you an opportunity to be heard.

In England and Wales, if you can show reasonable cause for not appearing, you may request the tribunal to review its decision (see p266). The request must be made within four weeks of the notice of the decision being given.[95]

In Scotland, if you have a reasonable excuse for your absence, the valuation appeal committee may set a new date, time and place for the hearing.[96] It must give all parties at least seven days' notice. For a hearing to be recalled in this manner, you must write to the committee (normally within 14 days of being notified that the original appeal was dismissed), requesting a new hearing date and setting out the reason for the original absence. If the committee considers that there are special circumstances, it may allow an out-of-time request.

If any party does not appear at the hearing, the tribunal or committee may hear and determine the appeal in her/his absence.[97] Local authorities vary in their willingness to appear. Whether the local authority sends a representative or not, always send it a copy of the documents you plan to use in an appeal well before the hearing.

Order of the hearing

The VTE/VTW or a valuation appeal committee may determine the order of the hearing – ie, which party puts its case first. The 'model procedure' practice statement provides that usually you are to open your case first.[98] However, sometimes the billing authority is invited to present its case first. Certainly, if you are unrepresented, the panel is entitled to invite the local authority or listing officer to go first, where it is thought that to do so will result in a fairer hearing.

The panel must, however, ensure that the local authority or listing officer is not prejudiced and is given the opportunity to respond to your case. In all cases, you must be given the final opportunity to address the panel.[99] You are given an opportunity to put questions to the local authority. Parties at the hearing may examine and cross-examine any witness and call witnesses. Evidence can be given in written submissions, including in witness statements.[100] Witness statements are often the best way to provide evidence at hearings, with the person reading from her/his statement and answering any questions which the other side may have about the information it contains. Where you are unrepresented and are having difficulty in formulating questions, the clerk (or the chair) may assist you, but not to the point where s/he becomes your advocate.[101]

After the close of the cases of both sides and the end of questioning, each side is entitled to make a closing submission. It is best to make closing submissions fairly short, as all the evidence should have been put forward to the panel by this stage. The aim of the summing up is to succinctly review the case and explain why your case should be preferred, not to repeat the evidence that the tribunal has already heard. You should not seek to introduce any new material to the panel in a closing speech.

At the end of the hearing, the tribunal or committee will normally retire to consider its verdict or the parties to the appeal will be asked to leave the room. The clerk can advise the tribunal or committee, but no other person should be present while it is engaged in deliberations. If any other person is present, the decision may be challengeable on grounds of breach of natural justice.

Adjournment and dismissal

A hearing may be adjourned for such time, to such a place and on such terms (if any) as the tribunal or committee thinks fit. Reasonable notice of the time and place to which the hearing has been adjourned must be given to every party.[102]

In England, an application for an adjournment must be made in writing to the clerk. The clerk considers the request and takes into account relevant factors including:

- the reasons;
- the other parties' comments on the request;
- the length of notice that was given for the hearing;
- the preparation for the hearing that the parties have undertaken;
- the time remaining before the hearing;
- whether the appeal has previously been listed for hearing.

If the clerk refuses the adjournment, an application can be made to a member or to the VTE itself on the day. Adjournments will only be rarely granted at the hearing, however, as parties are expected to be prepared.

In Scotland, a valuation appeal committee may request representations from both parties and then adjourn as it sees fit.

In some cases, an appeal may be dismissed if the listing officer or assessor fails to show that you have been properly served with notices and documents.

Witnesses

The VTE may summons a person to attend as a witness and order her/him to produce any documents or answer any questions relating to the proceedings.[103] A summons must normally be given with 14 days' notice (or a shorter period if the tribunal directs). A summons or order must state that a person may apply to vary or 'set aside' the summons or order if s/he has not had the opportunity to object to it, and must state the consequences of non-compliance. There is currently no equivalent rule in Wales or Scotland.

Evidence

England and Wales

Tribunals are not bound by any rules on the admissibility of evidence before courts of law; rather, they are concerned with the weight of any evidence.[104] For example, what someone else has been heard to say (hearsay) would be admissible at a hearing, but given less weight than the direct evidence of a witness.

Evidence can be given orally or in written form, such as valuation reports. Make sure that you have multiple copies of any documents wherever possible. If the valuation of a dwelling is in question, evidence could include photographs or a video. Occasionally, physical evidence may even be produced.[105]

You should expect to be asked questions by members of the tribunal and by the listing officer or local authority representative. For example, if you allege that your property value is affected by blighting or a nuisance of some kind, you may be asked what steps you have taken to remedy the problem. If you have taken no such steps, the conclusion might be drawn that the problem is not sufficiently serious as to make an impact on the property's value.

In appeals that do not relate to valuation matters, the local authority must give the other parties two weeks' notice if it wishes to produce evidence of information supplied in connection with a disability reduction or information in relation to liability. This information may be inspected and copies taken if at least 24 hours' notice is given to the local authority.[106] In a valuation appeal, the listing officer must give at least two weeks' notice of information s/he proposes to use at the hearing. Again, you and any other party to the appeal may, having given 24 hours' notice, inspect the documents and make a copy of all the documents, or an extract, if you wish.[107]

You have the right to inspect the relevant documents and to request information relating to a maximum of four comparable dwellings or, if the listing officer specifies more, the same number as is specified by the officer. The listing officer has a duty to produce both sets of documents at the hearing.[108]

Historic values

The government has indicated that it is prepared to allow the Valuation Office Agency greater freedom in the future to release information to taxpayers concerning property values obtained before 2000. This information could be of use, particularly with appeals in England where you may be able to show a trend in rising house prices for properties with a particular banding and argue that her/his property is similar. Currently, such information is shared only once an appeal proceeds to a tribunal, but the government has proposed to make pre-2000 sales information available at an earlier stage.

Scotland

In Scotland, a valuation appeal committee may require a party to provide the other parties, by a set date, with:[109]
- a written statement outlining the evidence to be given at the hearing; *and*
- copies of all documents which are to be produced for the hearing.

If a committee has made such a requirement, no other material may be produced unless the committee allows it.[110]

If there is to be a hearing, the committee has the power to grant to any of the parties the same rights of access to documents as could be granted, or provided, by the Court of Session.[111] The committee may require:[112]
- someone's attendance at the hearing as a witness; *or*
- the production of any document relating to the appeal.

If someone fails to comply with such a written requirement, s/he is liable on summary conviction to a fine not exceeding level 1 on the standard scale.[113] No one need produce any material or answer any questions which s/he would not need to answer in a court of law (eg, professional confidences)[114] or questions that might incriminate a person to a criminal charge. Additionally, if someone is required to appear as a witness at the hearing and it takes place more than 10 miles from her/his home, s/he does not have to appear unless her/his necessary expenses are paid.[115]

Caselaw

As well as evidence, it is possible to raise points of law at a tribunal, including law found in cases decided by the courts. If you are raising a point of law before the tribunal, you are expected to produce a copy of the judgment and provide a copy for the clerk and any other party to the hearing.

Case references should normally be provided in advance of the hearing to the other parties and to the tribunal, so that these cases may be studied prior to the hearing. Any cases not available online should be provided in a hard copy. It is best to bring multiple copies to the hearing, as the tribunal may not have facilities to make photocopies. It is not expected that multiple copies of well-known caselaw should be brought in a non-contentious case but, if you intend citing the case, you should have at least one full copy with you.

Failure to agree

Where an appeal has been heard by a panel with an even number of members who, at its conclusion, are unable to agree, a completely new panel will be selected to hear the appeal afresh.[116]

Decisions

Following a hearing, the VTE/VTW or a valuation appeal committee has the discretion to give an oral decision to the parties concerned.[117] Whether or not an oral decision is given, a written decision, together with a statement of reasons, must be supplied to the parties.

In England and Wales, this should be done as soon as is reasonably practicable after the decision has been made. If the tribunal does not give written reasons, you may request reasons in writing. Your request must be made within two weeks of the date on which the tribunal sent or provided you with a final decision notice.[118] Sometimes a handwritten copy is given to the parties on the day, with a more formal typed copy supplied afterwards. In Scotland, it must be done within seven days of the decision.[119] After the tribunal or committee has made a decision, it has the power to make orders to give effect to it, such as ordering the billing authority to reverse its decision.[120] An order may include a direction for the local authority to repay you any council tax owing or any bailiffs' fees or other charges, with interest from the date(s) of payment.

Tribunals are expected to give reasons for their decisions. If a tribunal or committee fails to give adequate reasons, the decision is invalid. In Scotland, the valuation appeal committee is expected to give reasons for its decision, by providing clear and sufficient grounds to indicate why it reached the decision it did.[121]

The tribunal's decisions become public documents. In addition to being sent to the parties, they are placed on the website, except that, in the case where you are appealing about council tax liability decisions, your name and other identifying information is removed from the online version in the interests of privacy.[122] You can request material to be omitted ('redacted') from the published decision, or ask that names and other identifying information be omitted.[123] It is up to you to satisfy the tribunal that information should not be published.

. . . .

Previous tribunal or committee decisions

You may be told at some stage of the appeal process that a valuation tribunal or committee has already decided a particular matter and that your attempt to appeal on the same grounds will fail. You should not accept this as a reason for abandoning an appeal. Although local authorities and listing officers have tended to treat previous decisions involving points of law as binding, it should not be assumed that a tribunal or committee will automatically find against you. Just because one appeal has been decided in a particular way does not necessarily mean that the same approach will be taken with a different appeal. Tribunals are not precedent-making bodies that are expected to follow decisions of earlier tribunals. Your case should be looked at on its merits.[124]

Records of decisions

In England and Wales, the clerk has a duty to make arrangements for the tribunal's decisions to be recorded. The record may be kept in any form, whether documentary or otherwise. The record should contain the following information in appeals about proposals:[125]

- your name and address;
- the matter appealed against;
- the date of the hearing or determination;
- the names of the parties who appeared (if any);
- the decision of the tribunal and its date;
- the reasons for the decision;
- any order made in consequence of the decision;
- the date of any such order;
- any certificate setting aside the decision;
- any revocation.

Records of decisions are published at http://info.valuation-tribunals.gov.uk. For other appeals, the record must also contain:[126]

- the date of the appeal; *and*
- the name of the billing authority whose decision was appealed against.

A copy of the relevant entry in the record must, as soon as is reasonably practicable, be sent to each party to the appeal. Each record must be retained for six years.[127]

Anyone may inspect the records free of charge. If a person with custody of records intentionally obstructs someone from inspecting the records, without a reasonable excuse, s/he is liable on summary conviction to a fine not exceeding level 1 on the standard scale.[128]

The member who presided at the hearing or determination of an appeal may authorise that any clerical errors be corrected in the record. A copy of the corrected entry must be sent to the people to whom a copy of the original entry was sent.[129]

The production of a document certified by the clerk or the president is evidence of the decision and the facts it records in any proceedings in any court of law.[130]

In Scotland, each party has the right to make a recording of the hearing at her/his own expense. The committee should be informed of the intention to make a recording before the hearing begins.[131] In Scotland, decisions are on the Scottish Valuation Appeal Committee's website at http://scotvac.org.

6. Reviews of tribunal and committee decisions

There are limited circumstances in which a decision of the Valuation Tribunal for England (VTE), the Valuation Tribunal for Wales (VTW) or a valuation appeal committee decision in Scotland can be reviewed.

In England and Wales, except where a decision has been the subject of an appeal to the High Court, a tribunal may review its decision or set it aside.[132] This may only be done following a written application from any of the parties, provided it is in the interests of justice to do so, on the grounds that:
- a document relating to the proceedings was not sent to, or was not received at an appropriate time by, a party (or a party's representative); *or*
- a document was not sent to the VTE/VTW; *or*
- a party did not appear and can show reasonable cause for this; *or*
- the decision is affected by a decision of, or on appeal from, the High Court or the Upper Tribunal; *or*
- there has been procedural irregularity; *or*
- in relation to a decision on a completion notice, new evidence has become available (unless it could have been established by reasonably diligent inquiry or foreseen previously).

In England and Wales, you may request reasons for the decision which the tribunal has made. Normally, only a summary of reasons may be given, but you may request a full statement of reasons within two weeks of being sent the decision notice.

An application for a review (or 'set-aside') must normally be made within 28 days of the day on which written notice of the decision was sent. In exceptional cases where there is a good reason, an application may be made outside 28 days.

The application must be considered by the tribunal president, who will decide whether one or more of the grounds are satisfied.[133] This is normally done without a hearing, but the president may call a hearing for the parties affected to make submissions.

All relevant parties are informed that a review is to take place and be invited to submit representations in writing within 14 days. A party may opt for a hearing to take place, which is then held within 28 days.

If a decision is to be set aside, the matter may be reheard or reconsidered by a differently constituted tribunal or, in England, treated as an appeal.[134] This can be done immediately if the parties consent.

As soon as is reasonably practicable after the outcome of the request for a review is known, the clerk must write to all parties informing of the outcome. Additionally, if an appeal to the High Court remains undetermined, the clerk must also notify the High Court as soon as reasonably practicable after the decision has been made.[135]

Appeals to the High Court

If you are unsuccessful in the valuation tribunal, there is no further right of appeal except on a point of law – ie, where the law has been interpreted incorrectly. In England and Wales, this is made to the High Court; in Scotland, it is made to the Lands Valuation Appeal Court. You, the listing officer, assessor and local authority all have an equal right of appeal. In England and Wales, the High Court has made it clear that it will not normally interfere with findings of fact made by a tribunal, unless it can be shown that it has acted perversely – eg, the errors of fact are so severe that they amount to mistakes of law, and thus come within the jurisdiction of the High Court.[136]

It is not enough that you simply disagree with the tribunal's decision or that, having heard the evidence, the tribunal made a finding of fact which you dispute. It must be shown that the tribunal was irrational in that either there was no supporting evidence or that it left out relevant facts or considered irrelevant ones.[137]

In arguing that errors of fact have become an error of law, it is necessary to:[138]
● identify the finding which is challenged;
● show that it was significant in relation to the conclusion;
● identify the evidence (if any) relevant to the conclusion;
● show that the finding, on the basis of the evidence, was one the tribunal was not entitled to make.

Appeals may also be made if the tribunal fails to observe the rules of what is known as 'natural justice'. Examples of breaches of natural justice include the involvement of a person in the hearing who is barred from appearing, bias, denial of cross-examination of witnesses or an opportunity to look at the evidence produced by the other side. A valuation tribunal which introduces legal points not made by parties of its own volition does not breach natural justice.[139]

The appeal proceeds by way of review unless the court considers that it would be in the interests of justice to hold a rehearing.[140] The scope of the court's powers on a review in most cases renders it unnecessary to hold a rehearing.[141]

Seek legal advice before embarking on this course of action, as costs are likely to be in excess of £1,500 and could be much higher depending on the complexity of the case and whether the appeal is contested. The High Court has the discretion whether or not to award costs against an appellant, but the normal rule is that the loser pays the costs of the other side. However, the court's decision depends on the facts and the conduct of the parties, whether they choose to appear and whether the matter could have been settled otherwise.[142]

If the listing officer or the local authority brings the appeal, different rules apply. Costs cannot be awarded if the listing officer has brought the appeal, or if you do not contest the appeal or attend the hearing. In cases where the local authority appeals to the High Court against a decision, the liability for costs will fall against the tribunal and not you.

In England and Wales, an appeal on a point of law to the High Court must be made within four weeks of:
- the date on which notice is given of the decision or order; *or*
- the date of a decision following review; *or*
- a determination by a tribunal that it will not review its decision where the application for review was made within four weeks of the original decision.

The High Court can hear appeals which are out of time (by judicial review) but this should not be relied on, as the right is purely discretionary.[143]

If the VTE/VTW or valuation appeal committee has acted in breach of natural justice, an application for judicial review may also be made. Strict compliance with the time limits is expected.[144] You are required to complete and submit a form for a statutory appeal together with a skeleton argument. The High Court may place a stay on an application for a liability or any order until the appeal is determined.

The High Court may confirm, vary, set aside, revoke or remit the decision or order, and may make any order the tribunal could have made.

In Scotland, an appeal from a committee decision must be made within 14 days. The appeal is started by writing to the secretary of the committee to state a case for the Lands Valuation Appeal Court or to the Court of Session. Six copies of an appeal case must be lodged in the court and six copies must be delivered to the solicitor for any other party to the appeal.

The Court of Session may intervene where a valuation appeal committee errs in the procedure it adopts and reaches conclusions that are illogical, erroneous in law and based on inadequate findings in fact.[145]

Notes

1. Valuation tribunals and valuation appeal committees
1 Reg 90 CTR(S) Regs
2 **E** Regs 3 and 4 Valuation Tribunal for England (Membership and Transitional Provisions) Regulations 2009 No.2267
   W Regs 4-14 VTW Regs
3 Sch 11 para A18A LGFA 1988, inserted by Sch 4 para 2 LGFA 2012
4 VTE CPS 2017, Part 1, para 2 citing Supreme Court in *BPP Holdings v HMRC* [2017] UKSC 551

2. Matters that can be appealed
5 Reg 10(2) VTE(CTRA)(P) Regs
6 **E** Reg 10(2) CT(ALA)(E) Regs
   W Reg 13 CT(ALA) Regs
7 **E** Reg 10(3) CT(ALA)(E) Regs
8 **E** Reg 7(6) CT(ALA) Regs
   W Reg 8(6) CT(ALA) Regs
9 **E** Reg 7(7) CT(ALA)(E) Regs
   W Reg 8(7) CT(ALA) Regs
10 **E** Reg 9(3) CT(ALA)(E) Regs
   W Reg 10(3) CT(ALA)
11 *Coll (LO) v Brannan* CO/5268/2014; *Coll (LO) v Kozak and Tsurumaki* [2015] EWHC 920 (Admin) CO/5270/2014
12 **EW** s16 LGFA 1992
   S s81 LGFA 1992
13 **S** s81 LGFA 1992
14 **EW** s16 LGFA 1992
   E Reg 21 VTE(CTRA)(P) Regs
   W Reg 29 VTW Regs
15 **E** Reg 21(6) VTE(CTRA)(P) Regs
   W Reg 29(5) VTW Regs
16 s81 LGFA 1992
17 Reg 7 CTR(S)A(No.2) Regs
18 Reg 90A(4)(c) CTR(S) Regs
19 Reg 90B CTR(S) Regs
20 **E** Reg 21(5) VTE(CTRA)(P) Regs
   W Reg 29(4) VTW Regs
21 **E** Regs 10 and 21(6) VTE(CTRA)(P) Regs
   W Reg 29(5) VTW Regs
22 Reg 10(6) VTE(CTRA)(P) Regs
23 **E** Regs 25 and 28(2) VTE(CTRA)(P) Regs
   W Reg 40(5) VTW Regs
24 Reg 24 CT(ALA)(S) Regs
25 Reg 24 CT(ALA)(S) Regs
26 Reg 24 CT(ALA)(S) Regs
27 **E** Reg 21(4) VTE(CTRA)(P) Regs
   W Reg 29(3) VTW Regs
28 **E** Reg 21(6) VTE(CTRA)(P) Regs
   W Reg 29(5) VTW Regs
29 Reg 30 VTW Regs
30 **E** Reg 28 VTE(CTRA)(P) Regs
   W Reg 30(5) VTW Regs
31 Reg 23 CT(ALA)(S) Regs
32 Reg 23 CT(ALA)(S) Regs
33 Reg 23 CT(ALA)(S) Regs
34 s13A(1)(c) LGFA 1992
35 See the judgment in *Morgan v Warwick District Council* [2015] RVR 224
36 *S and CW v East Riding of Yorkshire Council* VTE, Appeal nos. 2001M113393 and 2001M11750327 May 2014
37 *British Oxygen Ltd v Board of Trade* [1971] AC 610
38 *Associated Provincial Picture Houses v The Wednesbury Corporation* [1948] 1 KB 223
39 VTE CPS 2017, PS10, para 3

3. How to appeal
40 **EW** Reg 37 VCCT(Amdt) Regs
   E Reg 20A VTE(CTRA)(P) Regs
   W Reg 30(1) VTW Regs
41 **E** Reg 20A VTE(CTRA)(P) Regs
   W Reg 30 VTW Regs
42 Reg 17(2)(b)(i) VTE(CTRA)(P) Regs
43 Regs 10(1) and 17(2)(b) VTE(CTRA)(P) Regs; Council Tax Reduction Appeals Practice Statement, VTE/PS/A11, President's Note, para 13
44 Reg 22 CT(ALA)(S) Regs
45 Reg 22 CT(ALA)(S) Regs
46 Reg 22 CT(ALA)(S) Regs

4. How appeals are dealt with
47 **E** VTE(CTRA)(P) Regs
   W CT(ALA) Regs; VTW Regs
   S CT(ALA)(S) Regs
48 **EW** Reg 20 CT(ALA) Regs
   E Reg 29(1) VTE(CTRA)(P) Regs
   W Reg 33 VTW RegsS Reg 27 CT(ALA)(S) Regs
49 **E** Reg 6(1) VTE(CTRA)(P) Regs
50 **E** Reg 6(2) VTE(CTRA)(P) Regs
51 Reg 13 CT(ALA)(E) Regs; reg 19(7) VTE(CTRA)(P) Regs

52 Reg 33(1) VTW Regs
53 **E** Reg 20 CT(ALA) Regs; reg 29(1)
VTE(CTRA)(P) Regs
W Reg 33(1) VTW Regs
S Reg 27 CT(ALA)(S) Regs
54 Reg 27 CT(ALA)(S) Regs
55 Reg 27 CT(ALA)(S) Regs
56 Reg 27 CT(ALA)(S) Regs
57 **E** Reg 6 VTE(CTRA)(P) Regs
W Reg 21 CT(ALA) Regs
58 Reg 21 VTE(CTRA)(P) Regs; reg 10
CT(ALA)(E) Regs
59 VTE CPS 2017, PS1, para 7
60 VTE CPS 2017, PS1, para 9
61 Reg 7(3)VTE(CTRA)(P) Regs
62 Reg 7(4) (CTRA)(P) Regs
63 **E** Reg 19 VTE(CTRA)(P) Regs
W Reg 32(1) VTW Regs
64 Reg 32(1) VTW Regs
65 Reg 26 CT(ALA)(S) Regs
66 Reg 19(4) and (5) VTE(CTRA)(P) Regs
67 *Wiltshire Council v Piggin* [2014] EWHC
4386 (Admin)
68 Reg 19(8) VTE(CTRA)(P) Regs
69 Reg 2 VTE(CTRA)(P) Regs

5. **Appeal hearings**
70 VTE CPS 2017, PS4
71 VTE CPS 2017, PS4, para 4
72 *The Governor and Company of the Bank of
Ireland v Jaffery* [2012] EWHC 734
73 VTE CPS 2017, PS4, para 6
74 VTE CPS 2017, PS4, para 7
75 Reg 30 VTE(CTRA)(P) Regs. The
president, vice presidents and
nominated senior members may sit
alone as the tribunal.
76 **E** Reg 30 VTE(CTRA)(P) Regs
W Reg 34(1) VTW Regs
77 Reg 28 CT(ALA)(S) Regs
78 Reg 32(2) VTW Regs
79 Reg 28 CT(ALA)(S) Regs
80 **W** Reg 33(3) VTW Regs
S Reg 28 CT(ALA)(S) Regs
81 **E** Reg 13 VTE(CTRA)(P) Regs
W Reg 36 VTW Regs
S Reg 34 CT(ALA)(S) Regs
82 **E** Reg 13 VTE(CTRA)(P) Regs
W Reg 36 VTW Regs
83 Reg 13 Valuation Appeal Committee
(Procedure in Appeals under the
Valuation Acts) (Scotland) Regulations
1995 No.572; reg 34 CT(ALA)(S) Regs
84 **EW** Reg 25 CT(ALA) Regs
E Reg 32 VTE(CTRA)(P) Regs
W Reg 37(2) VTW Regs

85 Practice Statement: Council Tax
Reduction Appeals, VTE/PS/A11: 1
November 2015, para 34
86 Reg 17(2)(b)(i) VTE(CTRA)(P) Regs
87 Reg 17(2) VTE(CTRA)(P) Regs
88 VTW Best Practice Protocol 1F –
Evidence, para 4
89 Reg 6(1)(i) VTE(CTRA)(P) Regs
90 Reg 31(1) VTE(CTRA)(P) Regs
91 **EW** Reg 25 CT(ALA) Regs
E Reg 31 VTE(CTRA)(P) Regs
W Reg 37 VTW Regs as amended by reg
2(6) VTW(A) Regs
92 Reg 32 CT(ALA)(S) Regs
93 VTE CPS 2017, PS12
94 **EW** Reg 25 CT(ALA) Regs
E Reg 10 VTE(CTRA)(P) Regs
W Reg 32A(1)-(3) VTW Regs
S Reg 31 CT(ALA)(S) Regs
95 **E** Reg 40 VTE(CTRA)(P) Regs
W Reg 42(5)(b) VTW Regs
96 Reg 31 CT(ALA)(S) Regs
97 **EW** Reg 25(5) CT(ALA) Regs; reg 44(4)
VCCT(A) Regs
E Reg 32 VTE(CTRA)(P) Regs
98 VTE CPS 2017, PS8, para 12
99 VTE CPS 2017, PS8, para 15
100 **E** Reg 17(1)(e) VTE (CTRA) Regs
S Reg 33 CT(ALA)(S) Regs
101 VTE CPS 2017, PS8, para 13
102 **E** Regs 6 and 30 VTE(CTRA)(P) Regs; VTE
CPS 2017, PS4, para 11
W Reg 34(4) VTW Regs
103 Reg 18 VTE(CTRA)(P) Regs
104 **EW** *Garton v Hunter (Valuation Officer)*
[1969] 2 QBD 37
E Reg 17 VTE(CTRA)(P) Regs
W Reg 37(9) VTW Regs
105 *Morgan v Dew* [1964] RA 294
106 **E** Reg 17 VTE(CTRA)(P) Regs
W Reg 38 VTW Regs
107 Reg 17 VTE(CTRA)(P) Regs
108 Reg 17 VTE(CTRA)(P) Regs
109 Reg 29 CT(ALA)(S) Regs
110 Reg 29 CT(ALA)(S) Regs
111 Reg 30 CT(ALA)(S) Regs
112 Reg 30 CT(ALA)(S) Regs
113 Reg 30 CT(ALA)(S) Regs
114 Reg 30 CT(ALA)(S) Regs
115 Reg 30 CT(ALA)(S) Regs
116 VTE CPS 2017, Part 1, para 15 VTE
117 **E** Reg 36 VTE(CTRA) Regs
W Reg 40(2) VTW Regs
118 **E** Reg 37 VTE(CTRA)(P) Regs as
amended by reg 2(6) VTE(CTRA)(P)(A)
Regs
W Reg 40(3) VTW Regs
119 Reg 36 CT(ALA)(S) Regs

120 **E** Reg 38(1) VTE(CTRA)(P) Regs
W Reg 41 VTW Regs
121 *George Davidson v Central Scotland Valuation Joint Board* [2011] CSIH 15
122 VTE CPS 2017, PS15, para 1(ii)
123 VTE CPS 2017, PS15
124 **E** *West Midlands Baptist (Trust) Association (Incorporated) v Birmingham City Council* [1967] RVR 780 (CA)
S *Assessor for Highland and Western Isles Valuation Joint Board v Fraser* [2001] SC 473
125 **E** Reg 41 VTE(CTRA)(P) Regs
W Reg 31 and Sch 4 CT(ALA) Regs
126 **E** Reg 41 VTE(CTRA)(P) Regs
127 **E** Reg 41 VTE(CTRA)(P) Regs
W Reg 43 VTW Regs
128 **E** Reg 41 VTE(CTRA)(P) Regs
W Reg 50 VTW Regs
129 **E** Reg 39 VTE(CTRA)(P) Regs
W Reg 43(7) VTW Reg
130 **E** Reg 41(6) VTE(CTRA)(P) Regs
W Reg 42(1) VTW Regs
131 **S** Reg 35 CT(ALA)(S) Regs

6. Reviews of tribunal and committee decisions

132 **E** Reg 40 VTE(CTRA)(P) Regs
W Reg 42(1) VTW Regs
133 **E** Reg 40 VTE(CTRA)(P) Regs
W Reg 49 VTW Regs
134 **E** Reg 40(7) VTE(CTRA)(P) Regs
W Reg 44(2) VTW Regs
135 **E** Reg 41(10) VTE(CTRA)(P) Regs
W Reg 42(9) VTW Regs
136 *Bracegirdle v Oxley* [1947] 1 KB 349; *Edwards v Bairstow and another* [1956] AC 14; *Hayes v Humberside Valuation Tribunal and Kingston Upon Hull City Council* [1998] RA 37
137 *Vaughan v Valuation Tribunal* [2013] EWHC 1885 (Admin)
138 *Georgiou v Customs and Excise Commissioners* [1996] STC 463, per Evans LJ at p 476; *Ramdhun v The Valuation Tribunal of England* [2014] EWHC 946 (Admin)
139 *Macattram v London Borough of Camden* [2012] RA 369
140 CPR 52.21(1); *Salsbury v Law Society* [2008] EWCA Civ 1285, reported as [2009] 1 WLR 1286

141 *Adesemowo v Solicitors Regulation Authority* [2013] EWHC 2020 (Admin)
142 See *Wiltshire Council v Piggin* [2014] EWHC 4386 (Admin)
143 *R v London South Eastern Valuation Tribunal and Neale (LO), ex parte Moore* [2001] RVR 94
144 *R v London South West Valuation Tribunal ex parte de Melo* [2000] RVR 73
145 *Dundee City Council v Dundee Valuation Appeal Committee and another* [2011] CSIH 73

Chapter 12

....

Complaints about council tax administration

This chapter covers:
1. Complaints to the Ombudsman (below)
2. Complaints to the local auditor (p290)
3. Action through the courts (p291)

_____

1. Complaints to the Ombudsman

The role of the Ombudsman is to investigate complaints of maladministration by government departments, including avoidable delays, failure to advise about appeal rights or refusal to answer reasonable questions or respond to correspondence, discourteousness, racism or sexism. The Parliamentary and Health Service Ombudsman deals with complaints about central government and the Local Government and Social Care Ombudsman (in England)[1] or the Public Services Ombudsman (in Wales and Scotland)[2] hear complaints about local government.

The Ombudsman has the power to look into many different types of error which do not generate a right to take court action, but nonetheless give grounds for complaint. It is a free, independent service and complaints can be submitted online.[3]

You can only refer your complaint to the Ombudsman if you have tried to resolve it with the local authority first, or 12 weeks have passed since you first made your complaint and the local authority has not responded.

The Ombudsman may investigate maladministration by any district, borough, city or county council and, therefore, can deal with mistakes by billing authorities in administering council tax. In 2016/17, the Ombudsman in England investigated 2,109 complaints relating to local taxation and benefits.

The Ombudsman has statutory power to commence investigations into complaints that fall within the jurisdiction granted by statute and also stop investigations when considered appropriate,[4] though following reforms in 2012 there has been an apparent decline in the number of cases published upholding complaints in respect of council tax in England.

What is maladministration

'Maladministration' is an open-ended term covering a wide range of bureaucratic mistakes and abuses. It is not defined in statute and when the term was first introduced into parliament, it was considered to include 'bias, neglect, delay, incompetence and inaptitude, arbitrariness and so on' on the part of public authorities.[5] It has been judicially considered that maladministration 'in the context of the work of a local authority, is concerned with the *manner* in which decisions by the authority are reached and the *manner* in which they are or are not implemented'.[6]

Maladministration can thus cover many forms of bureaucratic wrongdoing which may not be serious enough to justify court proceedings, but which nonetheless can cause injustice – eg, delays in answering letters or losing records. It can include many forms of improper behaviour by local government staff, whether through lack of care or deliberate wrongdoing. Other examples of maladministration include:[7]

- rudeness;
- bias;
- knowingly giving misleading advice;
- falsifying records and documents;
- failing to mitigate the effects of rigid adherence to the law where this results in inequitable treatment;
- not acting in a timely way;
- late enforcement action long after an alleged liability arose;
- sending documents to the wrong address;
- allocating payments to the wrong account;
- generating numerous confusing and contradictory documents;
- wiping computer records or inserting inaccurate data;
- failing to notify a person of her/his loss of appeal rights;
- delays in referring an appeal to a tribunal or failing to refer an appeal at all;
- commencing enforcement action where an undertaking has been given by the local authority not to do so;
- seeking a liability order against a person after an undertaking has been given not to obtain one or obtaining an order against a person who has offered to pay the sum in full;
- taking disproportionate redress;
- refusing applications for discretionary relief without proper consideration;
- failing to follow paragraphs 70–78 of the *Taking Control of Goods: National Standards* regarding vulnerable people (see Appendix 2).

Specific examples of maladministration relating to council tax include instances where an authority:

- fails to give you information relating to entitlements to reductions in the tax or your right of appeal to the valuation tribunal;
- fails to tell you about, or consider, an application for a discretionary reduction in the council tax;
- fails to act on information provided which affects liability to council tax or entitlement to discounts or exemptions;
- permits or allows delays in dealing with disputes;
- makes mistakes in dealing with payments (eg, failing to credit them to your account, allocating them to a wrong account, or failing to pay in council tax support you have been awarded);
- continues to take recovery action after any debt is paid or where an agreement to pay a debt is kept.

The Ombudsman will not challenge council policy but will consider whether its stated policy is being carried out reasonably and correctly.

The Ombudsman may not investigate a complaint if it is a matter where you have a right of appeal or have appealed to a tribunal.[8] However, s/he may decide to investigate a complaint if s/he considers it would be unreasonable for you to have to do so or if there are other issues outside the scope of the tribunal.[9]

Injustice

The Ombudsman intervenes in cases which have resulted in injustice, caused by a local authority but which it has failed to redress adequately or at all. As with maladministration, the concept of **'injustice'** is a wide one and open to different interpretations. Arguably, it should mean more than a trivial problem or minor inconvenience, although much will depend on the actual effect of the error on the individual taxpayer concerned. Maladministration causing you nuisance, embarrassment, financial loss or serious inconvenience and distress falls within the remit of injustice. For example, a delay in replying to correspondence which results in extra charges or fees could amount to injustice.[10]

However, a complaint to the Ombudsman should not be used simply as a way of 'getting back' at a local authority or simply to get particular officials into trouble. Neither should a complaint be brought simply because you believe a decision to be wrong. Similarly, if a local authority has taken steps to correct an injustice and you are satisfied, the Ombudsman cannot be expected to take the matter any further.

Because of its complexity, the administration of council tax can frequently generate errors which, if uncorrected, may result in inconvenience, stress and embarrassment to taxpayers. Even when a mistake is discovered, the local authority may not act properly or quickly enough to remedy the problem.

For example, a local authority may fail to record an entitlement to a discount, repeatedly list the wrong person on a bill or fail to award payment to the correct account. This may result in sending reminder notices to, and summonses against, a person who has actually paid the tax or who is exempt. The authority may delay sending information or bills, causing 'prejudice' to the taxpayer (see p174) and unnecessary enforcement action. Problems may also be caused by sending demands in the names of people who have died after the local authority has been informed of the death, or failing to record that someone is severely mentally impaired. In such cases, it is often unrealistic to expect taxpayers to be able to contend with court and tribunal proceedings as an alternative to bringing a complaint but it may be difficult to achieve a remedy through the Ombudsman as an alternative.

Outsourced services

With more councils outsourcing services, it can be more difficult to make effective complaints. The Ombudsman noted in its 2014/2015 report that with many councils using the services of private companies to operate council tax 'the traditional lines of accountability and routes to complaining when things have gone wrong are more complex'. The Ombudsman welcomes measures by some councils in 'ensuring that an effective and accessible complaints service forms part of the contract with commissioned service partners'.[11]

Both the outsourced company and the council can be liable for errors and mistakes; ultimately the council can be liable for having selected a negligent subcontractor to perform its functions or for failing to control a subcontractor properly.

Interdepartmental inefficiency

Inadequate liaison between accounts, enforcement and the reduction sections in a local authority may generate problems. For example, although court action may be suspended, computerised enforcement systems may continue to issue warning letters even when the local authority has assured a person the mistake has been remedied. A local authority is not entitled to hide behind an excuse of 'computer error' to cover up inefficiency in such cases.

Delays in processing council tax reduction applications

Another form of maladministration is an unreasonable delay in processing a council tax reduction (CTR) application. Although you may ultimately receive CTR after a long delay, you may face considerable inconvenience, stress, financial difficulty and embarrassment in the meantime. Significantly, the Ombudsman does not consider automatically issuing a summons against a person who is waiting for her/his CTR to be calculated to be 'fair or reasonable' and that a local authority 'should take into account the circumstances of the individual before taking such action.'[12]

Refusal to accept evidence

In some cases, maladministration occurs where the authority refuses to accept evidence submitted in an application for CTR or makes repeated requests for information that has already been supplied.

In such a case, you may serve a witness statement for establishing the truth of what you are saying, and also give notice of an intention to escalate the complaint to the civil courts or tribunal if the issue is not resolved in your favour.

A witness statement should set out the facts and calculations and deal with any matter the local authority has hitherto refused to be satisfied about. It may also include copies of documents as exhibits and must carry a statement of truth.[13]

The witness statement should include the address of the local county court, as that is where an action may be founded against the authority and its staff, or alternatively, the valuation tribunal where an appeal may be heard.

A sworn witness statement is evidence for all purposes in civil and criminal proceedings and is the strongest evidence that can be provided, save for sworn evidence given orally in proceedings. It is to be preferred to anything that a local authority may say or provide that is unsworn. Furthermore, it must be accepted by any court or tribunal as the truth, unless contrary evidence is provided which undermines the truth of the statement or the witness is discredited by cross-examination.

Since a witness statement is the most conclusive evidence that you can provide, the local authority will err in law if it refuses to act upon the information contained in it. Refusal by the local authority to consider evidence placed before it can place the local authority in breach of its statutory duties, generating grounds for a complaint and potential legal action against the authority or officials concerned.

Late billing and enforcement

An increasingly common form of maladministration is late enforcement action, sometimes years after an alleged liability arose (see see p200). The problem was first highlighted in the *Digest of Cases 2008/09*, which stated:

> The Ombudsman receives many complaints about the way councils take recovery action over failure to pay council tax. Sometimes people receive summonses when they should not have done, and the consequences of that action can lead to councils granting liability orders that enable them to refer alleged debts to bailiffs. Where unjustified recovery action has been taken, the Ombudsman would expect an appropriate remedy to be provided.

Increasingly, complaints also relate to enforcement action once a case has been passed to enforcement agents. Although the system of new fees allows court action to be taken in a case of excessive charging, the Ombudsman is nonetheless prepared to investigate the conduct of a billing authority which has instructed the enforcement agents concerned.[14]

A complaint can sometimes be the most effective way to challenge a decision to send out a bill or begin an enforcement proceeding several years after the alleged liability. The complaint means that the alleged liability will be investigated, aside from any question of an appeal to the valuation tribunal. The investigation of the complaint can look into the circumstances as to why the delay in enforcing an old liability arose, whether there was proper record keeping and the reasonableness of any decision to pursue an old liability on the facts. For example, where a local authority suddenly serves a demand notice, an investigation should be commenced into why it was suddenly decided that money was outstanding and the failures which led to the delay in taking a decision.

The Ombudsman will not usually interfere with a correct decision to implement an enforcement measure but may order redress where the service has been poor. For example, in a complaint against Birmingham City Council in 2013, the Ombudsman criticised the failure of the council to keep a proper record of payments made by an employer after an attachment of earnings order was obtained against a debtor but credited to the wrong account. The debtor spent nine months trying to resolve the matter and the council failed to respond adequately to her complaint, gave incorrect advice and delayed in tracing the money and resolving the situation. Following the Ombudsman investigation, the council apologised and paid compensation.[15]

The Ombudsman may also consider whether enforcement action has been excessive, disproportionate or unjustified. In a case in Birmingham in 2014, the Ombudsman found injustice where the council had failed to properly consider the debt situation of a man willing to pay and his offers to pay and issued a summons and used bailiffs. A settlement was agreed, leading to the quashing of the court costs and the payment of £250 for the unnecessary enforcement action.[16]

Matters that the Ombudsman cannot examine

Matters that the Ombudsman cannot investigate include:
- the amount of tax set by the local authority;
- decisions of courts or the Valuation Tribunal for England (VTE), Valuation Tribunal for Wales (VTW) and valuation appeal committees in Scotland;
- who is liable for council tax;
- decisions about banding;
- the conduct of court proceedings. These matters can only be challenged through the High Court or the VTE/VTW or valuation appeal committees in Scotland when they are within the specific jurisdiction of these bodies – eg, whether you should be liable for council tax. The Ombudsman expects councils to signpost to the correct place to go where the complaint should be pursued as an appeal, unless it would be unreasonable to expect you to be able to do this – eg, due to disability;[17]
- cases where the remedy is a proceeding in a court of law or where an appeal lies to a Minister of the Crown.[18]

Matters that are outside the jurisdiction of the Ombudsman, such as alleged breaches of the Data Protection Act, cannot be investigated, as these fall within the remit of the Information Commissioner.[19]

Making a complaint to the Ombudsman

The Ombudsman investigates complaints from:
- individuals;
- family members of individuals;
- advice agencies acting on behalf of individuals.

The Ombudsman expects you to have fully exhausted the local authority's complaints process first. Most local authorities have a three-stage procedure, with officers at increasing levels of seniority examining the case, usually ending at the office of the chief executive.

Normally, details of the procedure can be obtained either by writing to the local authority or from its website.

The initial complaint to the local authority should set out the specific details of what has taken place and the effect it has had on you. It is best that such complaints are written in clear and polite language and without using emotive or abusive language. (Extremes of language or unsubstantiated allegations are only likely to result in a complaint being viewed in a less favourable light on any impartial review.) **Note:** you should not threaten legal action generally against the local authority as an alternative to investigation by the Ombudsman, as the Ombudsman's jurisdiction only arises where there is no practical alternative or where it would be unreasonable to expect you to pursue legal action.

Information to support complaints can be obtained by way of requests under the Freedom of Information Act 2000. Use may be made of the Data Protection Act 1998 and subject access requests for personal data; subject access requests can be made by individuals and are often used by journalists. Where an authority declines to answer a request for information, you may make an application to the Information Commissioner or the Scottish Information Commissioner.[20]

If you remain unhappy with the final outcome, or the council is taking too long to look into the matter (12 weeks is considered reasonable), you can complain to the Ombudsman. You should usually make your complaint within 12 months of realising the maladministration. The Ombudsman issues guidance on bringing a complaint – available at www.lgo.org.uk.

You can telephone the Ombudsman's helpline (see Appendix 1) to discuss your complaint with an adviser, or you can complete an online complaint form.

For CTR complaints, the Ombudsman in England has issued a fact sheet.[21]

When bringing a complaint, it is usually a good idea to include a short chronology of events and correspondence, to provide a summary of key dates and the history of the matter, particularly if the case is complex. In the chronology, you should list the dates as accurately as possible and the event which occurred – eg, what the local authority did or did not do. Copies of all the relevant correspondence should also be submitted with the initial application, in order that the Ombudsman may begin analysis of the case with all the relevant information.

On receipt of your application, the Ombudsman will normally assign a caseworker to deal with your complaint. The caseworker will contact you or your adviser as well as the local authority.

The Ombudsman may decide not to start or continue with an investigation if it is believed:

- it is unlikely fault by the council would be found;
- the injustice is not significant enough to justify the cost of involvement;
- it is unlikely anything may be added to any previous investigation of the council;
- the outcome you want cannot be achieved.

If the Ombudsman is satisfied with a council's actions or proposed actions, the investigation can be completed and a decision statement issued.[22]

Local authority complaints process

Complaints are normally dealt with in a three-stage process and may take 12 weeks or more to clear all three stages, ending at the level of chief executive. Chief executives vary in competence or understanding but seem to be highly media conscious. Where there is a complaint there is also scope for publicity, particularly with the local press.

To expedite or increase the effect of a complaint in a council tax matter, it can be worth copying the complaint directly to the chief executive. This may also be combined with a request to the local authority to exercise its discretionary powers to reduce or remit a sum in council tax.

Where an outsourced company is involved, a complaint should be taken to the senior officer in the authority responsible for contract compliance and liaison between the council and the contractor.

Where a local authority is acting in breach of any statutory duty or rule of law, a complaint may be made to the monitoring officer of the authority who is responsible for investigation and producing reports. The monitoring officer may also look into maladministration, though the duty only arises where the Ombudsman has investigated.[23]

Action the Ombudsman can take

Where the Ombudsman finds that the local authority is at fault, it can ask the council to:

- take action to put the matter right – eg, issuing the correct bill;
- ensure that payments you have made or CTR awards are properly credited to your account;

- deal with your correspondence or appeal;
- withdraw enforcement action and waive costs where appropriate; *or*
- pay you compensation.

There is no system to enforce an award of compensation but, in practice, local authorities usually accept the findings made by the Ombudsman and it is rare for a local authority to refuse to pay. In addition, an authority in England and the London Assembly has a specific power to pay compensation.[24] It should be noted that sums recommended in compensation have not kept up with inflation. For example, in a case reported in January 2005 concerning delays in processing housing and council tax benefit the Ombudsman found maladministration and made a recommendation that the Council pay £500 in respect of stress and court costs.[25] In 2017, the largest published award for council tax maladministration remained at £500 for a case where bankruptcy proceedings had been instigated.[26]

Directions may also be issued to local authorities to change their procedures to prevent the problem reoccurring.

Examples of Ombudsman complaints and settlements

The following cases are examples of complaints of maladministration involving council tax which have been upheld. Cases often depend on their individual facts, but the settlement figures give an indication of the size of any award.

Suicide of taxpayer
Southwark Borough Council (00/A/19293 [2002] RVR 289) September 2002

The complaint was brought by relatives of a taxpayer who had committed suicide after receiving a summons for non-payment of council tax. The taxpayer was a single man with learning difficulties receiving benefits. In October 2000, his council tax benefit (CTB) was cancelled and he was sent a fresh form to complete. Four days later he was sent a demand for £235.10 payable in instalments. The taxpayer visited the local authority's office and submitted a claim form, but the local authority continued recovery action. The taxpayer applied again for CTB and provided information on his entitlement to jobseeker's allowance. Nonetheless, a summons was issued again for £235.10. The summons was accompanied by an additional sheet warning that bailiffs or imprisonment could follow the granting of a liability order. The taxpayer hanged himself in his flat. Police called to the scene found the opened summons and a suicide note referring to his debt problems. Relatives of the deceased complained to the council but did not receive a satisfactory response.

Outcome: it was considered that the three-and-a-half-month delay in processing benefit amounted to maladministration. Further maladministration was found in sending out a summons while the relevant benefit claim had yet to be determined. The Ombudsman said that the summons had contributed to the distress and anxiety suffered by the deceased. The way in which the local authority had responded to relatives was also criticised. A settlement of £3,200 to the family of the deceased and £1,000 payment to a charity of their choice was approved.

Unnecessary recovery action
Hackney Borough Council (03/A/09613) 7 October 2004

The complainant, Ms Murray (pseudonym), set up a standing order to pay council tax in April 1998. In July 1998, Hackney Council realised that, because there was no council tax reference number on the standing order form, payments received were not being allocated to Ms Murray's account. Despite assurances from Hackney on several occasions that it would rectify the problem, this was not achieved until January 2004. Arrears for 1998/99 were wrongly carried forward each year and it began unnecessary recovery actions including summonses, liability orders and letters from bailiffs.

Outcome: the Ombudsman found maladministration and recommended that the council pay £1,800 compensation and undertake changes to its accounting systems.

Wrongful attribution of liability
Oxford City Council and Southwark Borough Council (02/B/09186 and 02/B/16542) 8 October 2003

A complaint was brought by Mr D Parry (pseudonym) that Oxford City Council was making deductions from his benefit for arrears of council tax. Mr Parry had been a student in Oxford over 30 years earlier but had not lived there since. The Ombudsman found that Oxford Council had believed that its debtor, another Mr D Parry, had moved from Oxford to London NW2, but when they could not find him there, they found the complainant living in SE15. This alone convinced it that it was the same debtor and it contacted Southwark Borough Council. Although Mr Parry had been a council tenant with Southwark for many years, Southwark Borough Council released information to enable deductions from his benefit and further compounded the error with delays in refunding his benefit.

Outcome: the Ombudsman found maladministration in the 'bizarre treatment' of the complainant and considered that depriving him of money while he was on a very low income must have resulted in difficulty. It was recommended that Oxford City Council pay £750 and Southwark pay £250 to the complainant.

Rating list errors and failures
Torbay Council (00/B/10806 1 August 2001 reported at [2001] RVR 194)

The Ombudsman held that Torbay Council should have taken reasonable steps to ensure that all the information about properties was accurate and that failure to do so was maladministration, the complainants having experienced considerable aggravation, uncertainty, time and trouble in pursuing the matter.

Outcome: the Ombudsman recommended an ex gratia payment of £1,000 in compensation.

Unnecessary enforcement and attendance at court
Sandwell Metropolitan Council (No 03/B/12862) September 2004

Sandwell Council issued a summons when a CTB claim was pending, the complainant having provided all the necessary information. It proceeded with court action even after the benefit claim had been assessed and the complainant did not owe the money that was being sought. As a result, the complainant overpaid his council tax by £400. A further incorrect bill was issued requiring the complainant to pay another £196. The taxpayer complained to Sandwell Council and the sums were later credited and repaid to him, but not for several months. The taxpayer was forced to attend an unnecessary court hearing and the local authority delayed in answering correspondence.

Outcome: although the local authority had refunded money to the taxpayer, the Ombudsman found maladministration causing injustice. There had been inadequate liaison between the accounts and benefits sections of the revenues department and the taxpayer had experienced stress, inconvenience and an unnecessary attendance at court. Sandwell Council had also delayed in replying to the taxpayer's complaints. The Ombudsman recommended £400 compensation be paid and that Sandwell Council review its procedures.

Delayed appeal and bailiff action
Waltham Forest Borough Council (03/A/01900) 28 October 2003

Mr Gower (pseudonym) complained that Waltham Forest Council had unreasonably delayed assessing claims for housing benefit (HB) and CTB, did not provide reasons on appeal and unreasonably took recovery action before his appeal had been determined. The Ombudsman considered that a delay of three months in assessing his claim was unreasonable and amounted to maladministration. The Ombudsman found that Mr Gower was caused prolonged anxiety by the slow progress of his claims and the growth in his rent and council tax arrears. Recovery action caused further stress, which was compounded when, after being told that the council would suspend bailiff action, he was nonetheless served with a bailiff notice threatening distress and removal of goods.

Outcome: the Ombudsman considered that an offer of £225 in settlement by the council was too low and recommended £500, together with a review of the way in which it communicated with its bailiffs.

Refusal of discretionary reduction
Redcar and Cleveland Borough Council (05/C/03367) 27 September 2006

In December 2004, the council decided that all empty homes in its area should pay the maximum 90 per cent council tax. Mr and Mrs Weaver (pseudonyms) bought a bungalow in the local authority district and renovated it, but then faced hostility from people in the area and decided not to move in. When they received a bill, Mrs Weaver wrote to explain their circumstances. The council refused the reduction, stating that it had set the maximum discount and that the scheme 'does not allow for any individual discretion'.

Outcome: the Ombudsman ruled that the blanket policy adopted by the council was wrong in law, and that the local authority had no basis for claiming it had no discretion on whether to grant a discount or not in individual cases. Parliament had given it a discretion and the Ombudsman said that a local authority should consider cases on an individual basis. The failure to do so amounted to maladministration, and the Ombudsman directed the authority to give proper consideration to Mrs Weaver's request and invite her to state her reasons for seeking the reduction. Having considered her reasons, the council was directed to give its reasons for either accepting or rejecting the application, as well as establishing proper arrangements for considering such cases in future.

Failure to record a verbal agreement
Aberdeen City Council (200502645) 30 November 2006

The complainant (Mrs C) alleged that a verbal payment agreement for council tax was not recorded or honoured by Aberdeen City Council. A verbal agreement reached between Mrs C and a member of staff about her payment schedule for council tax was not recorded with the result that a summary warrant was issued.

Outcome: the Ombudsman recommended that the council devised and pilot a clear procedure for staff updating customer records once a verbal payment agreement has been reached via a face to face discussion. Ideally, this would include the production of a signed agreement which both parties could keep as a record. This would clearly prevent similar complaints from arising again. The council was directed to write an apology to Mrs C for the inconvenience and distress caused by the issue of an unnecessary summary warrant.

Failure to communicate with taxpayer and inadequate record keeping
East Dunbartonshire Council (200600109) 19 December 2007

East Dunbartonshire Council failed to keep proper records and communicate about the account of Ms C, who disputed owing a sum of £242.

On investigation, the Ombudsman found the communication and advice from East Dunbartonshire Council was poor and its record keeping in relation to council tax was inadequate.

Outcome: the Ombudsman recommended that East Dunbartonshire Council should ensure the accuracy of account details before taking recovery action on council tax accounts, and that an apology should be issued to Ms C, together with a payment equal to the disputed sum of £242.

Failure to respond properly to a liability appeal and complaint
City of Edinburgh Council (200603479) September 2007

The complainant (Mr C) raised a number of concerns about the way in which City of Edinburgh Council had dealt with his correspondence and subsequent appeal over council tax liability, and its complaints handling system. The council failed to respond to letters and to refer an appeal to the appeals committee or advise the complainant of his right to pursue the appeal.

Outcome: the Ombudsman upheld Mr C's complaint that the council had unreasonably failed to treat a letter as an appeal and that the administration of his correspondence and the investigation of his complaint were inadequate. The Ombudsman recommended that the City of Edinburgh Council introduce a system to record all council tax appeals on receipt and set target dates for all appeals to be actioned within 10 days and, where cases are referred to the valuation appeal committee, within two months of receipt unless additional information has been requested. The Ombudsman also recommended a review of the complaints process.

Bankruptcy as a disproportionate method of enforcement

Wolverhampton City Council (06B16600) 31 March 2008

The local authority issued bankruptcy proceedings against a debtor owing council tax on a disputed debt of less than £2,000. This increased the debt to £38,000.

Outcome: the Ombudsman recommended that the council meet the costs of annulling the bankruptcy order. In his report, the Ombudsman said that a charging order should have been considered. The Ombudsman stated: 'The Council cannot, it seems to me, turn a blind eye to the consequences to the debtor of any recovery option it pursues. Some courses will no doubt be administratively more convenient and less costly than others. But in selecting those options, the impact on the debtor should be weighed in the balance. The dire and punitive consequences of bankruptcy, involving a multiplication of the original debt many times over and frequently incurring the loss of the debtor's home, must be a factor to be taken into account in deciding that the 'last resort' is indeed appropriate. I have seen no evidence that this relevant consideration was taken into account. And that too was maladministration.'

Maladministration causing injustice

London Borough of Camden (07A12661) 10 July 2008

Camden Council's revenue team commenced bankruptcy proceedings for council tax arrears against a woman who, because of mental health difficulties, was unable to conduct her own affairs. Before doing so, it did not adequately record what checks it had made and did not check with the social care department, which would have shown that bankruptcy was not an appropriate recovery method.

Outcome: the Ombudsman found that one department of Camden Council knew of the woman's problems, but the revenue department did not find this out because it failed to make effective internal enquiries. Had it done so, Camden Council would most likely have taken different steps, with less serious consequences.

The Ombudsman ruled: 'I do not think it unreasonable for revenue officers to look beyond their own departmental information and consider a council's records as a whole.' This was in line with data protection guidance issued by the Information Commissioner.

The Ombudsman ruled that the failure to make checks led to unwarranted action and found maladministration causing injustice. Camden Council agreed to apply to court to annul the bankruptcy. On annulment, the Ombudsman recommended that the council should contact credit rating agencies to advise them of the position and that it should change its procedures to make stringent checks for potential vulnerability before taking action leading to bankruptcy, a charging order or committal.

Wrongful pursuit of council tax debt after liability ceased

(Case reference confidential)

The taxpayer 'Mr J' was involved in a long-running dispute with the council about liability for council tax on a property. He received a summons for two years' worth of arrears. Shortly before the hearing, the council issued a letter accepting he did not have sole or main residence and that liability was with a 'Mrs K'. The council requested details of when

Mrs K vacated the property and a forwarding address. Nonetheless, the council pursued a liability order against Mr J and he was threatened with bailiffs. Mr J made a complaint, but received no reply for three months. The council still served four demand notices covering the previous three years.

Outcome: on investigation, the Ombudsman learned from the council that it had continued to pursue Mr J because he failed to provide the information on Mrs K. The Ombudsman found that this approach was incorrect. While not criticising the council for asking Mr J for that information, liability for the tax was not determined by the supply of information. The council had no legal basis on which to pursue Mr J for arrears arising after the date from which it had decided he was no longer the liable person. The council should not have proceeded with the court action. The council agreed to settle the complaint by apologising to Mr J for its errors and paying him £350 compensation.

Council tax recovery action against vulnerable woman with no income
Slough Borough Council (08 009 315) 4 April 2009

Slough Borough Council's council tax department failed to suspend bailiff action against a woman after being advised she was totally dependent on its own social services and had no means to pay. 'Mrs Carter' (pseudonym) had entered the UK as a student in 2002 but was prevented from studying after developing cancer and was prohibited from working or claiming benefits. She was totally reliant on the council's social services department, who provided accommodation and a subsistence allowance, and she had no income or belongings other than those they provided. She built up council tax arrears. In spite of being informed of these facts by Mrs Carter's social worker, the council instructed bailiffs to collect the council tax arrears, even though it had evidence that she was vulnerable, had no income, and was being supported by a different council department.

Outcome: the Ombudsman found the council at fault in failing to consider the information provided by the social worker and for failing to pass Mrs Carter's case to its welfare team. If the department had acted on the information provided, it is unlikely that bailiffs would have been involved and distress caused would have been avoided. The council was also criticised for the lack of effective liaison between different departments and for failing to have a written policy on dealing with vulnerable people.

The Ombudsman recommended that the council should write off Mrs Carter's council tax arrears; pay her £250; implement a written policy on dealing with vulnerable people, and a policy on how to deal with people who are reliant on support from social services; and establish a formal link between the council tax welfare team and social services.

Failure to administer council tax benefit and housing benefit and wrongful enforcement
Wandsworth Borough Council (09 008 990) 16 March 2010

The complainant (Mr L) had experienced repeated failures in the administration and payment of HB and CTB over a seven-year period. Shortfalls in HB resulted in rent arrears and eviction proceedings being commenced against Mr L, and failures to pay CTB resulted in three liability orders. Mr L attempted to settle the liability orders, whereupon bailiffs employed by Wandsworth Council imposed three sets of costs in respect of one levy. On receiving another summons, Mr L approached the authority before the hearing and was told that he would have to pay an additional £20 for seeking to make a repayment arrangement.

Mr L lodged a formal complaint which went through the three stages of Wandsworth Council's complaints procedure; he also complained separately to the bailiffs. The latter complaint resulted in bailiffs refunding the excessive charges, but the responses given by Wandsworth Council at each level to the wider issues of maladministration were inadequate and did not constitute a remedy.

Outcome: the council offered a settlement of £630 to Mr L, which was accepted. Excessive bailiff fees of £50 were also repaid separately.

Charging of fees not permitted by law
Thurrock Council (09 006 694) 3 February 2010

Thurrock Council served a statutory demand for arrears of £1,367.57 and a further £400 for administrative costs for settling the debt. The complainant disputed the £400 fee. After a complaint failed to resolve the issue, an investigation took place by the Ombudsman who ruled that the council had no power to charge a £400 fee since neither the Insolvency Rules, nor any other legislation, permitted recovery of fees for a statutory demand or an arrangement unless a bankruptcy order was made.

Outcome: the Ombudsman found there had been maladministration. The council accepted it was not entitled to charge the fee and it ceased to do so in similar cases. It refunded the £400 to the complainant, restored the right to pay in instalments, waived an additional £42.50 in bailiff fees incurred and made a £40 goodwill payment in compensation.

Bailiffs charging excessive fee for seizing a doormat
Slough Borough Council (10 007 469) 4 April 2011

A complaint was made against Slough Borough Council's bailiffs about a threat to remove a doormat and charge £230 in fees. The complaint was made by a man who had arrears of council tax and who was visited by bailiffs who could not gain entry. When he complained to the bailiff firm and then Slough Council, he was told the fees were legal.

Outcome: the Ombudsman considered that the levy on the doormat should not have been made. As the levy should not have been made, the fees should not have been charged. The bailiff was also at fault in charging an excessive amount for the levy. The Ombudsman found that the levying on such a low-value item as a doormat, the charging of the fees for this, and the lack of consideration of the reasonableness of this action amounted to maladministration. She noted the action the council and the bailiffs had taken in acknowledging they were wrong and withdrawing the fees. Given this, and taking into account the complainant's failure to pay his council tax, she did not consider that any further remedy was needed.

Failure to follow proper processes
Torbay Council (10 002 564) 12 May 2011

Torbay Council commenced bankruptcy proceedings against a man with mental health problems (given the pseudonym of 'Mr Castle') who owed a council tax debt of £2,248. He complained to the Ombudsman that the council had failed to have regard to his mental health issues.

Investigation by the Ombudsman established the council had difficulties engaging with the complainant. It was known that he did not open his post but left it to accumulate over a long period. None of the council's own officers visited Mr Castle at home. The council ignored the findings of a bailiff which indicated illness on the part of Mr Castle. The bailiff advised the council's solicitor that Mr Castle was suicidal.

While recognising that the council was short of enforcement options and that there was a duty to collect council tax, the Ombudsman found maladministration in its failures to keep proper records and the decision to commence bankruptcy proceedings.

Outcome: maladministration was found. The council had not followed proper processes or kept accurate records. The council had not reviewed its decision to commence bankruptcy proceedings when information came to light that Mr Castle might be considered suicidal. The Ombudsman considered that, had such failings not occurred, then the council would not have continued bankruptcy proceedings and Mr Castle would not have incurred the costs of some £24,000. The Ombudsman recommended that the council pay Mr Castle £25,000 and issue a formal apology.

Note: the bailiff appears to have acted in compliance with principles laid down in national standards. This requires an enforcement agent who discovers a vulnerable household to report it to the creditor for reconsideration. In this case the bailiff did, but the authority failed to act properly on receipt of the information.

Failure to control bailiff activity and fees
Blaby District Council (11 007 684) 18 July 2012

Mrs S owed arrears of council tax to Blaby Council. She complained that bailiffs employed by the council to collect her council tax arrears had not acted within the law and had overcharged her. She also complained that the council failed to properly respond to queries and complaints about these issues, including a serious allegation that four bailiffs tried to break into Mrs S's property and obtained money from her partner by clamping and taking occupation of a car that was not his.

Outcome: the Ombudsman found that the council failed to exercise proper control over the actions of its bailiffs and the fees it charged. The bailiffs had charged eight visit fees (because Mrs S had arrears for eight years – ie, there were eight accounts) on two occasions for one visit by one bailiff, and failed to carry out DVLA checks on the ownership of the vehicles. The council also failed to properly investigate Mrs S's complaints until she complained to the Ombudsman.

Once the Ombudsman became involved, the council reduced the fees charged by £630.50; carried out DVLA checks on the vehicles, which showed they did not belong either to Mrs S or her partner, so removed the remaining levies and associated fees; and set out a new contract under which bailiffs could only charge one fee per levy.

The council agreed to pay £300 to Mrs S for the distress and inconvenience she was caused, which it offset against the outstanding council tax arrears. The Ombudsman also urged Mrs S to enter into a reliable regular payment arrangement with the council to avoid future action, such as an attachment of earnings.

Pursuit of council tax debt at wrong address

Bassetlaw District Council (13 007 651) 11 November 2013

Mr X complained that the Council failed to properly explain council tax charges for a previous property and sought an attachment of earnings without first giving him an opportunity to pay the debt.

Outcome: the Ombudsman requested that the council apologise to Mr X, provide a breakdown of all charges and costs, reimburse all summons and bailiff costs, and pay £150 in compensation in respect of failings and inconvenience which could be offset against any outstanding debt.

Wrongful pursuit of arrears and mishandling complaint

London Borough of Newham (13 014 323) 24 April 2014

Ms X complained to the council that it had wrongfully pursued her for arrears she did not owe. The council issued three summonses for non-payment and the magistrates' court made liability orders. This resulted in costs being added to her council tax account. The council did not properly investigate her complaints.

Investigation by the Ombudsman showed that Ms X had paid council tax due under an instalment plan and the authority could not explain why summonses were issued and that it had compounded its errors by its poor handling of Ms X's complaint.

Outcome: the council agreed to apologise, write off remaining arrears, withdraw all summonses, refund amounts wrongly transferred between accounts and pay Ms X £200 in respect of the time and trouble taken in complaining.

Failure to accept reasonable offers of payment and allowing unnecessary enforcement action

Birmingham City Council (13 016 986) 3 June 2014

The council failed to properly consider attempts and proposals by Mr X to pay his council tax. Even though Mr X was paying sums off towards instalments and offering to pay, the council allowed unnecessary enforcement action to take place, adding costs to his account even though he had paid his liability by the end of the year.

Outcome: the Ombudsman considered that although the actions were legally available to the council, it did not mean it was reasonable to take them. The council had acted in a heavy-handed and disproportionate manner by referring the matter to the bailiffs and adding costs despite Mr X's payment.

Erroneous enforcement action and failure to advise taxpayer correctly

Sandwell Metropolitan Borough (14 006 452) 19 November 2014

Mrs B suffered 'a catalogue of errors' including making an attachment of earnings order against council tax arrears for the wrong address, the incorrect issue of summonses and erroneous advice. The Ombudsman found Mrs B had to chase up the council on too many occasions to get a proper response. The council was also at fault in allowing a particular officer to contact her and for issuing a cheque of £150 in compensation which she had refused. The council had also failed to advise her about the welfare team who could have assisted with the financial hardship she had been caused.

Outcome: the Ombudsman directed that the council should implement changes to its procedures, remind staff of the importance to taking action promptly and pay £300.

Excessive and unjustified bailiff fees

London Borough of Haringey (13 012 969) 14 January 2014

There was fault by the bailiffs who collected council tax on behalf of the council. The bailiffs charged excessive fees, seeking to claim for multiple visits which were not covered by the service agreement or justified under the enforcement regulations.

Outcome: the council agreed to waive some of the fees, refund £127.50 and review the service agreement between bailiffs and the council.

Failure to advise disabled taxpayer correctly and properly consider discretionary and disabled reductions

Medway Borough Council (14 000 985) 5 March 2015

The council failed to deal correctly with an application by Mr J for a discretionary council tax reduction, imposed an additional requirement on an application for a disabled band reduction and failed to answer correspondence in an accurate and timely manner, including informing the taxpayer of his right to appeal to the Valuation Tribunal for England.

Outcome: the council paid compensation of £420 for its failure in handling the discretionary reduction application correctly. Following investigation, the council agreed to revise and correct its disabled band reduction form, and the Ombudsman recommended the council apologise and review Mr J's application and pay him a further £75 for giving the incorrect information on its form and for its delays.

Delay in reaching decision on backdating of CTR claim

South Ribble Borough Council (17 002 063) 31 January 2017

Mr X, who was in receipt of universal credit, applied for backdated CTR. The council failed to comply with the 14-day time frame to deal with CTR applications set out in its scheme. It took an extra 10 weeks to give Mr X its decision on his backdated claim. The council also applied for an attachment of earnings order despite an agreement to pay £30 a month in respect of payments being in place when he obtained paid employment.

Outcome: the Ombudsman found fault causing an injustice to Mr X that needed redressing. It recommended the council apologised to Mr X and pay £100 in respect of the stress and delay in determining the claim and a further £100 in seeking a second attachment of earnings order in May 2017.

Wrongly imposed fees on enforcement for a liability
Aylesbury Vale District Council (17 008 183) 8 May 2018
The council imposed fees on the taxpayer on a outstanding council tax liability in respect of one financial year. The Ombudsman identified the council had increased the amounts owed by the addition of extra enforcement fees. It subsequently removed an enforcement agent compliance fee but added a further £480 the following year, including a £110 summons fee, £60 liability order charge, £75 compliance fee and £235 enforcement visit charge by enforcement ages. The council did not properly consider Ms B's request for a reduction in the level of deductions from an attachment of earnings order, failed in its communication with her and did not send her a copy of an attachment of earnings notice.
Outcome: the Ombudsman directed the council to refund the charges associated with enforcement, apologise and pay Ms B £410.

2. **Complaints to the local auditor**

You can make a complaint about the local authority to the local auditor or request an investigation into the local authority's financial conduct. Local authorities are required to ensure that public money is properly accounted for and that financial activities conducted in accordance with the law and proper standards, and that public money, such as council tax, is safeguarded and properly accounted for, and used economically, efficiently and effectively. County councils, district councils, borough councils and parish councils are all bound by these obligations and, in discharging their responsibilities, local authorities must have proper arrangements in place for the governance of their financial affairs and the stewardship of the resources at their disposal. They are also required to report on their arrangements in their annual published governance statements and accounts. Where there are concerns, the matter may be reported to the auditor. Examples involving council tax might include the excessive imposition of costs for liability orders not justified by law, the treatment and accounting of monies received or recovered, any refusal to accept money offered in settlement of a council tax debt which results in extra costs to the taxpayer, the imposition of unjustifiable charges or other accounting irregularities with the collection of local taxes.

The auditor has a range of powers including:
- issuing a public interest report on any matter that it is considered should be brought to public attention;[27]
- issuing an advisory notice;
- applying to the court for a declaration that an item of account is unlawful or if there is reason to believe that unlawful expenditure has been or is about to be incurred by an audited body.[28]

Where the auditor conducts an investigation, the cost is covered by the local authority. Although the auditor is paid by the local authority, the investigation is required to be wholly independent. Following the case of *Nicolson v Tottenham Magistrates' Court* (see p203), referrals to the auditor may be made concerning the costs being charged for seeking liability orders.

The current law on the auditing of local authorities in England is governed by the Local Audit and Accountability Act 2014 and by a Code of Practice issued by the National Audit Office (available at www.nao.org.uk). Auditors must give electors an opportunity to raise questions about the accounts of the local authority, including objections about items appearing in the accounts. The period for inspection, objection and questioning of local auditors, in relation to the accounts, are set out in regulations.[29]

The Secretary of State may also appoint an inspector to carry out inspections in respect of a local authority's compliance with best value practices.[30]

In Wales, responsibility for auditing lies with the Wales Audit Office, established under the Public Audit (Wales) Act 2004 as amended by the Public Audit (Wales) Act 2013. Its code is available at www.audit.wales/publication/code-of-audit-practice.

In Scotland, responsibility for auditing local authority finance lies with Audit Scotland, which provides the Auditor General and the Accounts Commission with services for checking financial conduct on the part of local government.[31]

3. Action through the courts

The role of the Ombudsman is generally to supplement the jurisdiction and not to act as a substitute for the courts.[32] The use of the civil courts is the ultimate recourse of the citizen who is a victim of bureaucratic wrong-doing.[33] The council tax enforcement regulations give a specific right to recover sums overpaid, but more generally a local authority will fall within the general jurisdiction of the civil courts, including the arbitration procedure or 'small claims court'. Each billing authority is liable for acts and defaults by its employees or servants in civil law, as with disputes between private parties. Local authorities may be sued for negligence, breach of statutory duty (eg, in refusing to process a council tax reduction application) or harassment in cases of wrongful debt recovery or for misfeasance in a public office.[34] For a claim of misfeasance in a public office to be sustainable, you must allege that conduct by a public servant was motivated by malice or ill-will or knowing illegality.[35] In addition to public authorities being liable in civil law, individual officials can be proceeded against on a personal basis where an individual officer has acted unlawfully, in bad faith or abused a position of trust.[36] Specific claims in tort may lie such as instigating malicious civil process or malicious instigation of bankruptcy proceedings or misfeasance in a public office. Misfeasance in a public office is recognised in Scotland, supported by English law authorities.[37]

Damages may be sought under a wide range of headings in respect of personal injuries of the individual.

In particular, the small claims jurisdiction of the county court may be used for acts and omissions by local authority departments, as it is relatively cheap to use and if you have a low income or are on benefits, you may be entitled to obtain a fee waiver.[38] The local authority faces the further problem that neither side in a claim for under £10,000 can claim for legal costs and, if the council does nothing in response to the issue of proceedings, a default judgment may be entered against the authority and any officer of the council named as a defendant.

In a small number of cases, maladministration may also involve the deliberate commission of corrupt or criminal actions or defaults. Liability may also attach to individuals and outsourced companies and agents employed by a local authority, although in some cases liability may be limited by statute.

Victims of maladministration have taken the matters to the police where maladministration has gone beyond negligence. There is a range of potential criminal offences that can arise from the production of false documents, various offences involving theft or fraud, offences under the Criminal Attempts Act 1981 and the common law offence, misconduct in a public office. The police are under a duty to investigate when a matter is reported, though officers may suggest that the matter be pursued as a civil matter. A private prosecution can also be commenced if the police fail to act.[39]

Judicial review in the High Court or Court of Session

Judicial review is a specialised form of legal remedy to mistakes in public administration. Judicial review proceedings may be available to challenge decisions of the local authority in the High Court in England and Wales or the Court of Session in Scotland.

Legal advice should be sought as this type of action can be costly, and the financial factor must be considered before embarking upon them as legal aid has been withdrawn since 2013. Judicial review may be available when no other option is available and should only be used as a last resort.

Judicial review is a three-stage process which requires action within three months of the wrongful decision or such longer period as the Court considers equitable.

The first step involves serving a letter on the authority, warning it of your intention to seek judicial review and providing 14 days for it to respond. If the response of the local authority is unsatisfactory, an application for leave for judicial review may be commenced in the Administrative Court, part of the High Court in England and Wales. In Scotland, an application is made to the Court of Session.

In England and Wales, the court can make an order cancelling the wrongful decision (a 'quashing order') or requiring the authority to do or cease doing something unlawful (a 'mandatory order' or 'prohibitory order'). In Scotland, a decision can be quashed by 'reduction' and a 'declarator' (known as a 'declaration' in England and Wales) can be established to ascertain the legal position.

In England and Wales, you must seek leave (ie, permission) for judicial review. The papers are put before a High Court judge who considers the merits of the case. If an arguable case is revealed, the judge may grant leave for judicial review and give directions to you, the local authority and the magistrates' court if enforcement by a liability order or committal to prison has been commenced. If the matter is not settled after the leave stage, the application may proceed to a full judicial review hearing. This takes the form of legal argument before a judge, or judges, of the Administrative Court reviewing the decision. Costs are at the discretion of the court. Any party which takes part in an appeal may be subject to a costs order if the case is contested. However, in some cases where a local authority or public body has acted badly, costs may be refused.[40] In exceptional cases, costs may be made against magistrates, clerks and tribunals where a decision is deemed to have been made in bad faith.[41]

Notes

1. **Complaints to the Ombudsman**
   1 s23 Local Government Act 1974
   2 **W** s1 Public Services Ombudsman (Wales) 2005
      S s1 Scottish Public Services Ombudsman Act 2002
   3 www.lgo.org.uk/forms
   4 ss24A(6) and 34B(8) LGA 1974
   5 House of Commons debates; Parliamentary Commissioner Act 1967
   6 *R v Commissioner for Local Administration, ex parte Eastleigh Borough Council* [1988] 3 All ER 151, per Lord Donaldson MR
   7 UK Parliamentary Ombudsman Report 1993
   8 s26(6)(c) LGA 1974
   9 s26(6) LGA 1974
   10 Ombudsman Report 14 001 797, Adur DC, 11 February 2015, para 37
   11 Local Government Ombudsman, *Review of Local Government Complaints 2014/2015*, p10
   12 Report by Commissioner Jerry White, Complaint 03/B/12862, 29 September 2004
   13 CPR rule 328 and Practice Direction 32
   14 Complaint and decision 17 011 640, London Borough of Merton, 4 May 2018
   15 Ombudsman Report 13 000 723, Birmingham City Council, 18 December 2014
   16 Ombudsman Report 13 016 986, Birmingham City Council, 3 June 2014
   17 Ombudsman Report 13 011 879, Rochdale MBC, 21 August 2014

18 **E** s26 Local Government Act 1974
   W s9 Public Services Ombudsman
   (Wales) Act 2005
   S s7(8) Scottish Public Services
   Ombudsman Act 2002
19 Ombudsman Report 13 007 295,
   Medway Council, 18 December 2014
20 ss50 and 76A Freedom of Information
   Act 2000
21 www.lgo.org.uk/make-a-complaint/
   fact-sheets/benefits-and-tax/council-
   tax-support-claims
22 ss30(1B) and 34H(i) Local Government
   Act 1974, as amended
23 s5 Local Government and Housing Act
   1989
24 s92 Local Government Act 2000
25 Allerdale DC (03/C/07422) 12 January
   2005
26 London Borough of Enfield (16 012 473)
   27 Sept 2017

2. Complaints to the local auditor
27 Sch 7 Local Audit and Accountability Act
   2014
28 s28 and 29 Local Audit and
   Accountability Act 2014
29 Part 5 The Accounts and Audit
   Regulations 2015 No.234
30 ss10-11 Local Government Act 1999
31 www.audit-scotland.gov.uk

3. Action through the courts
32 Auburn, Moffatt and Sharland on
   Judicial Review: Principles and
   Procedure (2013), paragraph 26.110
33 *Ferguson v British Gas Trading Ltd* [2009]
   EWCA Civ 46
34 *Three Rivers DC v Bank of England (No.3)*
   [2003] AC 1, [2000] 3 All ER 1
35 *Coghlan v Chief Constable of Greater
   Manchester Police* [2018] EWHC 1784
   (QB)
36 *Three Rivers DC v Bank of England (No.3)*
   [2003] 2 AC 1

37 *Robert Francis Phipps (AP) Pursuer v the
   Royal College of Surgeons of Edinburgh
   Defenders* [2010] CSOH 58
38 Form Ex160, www.gov.uk/government/
   publications/apply-for-help-with-court-
   and-tribunal-fees
39 *R v Stewart* [1896] 1 QB 300
40 *Wiltshire Council v Piggin* [2014] EWHC
   4386 (Admin)
41 *R v Newcastle Under Lyme Magistrates'
   Court ex parte Massey* [1995] 1 All ER
   125; *R (on the application of Desouza) v
   Croydon Magistrates' Court* [2012]
   EWHC 1362 (Admin)

Appendix 1

Useful addresses

Valuation Office Agency

www.voa.gov.uk

England

Telephone: 03000 501 501

Wales

Telephone: 03000 505 505

Assessor for Central Scotland Valuation Joint Board

Hillside House
Laurelhill
Stirling FK7 9QJ
Tel: 01786 892200
Email: assessor@centralscotland-vjb.gov.uk
www.saa.gov.uk/central

Valuation Tribunal for England

www.valuationtribunal.gov.uk

Doncaster office

3rd Floor, Crossgate House
Wood Street
Doncaster DN1 3LL
Tel: 0300 123 2035
Email: vtdoncaster@vts.gsi.gov.uk

London office

2nd Floor
120 Leman Street
London E1 8EU
Tel: 0300 123 2035
Email: vtwhitechapel@vts.gsi.gov.uk

Council tax reduction team

3rd Floor, Crossgate House
Wood Street
Doncaster DN1 3LL
Tel: 0300 123 2035
Email: appeals@vts.gsi.gov.uk

Valuation Tribunal for Wales

www.valuation-tribunals-wales.org.uk

East Wales Region

22 Gold Tops
Newport NP20 4PG
Tel: 01633 266 367
Email: VTWaleseast@vtw.gsi.gov.uk

North Wales Region

Government Buildings Block A(L1)
Sarn Mynach
Llandudno Junction LL31 9RZ
Tel: 03000 625 350
Email: VTWalesnorth@vtw.gsi.gov.uk

South Wales Region

22 Gold Tops
Newport NP20 4PG

Tel: 01633 255 003
Email: VTWalessouth@vtw.gsi.gov.uk

West Wales Region
Llys y Ddraig
Penllergaer Business Park
Swansea SA4 9NX
Tel: 03000 254 530
Email: VTWaleswest@vtw.gsi.gov.uk

Council Tax Reduction Review Panel (Scotland only)
Glasgow Tribunals Centre
20 York Street
Glasgow G2 8GT
Tel: 0141 302 5840
Email: ctrrpadmin@
scotcourtstribunals.gov.uk
http://counciltaxreductionreview.
scotland.gov.uk

Local Government and Social Care Ombudsman
England
PO Box 4771
Coventry CV4 0EH
Tel: 0300 061 0614 or 0845 602 1983
You can text 'call back' to
0762 481 1595
www.lgo.org.uk

Public Services Ombudsman for Wales
1 Ffordd yr Hen Gae
Pencoed CF35 5LJ
Tel: 0300 790 0203
Email: ask@ombudsman-wales.org.uk
www.ombudsman.wales

Scottish Public Services Ombudsman
Freepost SPSO (this is all you need to write on the envelope)

4 Melville Street
Edinburgh EH3 7NS
Tel: 0800 377 7330
www.spso.org.uk

Parliamentary and Health Service Ombudsman
Millbank Tower
30 Millbank
London SW1P 4QP
Tel: 0345 015 4033
You can text 'call back' to
07624 823 005
Email:
phso.enquiries@ombudsman.org.uk
www.ombudsman.org.uk

The Adjudicator
The Adjudicator's Office
PO Box 10280
Nottingham NG2 9PF
Tel: 0300 057 1111
www.adjudicatorsoffice.gov.uk

Appendix 2

Taking Control of Goods: National Standards

Vulnerable situations

70. Enforcement agents/agencies and creditors must recognise that they each have a role in ensuring that the vulnerable and socially excluded are protected and that the recovery process includes procedures agreed between the agent/agency and creditor about how such situations should be dealt with. The appropriate use of discretion is essential in every case and no amount of guidance could cover every situation. Therefore the agent has a duty to contact the creditor and report the circumstances in situations where there is evidence of a potential cause for concern.

71. If necessary, the enforcement agent will advise the creditor if further action is appropriate. The exercise of appropriate discretion is needed, not only to protect the debtor, but also the enforcement agent who should avoid taking action which could lead to accusations of inappropriate behaviour.

72. Enforcement agents must withdraw from domestic premises if the only person present is, or appears to be, under the age of 16 or is deemed to be vulnerable by the enforcement agent; they can ask when the debtor will be home – if appropriate.

73. Enforcement agents must withdraw without making enquiries if the only persons present are children who appear to be under the age of 12.

74. A debtor may be considered vulnerable if, for reasons of age, health or disability they are unable to safeguard their personal welfare or the personal welfare of other members of the household.

75. The enforcement agent must be sure that the debtor or the person to whom they are entering into a controlled goods agreement understands the agreement and the consequences if the agreement is not complied with.

76. Enforcement agents should be aware that vulnerability may not be immediately obvious.

77. Some groups who might be vulnerable are listed below. However, this list is not exhaustive. Care should be taken to assess each situation on a case by case basis.
- the elderly;
- people with a disability;
- the seriously ill;
- the recently bereaved;
- single parent families;
- pregnant women;
- unemployed people; and,
- those who have obvious difficulty in understanding, speaking or reading English.

78. Wherever possible, enforcement agents should have arrangements in place for rapidly accessing interpretation services (including British Sign Language), when these are needed, and provide on request information in large print or in Braille for debtors with impaired sight.

Issued by the Ministry of Justice in April 2014. The full document is available at www.gov.uk/government/publications/bailiffs-and-enforcement-agents-national-standards.

Appendix 3

Adjournment letter

TO: The Magistrates' Chief Executive
The [NAME] Magistrates' Court
[ADDRESS OF MAGISTRATES' COURT]

Dear Sir/Madam

RE: Summons number [INSERT REFERENCE NUMBER]
RE: Liability order application – Hearing date [STATE DATE]
RE: [NAME OF COUNCIL] v [NAME OF TAXPAYER]

I hereby apply to the court sitting at [GIVE NAME OF MAGISTRATES' COURT] for an adjournment of the above proceedings for the recovery of council tax to be heard on [STATE DATE CONTAINED ON SUMMONS].

The basis for seeking the adjournment is:
[GIVE DETAILS OF WHY ADJOURNMENT IS REQUESTED]
[IN A CASE WHERE AN APPEAL IS MADE TO A VALUATION TRIBUNAL ABOUT LIABILITY, EXEMPTION OR AN AMOUNT OF TAX, GIVE DETAILS OF THE APPEAL]

Accordingly, I have made an appeal to the valuation tribunal under section 16 of the Local Government Finance Act 1992 against this decision, and I would ask that the magistrates' court please consider adjourning this case until the tribunal has determined this matter.

Naturally, I hope that it will be possible to settle this matter without unnecessary proceedings and I await hearing from you with your decision.

Thanking you for your attention, I await hearing from you.

Yours faithfully
[NAME]

Note: a copy of the request should also be served on the local authority.

Appendix 4

Abbreviations used in the notes

AAC	Administrative Appeals	para(s)	paragraph(s)
All ER	All England Reports	PS	Practice Statement
Art(s)	article(s)	QB	Queen's Bench Reports
CA	Court of Appeal	QBD	Queen's Bench Division
Ch	Chancery Division	r(r)	rule(s)
CO	Crown Office	RA	Rating Appeals
COD	Crown Office Digest	Reg(s)	Regulation(s)
CPR	Civil Procedure Rules	RVR	Rating and Valuation
CS	Court of Session		Reports
CSIH	Scotland Court of Session,	S	Scotland
	Inner House	s(s)	section(s)
E	England	Sch(s)	Schedule(s)
EWCA	England and Wales Court	UKUT	UK Upper Tribunal
	of Appeal		(Administrative Appeals
EWHC	England and Wales High		Chamber)
	Court	VOA	Valuation Office Agency
HC	High Court	VTE	Valuation Tribunal for
HLR	Housing Law Reports	CPS	England Consolidated
JP	Justice of the Peace Reports	2017	Practice Statement 2017,
LJ	Lord Justice		effective from 1 April 2018
KB	King's Bench Reports	W	Wales
LC	Lands Chamber	WLR	Weekly Law Reports

Acts of Parliament

CSPSSA 2000	Child Support, Pensions and Social Security Act 2000
LA 2011	Localism Act 2011
LGA 1992	Local Government Act 1992
LGA 2003	Local Government Act 2003
LGFA 1988	Local Government Finance Act 1988
LGFA 1992	Local Government Finance Act 1992
LGFA 2012	Local Government Finance Act 2012
SSAA 1992	Social Security Administration Act 1992
TCEA 2007	Tribunals, Courts and Enforcement Act 2007

Regulations and other statutory instruments

Each set of regulations has a statutory instrument (SI) number and date. You ask for them by giving their date and number.

CCCTNR(E)(MC) Regs	The Community Charges, Council Tax and Non-Domestic Rating (Enforcement) (Magistrates' Courts) England Regulations 2000 No.2026
CT(AE) Regs	The Council Tax (Administration and Enforcement) Regulations 1992 No.613
CT(AE)(A)(E) Regs	The Council Tax (Administration and Enforcement) (Amendment) (England) Regulations 2004 No.297
CT(AE)(A)(No.2)(E) Regs	The Council Tax (Administration and Enforcement) (Amendment) (No.2) (England) Regulations 2012 No.3086
CT(AE)(A)(W) Regs	The Council Tax (Administration and Enforcement) (Amendment) (Wales) Regulations 2007 No.582
CT(AE)(AEO)(W) Regs	The Council Tax (Administration and Enforcement) (Attachment of Earnings Orders) (Wales) Regulations 1992 No.1741
CT(AE)(S) Regs	The Council Tax (Administration and Enforcement) (Scotland) Regulations 1992 No.1332
CT(ALA) Regs	The Council Tax (Alteration of Lists and Appeals) Regulations 1993 No.290
CT(ALA)(A)(W) Regs	The Council Tax (Alteration of Lists and Appeals) (Amendment) Wales Regulations 2010 No.77 (W.10)
CT(ALA)(E) Regs	The Council Tax (Alteration of Lists and Appeals) (England) Regulations 2009 No.2270
CT(ALA)(E)(A) Regs	The Council Tax (Alteration of Lists and Appeals) (England) (Amendment) Regulations 2013 No.467
CT(ALA)(S) Regs	The Council Tax (Alteration of Lists and Appeals) (Scotland) Regulations 1993 No.355
CT(APDD) Regs	The Council Tax (Additional Provisions for Discount Disregards) Regulations 1992 No.552
CT(APDD) Amdt Regs	The Council Tax (Additional Provisions for Discount Disregards) Amendment Regulations 1996 No.637
CT(CD)O	The Council Tax (Chargeable Dwellings) Order 1992 No.549
CT(CVL) Regs	The Council Tax (Contents of Valuation Lists) Regulations 1992 No.553
CT(D)(S)(A) Regs	The Council Tax (Discounts) (Scotland) Amendment Regulations 1995 No.597
CT(D)(S)(A)O	The Council Tax (Discounts) (Scotland) (Amendment) Order 1993 No.343
CT(D)(S)(A) Regs	The Council Tax (Discounts) (Scotland) Amendment Regulations 1993 No.342

CT(D)(S)CAO	The Council Tax (Discounts) (Scotland) Consolidation and Amendment Order 2003 No.176
CT(D)(S)O	The Council Tax (Discounts) (Scotland) Order 1992 No.1408
CT(D)(S) Regs	The Council Tax (Discounts) (Scotland) Regulations 1992 No.1409
CT(DD)O	The Council Tax (Discount Disregards) Order 1992 No.548
CT(DD)(A)(E)O	The Council Tax (Discount Disregards) (Amendment) (England) Order 2006 No.3396
CT(DD)(A)(W)O	The Council Tax (Discount Disregards) (Amendment) (Wales) Order 2006 No.580
CT(DDED)(A)O	The Council Tax (Discount Disregards and Exempt Dwellings)(Amendment) Order 1995 No.619
CT(DIS) Regs	The Council Tax (Deductions from Income Support) Regulations 1993 No.494
CT(DN)(E) Regs	The Council Tax (Demand Notices) (England) Regulations 2010 No.2990
CT(DN)(E) Regs 2011	The Council Tax (Demand Notices) (England) Regulations 2011 No.3038
CT(DN)(E)(A) Regs	The Council Tax (Demand Notices) (England) (Amendment) Regulations 2012 No.3087
CT(DN)(W) Regs	The Council Tax (Demand Notices) (Wales) Regulations 1993 No.255
CT(DN)(W)(A) Regs	The Council Tax (Demand Notices) (Wales) (Amendment) Regulations 2013 No.63
CT(DPRS)(S) Regs	The Council Tax (Dwellings Part Residential Subjects) (Scotland) Regulations 1992 No.2955
CT(DUD)(S) Regs	The Council Tax (Discounts for Unoccupied Dwellings) (Scotland) Regulations 2005 No.51
CT(Dw)(E) Regs	The Council Tax (Prescribed Classes of Dwellings) (England) Regulations 2003 No.3011
CT(Dw)(S) Regs	The Council Tax (Dwellings) (Scotland) Regulations 1992 No.1334
CT(Dw)(S) Regs 2010	The Council Tax (Dwellings) (Scotland) Regulations 2010 No.35
CT(ED)O	The Council Tax (Exempt Dwellings) Order 1992 No.558
CT(ED)(A)(E)O	The Council Tax (Exempt Dwellings) (Amendment) (England) Order 2006 No.2318
CT(ED)(A)(E)O 2005	The Council Tax (Exempt Dwellings) (Amendment) (England) Order 2005 No.2865
CT(ED)(A)(W)O	The Council Tax (Exempt Dwellings) (Amendment) (Wales) Order 2000 No.1025
CT(ED)(E)(A)O 2012	The Council Tax (Exempt Dwellings) (England) (Amendment) Order 2012 No.2965

CT(ED)(S)O 1992	The Council Tax (Exempt Dwellings) (Scotland) Order 1992 No.1333
CT(ED)(S)O 1995	The Council Tax (Exempt Dwellings) (Scotland) (Amendment) Order 1995 No.598
CT(ED)(S)O 1997	The Council Tax (Exempt Dwellings) (Scotland) Order 1997 No.728
CT(ED)(S)O 2002	The Council Tax (Exempt Dwellings) (Scotland) Order 2002 No.101
CT(ED)(S)(A)O	The Council Tax (Exempt Dwellings) (Scotland) (Amendment) Order 2006 No.402
CT(ED)(S)(A)O 1995	The Council Tax (Exempt Dwellings) (Scotland) Amendment Order 1995 No.598
CT(ED)(S)(A)O 2012	The Council Tax (Exempt Dwellings) (Scotland) Amendment Order 2012 No.339
CT(EDDD)(A)O	The Council Tax (Exempt Dwellings and Discount Disregards) (Amendment) Order 1998 No.291
CT(LO) Regs	The Council Tax (Liability of Owners) Regulations 1992 No.551
CT(LO)(A)(E) Regs	The Council Tax (Liability of Owners) (Amendment) (England) Regulations 2003 No.3125
CT(LO)(A)(W) Regs	The Council Tax (Liability of Owners) (Amendment) (Wales) Regulations 2004 No.2920
CT(LO)(S) Regs	The Council Tax (Liability of Owners) (Scotland) Regulations 1992 No.1331
CT(PCD)(E) Regs	The Council Tax (Prescribed Classes of Dwellings) (England) Regulations 2003 No.3011
CT(PCD)(W) Regs	The Council Tax (Prescribed Classes of Dwellings) (Wales) Regulations 1992 No.3023
CT(RD) Regs	The Council Tax (Reductions for Disabilities) Regulations 1992 No.554
CT(RD)(S) Regs	The Council Tax (Reductions for Disabilities) (Scotland) Regulations 1992 No.1335
CT(RDTA)(W)(A) Regs	The Council Tax (Reductions for Disabilities and Transitional Arrangements) (Wales) (Amendment) Regulations 2005 No.702
CT(SVD) Regs	The Council Tax (Situation and Valuation of Dwellings) Regulations 1992 No.550
CT(SVD)(W)(A) Regs	The Council Tax (Situation and Valuation of Dwellings) (Wales) (Amendment) Regulations 2005 No.701
CT(TA)(W) Regs	The Council Tax (Transitional Arrangements) (Wales) Regulations 2004 No.3142
CT(VALA)(E) Regs	The Council Tax (Valuations and Alterations of Lists and Appeals) (England) Regulations 2008 No.315
CT(VD)(S) Regs	The Council Tax (Valuation of Dwellings) (Scotland) Regulations 1992 No.1329

CT(VD)(S)(A) Regs	The Council Tax (Valuation of Dwellings) (Scotland) (Amendment) Regulations 1993 No.354
CT(VUD)(S) Regs	The Council Tax (Variation for Unoccupied Dwellings) (Scotland) Amendment Regulations 2016 No.369
CTNDR(DN)(E) Regs	The Council Tax and Non-Domestic Rating (Demand Notices) (England) Regulations 1993 No.191
CTR(S) Regs	The Council Tax Reduction (Scotland) Regulations 2012 No.303
CTR(S)A(No.2) Regs	The Council Tax Reduction (Scotland) Amendment (No. 2) Regulations 2013 No.218
CTR(SPC)(S) Regs	The Council Tax Reduction (State Pension Credit) (Scotland) Regulations 2012 No.319
CTRS(DFE)(E) Regs	The Council Tax Reduction Schemes (Detection of Fraud and Enforcement) (England) Regulations 2013 No.501
CTRS(DFE)(W) Regs	The Council Tax Reduction Schemes (Detection of Fraud and Enforcement) (Wales) Regulations 2013 No.588
CTRS(DS)(E) Regs	The Council Tax Reduction Schemes (Default Scheme) (England) Regulations 2012 No.2886
CTRS(DS)(W) Regs	The Council Tax Reduction Schemes (Default Scheme) (Wales) Regulations 2012 No.3145
CTRS(PR)(E) Regs	The Council Tax Reduction Schemes (Prescribed Requirements) (England) Regulations 2012 No.2885
CTRSPR(W) Regs	The Council Tax Reduction Schemes and Prescribed Requirements (Wales) Regulations 2012 No.3144
DFA Regs	The Discretionary Financial Assistance Regulations 2001 No.1167
LA(CR)CTI)(E) Regs	Local Authorities (Conduct of Referendums) (Council Tax Increases) (England) Regulations 2012 No.444
LGFE(SP)O	Local Government Finance England (Substitution of Penalties) Order 2008 No.981
TCG Regs	The Taking Control of Goods Regulations 2013 No.1894
TCG(F) Regs	The Taking Control of Goods (Fees) Regulations 2014 No.1
VCCT(Amdt) Regs	The Valuation and Community Charge Tribunals (Amendment) Regulations 1993 No.292
VT(A)(E) Regs	The Valuation Tribunals (Amendment) (England) Regulations 2000 No.409

VTE(CTRA)(P) Regs	The Valuation Tribunal for England (Council Tax and Rating Appeals) (Procedure) Regulations 2009 No.2269
VTE(CTRA)(P)(A) Regs	The Valuation Tribunal for England (Council Tax and Rating Appeals) (Procedure) (Amendment) Regulations 2013 No.465
VTENDRCT(E)(A) Regs	The Valuation Tribunal for England, Non-Domestic Rating and Council Tax (England) (Amendment) Regulations 2011 No.434
VTW Regs	The Valuation Tribunal for Wales Regulations 2010 No.713
VTW(W)(A) Regs	The Valuation Tribunal for Wales (Wales) (Amendment) Regulations 2013 No.547

Index

How to use this Index

Entries against the bold headings direct you to the general information on the subject, or where the subject is covered most fully. Sub-entries are listed alphabetically and direct you to specific aspects of the subject.

A

action of furthcoming 233
adjustment notice 187
agricultural property
Scotland 62
alteration of valuation
withdrawal of appeal 253
alterations
creating a new dwelling 19
disability reduction 93
alternative maximum council tax reduction
see: second aldult rebate
amount of council tax
appeals 191, 243
bills 176
capping
Wales 4
daily liability 72
discounts 101
discretionary reductions
England and Wales 167, 176
Scotland 114
excessive increases
England 4
referendums
England 4
valuation bands 42
appeals 239
amount of council tax payable 243
amount of the bill 191
bankruptcy orders 225
completion notices 20, 245
council tax reduction schemes 165, 243
England and Wales 165
Scotland 166
decisions 264
previous decisions 264
reasons for decision 266
record of decision 265
review of decision 266
setting aside decisions 266
directions
England and Wales 250

disability reduction 98, 243
discounts 120, 243
discretionary reductions 247
evidence 258
England and Wales 262
Scotland 263
exempt dwelling 67, 243
form of appeals
England and Wales 249
Scotland 250
hearings 255, 257
adjournment 261
caselaw 263
extraordinary venues 260
failure to attend 260
notice 257
order of hearing 260
postponement 256
public 259
representation 257
serving documents 258
High Court 241, 267
interested person 255
invalid proposal to alter valuation
Scotland 38
invalidity notices
England 38
Wales 39
Lands Valuation Appeal Court 267
lead cases 253
liability 88, 243
Scotland 232
payments pending appeal 254
penalties 246, 254
procedure 250
pre-hearing review 252
written representations 252
reinstatement 254
striking out 260
time limits 252
England and Wales 244
Scotland 245
valuation appeal committees 41, 239

Valuation Tribunal for England 39
Valuation Tribunal for Wales 39
valuation tribunals 39, 239
valuations 29
  England 39, 241
  Scotland 41, 242
  Wales 39, 241
what can be appealed 241
withdrawal 253
witnesses 262
applicable amounts 142
apprentices 107
armed forces
  accommodation counted as dwelling
    Scotland 18
  attachment of earnings orders 213
  discounts 112
  exempt dwellings
    England and Wales 58
    Scotland 64
arrestment 233
assessor 23
  powers 25
  right of entry 25
  valuation lists 30
asylum seekers
  liability 82
attachment of earnings orders 211
  administrative costs 212
  complaints 212
  deductions from earnings 213
  form of order 212
  notifying employment changes 212
  priority between orders 214

B
backdating
  disability reduction 96
  discounts 112
  exempt dwelling status 67
  liability 85
bailiffs
  see: enforcement agents
bankruptcy 223
  annulment of bankruptcy order 226
  appeals against bankruptcy order 225
  exempt dwellings
    England and Wales 55
    Scotland 62
  paying the debt 224
  procedure evidence 224
  proving the debt 224
  rescission of bankruptcy order 226
  time to pay order
    Scotland 234
bed and breakfast accommodation
  England and Wales 11
  Scotland 18

benefits
  deductions from benefit 214
billing authority 2
bills 173
  adjustment notice 187
  appeals against amount of council tax 191
  calculation 176
  council tax reduction schemes 127
  couples 173
  date of issue 174
  discounts 101
  discretionary reduction 176
  explanatory notes 181
  incorrect bills 178
  information to be included 180
  invalid 182
  joint liability 83, 173
  late bills 174
    causing prejudice 175
    challenging late issue 175
    complaints 176, 276
  liability for bill 173
  payment of council tax penalties 189
  readjusted bills
    England and Wales 200
  revised bill 187
  service 179
boarding school accommodation
  Scotland 18, 82
brankruptcy
  trustee in bankruptcy 223
business property 15
  residential and business use
    England and Wales 16
    Scotland 19
  valuation of mixed-use properties 29

C
capital
  council tax reduction schemes 158
    definition 158
    disregarded capital 159
    notional capital 159
capping
  Wales 4
caravans
  England and Wales 15
  exempt dwellings
    England 58
    Wales 51, 58
  liability of owner 72
  Scotland 17
care
  exemption where former resident
    receives care
    England and Wales 54
    Scotland 61

Index

care homes – council tax reduction schemes
• •

care homes
discounts 110
liability of owner 78
resident's former home
England and Wales 53
Scotland 61
care leavers
discounts
Scotland 103
exempt dwellings
Scotland 61
carers
discounts 108
exempt dwellings
England and Wales 54
Scotland 61
change of circumstances
council tax reduction schemes 163
disability reductions 97
liability 85
charging orders 222
charities
discount for carers 108
exempt dwellings
England and Wales 50
Scotland 60
children
discounts
who counts 101
who is disregarded 103
Church Army hostels 110
civil partnerships
bills 173
liability 82
code of practice for enforcement agents 216
college leavers
discounts 103
company directors
job-related dwellings 116
complaints
action through the courts 291
council tax administration 272
examples of Ombudsman cases 280
formal complaint to local authority 279
injustice 274
judicial review 292
local auditor 290
making a complaint to Ombudsman 278
maladministration 273
Ombudsman 272
outsourced services 275
completion notices 20
appeals 20, 245
composite hereditaments 16
valuation 29
controlled goods agreements 218
convents 81

council tax administration 2
action through the courts 291
complaints 272
judicial review 292
local auditor 290
maladministration 273
council tax benefit
overpayments 97
council tax collection protocol 195
Council Tax Reduction Review Panel 166
council tax reduction schemes 124
appeals 165, 243
England and Wales 165
Scotland 166
applicable amounts 142
applications 161
amending or withdrawing 162
backdating 163
couples 162
forms 161
further information 162
in advance 161
band E-H reduction
Scotland 137
bills 127
calculation 141
capital 158
change of circumstances 163
date of entitlement 163
decisions 162
disability reduction 91
earnings 154
eligible council tax 142
extended reductions 160
future changes 168
income 150
income taper 157
joint liability for council tax 84, 130
liability before application is determined
England and Wales 199
local schemes
England and Wales 126
Scotland 126
maladministration 275
maximum reductions 142
national rules 125
non-dependants 147
pensioners 125, 131
requirements of schemes
England and Wales 127
temporary absence from home 130
who is eligible 128
who is not eligible 128
working-age adults 125
England 133
Scotland 137
Wales 137

council tenants
  payment arrangements 186
councillors
  deductions from allowances 214
  restrictions on voting 214
couples
  bills 173
  council tax reduction schemes 129, 162
  joint liability 82, 173
crofts 29

D
daily liability 72
death
  exempt dwellings
    England and Wales 52
    Scotland 61
  liability of personal representative 71
  of liable person 85, 197
debts
  council tax 189
deductions from benefit 214
demolition
  exempt dwellings
    Scotland 62
derelict dwellings
  England and Wales 12
diplomatic immunity
  exempt dwellings
    England and Wales 58
direct debit 188
disability
  exempt dwellings
    England and Wales 58
    Scotland 63
  fixtures affecting valuation 28, 33, 91
disability reduction 91
  appeals 98, 243
  applications 95
  backdating 96
  change of circumstances 97
  conditions for reduction 92
  definition of disabled person 92
  further help available 97
  how the reduction is made 97
  information required 96
  joint liability 95
  person entitled 95
  qualifying dwellings 92
  sole or main residence 76
discounts 100
  appeals 120, 243
  applications 112
  apprentices 107
  backdating 112
  care home residents 110

care leavers
  Scotland 103
carers 108
children 101, 103
council tax bills 101
duty to correct false assumptions 113
foreign language assistants 106
hospital patients 110
hostels 110
imprisonment/detention 111
international and defence organisations
  111
job-related dwellings 115
penalties for failing to notify authority that
  discount does not apply 113
procedure for obtaining discount 112
religious communities 111
school and college leavers 103
severe mental impairment 107
single person discount 100
sole or main residence 76
spouse/civil partner/dependant of foreign
  student 106
student nurses 107
students
  disregarded 104
  evidence of student status 105
unoccupied dwellings 114
visiting forces 112
who counts 101
who is disregarded 101
young people 101, 103
discretionary reductions
  appealing a decision 247
  applications
    England and Wales 167
  England and Wales 167
  hardship
    England and Wales 167
  scope of discretion
    England and Wales 167
  Scotland 114
  sole or main residence 76
disregarded for discount 101
disrepair
  exempt property
    England and Wales 12
distress
  see: taking control of goods
dwellings 9
  chargeable dwellings 9
  composite hereditament
    England and Wales 16
  definition
    England and Wales 10
    Scotland 17
  derelict 12
  disability reduction 92

excluded properties
England and Wales 10
Scotland 18
hereditaments
England and Wales 11
job-related dwellings 115
long-term empty properties 117
new and altered dwellings 19
non-domestic use
England and Wales 15 .
residential and business use
England and Wales 16
Scotland 19
self-contained units
England and Wales 13
shared facilities
England and Wales 14
situated in two local authorities
England and Wales 17
see also exempt dwellings

E
earnings
council tax reduction schemes 154
deductions
arrestment of earnings 232
attachment of earnings orders 211
earnings arrestment 232
electronic communication 3
employment and support allowance
deductions from benefit 214
empty properties
premiums 117
energy efficiency
valuations 30
enforcement 194
arrestment and action of furthcoming or
sale 233
attachment of earnings orders 211
bankruptcy proceedings 223
charging orders 222
costs of enforcement
England and Wales 202
Scotland 234
death of liable person 197
deductions from benefit 214
enforcement agents
taking control of goods 215
final notices
England and Wales 196
human rights 199
imprisonment 226
means enquiry 227
information from debtor
England and Wales 211
Scotland 231

joint liability
England and Wales 196
Scotland 230
late enforcement
complaints 276
liability orders 198
local authority policies 195
process of enforcement
England and Wales 195
Scotland 229
recovery methods
England and Wales 210
Scotland 231
reminder notices
England and Wales 196
Scotland 229
remission of debt 228
special payment arrangements 194
summary warrant or decree 230
time to pay order
Scotland 234
winding-up proceedings 223
write-offs
England and Wales 197
enforcement agents
code of practice 216
entry powers 217
fees 220
powers of entry
identification 218
method of entry 218
remedies for wrongful enforcement 222
removing goods 219
return of debt to local authority 221
securing goods 219
selling goods 219
taking control of goods 218
vulnerable households 216
entry, powers of
enforcement agents 217
listing officer and assessor 25
evidence
alteration of valuation 37
appeals 258
England and Wales 262
Scotland 263
applications for discounts 112
medical certificates 108
student certificates 105
bankruptcy procedure 224
refusal to accept 276
excessive amounts of council tax 4
referendums
England 4, 5
validity of bills 182
exempt dwellings 48
agricultural property
Scotland 62

appeals 67, 243
armed forces
    England and Wales 58
    Scotland 64
backdating of exemption 67
bankruptcy
    England and Wales 55
    Scotland 62
caravans
    England and Wales 58
    Wales 51
care home resident
    England and Wales 53
    Scotland 61
care leavers
    Scotland 61
carers
    England and Wales 54
    Scotland 61
charities
    England and Wales 50
    Scotland 60
death
    England and Wales 52
    Scotland 61
demolition pending
    Scotland 62
dependent relatives
    England and Wales 58
diplomatic immunity
    England and Wales 58
duty to correct false assumptions made
    by authority 66
dwelling cannot be let separately
    England and Wales 55
    Scotland 62
England and Wales 48
garages/storage premises
    Scotland 64
halls of residence
    England and Wales 56
    Scotland 64
hospital inpatient
    England and Wales 53
    Scotland 61
houseboats
    England and Wales 58
    Wales 51
housing associations
    Scotland 63
identification 65
imprisonment/detention of former
    resident
    England and Wales 51
    Scotland 61
ministers of religion
    England and Wales 53
    Scotland 62

mortgage lender in possession
    England and Wales 55
    Scotland 62
new dwellings 19
    Scotland 60
notification of exemption 65
occupied dwellings
    Scotland 63
penalties 66
prescribed housing support
    accommodation
    Scotland 65
prohibited occupation
    England and Wales 53
    Scotland 61
repairs/alterations
    England and Wales 48
    Scotland 60
Scotland 59
severe mental impairment
    England and Wales 58
    Scotland 64
students
    England and Wales 54, 57
    Scotland 62, 63
unfurnished dwellings
    England and Wales 50
    Scotland 60
unoccupied dwellings
    England and Wales 48
    Scotland 60
vacant dwellings
    England 48, 49
    Scotland 59
    Wales 48, 49, 51
visiting armed forces
    England and Wales 58
    Scotland 64
young people
    England and Wales 58
    Scotland 63

F
family
    council tax reduction schemes 129
farmhouses
    Scotland 29
final notices
    England and Wales 196
financial hardship
    discretionary reductions
        England and Wales 167
fines
    attachment of earnings orders 212
    failure to provide information 25
foreign language assistants
    discounts 106
freedom of information 4

G

garages
England and Wales 10
converted to accommodation 15
Scotland 18, 64

granny flats
England and Wales 13, 55
Scotland 62

H

halls of residence
exempt dwellings
England and Wales 56
Scotland 64
Scotland 18

hereditaments 11
composite hereditaments 11, 16, 29

High Court 241
appeals 267

HMRC Adjudicator 24

holiday accommodation
England and Wales 10
Scotland 18

hospital patients
council tax reduction schemes 131
discounts 110
inpatient's former home
England and Wales 53
Scotland 61

hostels
discounts 110
liability of owner 78
Scotland 18

hotels
England and Wales 10

houseboats
England and Wales 15
exempt dwellings
England 58
Wales 51, 58
liability of owner 72

household
council tax reduction schemes 129

houses in multiple occupation
liability 78

housing association
exempt dwellings
Scotland 63

human rights
imprisonment for debts 228
liability orders 199

I

immigration status
council tax reduction scheme 128

implementation letters 5

imprisonment
challenging imprisonment 229
council tax reduction schemes
remand prisoners 130
discounts 111
exempt dwellings
England and Wales 51
Scotland 61
judicial review 229
mothers with young children 228
non-payment of council tax 226
means enquiry 227

income
council tax reduction schemes 150
taper 157

income support
deductions from benefit 214

increases in council tax 4
referendums
England 4, 5
validity of bills 182

information
disability reduction 96
duty to provide 25, 86
establishing liability 86
included in the bill 180
liability orders 211
public bodies 86
summary warrant 231

instalments 183
amount 185
council tenants 186
liability changes 187
liability ends 186
losing the right to instalments
England and Wales 196
Scotland 229
number of instalments 183
requesting 12 instalments 185
revised bill 187

invalidity notice
appeals 242
England 37
Wales 38

J

job-related dwellings 115

jobseeker's allowance
deductions from benefit 214

joint liability 82
billing 83, 173
civil partnerships 82
council tax reduction schemes 84
couples 82
disability reduction 95
England and Wales 196
liability ends 186
polygamous marriages 83

Scotland 230
severe mental impairment 84
students 84
see also liability
joint tax payers' notice 83
judicial review 229, 268, 292

L
Lands Valuation Appeal Court 267
legal framework for council tax 3
liability 70
    appeals 88, 243
        Scotland 232
    asylum seekers 82
    backdating 85
    boarding schools
        Scotland 82
    caravans 72
    care homes 78
    change of circumstances 85
    daily liability 70, 72, 85
    death of liable person 85
    duty to provide information 86
    hierarchy of liability
        England and Wales 71
        Scotland 71
    hostels 78
    houseboats 72
    houses in multiple occupation 78
    identification of liable person 86
    managing agents 86
    ministers of religion 81
    more than one residence 77
    non-resident owner's liability 77
    owner's liability 77
    payment by instalments
        when liability changes 187
        when liability ends 186
    payment of bills 173
    person liable to pay 70
    religious communities 81
    second homes 81
    sole or main residence 72
        England and Wales 73
        Scotland 75
    squatters 71
liability orders 198
    adjournment 204
    adjournment of hearing 254
    attending court 205
    benefit claim pending 198
    costs 202
    evidence at hearing 207
    form of order 208
    grounds for making order 206
    hearing 205
    joint liability 196
        duty to provide information 211

summons 201
    obtaining an order 201
    outstanding amount is paid 204
    recovery methods
        attachment of earnings orders 211
        bankruptcy proceedings 223
        charging orders 222
        deductions from benefit 214
        deductions from councillors'
            allowances 214
        imprisonment 226
        taking control of goods 215
    representation at hearing 206
    setting aside 209
    summons 201, 204
    time limits 201
listing officer 23
    invalidity notice
        England 38
        Wales 38
    powers 25
    right of entry 25
    valuation lists 30
local authorities
    dwelling situated in two authorities 17
    provision of information 25
long-term empty properties 117

M
maladministration
    action through the courts 291
    complaints procedure 278
    definition 273
    examples of Ombudsman cases 280
married couples
    bills 173
    joint liability 82
McKenzie friend
    England and Wales 206
    Scotland 232
means inquiry 227
medical certificates
    severe mental impairment 108
ministers of religion
    exempt dwellings
        England and Wales 53
        Scotland 62
    job-related dwellings 116
    liability 81
monasteries 81
multiple occupation
    England and Wales 14
    liability 78
    refuges in Wales 15
    Scotland 19

N
new dwellings 19
  exempt dwellings
    Scotland 60
non-dependant deductions 147
non-domestic rates 15
Northern Ireland 2
notice
  appeal hearing 257
nursing students
  exempt dwellings
    England and Wales 57

O
Ombudsman 272
  action Ombudsman can take 279
  complaints 272
  complaints about bankruptcy 224
  complaints procedure 278
  examples of cases 280
  matters that cannot be examined 277
  role 272
overpayments
  council tax 178, 254
  incorrectly estimated bills 178

P
part-residential property 19
payment of council tax 183
  appeal pending 254
  arrangements for payment 183
  council tenants 186
  direct debit 188
  discounts for lump-sum payment 188
  discounts for non-cash payment 188
  incorrect payments 178
  instalments 183
  penalties 189
  special arrangements 188, 194
  underpayments 178
  who must pay 173
  see also overpayments
penalties 87
  appeals 88, 246, 254
  exempt dwellings 66
  failing to notify authority that discount
    does not apply 113
  failure to provide information 25
  payment 189
pension credit
  council tax reduction schemes 131, 142
  deductions from benefit 214
  pension age 132
pensioners
  council tax reduction schemes 125, 131
  income 151
polygamous marriages 83

postponement
  appeal hearing 256
practice notes 5
premiums 117
  discretionary reduction of premium
    England and Wales 120
  dwellings exempt from premium 119
  England 117
  Scotland 119
  Wales 118
prescribed housing support accommodation
  Scotland 65
property prices
  valuation of dwelling 26
proposals to alter valuation 34
  alteration differs from that proposed
    England and Wales 39
  appeals
    England and Wales 39
    Scotland 41
  invalid proposals 37
    England 37
    Scotland 38
    Wales 38
  joint proposal
    Scotland 37
  notification of alteration 42
    England and Wales 42
    Scotland 42
  procedure 35
  procedure following valid proposal
    England and Wales 39
    Scotland 40
  time limits 35
  who can make proposal 34
  withdrawal of appeal 253
  withdrawal of proposal
    England and Wales 40
    Scotland 41

R
recovery of unpaid council tax 194
  see also enforcement
referendums
  England 4, 5
    excessive levels of council tax 4
religious communities
  discounts 111
  liability 81
reminder notices
  England and Wales 196
  Scotland 229
remission of council tax debt 228
repairs
  exempt dwellings
    England and Wales 48
    Scotland 60
  reasonable repair 28

repossession
exempt dwellings
England and Wales 55
Scotland 62
representation at hearings 257
England and Wales 206
Scotland 232
residence 72
council tax reduction schemes 130
more than one residence 77
sole or main residence 72
revaluation 26, 34
Wales 43
reviews
appeal decisions 266

S
Salvation Army hostels 110
school leavers
discounts 103
second adult rebate 126, 138
calculation 140
definition of second adult 139
second homes
discounts 114
Scotland 114
liability 81
premiums 117
self-contained living accommodation
England and Wales 13
severe mental impairment
certificate of confirmation 108
discounts 107
exempt dwellings
England and Wales 58
Scotland 64
joint liability 84
shared facilities
England and Wales 14
sheds
converted to accommodation 15
short-stay accommodation
England and Wales 10
single person discount 100
small claims court 291
sole or main residence 72
council tax discounts and reductions 76
England and Wales 73
proving sole or main residence 76
Scotland 75
squatters 53, 71
staff accommodation
England an Wales 13
Scotland 62
storage premises
England and Wales 10
Scotland 18, 64

student nurses
discounts 107
students
definition 104, 105
discounts 104
evidence of student status 105
exempt dwellings
England and Wales 54, 56, 57
Scotland 62, 63, 64
exemption from joint liability 84
halls of residence
England and Wales 56
Scotland 18, 64
postgraduate students 106
second adult rebate 141
spouse/civil partner/dependant of foreign
student 106
summary warrants 230
costs 234
information from debtor 231
recovery methods 231
action of furthcoming 233
arrestments 233
earnings arrestment 232
time to pay orders 234
summons
liability orders 201, 204
withdrawal of summons 204

T
taking control of goods 215
code of practice 216
controlled goods agreement 218
entry 217
exempt goods 216
fees 220
goods 216
remedies for wrongful enforcement 222
removing goods 219
return of debt to local authority 221
securing goods 219
selling goods 219
ways of taking control 218
temporary absence from home
council tax reduction schemes 130
time limits
appeals 252
amount of council tax 191
completion notices 20
disability reduction 98
discounts 120
exempt dwellings 67
liability 88
invalid proposal to alter valuation
Scotland 38
invalidity notices
England 37
Wales 38

judicial review 229
liability orders 201
proposals to alter valuation 35
England and Wales 39
time to pay order
Scotland 234

U
underpayments 178
unfurnished dwelling
England and Wales 50
Scotland 60
universal credit
deductions from benefit 214
unmarried couples
joint liability 82
unoccupied dwellings 48
discounts 114
England and Wales 114
England and Wales 48
Scotland 59, 114
see also exempt dwellings

V
vacant dwellings
discounts 114
England 48, 49
Scotland 59
substantially unfurnished
England and Wales 50
Wales 48, 49, 51
see also exempt dwellings
valuation 23
alteration 32
appeals 29
England 241
Scotland 242
Wales 241
appointees 24
assessor 23
assumptions 27, 242
complaints procedure 24
duty to provide information 25
energy efficiency measures 30
farms and crofts 29
fixtures for disabled people 28, 33, 91
historic valuations 263
increase in valuation 32
listing officer 23
mixed domestic and business use 29
property prices 26, 29
proposal to alter 34
reasonable repair 28
reduction in valuation 33
revaluation 26, 34
theoretical and actual value 26
valuation lists 30

valuation appeal committees 41, 239
overriding objective 240
see also: appeals
valuation assumptions 27, 242
valuation bands 42
England 43
Scotland 43
time limits for proposing alteration 35
variation between bands 44
Wales 43
Valuation Joint Board 24
valuation lists
alterations 32
compilation 30
contents 31
maintaining the list 30
proposal to alter list 34
Valuation Office Agency 23
valuation roll 17
Valuation Tribunal for England 39
Valuation Tribunal for Wales 39
valuation tribunals 39, 239
overriding objective 240
vicarages 53
vulnerable households
enforcement agents 216

W
water charges
Scotland 72
winding-up proceedings 223
withdrawal
appeals 253
proposal to alter valuation
England and Wales 40
Scotland 41
witnesses
appeals 262
women's refuges
Scotland 18
Wales 15
working-age adults
council tax reduction schemes 125
England 133
Scotland 137
Wales 137
income 152

Y
young people
discounts
who counts 101
who is disregarded 103
youth trainees 103
exempt dwellings
England and Wales 58
Scotland 63